The 7th Tennessee Infantry in the Civil War

The 7th Tennessee Infantry in the Civil War

A History and Roster

William Thomas Venner

McFarland & Company, Inc., Publishers
Jefferson, North Carolina, and London

Library of Congress Cataloguing-in-Publication Data

Venner, William Thomas, 1950–
The 7th Tennessee Infantry in the Civil War :
a history and roster / William Thomas Venner.
p.   cm.
Includes bibliographical references and index.

ISBN 978-0-7864-7350-2
softcover : acid free paper ∞

1. Confederate States of America. Army. Tennessee Infantry Regiment, 7th.
2. Tennessee—History—Civil War, 1861–1865—Regimental histories.
3. United States—History—Civil War, 1861–1865—Regimental histories.
4. United States—History—Civil War, 1861–1865—Campaigns.   I. Title.
E579.57th.V46 2013   973.7'468—dc23   2013014659

British Library cataloguing data are available

© 2013 William Thomas Venner. All rights reserved

*No part of this book may be reproduced or transmitted in any form
or by any means, electronic or mechanical, including photocopying
or recording, or by any information storage and retrieval system,
without permission in writing from the publisher.*

On the cover: *foreground* Confederate Soldiers of the 7th Tennessee Infantry
of Archer's Brigade (Mathew Brady; Library of Congress); photo frame Jupiterimages/
Comstock/Thinkstock); *background* map of the battlefield of Gettysburg, 1863
(*Official Records of the Union and Confederate Armies, 1861-1865*)

Manufactured in the United States of America

*McFarland & Company, Inc., Publishers
Box 611, Jefferson, North Carolina 28640
www.mcfarlandpub.com*

This book is dedicated to the men of
the 7th Tennessee Infantry and to their families.
We must not let their memories fade.

Table of Contents

Introduction 1

PART I : HISTORY

  1. May 28, 1861: Early Afternoon 5

  2. August 2, 1861: Morning 15

  3. May 8, 1862: Morning 29

  4. August 20, 1862: Before Dawn 50

  5. December 14, 1862: Early Morning 69

  6. July 1, 1863: Morning 80

  7. July 3, 1863: Morning 95

  8. July 3, 1863: Sunset 112

  9. May 4, 1864: Morning 122

  10. October 20, 1864: Afternoon 143

PART II : 7TH TENNESSEE INFANTRY ROSTER 159

Part I Notes 207
Bibliography 221
Index 226

Introduction

How is it that a Californian would end up writing a history about a Tennessee infantry regiment?

As far as I know I have no ancestors who were in the American Civil War. My father's people came to the United States in the 1850s — Italians and Austrians — bent on escaping Europe's wars. They settled in northern Wisconsin and wanted no part of America's conflict. My mother's family — German immigrants — arrived in the 1880s and immediately headed for America's Great Plains. So, as the old saying goes, I didn't have a dog in the fight.

But I've always been fascinated by our nation's past. In fact, even today, fifty years later, I can still recall the first time I became conscious of the Battle of Gettysburg. It was the summer of 1963, I was 12 going on 13 and sitting on a stool in our small town's one-room library. The librarian handed me the July issue of *National Geographic* and inside was a story about the Battle of Gettysburg. I still remember sitting there, leaning up against the cold spines of shelved books, closing my eyes, and trying to envision what it was like to have been there. The graphic, fold-out maps gripped my imagination with such force; from that moment on the study of the Civil War grew into one of my passions.

I became obsessed with trying to conjure up the sights and sounds of Pickett's Charge. I poured over maps, and read and reread the *American Heritage Picture History of the Civil War*. My parents bought me a Marx Civil War Playset with its scores of plastic soldiers and I recreated every major battle, as well as creating countless battles of my own. I then acquired the Avalon Hill Gettysburg board game with its squared-off grid map, rectangular gray and blue combat pieces, and its colored Order of Appearance cards. I learned the names of the brigade commanders and strategized as I pushed infantry, artillery, and cavalry units across Gettysburg's landscape. I seem to have spent a good chunk of my childhood moving plastic Civil War figures through the sand in the backyard, or tiny cardboard pieces across a board map, all the while trying to replicate what it must have been like to have been there.

When I was a junior in high school my mother and I traveled from California to Pennsylvania and we spent several incredible days exploring Gettysburg. I walked the fields, my feet treading upon the very ground my imagination had envisioned; I gazed where the soldiers looked and tried to feel what they did. I left Gettysburg with a better sense of the geography but with hardly any more understanding of what it was like to have been there. Then I went off to college, leaving behind my board games and plastic soldiers, but I didn't forget the Civil War; indeed — I earned a master's degree in American history.

I became a high school teacher in Southern California and taught history. I turned to living history as one of my teaching methods in an attempt to make the past interesting and relevant. I discovered Civil War re-enacting and used this activity as a way to widen my students' interest in history and push them toward trying to fathom that question, "What was it like to have been there?"

I continued re-enacting, and since I lived in California and had no ancestors demanding I choose one side or the other, I selected the best-led unit I could find — it turned out to be the 19th Indiana Infantry, a unit based in Los Angeles. We were a small unit, no more than two dozen at the very most, but we were deeply interested in trying to get it right. We each took the name of a soldier from the regiment — my Hoosier was James Van Tooth — and we took it upon ourselves to learn about that person. My research determined that Van Tooth was a brick maker from Plainville, Indiana. He enlisted as a private, rose through the ranks to sergeant, and was killed during the Cold Harbor campaign in June 1864.

Unexpectedly, my research on Van Tooth led to something much larger. Once again I was that young boy sitting on a stool in the library, but now I had more tools to aid my quest; I wrote to the Indiana State Library, dug through microfilms, perused old newspapers, and intensely read letters and journals. Ultimately I published five books about the 19th Indiana and the Iron Brigade. By the time my research ended I felt I had gained a small insight into James Van Tooth and his fellow soldiers and hopefully had shared that information with others.

Nonetheless, I knew in my heart I had not answered my question, "What was it like to have been there?" I realized the Hoosiers were only half the story. I had studied this single collection of Indiana soldiers —1,200 in all — and now understood a little about their lives and experiences, but these men did not act in a vacuum. They also were defined by those they fought. I was compelled to learn about the men they faced. Since the war's most important battle was Gettysburg it only seemed natural to investigate a unit the 19th faced in that battle. However, once I had settled upon Gettysburg the question followed — what to investigate? Gettysburg's historians have reveled in the classic fight between the Iron Brigade and the North Carolina regiments on the battle's first day — a confrontation spawning many well-crafted literary works. I figured one more book about the Iron Brigade versus North Carolina would not broaden our knowledge about what took place on July 1, west of Gettysburg.

Fortunately as I studied the record of that day's conflict I noticed much less had been written about the morning clash between the Iron Brigade and Archer's Brigade. To me, there appeared to be a historical gap and an opportunity for me to help further our understanding of what happened. I investigated the regiments in Archer's command and discovered little had been recorded about the 7th Tennessee. I now had the other half of the account to complete the story — the 7th Tennessee Infantry.

My research took me to Nashville and the Tennessee Archives. I invested a small fortune in photocopies, and purchased a set of microfilm reels containing the 7th Tennessee's personnel and payroll records. I returned to California and began assembling the regiment, man by man. This study took over a year as I spent hours on microfilm readers at the local Mormon Family History center. I became familiar with many of those soldiers, and one such man — Archibald Norris — became my guide and mentor into the intrigues of the 7th Tennessee.

"Archie" Norris left behind a journal, chronicling his experiences and thoughts, giving me the means by which to glean an inkling about what he thought it was like to be there. Archie was a sharp, quick thinking, and contemplative young man. He grew up in Wilson County, Tennessee, attended the local schools and eventually graduated from Pennsylvania's Allegheny College. Norris returned home and became a teacher in Rome, Tennessee. When the war began Archie reluctantly enlisted, writing, "I owe allegiance to my State and though I may regret the steps which my State may take, yet it is my imperative duty to support it." Surprisingly, this teacher-turned-warrior developed into a capable soldier. He earned the admiration and respect of his comrades and they elected him captain of his company. Archie served in the regiment for the entire war until being captured a week before Appomattox.

Archie Norris was just one of the nearly 1,000 Tennesseans serving in the 7th Tennessee, but it was through his assistance that I became immersed in the regiment. I had great plans to quickly finish my research and put the Tennesseans' thoughts and actions to paper, but life interfered and for the next fifteen years Norris and his pards remained packed away in file boxes. Remarkably, the Tennesseans refused to go away. Their whisperings echoed too loudly to ignore and finally I reopened my long-ignored file boxes and blew the dust off their papers. I reread everything and prepared to write, but the world had changed since I first had begun this Tennessee journey — the Internet had been invented.

My stepson helped me set up a website and soon descendants of the men of the 7th Tennessee were writing me, sharing their family stories, lending me photographs, and willing me to get the story right. Presently there have been three dozen descendants who've contacted me, representing nearly sixty men who were in the regiment. Some descendants did even more than just send me their family records. Jack and Ruth Cato, descendants of Sgt. William Cato, invited me to come and visit. I took them up on their offer and they proved to be delightful hosts. Jack shared with me his ancestor's world. He took me on back roads and showed me ancient farmhouses — the homes of the 7th Tennessee boys; we walked across the fragrant deep bottom farmlands — the very fields the Tennessee boys worked before they set down their farm tools and took up muskets; and we went to the family cemeteries where these civilian-soldiers now rested. I know now this book is so much richer because of the Catos and all the 7th Tennessee descendants. It is almost as if the spirits of those old boys played a part in helping me to get it right.

The 7th Tennessee Infantry came from four counties: Wilson, Smith, Dekalb, and Sumner, and basically was centered around the town of Lebanon. A writer for the *Lebanon Herald* called them "the very flower of Lebanon and vicinity." These exuberant men filled the regiment's ranks at war's start clamoring to get at the Yanks. They vowed their thousand rifles would bring victory to the Southern cause and were, as Lt. Col. John Goodner wrote, "anxious to confront the enemy on the battle front."

The 7th Tennessee was part of Robert E. Lee's Army of Northern Virginia and these soldiers fought in every battle in the three years between May 1862 and April 1865. The thousand Tennesseans suffered nearly 800 casualties, with some men enduring as many as five different wounds. One worn-out veteran, not long before the war ended, wrote, "Who of us will be the last to go?" This wearied young man had seen so many of his friends fall. Seventy-nine Tennesseans were killed in action and another 61 died from their battle injuries. Sixty-seven men died from disease and 16 more were buried while in prisoner-of-war camps. And finally, two died from accidental shootings, a third drowned, and a fourth was murdered while at home. In all, just a little less than one out of four of those excited volunteers in May 1861 did not live to see peace return to Tennessee. The regiment finished the war with just three dozen men standing in formation at the Appomattox surrender ceremony. These survivors, just like all their missing brothers, had done the best they could. They all possessed this incalculable quality — Tennessee valor.

Years ago I began this project, haunted by the challenge to discover what war was like. Personally, I have never been in harm's way so I will never know the emotions that fill a soldier's soul. All I can attempt to do is listen to what the soldiers say about what happened and what they did. This book lets those men (and their family members) talk about what happened. We are fortunate so many wrote down their thoughts. This book has nearly 1,000 quotes — 1,000 thoughts by those directly involved — and I have matched these pieces of personal history with what the regimental documents reveal — this is a view of war as seen through the eyes of civilian-soldiers. This is not a look at the big picture. This is an intimate close-up about war and what it does to individuals.

My quest today in 2012 is exactly the same as it was back in 1963 when that skinny youngster tried to figure out, "What was it like to have been there?" I have tried to get it right.

Part I : History

Chapter 1

May 28, 1861: Early Afternoon

"My regiment will be moved shortly."

The 7th Tennessee Infantry Regiment mustered into existence on May 28, 1861, with Colonel Robert Hatton as the commander.[1] Hatton, a 36-year-old politician, possessed no military experience but did have considerable expertise in influencing and commanding others. He grew up in Nashville until, at the age of fourteen, he moved to Gallatin, Tennessee, to clerk in a store. Later, he would declare, "I learned to do work, to stand the sun and the winter's winds, [and] to do what was exceedingly painful to me at the time."[2] The industrious Hatton taught school and saved enough money to attend Cumberland University. He finished at the head of his class and entered the Law Department, where he graduated with first honors.

Robert Hatton hung out his attorney's shingle in Lebanon, Tennessee, and because of his excellent standards and successful results, earned broad praise. Hatton always reminded those around him, "Endure hardship…. This is essential to success."[3] In 1848, at the age of twenty-two, Hatton garnered his first term in the Tennessee state legislature. Hatton remained in Tennessee's state Congress for the next eight years before winning his party's nomination as candidate for governor. He campaigned on a platform of fiscal responsibility and strong educational pursuits, believing those two forces would create a strong state. His opponent, Isham Harris, argued differently, maintaining Tennessee need not concern itself with financial restraints, as the state could pay for its ventures by distributing excess lands.

Hatton and Harris squared off in a widely-attended debate a few weeks before the election. Isham Harris spoke first. Then, when it was Hatton's turn to speak, Harris interrupted him repeatedly. Finally, Hatton could take no more of Harris' disruptions and stomped off the podium and approached him. As one bystander recorded, "Harris struck him, and both came to the ground in a scramble."[4] Eventually supporters snatched them apart and after a short break, Hatton resumed his speech — and without any more interruptions. Spectators remarked how powerfully and eloquently Hatton spoke. Unfortunately his presentation did not accomplish his goal. Hatton may have won the fist fight, but Harris won the election.

In 1859, Robert Hatton was elected to Congress as a member of the Know-Nothing Party, and he immediately became embroiled in the politics of a divided nation. He joined forces with the side struggling to maintain a united country and argued against secession. His speech before Congress in January 1861 was one of the last in behalf of the Union, when he pleaded for restraint, saying, "Each side, North and South, seem[s] to bristle up and show fight — nothing but fight."[5] His appeal and those of others were ignored and the country soon split apart. Finally, when it became obvious Tennessee had chosen to secede, Hatton reluctantly decided to go with his home state.

Returning to Lebanon, Robert Hatton raised a company of volunteers called the Wilson Blues and brought them to Camp Trousdale, one of Tennessee's main mustering-in centers. Hatton's Wilson Blues, along with nine other locally raised companies, were organized into a regiment and on May 28, 1861, he became the formation's colonel. That evening the politician-turned-soldier wrote his wife, Sophie, "My election was unanimous. The regiment seemed delighted."[6]

ISHAM G. HARRIS. Isham Harris was born in 1818 and was Tennessee's governor in 1861. The next year when the Federal army controlled much of the state Harris became a staff officer for Gen. Albert Johnson. When the war ended Harris fled to Mexico but returned to help Tennessee re-enter the Union. Isham Harris died in 1897 (Library of Congress collection Photographs Division LC-USZ62-123456).

Hatton's regiment mustered into the Confederate army as the 7th Tennessee Infantry, and Hatton's old nemesis, Governor Isham, was forced to commission him as colonel.[7] The 36-year-old colonel took command of his force of 988 volunteers, calling them "a noble set of fellows."[8] The 7th Tennessee consisted of six companies from Wilson County, two from Sumner County, one from Dekalb County, and one from Smith County.

The mustering-in ceremony included the presentation of a flag, an elegant ensign sewn by Captain Samuel G. Shepard's sister — Fannie Shepard.[9] The 26-year-old woman proudly handed the regiment's colors to a beaming Private William Stott (Co. B).[10] He humbly raised the banner above his head to a thunderous ovation. It was the first of four flags the regiment would use throughout the war. This original banner was patterned after the Confederate national flag. It was large, measuring 83¾ by 54½ inches. The pennant had a blue canton in the upper left corner, just as the American flag, however there were only eight stars in the field, and they were arranged in a circle, with a space at the bottom for another star. The American flag's thirteen stripes were replaced by three bars, arranged in a red-white-red pattern.[11] The new soldiers revered their pristine banner and venerated their womenfolk. A local newspaper reported, "The ladies of Lebanon who have here-tofor been regarded as angels of peace and for the 'Union' ... are becoming thoroughly involved with the war spirit. They have been busily engaged for the past week in making up the uniforms for the volunteer companies. They are the 'heart and soul' in the Southern Cause."[12]

Once the speeches ended the colonel and the governor warily shook hands. Then Col. Hatton turned his back on the governor and, with an energetic brass band leading the way, marched the 7th Tennessee Infantry Regiment back to its quarters at Camp Trousdale. Hatton became busy, as he now had to outfit and train his exuberant volunteers. Colonel Hatton turned the regimental operations over to his second in command, Lieutenant Colonel John Goodner, and immediately set out in pursuit of weapons for his men. Hatton soon discovered Isham Harris would not support him. The restless regimental commander wrote his wife, "I go this evening, again to Nashville, to see about getting up my guns. I am terribly troubled about it."[13] Eventually the persistent colonel succeeded; Hatton acquired Mississippi rifles, which he declared "the best gun in the service."[14]

Colonel Hatton knew nothing about military tactics and strategy, nor did he understand the powerful effects modern weapons could wreak upon the formations his volunteers were struggling to master. He was similar to every other neophyte commander, possessing no clue what was going to happen. Yes, there were a few veterans from the Mexican War, but these old timers' experiences did little to prepare the naïve volunteers for the horrors facing them. The Tennesseans, just like tens of thousands of new recruits all across the divided nation, were completely ignorant of the alien world they had entered.

The 7th Tennessee, along with a collection of other regiments and battalions, remained at Camp Trousdale, in Sumner County. This location, convenient because of its close proximity to the tracks of the Louisville and Nashville Railroad, was surrounded by level and

ROBERT H. HATTON. Robert Hatton was born in 1826 in Ohio and attended Cumberland University, in Lebanon, Tennessee. An attorney, he also served as a Tennessee state representative in the Congress. Hatton was married to Sophie K. Reilly. He was elected the regiment's first colonel and was promoted to brigadier general (5/23/1862). Robert Hatton was killed at Seven Pines (5/31/1862) (Library of Congress collection Prints & Photographs Division LC-USZ62-83419).

open fields. Here, upon these smooth and grassy grounds, Tennessee's boisterous farm boys and shopkeepers struggled to learn the rudiments of military life and infantry drill.

As Hatton's Tennesseans strained to learn company and battalion drill, one of them, Private Archibald Norris (Co. K), discovered military life much more exciting than he could have imagined. Archie, as his companions called him, was a graduate of Allegheny College in Pennsylvania and had been teaching school in Lebanon. Though a reflective and thoughtful young man, Archie Norris had held his own with school ruffians, once noting, "My troubles in the classroom thicken. I had to punish today two of my scholars. It was a painful duty."[15] Archie relished his freedom from the classroom and enjoyed the rough and tumble life of a soldier.

Private Norris was immensely proud of Robert Hatton and vowed to follow him anywhere. At first, Archie had been reluctant to enlist, arguing, "The evils which our once happy but now distracted country is suffering, have all been the work of demagogues and politicians."[16] However, once Norris had joined Hatton's company, he became confident in Hatton's abilities. Norris had also argued against secession, but he also believed he must defend his home state.[17] Patriotism aside, Norris also enlisted because believed he had reached a defining point in his life. Norris knew he was a decent teacher, but he felt there was more to life than disciplining schoolhouse hooligans. Archie Norris wanted to experience the world and face life's challenges. He recorded in his journal, "My prospects in life seem gloomy indeed. I will soon be thrown out on the cold charities of the world. When I think of the difficulties by which my way is beset I almost shrink from the encounter with life's battles."[18]

Another teacher in Company K and a close friend of Archie Norris was 22-year-old David Phillips. He also joined hoping to experience new horizons. David Phillips was described by his peers as, "A tall youth, a fine physical specimen of young manhood, abundantly capable of mastering the

ARCHIBALD D. (ARCHIE, A.D.) NORRIS. Archibald Norris was born in 1838 near Rome, Tennessee. He attended Allegheny College, Pennsylvania, and was a teacher before the war. He enlisted into Company K as a rifleman and was elected captain (4/26/1862). In 1864 he often led the regiment but was captured at Hatcher's Run (4/2/1865). He married Sarah Baird and they had four children. He became the Wilson County school superintendent and a Tennessee state representative. Archibald Norris died in 1911 (Ruth and Jack Cato family collection).

most stubborn student, yet was a sympathetic, earnest, understanding teacher who challenged the best and inspired ambition in the pupils under his tutelage."[19]

Of the hundreds of farm boys, two brothers, Martin Van Buren Coe and Andrew Coe, also hoped their military experiences would include adventure. They, like so many young men joining the 7th Tennessee, savored their escape from farming's wearisome routines. Martin, the younger of the two, stood five-foot-ten and had strikingly dark eyes, and he danced at the chance to leave his father's prosperous farmstead in Tucker's Crossroads, Tennessee. Though the young man missed his brother and two sisters, he yearned for action, wanting to make something of himself. Martin, as did numerous young Tennesseans, was convinced he had something to prove. Archie Norris described Martin's attitude, writing, "I look back over my past year and see nothing of profit I have done. May my hour of usefulness soon come? I am tired of doing nothing and gaining nothing."[20] Believing they had much to prove, Martin and his brother Andrew eagerly awaited the command sending their regiment to fight the Yankees. They keenly absorbed every rumor suggesting the regiment would quickly be transported to the center of the war.

Other youthful men joined the regiment, and some of them were so young they were legally ineligible to participate. But these fervent adventurers found ways to circumvent the new nation's enlistment guidelines. One of these young volunteers, 16-year-old James Phillips had run away from home, lied about his age, and secured himself a place on the roster of Company F.[21]

Regardless of everyone's anxiety to get at the Yankees, the 7th Tennessee remained at Camp Trousdale until the middle of July 1861, drilling constantly. Colonel Robert Hatton, his staff, and his ten elected company commanders struggled to mold their farmers into fighting men. The officers led their clumsy volunteers in as many as six hours of drill each day, first in squad and platoon-sized entities, then company units and finally in battalion-sized formations. Colonel Hatton, forever the champion of his Tennesseans, wrote, "Boys drilling finely; a nobler set of fellows never set their tents."[22]

In Company B, the newly elected Captain John Fite grappled with his own problems of mastering the drills and then communicating them to his lieutenants and NCOs. Fite, a lawyer before the war, had practiced law with his brother in Carthage, Tennessee, and tackled each day's problems head-on. The 29-year-old had always been that way. Once, years earlier, while Fite attended Lebanon, Tennessee's Cumberland University, one of his professors had taken a dislike to him. Fite, never one to shy away from a confrontation, grew annoyed with the professor's harassment and retaliated. Fite bragged, "I got tired of it finally, and [one day] sitting in the class, I winked at him."[23] The shocked professor reported the incident to the administration and a reprimand soon followed. However, the altercation worked, the instructor never bothered Fite again.

John Fite discovered Lieutenants John Allen and Jack Moore were fast learners and adept at drilling the company, however, the other lieutenant, Joe Greer, appeared not to care. One evening, after a long day's drill, Captain Fite decided to have some fun with his lazy lieutenant. John Fite told Allen and Moore he was going to turn the company over to Greer as they marched back to camp. Fite instructed Allen and Moore, and the company's first sergeant, James Corder, "not to pay attention to any order that came unless [Greer] gave the proper order." Fite then turned the company over to the lieutenant.

The languid officer gave the command to march, but did not know how to give the correct orders to turn the unit around. Fite watched as Greer "marched them a little piece and told them to halt. He stood a while trying to see what he was going to do, but could not get them to turn around." Fite wrote that Lt. John Allen "laid down on the ground and roll[ed] over and liked to killed himself laughing. Finally, someone whispered the proper command to Greer and he got the company properly moving and back to camp."[24]

Unfortunately Lieutenant Greer never grasped the dexterity required for leadership and his situation became arduous as the boys in the company began to make his life difficult. Fite could not change Greer, so, as time passed, he gave the inept lieutenant less and less to do. John Fite came to rely on the calm Lt. John Allen, who quickly had demonstrated soundness of judgment as well as his colorful vocabulary.

In Company G, a formation of volunteers who called themselves the Hurricane Rifles, the men quickly grew to like their leader, Samuel G. Shepard, an ex-teacher from Gladesville, Tennessee. George, as everyone called him, sported a thick, black beard, and a thoughtful, educator's disposition.[25] He led his riflemen with poise and deference. Shepard's Hurricane Rifles always preferred that their 31-year-old leader give the drill commands, a task he became proficient at. Sadly, Shepard's two lieutenants, James "Goat" Hobbs and Monroe Bond, appeared not to possess any leadership attributes. Fortunately 3rd Lt. William "Fox" Graves and 1st Sgt. James Bond stepped forward and eased Shepard's dire situation.[26]

One of Captain George Shepard's volunteers was an ill-dressed mountain man who became the brunt of his comrades' jokes. They liked to laugh, "He got his pants, hat, and shirt off a scarecrow." However, as Shepard observed the gangly soldier he realized the woodsman was extremely adept with his new 54-caliber Mississippi rifle so one day Shepard called the man out in front of the company. Shepard ordered the soldier to prepare to fire. As one soldier recalled, "[He] was ready so quick it sorter (*sic*) astonished us."[27]

Shepard cautioned his troops to watch the mountain fellow, saying, "If he makes a good shot you'll know how to profit by his example." A rumble of disrespect coughed its way along the company's battle line but Shepard ignored the sound. He ordered the woodsman to fire and the bullet went true and centered the target. Shepard said quietly, "We have a man here who knows how to handle a gun and shoot straight." He then took the company through its firing drill but few of the men even approached the fellow's accuracy. After repeated volleys, Shepard halted his troops and called the mountain fellow forward. "Now try to hit the target again," Shepard said, "We'll see if he's as good as he seems to be, or if his first shot was an accident." The fellow nailed the bull's-eye again. Shepard turned to his company and stated, "Evidently he's used to taking squirrels out of treetops. Imitate him, and you'll learn to shoot."[28] The Hurricane Rifles never bothered their sharpshooter again; in fact, from then on Shepard's Tennesseans protected their awkward-looking marksman when anyone came by intent upon pestering.

Though the Tennesseans endured countless hours of drill each day, life at Camp Trousdale was far from harsh. Nearly six thousand young men occupied the locality, making them a commanding focus for everyone within a day's ride. Relatives and loved ones called constantly, bringing picnic baskets and staying to visit. As one Tennessean noted, "Almost everybody, it seems, has been here."[29] For the young men, many away from home for the first time, the endless parade of visitors provided unending excitement, and especially the presence of countless flocks of gaily-dressed young women heightened their exhilaration. One recruit noted the girls, recording, "We were marched to the academy grounds where we rested and were treated to drinks of cold water by the beautiful [academy] girls."[30] Another cheery soldier boasted, "[I] escorted two young ladies to [the] drill grounds — [a] very pleasant day."[31]

Some of the interactions between the young soldiers and the local girls proved to have long-term significance. Private Jeremiah Turner (Co. F) met Sarah McGlothin, a teenager living not far from Camp Trousdale, most likely at one of the numerous dances held in the evenings. The two became close friends and wrote each other throughout the war. Then, once the war ended, Jeremiah Turner returned and the two married in February 1867.[32]

However, even though the camp was besieged by visitors, a few young men suffered homesickness and they slipped away to spend their nights at home. At first the casual coming and going of men was tolerated, but when recruits failed to return promptly their officers were forced to crack down. Most of the fledgling soldiers adhered to the new restrictions, but a few refused to conform to the military schedules, forcing stiffer penalties. Finally, an example had to be made. Archie Norris described the consequences, writing, "[I] witnessed the infliction of the first sentence of a Court Martial on a deserter named M. Henry. He was divested of his uniform, clad in calico breeches and shirt, pants rolled above his knees, head half shorn, uncovered, barefooted, shoes in hand and two huge horns projecting from his forehead. In this condition he was led along the line of regiments drawn up for his reception."[33] Another soldier observed this humiliation and remarked, "While I had the greatest contempt for him, I don't think I ever felt sorrier for a poor devil in my life."[34]

Even though the visitors were wonderful distractions, the most important discussion among all the young men was how they would do in battle. As one writer stated, "The pursuit of courage — and its obverse, the flight from cowardice — proved the ultimate sanction. Courage served as the goad and guide of men in battle."[35] Rumors swept through the company streets every day, tormenting the anxious recruits and intensifying their longings to fight the Northerners. The Tennesseans worried the war would end before they would have a chance to prove themselves. They groaned in frustration, waiting for the command to strike their tents. One soldier noted, "The prevailing opinion in these Tennessee units was that at most sixty days should see the end of their military careers and the full success of their cause. It would be absolutely essential to quickly reach the Virginia battlefield."[36] Lieutenant Colonel John Goodner seconded this concern, writing, "Some think Lincoln will sue for peace in less than three months."[37] A third remarked, "This little fracas will blow over in a few weeks and we'll be home again."[38]

Colonel Robert Hatton and his staff also wanted to get the regiment in motion, but for reasons other than proving Tennessee valor. Even though penalties continued to be handed out for absence and desertion, it was just too easy for the soldiers to dodge camp guards and slip out of camp. Hatton realized if the men were far from home, they would be less likely to sneak away. Robert Hatton wrote his wife, "If we get 2 or 3 hundred miles away from home they will abandon the idea of going home."[39] Therefore, when the order finally came for movement to Virginia, the 7th Tennessee boys were "nearly all ... delighted at the prospect of active service."[40] The volunteers did not worry where they were being sent; they just wanted to get in on the action. Colonel Hatton, relieved his men had been given orders, realized what had occurred; Governor Harris was sending the regiment far away from Tennessee.[41] But the excited soldiers did not worry about the politics of this move. They just savored the moment. As Archie Norris wrote, "[We] were roused up about midnight, struck our tents, packed our knapsacks and prepared to leave."[42]

Robert Hatton's volunteers packed gear, took down tents, and loaded the baggage into the cars of the Nashville and Chattanooga Railroad. This turned out to be a difficult endeavor, because as one recalled, "Most of the men were carrying tremendous amounts of personal baggage in huge trunks," and "a few of the officers and men even had personal body slaves to accompany them."[43] The confusion was sorted out and the 7th Tennessee traveled from Nashville to Chattanooga and on to Knoxville, a two hundred-fifty-mile journey, taking two days. This train ride became a great celebration. One Tennessean jubilantly remembered, "Passing through Nashville had been brief fun for the officers and men. The young ladies of Nashville had come out to honor the troops, flowers were carried by many of them and great baskets of home cook foods, and a good time was had by all."[44]

Amazingly, and to the troopers' dismay, once the regiment reached Knoxville, it went no farther. The soldiers unloaded from the train and set up camp outside of town, where they remained for nearly a week, waiting impatiently and drilling unenthusiastically. Here, to the Tennesseans' disappointment, they received telegraphs describing the great Battle of Manassas. The soldiers were astonished at the fight's results and appalled by the fact they had missed their chance to take part in the war. Archie Norris wrote sadly, "We would have been in the fight had we not stopped so long at Knoxville."[45] Colonel Hatton, as exasperated as his men, made sure his soldiers drilled each day and even conducted a parade through the town of Knoxville. Finally, to the Tennesseans' relief, orders came for the regiment to move. The formation left Knoxville at sundown on July 21, 1861, traveled 370 miles, and arrived in Charlottesville, Virginia, on the morning of July 24.

At one of the stops along the way two companies (B and E) were left behind under the command of Lt. Col. John Goodner. The boys in Captain John Fite's and in Dewitt Douglas' companies saw this freedom as an opportunity and scattered throughout the Virginia town, hunting adventure. Goodner turned to Captain Fite for help in rounding up the missing hooligans. Captain Fite recalled, "I was ordered by Colonel Goodner to take a squad of men and go into Lynchburg and hunt up all the stragglers ... I found them in all sorts of places."[46] The young captain also discovered an odd-looking new soldier wearing the regiment's uniform. The surprised officer inspected this new recruit. Captain Fite noted, "I was satisfied he wasn't a fellow. He was a woman dressed up in boys' clothes. I told her we didn't need any of that sort of recruit. I told her, she'd better put on her own clothing and stay at home, we didn't want no woman killed out there."[47]

Once the entire regiment reached Charlottesville, the men experienced their first encounters with the effects of war. Hundreds of wounded soldiers clogged the town, their ugly wounds shocking to see. Robert Hatton penned a note to his wife, "[Saw] a great number of sick and wounded, from Manassas, here [and] some dead." He continued, "Almost every house in the place is full."[48] Then the wide-eyed soldiers loaded back onto the train and traveled south to Staunton, a ride disappointing the Tennesseans. They wanted to fight the Northerners but now found themselves moving in the opposite direction. Some upset boys unhooked one of the boxcars and it raced down out of the mountains. A shaken John Fite recalled, "When we were nearly on top of the mountain somebody uncoupled the hind car, and it went whizzing back down the mountain. We expected every minute to see it jump the track and carry the whole load of fellows but it didn't leave the track." Fite continued, "If we had found out who did it the balance of the soldiers would have broken his neck."[49] Not surprisingly, the culprits never confessed.

Once the regiment arrived at Staunton, the men were placed within the brigade of Brigadier General Samuel Anderson, a 57-year-old Tennessean from Nashville. General Anderson was an experienced military man, having served as a lieutenant colonel in the 1st Tennessee Infantry during the Mexican War. However, once the war ended, he had served as Nashville's postmaster. Anderson was wealthy and a supporter of Governor Harris for governorship, therefore it was easy for Isham Harris to commission Anderson as brigadier general and place him in command of all Tennessee troops sent to Virginia—the 1st, 7th, and 14th Tennessee infantry regiments.[50]

The regiment remained at Staunton for almost a week and during this time the Tennesseans did little. In Company B, Lieutenant John Allen observed one of his men, an amusing character. Private Tom Lownsborough, now the regimental color-bearer, had a quick mind and a sharp wit. He discovered a sickly kitten and used it as a prop for a variety show, proclaiming it to be an exotic species from Africa, and warning, "I thank you ladies and gentlemen not to smoke here, he can smell it, and nothing makes him so ferocious as the smelling of tobacco smoke." Lownsborough continued with his spiel, saying, "He has been known to eat as many as three grown negroes in one morning ... under ordinary conditions he is mild and gentle, but if aroused he is the most dangerous animal in the world. Keep perfectly quiet ladies and gentlemen."[51] With a tale as inventive as this, it was easy to see why Lownsborough attracted large crowds.

Also during this delay Company B's Lieutenant John Allen was forced to deal with two men in his platoon, Isaac "Ike" Dawson and William James. Ike Dawson, a volunteer from a dirt-poor farm, disliked James; why, no one was certain—maybe because his neighbor was married and had title to his own farm, but who knows? For whatever the reason both 26-year-old riflemen were always quarreling. Whenever the two would get into it their comrades would step in and cool things off. Lieutenant Allen turned to his captain for advice. Captain Fite issued an order one night to Allen and to their company's first sergeant, James Corder, telling him that he "wanted that quarreling stopped, and to notify the gentlemen of that the next time they got to quarreling, they had to fight, but not to let them use any weapons." Not long after, the two "went to fighting ... [and] one of them grabbed a camp kettle and Corder took it away from him, [saying], 'You have to fight with your fists.' They had enough of that, walked off, and there was the end of that quarreling."[52] Ike Dawson, realizing he might actually have to fight Bill James, never bothered him again.

Finally on July 30, 1861, the bored Tennesseans piled into train cars and traveled to Millboro, Virginia. Once at Millboro, the soldier loaded their gear into wagons and the regiment marched to Warm Springs, Virginia, some fifteen miles away. General Anderson, concerned with the size of the brigade's wagon train, gave orders reducing the number of vehicles for each regiment. Colonel Hatton recorded this change, writing, "The baggage is cut down so that a single wagon carries all belongings to a whole company."⁵³ The officers though, continued to transport a lot of gear, but now not in the wagons. The regiment had many slaves taking care of their masters' belongings. Robert Hatton wrote of his personal servant, "Jerry ... is really as good a servant as ever was. He has more sense than any Negro in the regiment — there are some forty."⁵⁴

This march was the first time the men hiked to their next destination, a challenge they accepted with good spirits. The young men trekked westwards, marching steadily, even though it rained all day. That evening Archie Norris recorded in his journal, "Left camp this morning about seven o'clock in a heavy rain. Trudged through mud and water on our way to Warm Springs."⁵⁵ When the men reached their destination they delighted in the warm springs. Though tired and sore from their day's travels the soldiers explored the location's amenities, especially its heated pools. Captain John Fite wrote, "Warm Springs was a great summer resort, and at the spring they had a large house built over the pool, which the warm water ran through. The pool of water must have been about 40 or 50 feet square, and 4 or 5 feet deep. On the side of the pool were little dressing rooms. We all went down there and went in, it felt so good that some of the fellows stayed so long that when they got out they were so weak they could hardly walk."⁵⁶ The locality put the soldiers in such good spirits they were not bothered by the torrential rains drenching their camp, but instead declared, "They would no longer be troubled with dust."⁵⁷ Guilelessly, the soldiers discounted the downpours, ignoring them and delighting in music and dance. One Tennessean noted, "There was in most of the companies one or more who played on the violin, and at night could be heard the notes of the fiddle, and the call of the prompter, as the mazes of a 'cotillion' were gone through or the old 'Virginia Reel.'"⁵⁸

The 7th Tennessee did not stay at Warm Springs. They marched farther west, going up into the Allegheny Mountains, where, as the drenched Archie Norris grumbled, "[we] pitched [our] tents in the rain," near Huntersville, of what is now West Virginia.⁵⁹ Colonel Hatton established a regimental camp there and the farm boys-turned-soldiers settled in for a short period of inactivity. The officers vigilantly drilled their companies during the day, but once the soldiers were freed of their duties they hunted, fished, and gathered blackberries. As one Tennessean observed, "Here the soldiers, not having as yet entered upon the realities of war, spent several weeks resting themselves ... and indulged in hunting and fishing."⁶⁰ The men also found themselves clustering together into small groups, based upon growing friendships. They took to eating together in messes, as they called themselves. One soldier remembered, "[We] were divided into messes and took our cooking [together]."⁶¹ As of yet the war remained nothing other than an extended camping trip and the soldiers struggled to understand its seriousness. Private Ferguson Harris (Co. H) wrote, "[It] was my first night's experience on guard duty. I walked two hours incessantly on a steep hill, almost worn to a frazzle, when Joe Hamilton (Co. F) asked me why I did not come and sit down. When I went to him I found him with his back against a tree and he told me to watch out for the officer of the guard. We became careless and the officer of the guard, Capt. Lafayette Walsh, slipped up behind us while we were discussing Miss Lizzie Catron, of Rome [TN], and Miss Agnes Ragland, of Cherry Valley [TN]. Instead of having us shot as I expected, he commenced going through [our haversacks] looking for something to eat."⁶²

CHAPTER 2

August 2, 1861: Morning

"To die on the battlefield, is glorious."

The mid–August weather turned chilly and the rain continued. Lieutenant Colonel John Goodner recorded, "It rains in torrents every day and we have been wet so often and have slept in the mud on wet ground until we look more like hogs than men."[1] The soldiers' boots, uniforms and clothing fell apart, leaving the men unprotected from the elements. This exposure began to take its toll and the hapless soldiers started lining up for sick call in increasing numbers. Colonel Robert Hatton, alarmed at the mounting tallies of ailing soldiers, wrote, "Our men are suffering today more than for a month past. Have on the sick list this evening, over seventy case of sickness. Three days ago, our morning report showed only ten unfit for duty."[2]

A surprisingly early winter storm blew into the mountains, dropping temperatures and dumping frigid rain upon the men. Hatton recorded this calamity: "We have winter on us, this morning ... and the wind is blowing as cold as is usual in Tennessee in November."[3] Not only did the storm batter the unprepared soldiers, its continuous rain transformed the region's dirt roads into muddy quagmires, preventing wagon movement. The fledgling Confederate supply system collapsed and the men ran out of provisions. Suddenly, the boys' great summer adventure turned dark—the men were cold, wearing disintegrating clothing, wet, and hungry.

An influx of sick soldiers quickly overwhelmed the medical staff. Every available dry space was filled with suffering men wracked by pneumonia and dysentery. There was little the surgeons and hospital stewards could do but rely on their patients' tough constitutions. Most of these young Tennesseans were resilient, but some struggled vainly. As the conditions worsened Colonel Hatton observed, "Where we are, is so flooded with water, and so muddy, as to make it impossible for us to stand it [much] longer. A Tennessee hog pen would scarcely be more uncomfortable."[4]

Private William Johnson (Co. F), a 26-year-old from Statesville, Tennessee, was the first to die. Johnson, a farmer on his mother's small farmstead before the war, had enlisted, dreaming of glory and fame, but instead, he was buried in an isolated grave. Sadly, Johnson's funeral was not to be a solitary instance. He was quickly joined by Pvt. Leroy Perkins (Co. K) and 2nd Lt. William Martin (Co. D), and that was only the beginning; in the weeks to follow dozens more would be buried.

From then on, nothing went right. On August 17, 1861, the 7th Tennessee saw its first soldier killed. Private William Bruce (Co. D) was accidentally shot by a soldier from the 1st Tennessee. Captain John Fite recorded the event: "George Maney [colonel, 1st TN] had his regiment ... out drilling, and they were going through practicing arms, loading and firing but they did not load any [bullets]. One of the fellows evidently got a bullet in a gun some way, and while going through the manual of arms, fired his gun."[5] William Bruce, a 22-year-old from Rainy, Tennessee, was struck in the chest and died a few hours later. Colonel Hatton ordered the regiment to form and, as he described, "[William Bruce] was buried with the honors of war, today, on the side of the mountain, in a hard rain."[6]

Consequently, by the end of August 1861 the 7th Tennessee had lost five men, including Pvt. Elijah Grier (Co. I) who also perished due to pneumonia and dysentery. All five young men had enlisted, prepared to defend their state against Northern aggression, and now they were dead, having never even seen a Yankee. Colonel Robert Hatton summed up what so many Tennesseans felt: "To die on the battlefield, is glorious. To die, away from the comforts and endearments of home, on the ground, in a wilderness, and to be buried alone, without a stone to mark our resting place, is pitiable."[7] The sympathetic and meticulous regimental commander wrote to Harriet Bruce, the young soldier's mother, attempting, "to say something that might give her some comfort, in her sad bereavement."[8]

The rains continued to fall, keeping the Tennesseans wet and cold, as well as preventing supplies from arriving. The men, now out of rations, learned to forage. They scoured the surrounding countryside for food. Captain John Fite noted, "Somebody discovered a pretty fat steer close to where we were and we killed him. [Each] fellow would skin a piece and get him a chunk, and soon that steer was gone. I expect some of him was gone before he was good [and] dead." Fite continued, "Got an old hen and took it back to where we were stopping, cleaned it and stuck it on the end of a ram rod, and held it over the fire until I thought it was done."[9] Lieutenant Colonel John Goodner, frustrated by this nightmare complained, "I expected and sought a position where I could do something." He continued, "To be sent up into these mountains where it rains for a solid month without ceasing [and] rendering the mountain roads impassable. [We are] cooped up [and] can go neither forward nor backward."[10]

The ravenous soldiers were so intent upon foraging they often ignored their senior commanders. Captain John Fite had special problems with one of his recruits, Pvt. James Horn. Fite's rifleman, an 18-year-old farm boy from Chestnut Mount, Tennessee, saw no problem in slipping away from the company whenever he felt like so inclined. Jim Horn, an intelligent young man, saw everything with an eye for adventure. Having never been away from home, he possessed an intense craving to explore, and repeatedly ignored Fite's admonitions. John Fite assigned Horn to guard a supply wagon, warning, "I told him if he left that wagon I'd punish him." Fite recalled, "We hadn't gone far ... [and] Horn wasn't with it. He had left and gone on." The exasperated captain continued, "I saw no more of him until we got to Warm Springs when I looked up and in the porch of a hotel there stood Horn." Fite then "put him in the guard house."[11] Another soldier proficient at obtaining food was Cpt. Lafayette Walsh. A Tennessean wrote respectfully of Walsh's diligence; "Capt. Walsh stole a bee gum ... [however] the bees got down his collar but he still held onto the gum."[12]

Colonel Robert Hatton was aware of the suffering his soldiers endured and he agonized over his boys' situation, complaining, "The boys are out of tobacco, and a number of articles — not to mention whiskey. We eat beef, and bread, and coffee ... occasionally a little rice and a mess of potatoes." Hatton continued, "One of the boys shot a deer yesterday."[13] Another unit's officer watched the Tennesseans scavenge for food and told Colonel Hatton he had "the damnedest regiment he'd ever seen."[14]

In early September 1861, the 7th Tennessee, now numbering 800, marched toward Cheat Mountain as part of the Confederate force ordered to drive away Union troops occupying the region. The regiment arrived at Mingo Flats and approached Federal pickets so closely the men were not allowed to make any noise, or build any campfires. David Phillips (Co. K) recorded, "Camped quite close to the Yankee pickets, ours and theirs in sight."[15] But the Union picket line was not the Tennesseans' real adversary. The weather caught up with the regiment and it rained heavily, soaking everyone. The miserable soldiers waited for sunrise, fully expecting to assault the Yank position. They turned to their commanders, awaiting the commands to go into battle. It was at this time the Tennesseans got their first look at Robert E. Lee. Archie Norris wrote, "Saw Gen. Lee before a house in which the principal officers were quartered. He wore a slouch hat and looked more like a teamster than a general."[16]

The order to attack was never given, and though the Yankees took potshots at the Tennesseans, nothing happened all day. Finally, the companies were pulled back and marched two miles away. Here, in this new location, the men built monstrous fires to dry their clothes. Thankfully the rain quit, giving the tired men something to cheer about. But they still lacked rations, as the roads remained too muddy for wagon movement. David Phillips recorded, "Got nothing to eat till the next evening ... [and] had to go three miles and carry it on our backs."[17]

On September 9, 1861, a force of Union troops attacked the Confederate picket line at Mingo Flats, forcing Col. Hatton to rush the rest of the regiment to the line. The Tennesseans hustled to support their pickets but by the time they arrived the Yanks had withdrawn. Hatton left a reinforced picket guard along the line but nothing happened. For the soldiers on the picket line, the time was spent uncomfortably. One guard wrote, "I [was] with about 60 men under Captain Shepard [and] had to stand picket there the rest of the day and till 11 at night. It was clear and cool. We had no blankets nor anything to eat."[18]

The regiment pulled out of its bivouac and hiked along the base of Cheat Mountain. The trek took all day and into the night, and once again, did so beneath heavy rains. Discouragement burdened the disheartened men and some tossed their extra gear and clothing into the bushes. Soon a litter of discarded blankets, coats, and excess equipment marked their trail. Finally at about midnight, the worn out soldiers halted. David Phillips recorded, "Had to march on little farm paths which were crossed with logs and fences so that it made our march very slow."[19]

The next morning the men arose, ate "bread and boiled beef—half cooked," and continued their slow journey. Again, the rain fell, compelling the officers to whisper to their men, "Keep your powder dry."[20] The regiment rambled through the thick woods, often following no road or trail, but just marks left on trees by the scouts. That evening the Seventh was halted and the men spread out searching for cover from the rain. No fires were allowed and the soaked men made shelters of "leaves and arbors of bushes to sleep under." Then, later in the evening, the rains increased, drenching anyone who had gotten dry. One private wrote in disgust, "Scarcely any sleeping done, everybody and everything wet, completely wet."[21]

The next day the 7th Tennessee continued its trek. That afternoon Hatton's men heard volley after volley rolling through the mountain valley. The colonel ordered the regiment to load their Mississippi rifles. The excited Tennesseans rushed forward, prepared to engage their elusive enemy. But the shooting ceased and when the Tennesseans reached the picket line, they found everyone standing around, milling about in confusion. The Tennesseans grumbled in disappointment. Once again they had missed the action.

This was the wrong time to let down their guard. The Yanks, hidden safely among the thick foliage, fired a volley into the Tennesseans. Private Sam Hope (Co. C) took a Minié ball in his left side, the first 7th Tennessean to be injured by enemy fire. The Tennesseans scattered to places of protection, shocked by the sudden ambush. Private Phillips wrote of the incident, "The Yankees came stealing along unobserved [and] fired at one of Captain Baber's men, the ball taking effect in his left side, inflicting a severe wound."[22] The enraged Southerners tossed aside their blanket rolls and prepared to repel an attack.

Instead, the 1st Tennessee regiment filed through the Seventh's position and worked forward through the underbrush. Moments later, dozens of rifles opened fire. The boys in Hatton's regiment remained in their position, and as Pvt. Phillips recalled, "A tremendous volley shook the mountain sides [and] bullets went whirling and whizzing over our heads cutting limbs and leaves off the trees and bushes."[23] Maney's regiment made a bayonet charge, rushing straight into the Union rifles, and suffered nearly twenty casualties. Colonel Hatton sent a line of his eager boys forward to support the 1st Tennessee. They surged forward, screaming loudly, and helped force the Yanks deeper into the woods. Private J. P. Bashaw (Co. I) recorded, "[We] captured a few prisoners, also killed one man."[24]

Unfortunately in the confusion the severely wounded Sam Hope was forgotten and left behind; by the time order was restored, the unprotected Pvt. Sam Hope had been captured. Taking a bullet in his side only began his travails. Federal surgeons repaired the damage done by the Yankee Minié ball but there was little they could do for their captive when he was hauled off to a prisoner of war camp. Sam Hope, a farmer from Sweetwater, Tennessee, who was married and the father of two children, remained a prisoner for nearly a year before being exchanged at Vicksburg. Regrettably the prison's appalling conditions destroyed Sam Hope's health. The severely ill soldier was shipped to Atlanta and remained in a hospital until November 1863. Then the feeble rifleman rejoined the regiment during the winter of 1863-1864. Sadly his health would not rebound and he could not remain. Sam Hope was placed in a hospital in Staunton, Virginia, in January 1864 and would never return. He died in September 1864, a victim of that ambush three years earlier.[25]

The 7th Tennessee, not long after this confused skirmish, received orders to pull back and march to Mingo Flats. The regiment slipped away and trekked for several hours during the night. They resumed their movement the next day and continued until passing Mingo Flats, Brady's Gate, Valley Mountain, Big Springs, Greenbrier Bridge, Sewell Mountain, Lewisburg, and Frankfort. The Cheat Mountain campaign had been a disaster for the 7th Tennessee. Though the regiment had suffered only one battle casualty, the men's health had been devastated. Nearly half of the regiment was incapacitated by sickness and an entire wagon train had to be assembled just to haul the ailing soldiers back to Warm Springs. Captain John Fite observed, "All of the sick ... were put in wagons, 4, 5, or 6 in a wagon."[26] By the end of September eleven more Tennesseans died, including Martin Van Buren Coe (Co. A), who perished from pneumonia and dysentery. The once-excited recruit now joined his buried comrades in the growing cemetery in Huntersville, West Virginia. One Tennessean summed up their situation, proclaiming, "He had never understood what the word HELL meant until he passed through this Cheat Mountain Campaign."[27] Colonel Robert Hatton agreed, writing to his wife, "men, we can overrun and overcome. The elements are hard to conquer."[28]

The battered regiment remained in the Warm Springs–Greenbrier–Sewell Mountain area, resting and reorganizing. Reinforced companies were sent out to patrol the Union positions and would be gone for days at a time, before rotating back. Supplies and mail came up from Virginia and the 7th Tennessee slowly recovered. On October 6, 1861, rumors swept through the camps that the Yanks had retreated. The 1st and 7th Tennessee Regiments sent battalions forward to investigate and discovered the Federal troops had withdrawn, abandoning derelict wagons, equipment, and rations, leaving the Tennesseans the vicinity to themselves.

Colonel Hatton's regiment continued to occupy the mountainous region as October gave way to November. The soldiers received new uniforms, and a large shipment of packages from home. David Phillips exclaimed, "We ... got some goodies from home. Harper got some fine apples and sweet cakes and two-pound cakes which we ate in the memory of those at home."[29] The soldiers were also paid. An ecstatic Tennessean wrote, "We drew two months' pay which made me feel quite rich, it being the first money I have had in three months."[30]

Even though the soldiers' morale and health improved, weather conditions worsened. The lightly-equipped Tennesseans had little protection from the swirling winds, freezing rain, and biting cold. Their contentment vanished; the brutal mountain climate sapping everything away. Lieutenant Colonel John Goodner grumbled, "Cold weather [is] on us; very heavy frost and ice at night and but few blankets. Our [winter] clothes [have] not reached us yet."[31] In mid–November a brutal winter storm howled through the mountainous area, punishing the Tennessee boys. Private Phillips described their unpleasant conditions; "Our tents are rotten and the gales tear them and upset them, leaving us exposed to the merciless and bitter winds.... The wind blows the smoke of the whole encampment along the ground which makes the air dense with smoke everywhere." He concluded his grievances: "Camp life in cold weather is a very miserable one."[32]

Colonel Robert Hatton agonized over his troops' conditions, and lamented on his thirty-fifth birthday, "It is raining. Rained all last night. Wind blew hard.... We know nothing, as yet, as to what is to become of us."[33] He continued, describing his servant's failing health, and counseled his wife, "Jerry ... has pneumonia.... You must fulfill your part of the contract, to be kind to Jerry's children."[34] Hatton also grieved at the destruction the weather inflicted upon his men. He noted, "I am pained to say that we have lost another boy — young [Robert] Freeman [Co. D].... He was a handsome and spirited young man, and a first rate soldier." Hatton continued sadly, "Say to his mother, her son was as well cared for as if he had been at home, except he did not have the attentions of a mother."[35]

Winter attacked and the miserable soldiers' morale plummeted as they huddled inside their decaying tents. The disconsolate men endured the deepening chill, read letters from home, and counted the days they had left to serve in the Confederate army. One shivering rifleman wrote, "This morning begins the last six months of our service. Day gloomy and rainy. During the past six months we have endured innumerable ills such as soldiers alone are heir to."[36] A dozen more Tennesseans died during November. The soldiers, now believing they had been forgotten by the Confederate high command, clamored for escape from their windswept mountain campground.

Colonel Hatton pleaded with the high command but received no orders to relocate his regiment. Finally, he took matters into his own hands and decided upon movement. He ordered the men of nine companies to abandon their tents and move into structures around the town of Warm Springs. One company, though, he needed to position in Hot Springs as a mountain guard, and to protect the sick housed there. The march to this location required a miserable day-long, muddy trek, so whichever company assigned to that task would suffer. Hatton could not decide which unit to offend so he called in his company commanders and asked for a volunteer. The captains, all wanting to protect their men, shuddered at Hatton's request.

The quick-thinking Cpt. John Fite saw an opportunity in Robert Hatton's appeal. Fite took his colonel aside and whispered, "I [have] a fellow in my company by the name of Ben Ferguson who [is] as mean as the devil. I want to get rid of him." Fite pressed his demand, "If he'd discharge Ben Ferguson I'd take [my] Company."[37] And thus, Ben Ferguson, a 26-year-old disgruntled farmer-turned-soldier, was given his release and he immediately returned to his wife, child, and small farm in Granville, Tennessee — and Hatton got a volunteered company to perform an arduous duty.

The Tennesseans in the other companies were reluctant to walk away from their tents, which though miserable, were better than the unknown. They did not trust the news they were being shifted to better lodging. However, when the Tennesseans realized what Hatton had done, the boys quickly responded, and as one soldier boasted, "[Went] to my new home today. Owl's Nest is the name.... Found it to be a very nice place." He continued, "We went to fixing it up immediately. Our furniture consisted of two chairs, two beds-steads, four tables, safe and other articles of much household importance." He concluded, "We enjoyed ourselves finely."[38]

They were immensely pleased with their shelters and scattered about the region, collecting tables, beds, chairs, and other amenities. They took in loads of firewood and luxuriated in warmth, protected from the harsh outdoor weather. Therefore, when they received orders for the high command to march, none were pleased. One unhappy soldier wrote, "This is sad news to us of the Owl's Nest."[39]

On December 1, 1861, the 7th Tennessee began its movement down out of the mountains and arrived in Millboro and set up their tents just in time to be buried by a snowstorm. The regiment remained at Millboro for a week before the men climbed into a train and rode to Staunton. Then, they retrieved their baggage, set up camp, and waited six more days before being ordered to march to Strasburg, Virginia.

As the sullen troops shifted into marching formation, Lt. Col. John Goodner commanded the Seventh's band to play and the regimental colors to be unfurled. At first the Tennesseans refused to respond to their band's buoyant music, but when the lively tunes attracted the Virginian civilians along the road the Tennesseans threw back their shoulders and marched proudly through the towns and along the valley turnpike. They hiked northward most of day, covering about ten miles. The next day, again to the rhythm of their band, the regiment journeyed northward and again, the Virginians came out to the road, waving and cheering, and eased the soldiers' burden. However, by nightfall and after covering almost twenty miles the Tennesseans were tired and footsore. David Phillips summed up their condition: "Much suffering in the flesh on account of corns, blistered feet and sore bones. Everybody broke down and worn out."[40]

The Tennesseans, marching unprotected beneath an unrelenting winter sky, continued to sicken and die; another dozen perished. One of these Tennesseans to fall was Captain James Baber (Co. C), a 23-year-old son of a wealthy farmer near Gallatin, Tennessee. Colonel Hatton solemnly recorded, "Capt. Baber ... he is gone.... Was sick twelve days." Hatton then remarked, "My heart bleeds at the death of noble boys of my command.... If they must die, may it be on the battlefields, where their lives may be dearly sold."[41]

Barely pausing long enough to bury their dead, the formation continued on and passed through Harrisonburg, Lacey's Springs, Sparta, and into New Market. All along the turnpike, people came out to listen to the regiment's band, watch the soldiers pass, and to wave and cheer. Once in New Market, Lt. Col. Goodner halted the men and formed the companies in front of a house displaying Confederate flags. The inspired Tennesseans presented arms and gave honors to their new nation's colors.

One soldier, as he gave tribute to the Confederate flag, paid only half attention to the patriotic proceedings. Instead, he checked out the local women and remarked, "Virginia is noted for her handsome women with their bright eyes and rosy cheeks."[42] He, like many a Tennessean, had never seen so many different girls in his entire life. The regiment continued northward, hiking to Woodstock, where the boys were treated by the townsfolk. Private David Phillips gratefully remarked, "The girls and servants brought out bread and meats of any quantity. Everybody got plenty." He also noted, "Found clever folks and a pretty girl who seemed to be interested ... in soldiers. Got a splendid dinner of good things. Jim fell in love with the girl, Eliza."[43]

The troops returned to the turnpike and reached Strasburg about noon on December 21, 1861. The men bivouacked about a half mile outside town in a field beside a stand of cedar, of which many Tennesseans remarked, "Looks very much like some of our Wilson County country."[44] Two days later, the rest of the Tennessee brigade reached Strasburg, along with another winter storm. That night as the soldiers suffered beneath the ferocious winds, tragedy struck. Private Clark Harrison (Co. H), a 25-year-old teacher from Green Hill, Tennessee, was accidentally shot in the head. One of his comrades described the 6-foot-tall Tennessean's last moments; "There was a drunk soldier asleep on his gun in the hotel. [Clark Harrison] went to take up the gun which was loaded. It went off ... killing him instantly. Harrison was a fine man, liked by all."[45]

The regiment remained in camp and the resourceful Tennesseans took advantage of their nearness to Strasburg by finagling ways to obtain liquor. Soon, numbers of intoxicated soldiers staggered around camp, forcing Colonel Hatton to detail patrols just to guard against alcohol coming into camp. This contest to keep liquor out of camp was a never ending struggle, and the officers usually were on the losing side. One Confederate lamented, "Every load of forage has to be searched by running our ramrods through it in search of bottles or jugs, and sometimes five-gallon kegs. The soldiers have a lot of mysterious ways to get into camp with it. For instance, push a stopper down the neck of the jug, pour a little milk on it, and put in another stopper; or carry it in his gun barrel."[46]

Captain John Fite recorded one incident with an ingenious imbiber: "Charles Simpson [Co. F] [had] a keg of whiskey ... on his shoulders. I arrested him and took him around to Hatton's headquarters with his keg of whiskey. Hatton ... threatened him with all sorts of punishment [and] told me to put him in the guard house." The next day John Fite was ordered to take a platoon and go into town and round up the liquor salesmen. Fite was shocked to discover Charles Simpson staggering beneath the weight of a keg of whiskey. Captain Fite arrested Simpson, but to his amazement, the drunk responded, "Col. Hatton had allowed him to take [the keg] back and give it to the fellow and get his money." Fite then returned to his colonel, fuming, and was astonished when Robert Hatton told him, "He felt sorry for the poor fellow."[47]

Colonel Hatton eased up the struggle against drink on Christmas Eve and his Tennesseans took advantage of the situation. Many of the boys combined eggs with whiskey and by Christmas morning almost everyone was in a drunken stupor. Therefore, when orders came for the regiment to march, few men were in condition to go anywhere. When Cpt. John Fite assembled his company, he declared, "There were a great many so drunk that they couldn't walk. We put the drunkest ones in the wagon and hauled them along."[48] The befuddled Tennessean troops stumbled northward and arrived in Winchester that evening, only to remain there for almost a week. Why, wondered the tormented soldiers, had they been forced to march on Christmas morning? David Phillips grumbled, "I am tired of doing nothing and gaining nothing." The soldier summarized their situation: "I look back over my past year and see nothing of profit I have done. May my hour of usefulness soon come."[49]

On January 1, 1862, the 7th Tennessee struck their tents and marched toward Romney, some thirty-five miles west of Winchester. The Tennessee brigade had been assigned to Stonewall Jackson's command. The boys welcomed this change; they knew Jackson had a reputation for action and the Tennesseans still clamored to come to grips with the Yankees. Now, they hoped, Jackson would get them into battle.

The men trekked west and then northward and several days later ended up near Bath. When Col. Hatton heard gunfire he prepared his impatient soldiers for combat. They hustled toward the sounds of shooting, only to find nothing had happened. As one frustrated Tennessean complained, "We loaded and moved up the road in quick time.... We expected to have a fight every minute.... After dark we were about-faced and marched back a short distance and camped."[50] Not long afterward, snow began to fall. The Tennesseans, now used to weathering winter storms, took action to protect themselves. David Phillips wrote, "We got our rail fires built [and] went to a nearby house and got some hay and built ... a shelter in my mess with rails and covered it with hay." Sadly, their efforts did little to help. Phillips complained, "Had a very disagreeable time on account of the cold and the lack of blankets."[51]

Stonewall Jackson did not let the weather slow down his push forward. On January 4, 1862, the regiment was ordered to advance against the Union positions. Federal artillery opened fire, and as Pvt. Phillips remarked, "These were the first cannon I have heard during the war."[52] Colonel Hatton's boys were placed in support of the 1st Tennessee and followed along behind Colonel Maney's troops as they moved forward.

Orders came to detach a wing; Hatton immediately sent the companies commanded by John Fite (Co. B), George Shepard (Co. G), and Tom Bostick (Co. K) away from the regiment. The soldiers rushed toward the sounds of fighting. One of Bostick's men wrote, "We soon came to where the Yanks and militia had their skirmish in the morning. [I] saw where the bullets cut the trees."[53] The Tennesseans scrambled up the elevation and took shelter behind trees and stone fences. They were ready to fight! Captain Fite ordered the three-company battalion to give a holler and the men responded with a robust yell. A few minutes later the shooting diminished, and soon the area was silent. The Tennesseans pressed forward and came to where the Union troops had bivouacked but found the Yanks gone. Their campground was littered with baggage, equipment, and abandoned gear. One Confederate recorded: "[Our] troops had not advanced far before the enemy fled, leaving his baggage and stores."[54]

The three companies rejoined the regiment and moved toward Hancock at the double-quick. The Tennesseans hustled, covering the five miles in just over an hour. But events outpaced them; a fight had already occurred: Confederate cavalry leading the race to Hancock had been ambushed and driven back. There was nothing for the breathless Tennesseans to do but recover from their efforts, listen to the sounds of artillery, and watch the artillery muzzle flashes.

Later, Hatton's men were moved back a couple of hundred yards and bivouacked. Orders were given to build no campfires, so the men spent the night shivering in the cold. One Tennessean groused, "We had nothing to eat again that night. It was severely cold and I spent a cold, sleepless night ... not daring to lie down for fear of freezing."[55] The next day the regiment moved back about a mile and met up with their baggage train. The Tennesseans collected their gear, put up tents and cooked meals. A relieved Pvt. Phillips wrote, "We received orders to ... make ourselves comfortable for the night. We did so and I never had such sweet sleep in my life."[56]

Nothing happened for the next week. During this time the men huddled in their tents and listened to sporadic artillery fire. The only action during that time was when Captain John Fite received orders to take a platoon and cross the Potomac and tear up the railroad tracks. Fite and his volunteers paddled across the river in a boat, and as he noted, "We had pulled up some of the rails when I heard a train coming. We hurried back across the river ... when [the train] struck the rails we had loosened up, the whole trained jumped the track and ran down into the river." Fite sadly remembered, "It turned out to be a train of cattle, of course they were drowned."[57]

Eventually the regiment was shifted back to Bath where it became part of the advance guard for Jackson's army. Colonel Robert Hatton's regiment, and the 1st and 14th Tennessee moved in nearby, and all three formations were given permission to erect winter quarters. An excited Tennessean described his new abode, "Our mess commenced to raise winter quarters today. Expect to be employed for several days in fortifying against storm and snow.... The rain and sleet ceased about noon and we resumed our labors on our quarters. We completed them during the day and found ourselves very comfortable and happy, sitting around a fire in a chimney singing and making ourselves merry. We call our house, 'Pinefort.'"[58]

However, once the Tennesseans were comfortably situated, their good fortune vanished. The Confederate high command gave orders for the brigade to relocate. An exasperated Col. Hatton argued, but to no avail. He lamented, "[We] had no alternative but to obey, and we had to comply with the order."[59] On February 8, 1862, the regiment moved a short distance from where the men had constructed their cabins, and the frustrated Tennesseans were forced to rebuild. This relentless chaos and turmoil left the men "wearied almost to death."[60] During January and February the 7th Tennessee's regimental rolls were reduced by over fifty discharges, including eleven young men who died from pneumonia, dysentery, or tuberculosis. Three officers also resigned: Cpt. Thomas Bostick (Co. K), 1st Lt. James Hobbs (Co. G), and 3rd Lt. Benjamin Tarver (Co. K). And, one unfortunate rifleman, 29-year-old Frank Campbell (Co. H), was seriously injured when a tree fell on him. Colonel Hatton wrote his wife a lament many of his men also felt: "Oh, when will it be my lot to go home!"[61]

The disconsolate Tennesseans hibernated within their huts, attempting escape from the alternating cycles of sleet, icy rain, and snow. With little to do the men became consumed with thoughts of going home. As one unhappy soldier sighed, "Furlough fever continues to rage. A company is being made up from the regiment which is likely to secede."[62]

On February 13, 1862, Colonel Hatton's boys were dumbfounded by the news that Colonel Maney's 1st Tennessee regiment was to be shipped back to Tennessee. Colonel George Maney, the 36-year-old Tennessean from Franklin, had been pressuring the Confederate high command, arguing forcefully for movement of his regiment back to Tennessee. Maney, the son of a wealthy planter and a veteran of the Mexican War, employed his political connections and succeeded. Hatton's boys dejectedly watched Maney's troops pack up and head for home.

Then, as the Tennesseans picked through Maney's abandoned camp, they received word that Union troops had advanced into Tennessee. One wrote, "There was great excitement in camp on account of a report that the enemy had taken Nashville."[63] This news was soon updated — Fort Donelson had fallen, not Nashville. Hatton's boys were, "gloomy and dispirited over the news ... [and] doubly anxious to go to Tennessee."[64] Colonel Robert Hatton pulled every string he could as he fought to get his regiment reassigned to a command in Tennessee, but he failed. Hatton grumbled to his wife, "I get no reply to my application from Richmond ... nothing so far has been accomplished toward getting us home." Finally, after more of his pleas were rebuffed Hatton wrote, "I fear we have no longer any chance."[65]

The Confederate high command ordered the 7th Tennessee out of their winter quarters on February 22, 1862, and directed the men to hike to Manassas, some seventy miles away. The Tennesseans crossed the Shenandoah River the next day on ferryboats and camped near Snickersville. They marched southward and eastward for several days, crossing over the old battlefield of Manassas. The wide-eyed Tennesseans looked about in awe: "We passed through where the hottest of the fight was. Saw a great many skeletons of both men and horses. Saw a great many clothes that had been torn from the dead bodies of the enemy." Robert Hatton wrote, "The sight was almost heart-sickening, yet it must have been dreadful just after the battle."[66]

That next evening the regiment was put into railroad cars and transported to Fredericksburg, and from there, to Aquia Creek. The rapid movement went almost unnoticed — the Tennesseans had received terrible reports from home. David Phillips recorded; "Most disheartening news ... our army had fallen back to Huntsville."[67] The Tennessee boys muttered to each other in despair, "We are completely cut off from our homes," and as Pvt. Phillips noted, "Every man's heart seemed ready to burst with mingled emotions of regret and indignation ... suffering keenly with the pangs of total separation."[68]

Wilson County, Tennessee, was now under Yankee rule. On March 22, 1862, the Federal 23rd Kentucky Infantry, commanded by Colonel Marcellus Mundy, marched into Lebanon, Tennessee, took over the Cumberland University campus and quartered in the college's barracks. The Kentuckians, pleased to sleep under a roof, fanned out throughout the town, exploring the homes of so many soldiers who now camped so far away. Colonel Mundy's young men, many away from home for the first time, and excited to find a town so devoid of men their own age, but yet filled with young women, reveled in their circumstances. One of these young men, 24-year-old Thomas Hastings of Crittenden, Kentucky, moved among Lebanon's citizens, his heart set upon finding romance. Private Hastings, and many other lonesome soldiers like him, represented the Tennessean boys' ultimate fear: the invading soldiers targeting their women. Private Thomas Hastings would begin courting Sarah Jacobs, a cousin of 2nd Lt. Newborn Jennings (Co. G).[69]

Colonel Hatton redoubled his efforts and tried to speak one on one with Confederate president Davis. Hatton was tortured by the knowledge that Colonel Maney had personally seen President Davis and succeeded in getting his unit returned to Tennessee. Hatton argued, "Now that our homes are invaded, we feel that we should be sent there."[70] But there would be no re-assignment, and there would be no appeal; the 7th Tennessee would remain in Virginia. The exasperated officer wrote, "[I] have made every effort, consistent with propriety and soldierly bearing, to get my regiment ordered to Tennessee; have entirely failed — the President preferring to retain us here."[71] Hatton continued, his misery the same as hundreds of his men, "You can form ... no adequate conception of the anxiety, the pain, that I have experienced, in the thought that my home is now within the lines of the enemy; that my wife and children are within their reach, in their power — and I remote from them, separated by many cruel miles, from all I most love — barred away by the arms of an invading army."[72]

Accepting defeat, the heartsick Hatton called his officers together and urged them to hold the regiment together. The 7th Tennessee remained part of Anderson's brigade, now consisting of only two regiments. This problem was solved by the addition of the only other Tennessee regiment in Virginia. This formation, strangely, also called the 1st Tennessee, had been in Virginia almost from the start of hostilities. This 1st Tennessee, commanded by Col. Peter Turney, had been part of Barnard Bee's brigade at the time of the Battle of Manassas. Though the Tennesseans did not participate in that first battle the men moved with the swagger of battle-seasoned veterans. They quickly made themselves the "kings" of Anderson's Tennessee brigade, lording over the entire 2,000-man formation.

Hatton, observing the difference between his moody men and the self-confident cockiness of those under Colonel Turney, realized his troops needed to be shaken from their lassitude. Further instruction was the answer. Hatton ordered twice-a-day drills and a dress parade in the evening. His disheartened young men drilled and carried on. Private David Phillips noted this additional work: "Had company drill in the morning in the exercise of our [bayonets].... Had battalion drill in evening."[73] Hatton was correct the constant drill forced the Tennesseans out of their lethargy. After considerable drill, Phillips wrote, "Our good execution of marching to the front was a theme of praise by all."[74]

On April 6, 1862, the regiment was rousted from its tents and Hatton's men were told of a great victory in western Tennessee. At first, Gen. Anderson addressed the assembled troops but then had Maj. John Howard read the details of the great battle and victory of Pittsburg, Tennessee. The Tennesseans "gave three times three cheers for our glorious success."[75] Of course, successive dispatches would correct this earlier news — the Southerners had suffered a dramatic defeat in Tennessee, at Shiloh.

Colonel Hatton's men did not have much time to brood; two days later the brigade was ordered to march to Richmond, and of course, it began to rain the moment the Tennesseans lined up to march. David Phillips wrote, "It was a bitter pill to pull down one's tent and pack and march in the mud and cold rain. But we did it."[76] The troops halted outside of the city and camped for several days until being told to continue toward Yorktown. The weather turned hot and dry, causing the men to suffer, but they marched onward, driven by the hope of a coming battle. By April 20, 1862, the 7th Tennessee camped southeast of Williamsburg and near enough to Yorktown to hear artillery fire. The men waited for orders.

While bivouacked outside Williamsburg Hatton's boys learned the Confederate Congress had passed the Conscription Act, requiring the "conscription of all able-bodied males between 18 and 35 ... for three years or for the duration of the war."[77] Along with this legislation, the Confederate high command realized most of their soldiers had signed up for only one year's service and within the next couple months these volunteers would complete their terms of service. Accordingly, the Confederate Congress provided a fifty dollar bonus to each man who re-enlisted and for the opportunity to re-elect officers. This caused great excitement among the Tennesseans. A number of the original officers had proven to be inept, as well as unpopular. This was the perfect time to replace them with men of demonstrated leadership ability. Private David Phillips recorded, "The question of reorganization is being agitated considerably. Many officer seekers are making themselves prominent."[78]

Elections occurred throughout the 7th Tennessee, weeding out unpopular commanders and replacing them. Robert Hatton proudly wrote his wife, "I was re-elected without opposition." He added, "Col. Goodner and Maj. Howard were also re-elected." But then, in surprise, Hatton recorded, "Only four of our Old captains were re-elected."[79] Hatton's surviving captains were John Fite (Co. B), John Fry (Co. C), George Shepard (Co. G), and William Williamson (Co. H). Everyone else would be new to company command.

This far-reaching leadership transformation occurred throughout the regiment. New captains were elected by the men of Companies; A, D, E, F, I, and K. In Company K, Private David Phillips chronicled the change in command: "It soon became evident that the contest for captaincy would be hot and close. [Archibald] Norris and [Thomas] Bostick were candidates." Phillips described the dispute, writing, "On the first ballot they tied. The next vote became more exciting and interesting. Norris [won], having 39 votes to Bostick's 33."[80] Norris' elevation, along with many other newly-elected officers, remade the regiment's structure. The 7th Tennessee now had six new captains, and 22 rookie lieutenants.

Within the ranks of each company, re-elections for sergeants and corporals proved just as turbulent and resulted in considerable turnover among noncommissioned officers — there were 74 newly promoted sergeants and corporals. The regimental adjustments did not cease with the NCO exchanges; the Conscription Act also affected the riflemen. Volunteers who were over 35 or under 18 were discharged, as were many individuals who had become disabled or chronically ill. Private Enoch Brown (Co. B), a 51-year-old day laborer who had joined the regiment, was sent home, his release noted in his records as "discharged because of seniority." Another rifleman, 46-year-old Daniel Searcy (Co. I), was also sent to his farm where his wife and three children awaited him.

One Tennessean who was discharged, 46-year-old Joseph Lannom, returned home to Wilson County and resumed farming, only to be murdered. Lannom was killed by a man named Richard Mount, whom everyone knew simply as "Cedar Dick." The murder had been bloody, as Cedar Dick assaulted Lannom "with a large ... Bowie knife ... and killed Lannom [by] cutting and stabbing."[81]

Private Tom Rose (Co. C), a 16-year-old blacksmith's apprentice from Gallatin, was dismissed, his personnel file closed with the phrase "discharged, minority." And another youngster, 16-year-old Robert Allison (Co. A), was also cleared from the company rolls because of his age.[82] In all, 114 Tennessean volunteers were removed from the regimental rolls. Col. Hatton, along with his surgeons, Dr. Robinson Gutheridge and Dr. James Fite, also took this opportunity to cull from the regiment's ranks volunteers who were not able to withstand the physical demands of military life. Most of these men suffered chronic illnesses, were lame, or possessed deformities preventing them from full participation in regimental duties. One such Tennessean was Pvt. Eli Sellars (Co. G), a 24-year-old farm boy who was discharged because of deafness.[83] In all, another 107 Tennesseans were discharged.

Though the Tennesseans had been in the army for almost an entire year, they had experienced enemy gunfire only briefly, and to little effect. The men of the 7th Tennessee had marched over 1,500 miles, completing wearing out their boots and shoes.[84] They had suffered under enough rain and snow to destroy their uniforms, and they had endured many days without meals. Thus, combined with their new officers, the final result was a leaner, better led, and more efficient regiment. Their first year's experiences were over; there was no way the Tennesseans could foresee the violence lying ahead of them. However, they stood ready, just over 600 Tennesseans still eager to fight, though none could know the road they were about to travel.

CHAPTER 3

May 8, 1862: Morning

"If I should not return, be a mother to my wife and children."

The officers released from the 7th Tennessee headed to Richmond, and from there most went back to Tennessee. Many of the Tennesseans referred to this as "The Exodus."[1] The new company commanders began to drill their units, learning how to give the commands and how to deal with personnel problems. The men also got their first looks at their newly elected leaders. A rifleman in Company K evaluated his new captain, writing, "We have Camp Trousdale drill today, Captain Norris commanding a favorable impression."[2] Unfortunately there was little time for more training; orders came directing the regiment to move to the Chickahominy River.

On May 8, 1862, the 7th Tennessee, as well as the other two regiments in Anderson's brigade moved into the deep woods near Bottom Bridge, about a mile south of the Richmond and York Railroad tracks. Colonel Hatton's 600-man regiment worked its way through the heavy foliage, searching for contact with the enemy, a goal so many had sought for nearly a year. Today the Tennesseans would not be disappointed. Their skirmish line bumped into the Yanks and shooting erupted. Though the vegetation made vision difficult and movement strenuous the hungry-to-fight Tennesseans slowly pushed the Yanks back nearly 2,000 yards. An excited Southerner reported, "It was impossible to see over 30 or 40 yards ... and [the Federals left] many dead and wounded on the field."[3]

The bluecoats stiffened their resolve and held firm once beneath the protection of Federal gunboats floating on the Chickahominy. The riverboats' big guns opened fire, forcing Hatton's boys to, as one groused, "grab a root," and seek shelter. A couple of the Tennesseans refused to take cover and instead stood stoically above their brothers, because, as one put it, "A soldier ... was not brave if he did not stand out and let [the enemy] shoot at him." It did not take long, though before these fellows took cover and "hid behind almost anything [they] could find."[4]

The bombardment ceased at sunset and General Anderson notified Colonel Hatton to pull his Tennesseans back. The weary boys quietly crept from their hiding places and made their way through the underbrush back to where they had been earlier in the day.

The Tennesseans had been under fire for several hours. Though no one had been hurt Colonel Hatton's boys were subdued. Private David Phillips wrote solemnly, "By the Gracious Providence of God I am here sound and unhurt."⁵ Though the entire Tennessee brigade lost only four men, the day's action had been more severe than anything the Tennesseans had ever experienced; little did they know it was nothing compared to what was coming.

The next day Colonel Hatton's regiment inched backward, keeping aligned with the rest of Anderson's Tennessee brigade, part of a gradual Confederate retreat. By May 21, 1862, the Confederates found themselves along the Chickahominy River, about a dozen miles east of Richmond, near Bottom Bridge, assigned the duty of guarding the crossing. The location was quiet because the Union forces had not pursued and several miles separated the two battle lines. There was little for Hatton's riflemen to do except worry about things back home.

Shockingly, the boys from Wilson County received a report of a fight right in the streets of their home town — Lebanon. An astonished Robert Hatton wrote, "The Yankees are in Lebanon? My house surrounded by a hostile foe."⁶ This initial story was soon followed by successive accounts of the fight, each story providing details of appalling verity — not only had Confederate troops been defeated, they had run away! Colonel Hatton reacted: "[I am] disgusted at ... what I heard."⁷ David Phillips wrote, "Oh, how distressingly sad it is to be so completely cut off from home."⁸

ANDREW B. MARTIN. Andrew Martin was born in 1836 and attended Cumberland University. He practiced law before the war and enlisted into the 7th as a 3rd Lt. in Company H. He was relieved of duty and transferred to Brig. Gen. Joseph Wheeler's staff. After the war he married Cora Alice Ready and they had seven children. He practiced law and served in the Tennessee state legislature. Andrew Martin died sometime after 1920 (Loewentheil Family Photographic Collection).

The first Union troops that had occupied Lebanon had been transferred to another location, enabling Confederate colonel John Hunt Morgan to slip back into the town, along with nearly 800 of his troopers. Morgan then began using Wilson County as his base from which to attack Union supply trains. The Federal command responded to his attacks by sending a force to stop him. On the night of May 4, 1862, Col. Morgan quartered two companies of his cavalry in the Cumberland University's structures, and the rest in buildings surrounding Lebanon's courthouse square. The troopers' mounts, however, were picketed in livery stables throughout the town, a decision based upon convenience rather than military expediency. Morgan made his headquarters near the town's square, but the dashing and single 36-year-old Alabamian chose to spend the night at the home of Dr. Joseph Anderson, a 46-year-old physician, who along with his vivacious wife, Mary, and pretty 19-year-old daughter Sarah provided a pleasant and entertaining evening. Morgan's absence from his command, as well as the inopportune positioning of the unit's mounts, would lead to disaster.

During the night Northern troops under the command of Brig. Gen. Ebenezer Dumont crept to within four miles of Lebanon. Dumont's 600 men paused, waiting for sunrise before rushing the Confederate pickets posted as an advance warning. The Federals attacked the small force of defenders and overcame all but one, Trooper Pleasant Whitlock, who escaped and raced ahead of the attackers. Whitlock reached Lebanon's central square and gave the alarm before being shot from his mount. But Morgan's soldiers had no time to react. The Confederates bunking in the campus tried to get to their horses but Yank forces prevented them from reaching the livery stables. The shocked Southerners attempted to assemble a defense, but lacking mobility, they were crushed. The survivors fled to the safety of the town's buildings. Some of Morgan's men who had been quartered around the square had enough time to mount and respond. They fought the Federals in a running battle sweeping northward from the square.

By this time John Hunt Morgan rushed into the fight to give gave his soldiers critical leadership. He rallied his men and they pushed back against the Federals and for a few terrific moments the battle roared with horrific results. Three out of the four Union commanders were shot from their horses, and dozens of men were hit. The Confederates took sizeable casualties as well. Then unexpectedly, Morgan, an aristocrat known for his riding abilities, lost control of his horse. One Tennessean noted, "The curb of Black Bess' bridle slipped and the excitable mare ran away down the pike."[9] Morgan's soldiers, knowing their fearless commander as one of the best horsemen in the South, assumed he had given the command to retreat. Those men able to disengage from the battle fled northward, following their colonel.

Morgan eventually regained control of his horse, but by now it was too late. Union troops controlled the center of town and captured scores of stunned Confederates. John Hunt Morgan attempted to organize the few men accompanying him, but much of his force had been scattered. He realized the battle was over—he had been beaten. Morgan ordered a retreat at about the same time another force of Union cavalry arrived. The Northerners chased Morgan and his troops for nearly twenty miles before the Confederates were able to ferry across the Cumberland River to safety.

Meanwhile, back in Lebanon Union troops went from house to house, rooting out the remaining Confederates. One last resolute group holed up in the Old Fellows Hall, a stout brick building, and shooting from its many windows drove back attempts to assault the position. The Yankees, not wanting to suffer needless casualties, surrounded the building and from hiding places kept up a stiff fire upon the Confederates. The fighting raged for nearly an hour before a truce was arranged and the Confederates were convinced to surrender. Six officers and 60 men laid down their weapons and walked out of the hall, thus ending the battle for Lebanon. The Federals lost 6 killed and 25 wounded. Morgan's command suffered as many as 60 casualties and another 200 captured. One Yankee laconically wrote of the fight, "Our boys whipped them badly."[10] John Hunt Morgan was devastated. One Tennessean wrote of his reaction, "Tears were in the commander's eyes as he saw the result of the day's disaster."[11]

Regardless of how badly Morgan felt about the details of his defeat, the Tennesseans stuck in Virginia felt betrayed. Confederate troops had run away, leaving their families unprotected. Robert Hatton's men shook their heads in disgust; how could good Southern men of conscience run away and leave women and children behind? Colonel Hatton summed up their loathing, writing, "These are strange times, giving rise to strange things."[12]

But neither Colonel Hatton nor his men had time to dwell on the disaster striking their homes; there was a war going on in Virginia which they could not escape. Their brigade's commander, Brig. Gen. Sam Anderson, suffering from a serious illness, resigned his commission and returned to his home in Athens, Tennessee. Before he relinquished his command, Anderson wrote to the secretary of war, George Randolph, requesting Robert Hatton be given command of the brigade. Anderson's petition proved successful, and Pvt. David Phillips noted, "Colonel Hatton today received the command of this brigade."[13]

Robert Hatton's promotion caused tremendous excitement among the men in the Seventh. They were proud of their commander and celebrated his promotion. John Goodner was promoted to colonel, John Howard moved up to lieutenant colonel, and John Fite was approved for major. The regiment's new commanding officer, John Goodner, a 39-year-old farmer from Alexandria, Tennessee, had much more military experience than Robert Hatton. Goodner, a captain during the Mexican War, had led his squadron in 1846-47 and made a favorable impression on them. One of his veterans wrote years later, "I joined Captain Goodner's company [in] ... the 1st Tenn. Regt. of Mounted Infantry.... Our uniform was gray.... We fought ... at the battle of Vera Cruz [and] ... at Cerro Gordo. Then ... [we] guarded four wagon loads of gold and silver from Vera Cruz to Jalapa."[14]

Robert Hatton said good-by to his beloved regiment and began leadership of the brigade, which included the 1st, 7th, and 14th Tennessee infantry regiments, and a four-gun battery called Braxton's battery. The entire formation numbered 2,300 men.

The newly promoted general took his duties seriously. He immediately shifted men around, creating a team of assistants who could help him administer to the needs of his brigade. One of these assignments went to Rufus McClain, the sharp 25-year-old from Silver Springs, Tennessee. McClain, appointed as Hatton's chief brigade quartermaster, assumed the task of wringing supplies from the ineffectual Confederate commissary and quartermaster departments and would struggle with this unrewarding task for the rest of the war.

The Confederate high command ordered General Hatton to move his brigade to a low bluff overlooking the Chickahominy River, just beyond the eastern outskirts of Rich-

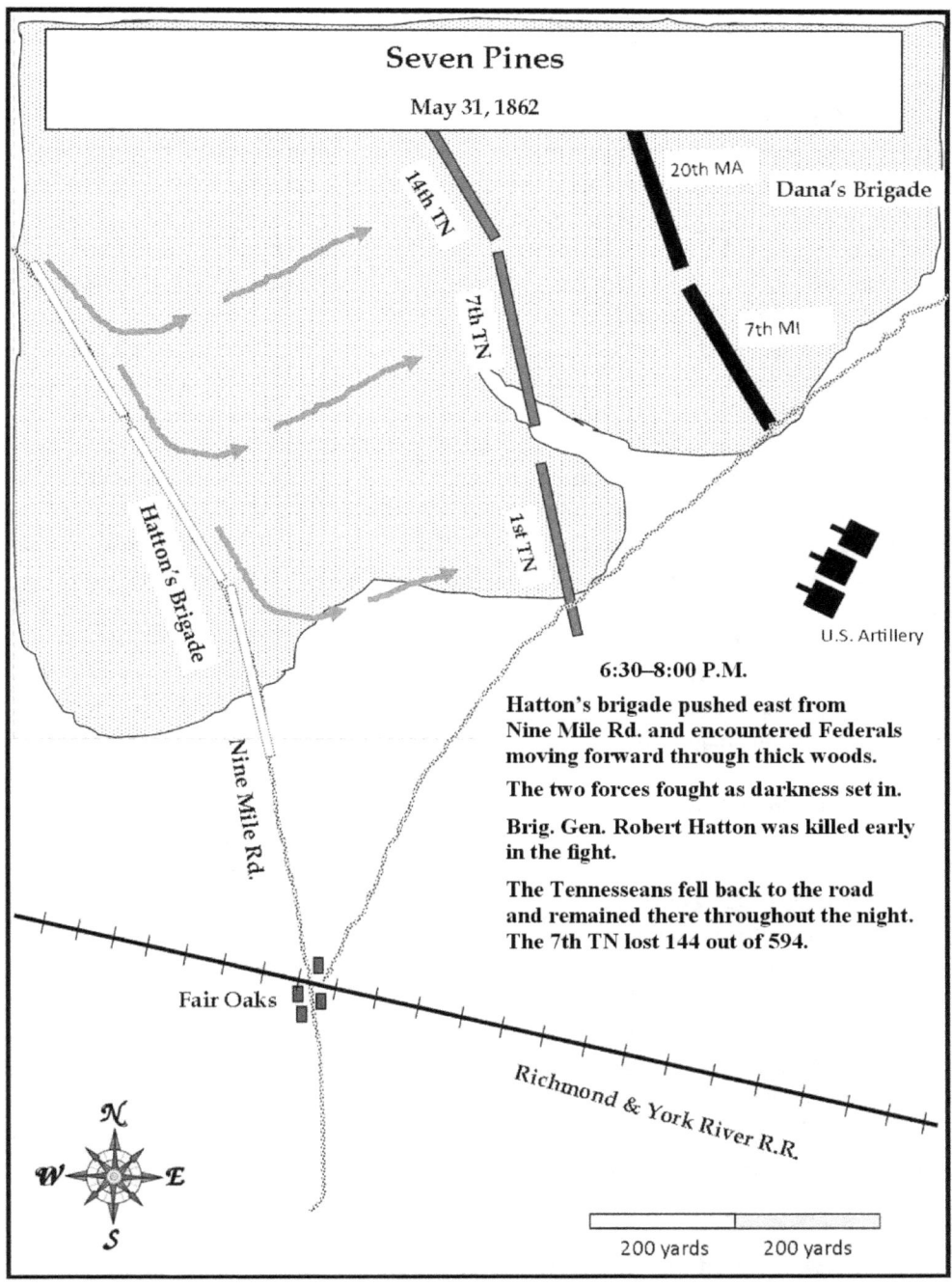

mond. Here, Hatton's boys remained until the end of May 1862. During this time they were occasionally shelled by Union artillery and scrapped against Yankee pickets. At one point the 7th Tennessee was forced to retreat to keep from being outflanked, an experience surprising to the still-untested soldiers. David Phillips recorded, "[It was] a good day's work if we did not have to run."[15]

On the night of May 30, 1862, General Hatton received word to prepare his troops for battle. He passed these orders on to his regimental commanders, Col. Peter Turney (1st TN), Col. John Goodner (7th TN), and Col. William Forbes (14th TN), and then retired to his tent. That evening, while sheltered from a thunderous rainstorm, Robert Hatton wrote personal instructions to his parents: "If I should not return, be a mother to my wife and children."[16] Convinced he would be killed in tomorrow's battle, he penned a last letter to his wife, Sophie, writing, "Would that I might bind my heart, before the battle, my wife.... That pleasure may never again be granted me.... Farewell; and may the God of all mercy be to you."[17]

The next morning General Hatton ordered the 7th Tennessee to march along the Richmond and Yorktown River Railroad tracks, heading east. The regiment traveled several miles before halting. The men stacked their muskets and lounged besides the tracks. The day's battle noises remained quiet until just after noon, when sounds of artillery and musketry erupted a couple of miles east of where the regiment waited. The Tennesseans sat apprehensively, torn between the desire to "see the elephant" and the longing to remain far from danger. General Hatton, not wanting to be alone, walked among the men of his cherished regiment. One soldier, not understanding Hatton's purpose, noted, "Gen. Hatton ... moved through the ranks of men in careful inspection of their readiness for the conflict."[18]

Around 2:00 P.M. Hatton received word to bring his boys to the fight. The 7th Tennessee shouldered its muskets and hustled toward Seven Pines. Major John Fite recorded, "We went there [at the] double quick."[19] The closer the men got to the battle, the louder the sounds of war grew. As the Tennesseans hurried toward the conflict they passed by President Jefferson Davis. One Confederate recalled, "Every boy snatched off his hat, and the wild Rebel yell rent the air as a salute to the gallant chieftain of the Confederacy."[20] The Tennesseans continued on, also catching glimpses of General Joseph E. Johnston and General Robert E. Lee before stopping not far from a little schoolhouse.

As the sun closed upon the western horizon General Hatton moved the brigade out into a field of oats and called the men to attention and gave them a short speech, exhorting his Tennesseans, declaring, "The occasion is at hand, and I confidently expect that you will acquit yourselves as noble heroes."[21] Hatton then gave the order to "load," "fix bayonets," and finally, "forward, guide center."[22] With that, the three Tennessee regiments aligned and moved northward toward a thick stand of trees.

A far off Federal battery opened fire upon the Tennesseans but could not get the range before the Seventh passed into a dip in the terrain. Colonel Goodner's 600 men marched in step, their alignment straight, and toward the sounds of heavy musketry. Clouds of choking gun smoke swirled through the air, obscuring the soldiers' vision, but the Tennesseans moved forward, tensely aligning on their colors. The regiment passed beyond the open field and entered a near-jungle of trees, tangled underbrush, and fallen branches. The ground was soupy from the heavy rains and thick mud clung to the soldiers' brogans. David Phillips recalled, "We crossed as best as we could."[23]

General Hatton rode his horse, some fifty feet or so, behind the 7th Tennessee color guard, waving his sword, and shouting, "Forward, my brave boys, forward!"[24] The Southerners advanced nearly two hundred yards, searching for the bluecoats. Unfortunately Yanks from the brigade of Brig. Gen. N. J. Dana, the 20th Massachusetts and the 7th

Michigan saw the Confederates first. These bluecoats unleashed a massive 1,000-man volley at a distance of about one hundred fifty yards. Major John Fite remarked, "We had gone but a short distance ... when we met the enemy's fire."[25] Minié balls shredded the vegetation around the Tennesseans. This was the first time the Tennesseans had ever been under massed rifle fire, and the results proved deadly. Many went down, including 2nd Lt. Cassius Ingram (Co. C), Pvt. Dan Sewell (Co. A), Cpl. John Peyton (Co. K), and Pvt. Tom Hardwick (Co. E) — all killed in less time than it took the Tennesseans to dive for cover. Lieutenant Jack Moore recorded, "We received one of the most destructive volleys ever discharged into a body of troops."[26]

More Federal volleys raked the 7th Tennessee. Bullets stuck Hatton's horse, killing it. General Hatton calmly climbed off his fallen mount and followed after his regiment. The Tennesseans returned fire, aiming at the muzzle flashes in the evening's darkness. Federal soldiers from Michigan began to fall. One Yankee noted that his regiment was "exposed to a galling fire from the enemy."[27] But the Federals refused to budge. They poured a heavy fire into the 7th Tennessee. More went down: Cpt. Jonathan Dowell (Co. A) was hit in the chest, Pvt. Jim Buck (Co. C) was struck in the leg, and Pvt. George Helleman (Co. D) was shot in the head and killed.

A Minié bullet crashed into Robert Hatton's chest, knocking him to the ground. At first no one noticed their leader's misfortune until a couple of Wilson County boys saw him. Private Squire Davis (Co. F) and Pvt. Tom Holloway (Co. H) gathered up their general and rushed him back to the surgeons. But the Tennessee statesman had already died. The surgeon, Dr. James Fite, recalled, "Dr. Lester quickly placed his ear to Hatton's heart ... [and I] came up at that time and asked, 'Jim is he dead?' Dr. Lester rising slowly, in a sad and subdued voice said: 'Yes,' without taking his eyes off his beloved commander." The two Tennesseans gazed at their dead friend for a moment before Dr. Lester said, "Jim we can do nothing for him let us look after the others."[28]

Not knowing of their leader's demise, the 7th Tennessee crept forward, the men dodging from tree to tree, and shooting as fast as they could load. Two of the 7th's companies (H and I) came upon a clearing, no more than ten yards wide but stretching in a straight line for hundreds of yards. When the regiment's advance stalled, these two companies remained out in the open, horribly exposed. A three-gun Federal battery, a half-mile away, had one of its cannons aimed to fire down the length of this road. The gunners loaded canister and slaughtered the Tennesseans.

That blast swept through Company I, killing Sgt. Jim Young, Pvt. Pleasant Eatherly, and Pvt. Al McClain. Private William Parker took canister to his hip while 3rd Lt. John Vivrett was struck in the left leg, and Pvt. Richard Davis was downed by grapeshot to his knee. The carnage continued; Pvt. Tom Beard was killed, Pvt. Henry Blair stunned, and Pvt. Stephen Turner's right hand and left arm damaged. Canister struck Private Bob Taylor and he was "all torn to shreds."[29] Private David Hamilton also suffered from the artillery projectiles, being struck "in the head, which fractured his skull, and in the left shoulder."[30] Private William Sewell (Co. A) watched in horror as his older brother, Watts, "got his head shot off with a cannon ball."[31] The survivors scattered into the trees, leaving casualties dotting the roadside, and a gap in the Tennessee line.

By now no Tennessean persisted in trying to prove his belief that faith in a just God was "a much better shield ... than steel armor."³² Instead, everyone hid the best he could behind trees or as low to the ground as possible. The slaughter continued, claiming more Tennessee boys; Sgt. Jim Vanatta (Co. A) was killed, as were Cpl. James Hubbard (Co. C), Pvt. Henry Wormack (Co. D), Pvt. Buck Edwards (Co. G), and Pvt. William Rice (Co. K). Private Tom Davis' (Co. A) left hand was shattered, while Pvt. Samuel Ragland (Co. D) was killed instantly, shot "through and through." Private Jimmy Patton (Co. H) took a bullet. One comrade recalled Patton "called out to me in a feeble voice to come and help him. I turned and saw him struggling to walk, with a wound in his neck."³³ Privates Henry Purcell (Co. E) and George Webb (Co. F) received serious injuries. Private Madison Buck (Co. C) was struck in the arm, Cpl. Sam Jennings (Co. D) was incapacitated by damage to his scalp, and Sgt. Ferguson Harris (Co. H) took a ball in his shoulder.

Though the Tennesseans loaded and fired rapidly the harried riflemen had little time to see the effects of their galling fire. Scores of bluecoats from Michigan and Massachusetts also experienced the agony and death caused by modern mid–19th century weaponry. Major John Richardson, commander of the 7th Michigan later wrote, "I have to report of the loss of this regiment in killed and wounded from 95 to 100."³⁴

The bloodbath raged on into the twilight, the two forces shooting at each other in the growing darkness. One soldier remembered, "We would shoot at the flash of the enemy's guns, and ... they would shoot at the flash of ours."³⁵ Colonel Goodner's men continued to fall. Sergeant Major Abram Bostick received a ball in the chest and died. Private James Turnage (Co. C) was hit in the leg, and Pvt. Jim Graves (Co. D) was wounded in the shoulder. Private Tom Buford was killed. A nearby comrade noted, "I heard the bullet strike Tom and looking around saw Bill McCorkle [Co. H] raise his cap, his brains were oozing out where the bullet had struck him square in the forehead."³⁶

The battle went for another thirty minutes before darkness and exhaustion forced the combatants to cease the killing. Since no brigade commander remained to give orders, each Tennessee regimental leader acted independently. Lieutenant Jack Moore recorded, "The effort to reform was fruitless. We were compelled to retire."³⁷ Colonel John Goodner called his company commanders together and told them to gather up their formations and withdraw. The 7th began sliding to the rear, but in the darkness and tangled foliage the withdrawal fell apart. Private Phillips recalled, "Every man in the retreat acted on his own judgment." Not all of the soldiers successfully escaped. The rifleman continued his description of the retirement: "I got behind the

THOMAS E. BUFORD. Thomas Buford was born in 1837 in Virginia and attended Cumberland University in Lebanon, Tennessee. He worked as a trader before the war. Buford enlisted into Company H and served as a rifleman. He stood 5-9 and had hazel eyes and dark hair. Thomas Buford was killed at Seven Pines (5/31/1862) (*Confederate Veteran* collection).

regiment and fell in with Jim Weaver [Co. K]. We were making our way out ... when we ran very suddenly upon a Yankee picket of six men. It was now dark; we were lost and there was no other alternative left but to surrender."[38]

The 7th Tennessee took up a position very close to where the regiment had been before making their assault. Major Fite summed up their position; "[We] were told to lie down. We did so. The dying and wounded were all around us."[39] The stunned officers sorted their men out, took roll to find out who was missing and put out pickets while Surgeons James Fite and David Jones struggled to deal with five dozen wounded.

One of these wounded, Pvt. John Johnson (Co. K), suffered from a mangled right shoulder. Doctor Fite stopped the bleeding and cleaned up Johnson's dangerous wound, and then ordered him, along with others, to be transported to the hospital in Richmond. Medical staff loaded the 29-year-old farmer from Lebanon into an ambulance and hauled him to the Chimborazo hospital complex. Johnson became one of thousands of wounded Confederate soldiers to be treated in the massive facility, consisting of nearly a hundred buildings, each 30 feet wide and 100 feet long and housing 50 patients each. John Johnson remained at Chimborazo for nearly six months before dying in November 1862.[40]

Meanwhile, while Doctors Fite and Jones wrestled feverishly among their shattered soldiers, supply sergeants worked to get their soldiers food, water, and ammunition. Other Tennesseans, those with energy, crept back to the battle line, searching for wounded and missing friends. These ambitious stalwarts retrieved some of their comrades. But sadly, for many Tennesseans, there was nothing to be done; they had been killed outright and now their bodies lay cooling in the night air. One battle-shocked soldier penned to his wife, "I can't describe my feelings when the battle began. I could but think of you at home so far away and me here with the balls flying around ... thinking that the next moment one might get me."[41] Richard Beard (Co. H) wrote, "This battle gave me a better conception of hell."[42]

Colonel John Goodner was horrified when the casualty count had been completed. Official records would eventually show his regiment had lost 144 — all shot down in the space of 90 minutes.[43] The stunned Tennesseans tried to make sense of what just occurred. Many of the young soldiers struggled with the unfairness and randomness of who was struck down and who survived. The losses had not been equally distributed throughout the regiment; Captain William Williamson's right flank Company H lost 15, as did Cpt. Jonathan Dowell's Company A. The color company, Cpt. John Allen's Company C, lost 14, and so did Cpt. William Curd's Company I. Other units, such as Cpt. James Franklin's Company E and Cpt. John Allen's Company B came out of the fight relatively unscathed, losing three and four respectively.[44]

Later that night the news of Gen. Robert Hatton's death reached the brigade. One discouraged Tennessean wrote, "Many of the men cried openly when they realized Hatton would never lead them in battle again."[45] The Battle of Seven Pines had been a dreadful experience — the adventure was over, the Tennessee boys now knew about war. Hatton's Tennessee brigade had taken devastating casualties; besides the 7th Tennessee's losses, the 1st Tennessee lost 96, and the 14th Tennessee lost 52. Hatton's brigade had suffered 292 casualties out of a total of 2,300 men.

There also were eight captured Tennesseans, and for them, the night was long and frightening. David Phillips penciled into his journal, "We were all crowded in a hen house for the night."⁴⁶ These Tennesseans were sent to Fort Delaware, a six acre facility located amid the marshes on Pea Patch Island, off the coast of Delaware. This pentagon-shaped structure would become one of the main prisoner of war facilities used by the Federals. Phillips and his pards became some of the first prisoners to be dumped into the prison's confines. A year later, following the Battle of Gettysburg, the number of Confederates housed there exceeded 13,000. Fortunately for these first 7th Tennessee fellows, they were exchanged in August 1862 and rejoined their regiment. The paroled Phillips happily wrote, "Freed again from the yoke of tyranny by exchange."⁴⁷

Fighting erupted the next morning, June 1, 1862, but not for the battered 7th Tennessee. During the night the Federals facing John Goodner's regiment slipped away. Colonel Goodner ordered a skirmish line to advance to determine the extent of this Yankee retreat and then the men rested, content to let the day go by without incident.

Two days later Colonel James J. Archer was promoted to brigadier general and given command of Robert Hatton's brigade. Archer, a graduate of Princeton University, was from Maryland. He was 45 years old and had served in the Mexican War as an infantry captain, and he quickly let everyone know he had been a hero at Chapultepec. James Archer had commanded the 5th Texas Infantry and distinguished himself at Seven Pines, especially for his aggressiveness. He was a strict disciplinarian and many of the Tennesseans who longed for their beloved Hatton disliked him.

One of Hatton's boys

ALEXANDER W. VICK. Alexander Vick was born in 1834 and attended Cumberland University in Lebanon, Tennessee, and earned a law degree. He enlisted into the 7th Tennessee as the regimental quartermaster captain and held this position into 1862. He served as a brigade quartermaster. After the war he returned to Lebanon and practiced law. He never married. Alexander Vick died in 1901 (Loewentheil Family Photographic Collection).

who developed an immediate animosity toward Archer was Major John Fite. His first interaction with Archer came when Maj. Fite was in charge of the brigade's picket line. General Archer approached Fite's picket headquarters, demanding to know which officer was actually out on the picket line. John Fite answered, naming a lieutenant but was interrupted by Archer who ordered him to go out and take physical command of the guard. Fite replied, "We hadn't been in the habit of having field officers in command of the picket." Archer, not listening to Fite, ordered him to "take charge of it [because] he didn't care what had been our practice."[48]

General Archer did not relieve Fite and two days later, Lt. Col. William McComb (14th TN) came out to the picket line, angrily spewing profanity. He had approached Archer, volunteering to send out a relieving unit for Fite and his men, but Archer rebuffed him, harshly replying, "When he wanted his services he'd call on him."[49] General Archer kept John Fite out on the picket line for four days. Eventually Fite and his pickets were relieved by Georgians from another brigade. Major Fite brought his detail back to the camp only to discover Archer had moved the entire brigade and left them behind. From that point on, Fite loathed James Archer.

Archer's Tennessee brigade shifted to the north of Richmond, along the Mechanicsville Pike and remained there for the next four weeks. During this time more Tennesseans learned about their new brigade commander. The general remained aloof and unapproachable and required his soldiers to follow bureaucratic procedures. One Tennessean wrote, "Archer kept his headquarters about one-half mile from his command and required all of the formalities of an old army officer."[50] Sergeant Ferguson Harris noted, "His exterior was rough and unattractive, small of stature and angular of feature. His temper was irascible, and so cold was his manner that we thought him ... a Martinet."[51] Another 7th Tennessean, Sgt. Maj. Abram Bostick, wrote, "Our newly appointed General is so much [Hatton's] inferior in every respect that the men really hate him."[52]

On June 26, 1862, Archer's Tennessee brigade lost its regional uniqueness when the 5th Alabama Battalion (Maj. Abram Van Graff) and the 19th Georgia (Col. William Boyd) were added. The 7th Tennessee, along with Archer's brigade, now part of Ambrose P. Hill's division, moved northward in preparation for an attack across the Chickahominy River; their goal was to drive the Union army from Richmond. The Tennesseans neared Meadow Bridge and halted. They spent most of the rest of the day in idleness as the Confederates waited for the arrival of Stonewall Jackson's forces. Finally, after hours of receiving no word of Jackson's whereabouts, the aggressive A. P. Hill ordered his men forward. Hill's Southerners crossed the Meadow Bridge and closed in on the settlement of Mechanicsville. A brief fight erupted before the Federals fell back, though the Tennesseans did not participate in this skirmish.

Beaver Dam Creek was a thousand yards north of Mechanicsville. This slow moving watercourse bordered by swamp on the southern side and a hilly region on the north. Here, the Yanks made their defense. When the Northerners opened fire General Archer ordered his brigade into a battle formation, positioning the 19th Georgia and 1st Tennessee in the front, and the 5th Alabama and the 7th Tennessee in the rear. Somehow the 14th Tennessee had lost contact with the brigade and drifted away, thus leaving Archer with four regiments and about 1,225 men.[53]

The brigade advanced and came under heavy artillery bombardment. Private John Williams (Co. D) recalled, "It wasn't long before we came in range of the enemy's cannon. We continued at a double-quick ... for ¾ of a mile."[54] Shells rained down upon the Tennesseans as Colonel John Goodner ordered his boys to advance at the double-quick. As the Tennesseans hustled forward a shell exploded among the ranks of Company A, killing Pvt. Chesley Chapman and wounding Pvt. Alphonso Emrique. Another round detonated between Companies F and G, wounding Pvt. Luke Robertson (Co. G) and seriously injuring Sgt. James Thompson (Co. F). Then a barrage of shells erupted, scattering Company I, killing Cpl. John E. Sullivan, Pvt. James E. Sullivan, and Pvt. John York. Four other Wilson County boys were also wounded.[55]

The men in Goodner's 7th Tennessee took refuge among the trees beneath an embankment overlooking the creek. The Union artillery preyed upon other Confederate formations, leaving the Tennesseans alone. Once the soldiers were assured of their position's security some chuckled nervously about their colonel's close call. Most of the regiment had seen Lt. Col. John Howard dive to the ground to dodge a bouncing cannonball. Ferguson Harris remembered, "A tremendous solid shot passed just over Col. Howard, which he missed by dropping quickly to the ground." The sergeant continued, "Had he dropped two seconds later his valued life would have gone out."[56]

Another bounding cannonball struck Major John Fite in the chest, knocking him unconscious. Later, he remembered, "I had squatted down and, while holding to a little pine bush, a spent cannon ball came along striking the ground and bouncing and struck me and knocked me down." Fite continued, "I did throw up great clots of blood. Brother Jim [Dr. James Fite] saw me and so did Dr. McGuire. They both came to me…. Jim pulled open my shirt and said, 'Brother you are ruined.' He and McGuire examined me and they decided that my breast bone was broken, and that some of my ribs were torn loose." Fite finished his account, writing, "They tore off a strip of a piece of domestic, about a foot wide, and wound that around me, I don't know how many times, and put me in an ambulance and sent me back to Richmond."[57]

Colonel John Goodner's men remained in position for the rest of the afternoon and evening, staying low to the ground as Union and Confederate artillery shells shrieked over their heads. Sergeant Harris wrote, "[We] lay back of that crest while the artillery swept its top, passing just over."[58] Finally the sun set and the gunfire ceased. The Tennesseans remained hunkered down, dozing fitfully and anxiously awaiting the coming morning's dangers. However, during the night the Yank formations slunk away, leaving the Southerners in control of the slow-moving creek.

General Archer sent his brigade forward, following behind Brig. Gen. Maxcy Gregg's South Carolinians. Gregg's brigade slowly pushed the Yankee rearguard backward. During this deliberate advance Col. Goodner's riflemen re-outfitted themselves, scrounging through the mountains of gear the Federal troops left behind. Worn-out accoutrements, clothing, boots, blankets, tents, and weapons were dumped when new replacements were located. One Tennessean noted, "[They] were able to obtain the more modern and efficient Springfield and Enfield rifles for their use."[59]

Archer's brigade trailed Gregg's brigade for several hours until the South Carolinians came to a halt bordering an area the locals called Boatswain's Swamp. This region, not far from the village of Gaines' Mill, was a horrible place for an attacking force. One Southerner described the terrain: "All the cleared ground visible to the Confederates led down to a boggy little stream ... bordered widely by almost impenetrable underbrush and by large trees.... South of the swamp, at a good elevation ... the Federals had their infantry and their artillery."[60] The Tennesseans could see thousands of Federals hustling to finish their defenses. One Confederate wrote in alarm, "Three lines [were] heavily entrenched with logs behind a dry ditch about six feet deep and equally as wide, with supporting entrenchments behind them and artillery on the hill."[61] And above the Federal infantry lines, higher on the hills, dozens and dozens of artillery pieces waited to spew death.

Colonel Goodner's men, now veterans of the bitter fight at Seven Pines, knew an assault against this position was madness. The Tennesseans quietly took their places in the underbrush. At 2:30, General Archer issued the attack order. Colonel John Goodner placed Company I out in front, to advance as skirmishers. Ferguson Harris watched the riflemen deploy and wrote, "The long line of sharpshooters advance[d] to the crest of that hill ... [led] ... by the manly form of Capt. Curd."[62] The grim Tennesseans arose and crept out of the underbrush and made their way into the clearing. The Federal entrenchments were about 1,200 yards away. The Tennesseans pushed against a thin line of Federal pickets, who easily gave way. One of the Yanks, a soldier from the 25th New York, noted, "Four companies of skirmishers were thrown forward to the crest of the hill in front, with instructions to fire a volley upon the foe upon their approach and then retire behind the barricade."[63] In this quick exchange of rifle fire, Captain William Curd was struck in the stomach and severely wounded. The 25-year-old farmer from Green Hill, Tennessee, would die three weeks later.[64] Command of the skirmish line now fell to 1st Lt. Oren Bass, a 24-year-old from Silver Springs, Tennessee.

Once the Yank skirmishers were out of the way, the Tennesseans let out a rebel yell and increased their pace to the double-quick. The Federals let the Southerners get within the kill zone. There were several minutes of quiet, save the sounds of hundreds of Confederates double-quicking across the open field.

The Northerners, soldiers from the 13th and 25th New York, opened fire when the Tennesseans were 500 yards away. Bullets thudded into the men of the 7th Tennessee. Lieutenant Colonel John Howard immediately fell, "shot through the lungs," as did 1st Sgt. James Johnson (Co. B), who was wounded both in the arm and in the lungs. Private Andrew "Jack" Coe (Co. D) died, killed by a bullet to his brain. Sergeant Ferguson Harris (Co. H) was hit in the hip, Sgt. Henry McClain (Co. I) was struck in the right thigh, and Sgt. William Eddins (Co. K) was killed when a Minié ball crashed into his heart.[65]

The New Yorkers fired as rapidly as they could load their weapons. The Tennesseans could only rush forward, hoping to reach the Union entrenchments. But the distance was now four hundred yards, and the blue-coats' musketry became increasingly more disastrous. One Tennessean recalled, "It was ... [a] carnival of death."[66] Private Jack Bradley (Co. B) was hit in the head, Pvt. John Crump (Co. C) was struck in the thigh, Pvt. William Shoemaker (Co. D) was shot through the chest, and Pvt. Tom Grissom (Co. G) was wounded in the left leg. Then, Col. John Goodner fell, struck by a bullet, leaving the regiment without a field officer.

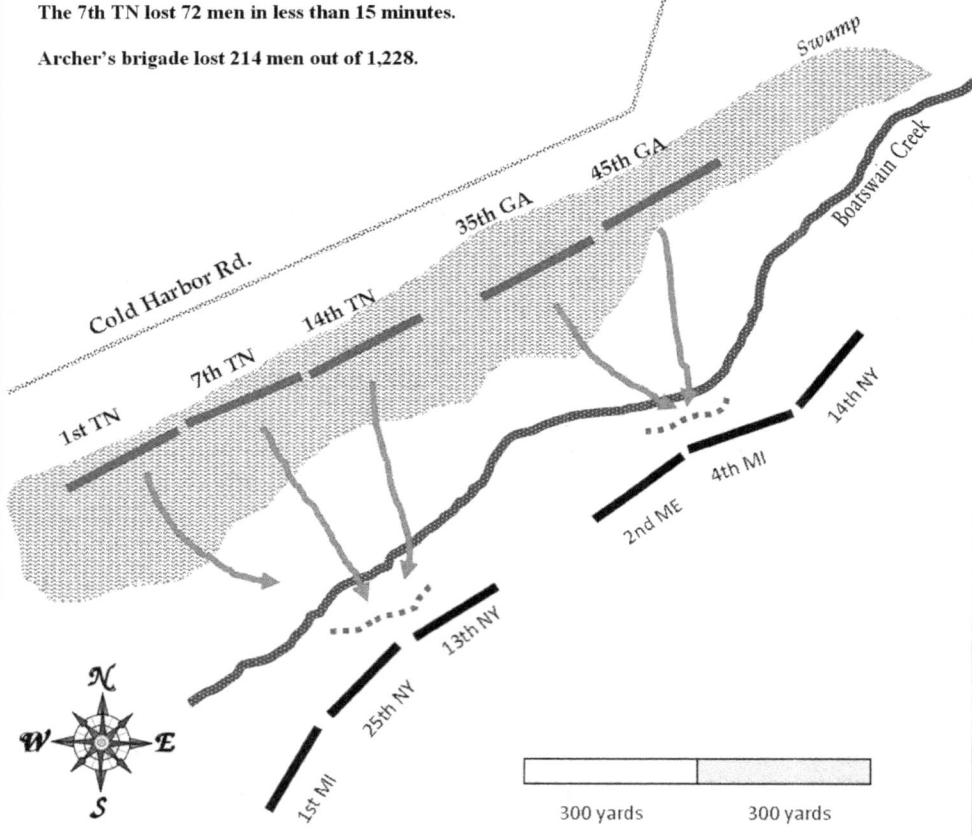

The Federals smothered the Confederates beneath a withering fire. More courageous Tennesseans went down. Corporal James Knight (Co. B) was mortally wounded, Pvt. Alex Piper (Co. B) took a bullet to his thigh, and Pvt. Buck Jones (Co. G) was hit in the head. Private Billy Matlock (Co. H) was struck in the hip and the knee, and Billy Bradshaw (Co. D) had his "head blown off."[67] More Tennesseans fell, including Cpt. Marcus Fayette Walsh (Co. D), who was seriously wounded. The men in the regiment were being butchered almost as methodically as if they were hogs in a slaughterhouse. The wounded Sgt. Ferguson watched as "a large number ... were killed and wounded in less time than it takes to tell it."[68]

The assault collapsed after barely ten minutes. The shattered Tennesseans dove to the ground. As one Confederate admitted, "The storm was too fierce for such a handful of men, and the advance stalled."[69] Then, the survivors, first in ones and twos, and finally in small groups, retreated from the deadly ground. One soldier remarked, "Had [we] remained in this valley of death for half an hour not a man would have been left to tell the tale."[70] A Federal officer noted their retreat, writing in admiration, "The enemy ... halted, tried bravely to hold their own, but soon retired."[71]

The Tennesseans gathered together behind the safety of a hillcrest and regrouped. It took a while to figure out who was in command; there were only four captains left, and the senior captain was George Shepard. Regardless of this loss in experienced leadership, the remaining officers and NCOs rallied their units together, took roll, and saw to their men's needs.

As they rested the Tennesseans were dismayed to learn the 1st Tennessean had lost their battle flag. The shaken soldiers looked at their own bullet-shredded colors in pride and told and retold the story of how their own ensign had been rescued once its bearer had been shot down: "The flag had hardly touched the ground when [Roger] Word [Co. H] sprang from his place, grabbed it up and raised it aloft.... When [he] could go no further he placed the staff beside him and fired one shot directly in their faces ... and bore the starry flag unfurled slowly from the field.... How he escaped is one of the mysteries of war."[72] "Cu," as everyone called him, basked in his comrades' admiration, but when alone, trembled as he pondered why he had not been killed.

Later that afternoon another assault was ordered. The weary men looked to each other for strength and courage. No one wanted to cross that open field again, but they knew it was their duty. As one Tennessean recalled, "I [was] afraid [and] I would have declined to go ... [Jim] said, 'let's go if it kills us all,' and so we did."[73]

Archer's bloodied Tennessee and Alabama regiments went forward, fortunately posted in the second rank of the attacking brigades as the entire division advanced. It was simply a case of others doing the dying. This massive fist of Confederates broke the Federal resistance and they retreated. One Yank noted, "The enemy came on us again in stronger force than before. Our men stood their ground manfully, holding the enemy in check until all their ammunition was expended, when we fell back."[74] By the time darkness ended the fighting the Tennesseans occupied the old Federal positions and had captured several Union artillery pieces. The boys in the 7th Tennessee spent the evening armed with "candles and lanterns, [searching] ... the field looking for their dead and wounded friends."[75]

General James Archer wandered among his troops, badly shaken by their horrific casualties. Archer felt sadness for the very men he had treated so callously. He realized it had been his commands which resulted in their traumatic losses. Archer reported, "My ... total loss in the two battles 542.... All the field officers of the Nineteenth Georgia, First and Seventh Tennessee Regiments, and the two senior captains successively in command of the Fifth Alabama Battalion were killed or wounded."[76]

The 7th Tennessee's surgeons, Doctors James Fite and David Jones, faced another nightmarish night, struggling to save their mangled friends' lives. Eight more Tennesseans required burial, and another thirty lay bleeding in their regiment's makeshift first aid station. Many of the wounded were in serious condition. Lieutenant Colonel John Howard was one of these mortally wounded Tennesseans. Barely a year earlier, the 35-year-old leader — Lebanon's clerk magistrate of the court — had left his wife and their one-year-old child to join Robert Hatton's regiment. Now, on the evening of June 27, 1862, he clung to life, his condition critical. Later, the badly injured lieutenant colonel was transported to Richmond where he died on July 9, 1862. Howard, along with ten other Tennesseans, would succumb to their wounds in the next couple of months. Lieutenant Jack Moore wrote of John Howard, "[his] daring and courage were only equaled by his popularity."[77]

Nothing happened the next day or the one following that. Private John Williams (Co. D) recalled, "The enemy fled during the night and burned up all their commissary."[78] The haggard soldiers were buoyed by news that the Union army was falling back, and they were content to let other brigades pursue the retreating Yankees. The 7th Tennessee had already done its part in the Seven Days' battle. The regiment and the rest of Archer's brigade hiked back to Richmond's outskirts and the men were given time to recover. In time, some of the wounded men recovered from their injuries and returned to the regiment. Their homecomings caused small bursts of celebration as these returning veterans were kindly greeted by their comrades.

Major John Fite was promoted to John Howard's position, and George Shepard advanced in rank to major. Since there was no word on whether Col. John Goodner was going to return to the regiment, his posting remained in his name. But Goodner's health did not improve and eventually the 7th's surgeon, Doctor James Fite, wrote, "I find him [John Goodner] incapable of preforming [sic] his duties."[79] Goodner realized he could not come back and reluctantly wrote in March 1863, "Sir, In consequence of protracted ill health ... [preventing] me to discharge the duties demanded of me, I am induced to tender this ... resignation."[80]

While the Tennesseans mended, their division commander, Gen. Ambrose P. Hill, got into a personal conflict with Gen. James Longstreet and Longstreet placed him under arrest. The passionate and excitable Hill, insulted by Longstreet's accusations, immediately challenged Longstreet to a duel. General Robert E. Lee heard of the impending duel and "act[ing] quickly and effectively, using his unvarying tact and great influence, brought matters, through other friends, to an adjustment honorable to both."[81] Lee also eased the pressure for each general by ordering A. P. Hill to take his division and reinforce Stonewall Jackson's army, up near Gordonsville. On July 26, 1862, the 7th Tennessee received orders to board a train and head northward, again another move dictated by politics.

The 415 men left in the 7th Tennessee rode railcars to Gordonsville and arrived there to find General Jackson's army farther north, near Culpepper. The Tennesseans were delayed at Gordonsville for a few days before moving northward again, this time to Orange Court House. Lieutenant Colonel John Fite, who because of his broken ribs would "have done anything on earth if [he] could have taken a long breath," marched his regiment to Orange Court House, arriving on the evening of August 7, 1862.[82]

The Tennesseans idled the next day, and took to the road before sunrise on August 9,

1862, a day which became blisteringly hot. Locals with thermometers announced to the sweating soldiers the temperature at nearly 100 degrees. Lieutenant Colonel John Fite recalled, "It was the hottest day I ... ever saw."[83] Dozens of men in Fite's regiment dropped from the marching column, felled by the intolerable heat.

That afternoon the sounds of battle came to the suffering soldiers. Couriers frantically shouted orders for Archer's brigade to hurry. Word reached the Tennesseans that Stonewall Jackson's men were in trouble.[84] Archer's brigade marched third in Hill's division; thus by the time they arrived, Hill's first two brigades had already reinforced Jackson's formation and ended the threat of a Confederate collapse. The 7th Tennessee formed into its battle line on the brigade's far-right flank. The Tennesseans abutted up against the 5th Alabama Battalion, with the 19th Georgia and the 1st Tennessee continuing the line to the right. General Archer ordered his 1000-man brigade to advance at the "right oblique."[85] His veterans worked their way toward the right, aiming for contact with the left flank of Brig. Gen. Lawrence Branch's North Carolinian brigade's left flank.

John Fite's regiment struggled up a slope, passing through a thick stand of vegetation. The left flank company maintained contact with the Alabama boys, while the rest of the regiment's companies dressed on them. Then, after battling with the underbrush for several minutes, the Tennesseans halted. The Seventh realigned its formation and waited; the regiment now stood at the edge of the woods.

The Tennesseans could see down into a valley before them. Fite described the terrain: "There was a wheat field in front of us, the wheat had been cut and shocked." Fite also noted, "I suppose our lines were about 250–300 yards apart."[86] The 14th Tennessee joined Lt. Col. Fite's battle line, forming on their left. Though heavy fighting could be heard off to their right, the Tennesseans had nothing to do except wait.

Suddenly, to the Tennesseans' surprise a large formation of Union cavalry deployed into attack formation and charged. Fite depicted what followed: "I saw the grandest sight I ever witnessed, at least 10,000 Federal Cavalry came charging across the field." Fite continued, "They came charging across the field and when they got about 50 or 75 yards from us we opened on them. They were evidently surprised, they halted, and we poured volley after volley into them, a great many of them fell off their horses."[87] Fite's estimation of the number of cavalry proved highly inflated. The Yank cavalry formation they slaughtered, the 1st Pennsylvania, numbered less than two hundred troopers. Another Confederate noted the Southerners "poured a devastating fire into the mass of horsemen. Out of 174 officers and men only 71 rode back."[88]

A Federal infantry unit emerged from the distant tree line and moved out into the wheat field. The Tennesseans directed their fire upon these soldiers. Fite remembered the bluecoats "advanced across the field, and we lit into them. They broke ranks and run everywhere, [while] some of them got behind wheat shocks."[89] This long-range shooting lasted only for a few minutes before General Archer gave the command for his brigade to advance. Now it would be the Tennesseans' turn to charge across the open field.

Two Union infantry regiments (nearly 800 men of the 27th Indiana and the 2nd Massachusetts) were hidden in the distant trees; they were veterans in Brig. Gen. George Gordon's brigade. The Yanks waited until the 7th Tennessee was about halfway across the wheat field—a range of about 150 yards. The 2nd Massachusetts' commander

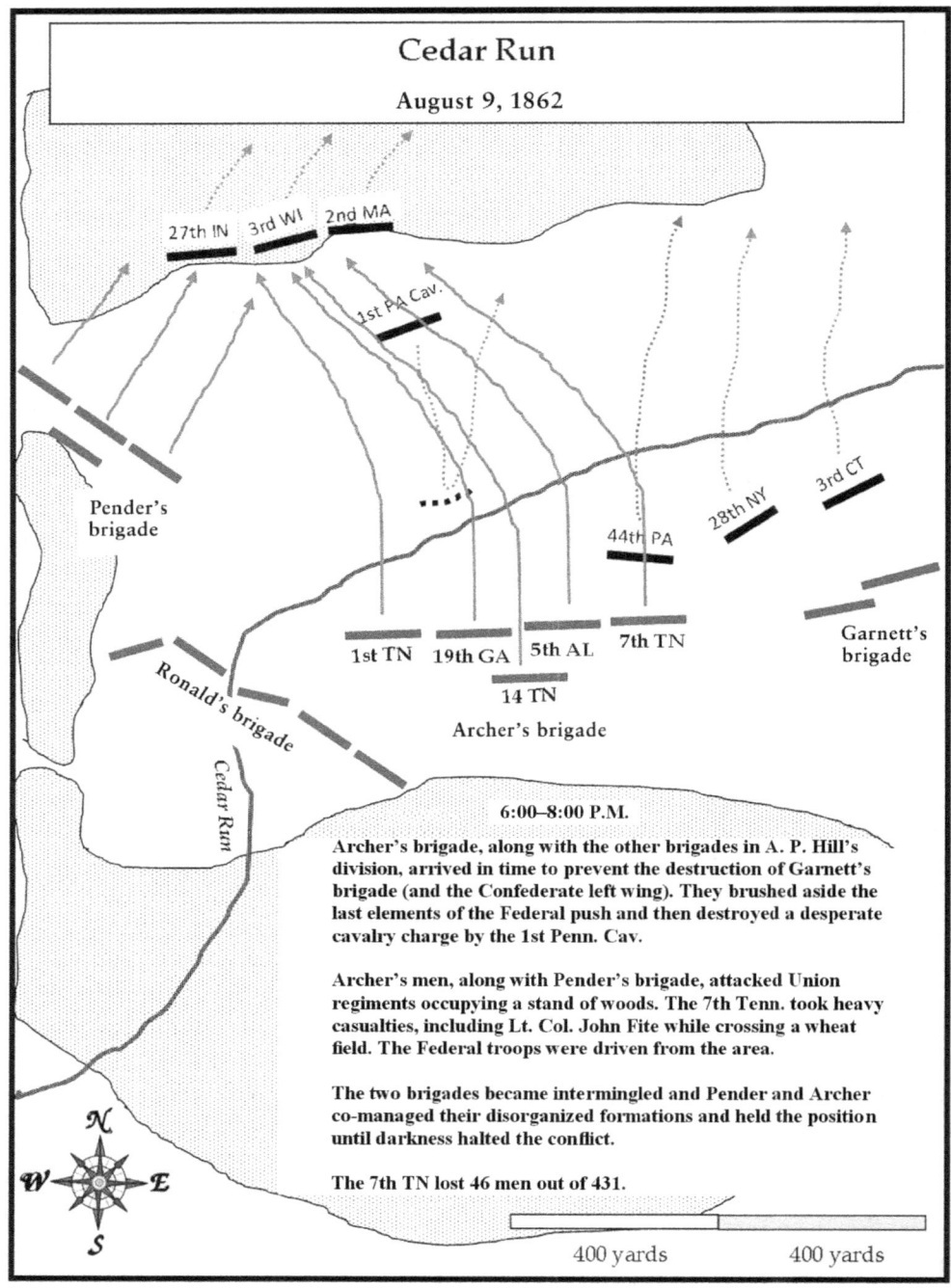

described his soldiers' shooting: "The regiment was mostly reserved until the advancing line of the enemy afforded a fair mark, when I ordered the fire by file, which was opened and continued with perfect coolness and great effect."[90] The musketry, disciplined and orderly, slashed into the Tennesseans, moving from one end of the regiment, to the other. Captain James Franklin (Co. E) was immediately struck in the foot, Cpl. Bailey Richards (Co. B) was hit in the neck, and Pvt. Lester Stroud (Co. F) had a bullet go through his right shoulder.[91] The Tennesseans did not waver, marching shoulder to shoulder with their comrades; they courageously followed Lt. Col. John Fite.

More lead slammed into Tennessee tissue. Private John Reeves (Co. H) took a bullet to his head and died instantly. Corporal John Cartwright (Co. K) went down with a Minié bullet smashing his leg. Private Littleton Johnson (Co. G) suffered a mortal wound to the chest.[92] Then a chunk of lead whacked into Lt. Col. John Fite. He described his malady: "About half way across the field ... my left leg was broken by a Yankee bullet."[93] The Seventh's commander crawled behind the protection of a pile of stone as the regiment continued forward, now in the hands of Major George Shepard.

The 7th Tennessee paused and Shepard's riflemen unleashed repeated volleys. Even though the Confederates fired as fast as they could, it seemed Yank bullets did all the damage. More Tennesseans fell. Private Richard Gibbs (Co. B) had lead rip through his knee. Private Tom Forrester (Co. C) was severely hurt with a wound to the stomach. Third Lieutenant John Wise (Co. E) died soon after taking a mortal wound, and Pvt. Henry Harkreader (Co. I) suffered an injury to his right forearm.[94]

The Tennessean riflemen could not know that their accurate musketry proved equally destructive to the bluecoats. In just a short period of time, five officers in the 2nd Massachusetts were killed, as were a dozen riflemen. The wounded quickly numbered above fifty. The Massachusetts colonel would eventually record his regiment "lost half of his officers and nearly 160 men out of 474."[95] The battered outnumbered Federal regiments' fire slackened.

When the Tennesseans noticed the diminishing fire they surged forward, shooting as they advanced; but the Yankees did not quit. More Tennessee fellows dropped among the trampled wheat. Private Jim Watkins (Co. D) was hit in the foot, and 1st Sgt. James Jewell (Co. F) was shot through the right thigh. Private James Walpole (Co. I) took a bullet through his foot, and Pvt. George Grisham (Co. H) died instantly, shot through and through.[96] Also, Pvt. James Ferrill (Co. B) was wounded, "shot through the knees and hips."[97]

The Union resolve melted as the Tennesseans neared the tree line. The commander of the 27th Indiana noted in alarm, "I soon saw symptoms of disorder in my ranks."[98] The Federals' shooting diminished, but many hardy bluecoats remained, firing resolutely at the Tennesseans. Private Tom Bailey (Co. D) suffered a wound to his head. Private Rufus Ayers' (Co. F) hip was shattered. Private Charles Wilkerson (Co. H) was severely hurt by a bullet to his shoulder, and Pvt. Andrew Thompson (Co. F) died instantly, shot through the heart.[99]

Still advancing, the Tennesseans reached the tree line. They poured a devastating close-range fire into the Yanks. The colonel of the 2nd Massachusetts recorded, "Their fire becoming more and more destructive, and finding my men falling rapidly to no purpose ... a retreat was ordered."[100] Once the Bay Staters fell back the Hoosiers' line cracked. The 27th Indiana's commander noted, "In spite of all I could do the regiment fell back, and was not rallied until it had reached the open ground on the other side of the woods."[101] Lieutenant Jack Moore recorded, "They ... broke and fled in confusion from the field."[102]

The bruised 7th Tennessee paused. Officers and sergeants frantically regrouped their formations, taking quick roll calls and assessing who was missing. Major George Shepard gathered his company commanders around him and they gave their reports; the advance across the wheat field cost nearly fifty Tennesseans.[103] The Confederates now held the tree line, but the Yankees were still around, having fallen back to another defensive position a few hundred yards away. The Tennesseans slumped to the ground, drained and heatstruck, wondering what made this piece of land so valuable it had to be captured by frontal assault.

General Archer did not worry about his men's concerns; instead the aggressive general ordered his brigade to drive into the woods and press the Federals. The worn-out Tennesseans helped each other to their feet, fell into line and complied. Later, Archer would only marginally consider the fate of his riflemen, writing, "In crossing this field I was exposed to a heavy fire from the enemy."[104] Right now, he shoved his tattered brigade forward, pushing his riflemen so they could align with the brigade of Brig. Gen. William Pender.

The two brigades bumped into each other and the soldiers became intermingled. Archer and Pender found themselves ruling over a mob of Tennesseans and North Carolinians. Neither general took the time to sort out the various units; instead they jointly commanded this horde. Luckily the Union forces did not strike at this disorganized rabble and darkness halted the Southerners' push. That night General Archer wrote lightly of the chaos, reporting, "General Pender and I commanded the two brigades together without regard to the proper brigades to which the regiments belonged, he taking the right and me the left." Archer completed his article; "I did not again meet with any opposition, but took a number of prisoners and continued the pursuit until night."[105] The tired infantry bivouacked for the night, ignoring the sounds of distant artillery. One Confederate who had the energy to watch wrote, "The cannonade continued until long after dark and was a splendid sight."[106]

Surgeon James Fite and his medical team went to work, setting up their first aid station beneath the illumination of a near full moon. Stretcher bearers brought in the badly injured, while those who could walk staggered in unassisted. One of the soldiers carted in and placed upon James Fite's operating table was his brother, Lt. Col. John Fite. The wounded officer recalled, "It was a perfectly bright moonshiney night [and] we had a great many wounded at the hospital.... Our head surgeon ... and brother Jim examined my wound by running their fingers in from both sides." Fite continued, noting the surgeon's comment, who decided, "We can't do anything for him tonight, that leg will have to come off." Fite reacted immediately, arguing, "I told him it would never come off and when I died I would die with that leg on.... I lay there until next morning, and they made another examination of it and brother Jim said he didn't think it would have to come off. They bandaged it up."[107]

Unfortunately, other Tennesseans were not as blessed; some had much more serious wounds. Six of the wounded eventually died from their injuries: Pvt. Thomas Bailey (Co. D), Cpl. Bailey Richards (Co. B), Pvt. Thomas Forrester (Co. C), Pvt. Elihu Donnell (Co. H), Pvt. Littleton Johnson (Co. G) and Pvt. Rufus Ayers (Co. F). There also were three dozen other wounded who endured their surgeon's ministrations. One of these Tennesseans, Pvt. Henry Harkreader (Co. I), came into the hospital tent, suffering from a badly damaged right forearm. The 25-year-old survived the night before taking transport to the hospital at Orange Court House. There, he recovered enough to be granted a medical furlough sending him to his home in LaGuardo, Tennessee. The young soldier recuperated in his own bed until being captured by the Union troops controlling Wilson County. Harkreader was shipped to Vicksburg and imprisoned. He eventually was exchanged but, "being unfit for active service ... was placed with A. P. Hill's Ordnance Department."[108] Finally, he was again able to rejoin the regiment toward the end of the war.

The remaining unhurt Tennesseans bedded down for the night, gloomily missing their absent comrades. The young soldiers from Wilson, Dekalb, Sumner, and Smith counties had faced danger and experienced the lethal violence of war. The soldiers had carried out their duty, completing another Archer-ordered frontal assault, which just like at Gaines Mill had produced grievous casualties. The Tennessean riflemen had learned a painful lesson — attack and die. The "Little Game Cock," as they called Archer, had become, as one Tennessean wrote, "one of the most intensely hated of men."[109] They rested beneath the bright moon, thinking about home and wondering what tomorrow would bring.

Chapter 4

August 20, 1862: Before Dawn

"Now is the time to test the fighting qualities of the two armies."

The 7th Tennessee moved out on August 20, 1862, their predawn start so quick the men did not cook breakfast. One soldier noted, "No time was to be lost after reveille."[1] The Southerners crossed the Rapidan River and marched toward Warrenton. They arrived and moved into a position near the Warrenton Springs Ford. Here, the brigade remained several days, listening to others do battle, though not getting involved except, as their general noted, "My brigade ... [was] exposed to heavy shelling from the enemy's batteries."[2] The Tennesseans did not suffer casualties from enemy fire. Their worst enemy proved to be the Confederate logistical system; supply trains could not reach the soldiers and they ran out of food. The hungry Tennesseans scoured the countryside. Lieutenant John Ingram (Co. G) remembered, "[When] ... the commissary wagon broke down and could not get to us: [we ate] roasting ears and such."[3]

On August 25, 1862, the Confederates moved northwest toward Amissville, and from there, to Henson's Mill. All along this route the men took "corn from the fields and apples from nearby trees."[4] Major George Shepard's Tennesseans did not know where they were going, but were consoled by the fact no one knew what Jackson planned. One rifleman wrote, "[We] ... knew nothing of [our] destination ... [and yet] strode on mile after mile, through field and ford, in the fierce heat of the August noon, without question."[5] Finally near midnight, the exhausted Tennesseans halted and were allowed to rest, having covered twenty-five miles. The next morning the men were back on the road, heading east. The August sun attacked the soldiers. One soldier noted, "There was no need for speech, no breath to spare."[6] The silent column trekked through Thoroughfare Gap and then on to Haymarket and Gainesville, with no sound other than, as one soldier noted, "Only the shuffling tramp of marching feet, the rumbling of wheels, [and] the creak and clank of harness and accoutrements."[7] The column turned southeast and made its way toward Bristoe Station. That evening the Tennesseans heard shooting up ahead but were too tired to investigate. They dropped their packs and sank to the ground, four miles from Manassas Junction, having hiked fifty-four miles in two days.[8]

The Tennesseans were on the road again early the next morning but traveled only a few miles before jamming into the chaos at Manassas Junction. Here, Jackson's army had captured an immense Federal supply depot, an entire square mile of railroad sidings lined with boxcars, sheds, warehouses, and canvas covered stacks of rations; it was a treasure house for the starving Southerners. They broke ranks and raced among the boxes and barrels, gathering plunder. One Tennessean wrote, "The men spen[t] most of their time filling haversack."[9] The hungry soldiers were taking care of themselves; others saw the pilfering in a different light. One of General Jackson's aides disgustedly remarked, "I witnessed an indiscriminate plunder of the public stores, cars, and sutlers' houses."[10]

When a Federal battery began to shell the area Brig. Gen. James Archer ordered his officers to round up their troops and form a line of battle. Jackson, seeing at least one brigade under control, told Archer to drive the Yanks away. Archer pushed five regiments forward and the artillerymen hastily withdrew. The Tennesseans jeered the fleeing Yanks but their taunts quickly ended when they noticed a large formation of blue-coated infantry emerge from the distant tree line.[11] Archer, realizing his 1,000-man brigade appeared to be greatly outnumbered, hurriedly addressed his men, saying, "Now is the time to test the fighting qualities of the two armies; maneuvering will not avail anything, and victory depends upon fighting."[12] The Tennesseans gritted their teeth and moved forward. Corporal William Clendening (Co. E) wrote, "Our brigade being in advance ... were deployed in line of battle, and charged."[13]

General Jackson observed this small brigade of stalwart Southerners facing off against the mass of Yanks and rushed in reinforcements. Pender's brigade moved up on Archer's right, and three batteries unlimbered their guns. The Confederate artillery opened fire upon the Northerners. The Union regiments, Yankees from the 2nd, 3rd, and 4th New Jersey fired a few volleys. Then, as one of their commanders noted, they were "forced by vastly superior numbers to retire under a galling fire from the enemy's artillery."[14] A relieved William Clendening (Co. E) noted, "The Yankee line immediately gave way."[15]

The Tennesseans pursued the withdrawing Federals, firing sporadically, but for the most part, advancing slowly and cautiously. Major Shepard's men occasionally gathered up a worn-out Yank. A Federal officer noted, "Fatigue of incessant marching over bad roads and continuous fire of the enemy had thinned my ranks, and many men had fallen out, unable to march.... These stragglers were captured by the enemy."[16]

Archer's easy advance ended when his men reached the banks of Bull Run. Union troops awaited the Confederates and opened fire when the Southerners came within range. Private Robert Ozment (Co. G) went down immediately. George Shepard's men returned fire and the exchange of musketry continued for a few minutes before disaster struck Captain William Williamson's Company H — a volley with surprising accuracy ripped through Williamson's men, striking six.[17] Sergeant Ferguson Harris was hit in the chest and Pvt. John Tucker in the stomach. Private Bob Jackson was seriously wounded, as was Cpl. George Thompson and Pvt. Robert Wormack. Private Parson McKenzie (Co. K) was also injured. The wounded Ferguson Harris recalled, "John Tucker, Bob Jackson, Parson McKenzie, and myself were all wounded in one volley and piled up on each other."[18] Lieutenant Jack Moore (Co. B) reported, "Almost the entire loss of the regiment fell upon ... Company H, [most of whom] were either killed or wounded."[19]

The Northerners withdrew after fighting for a few more minutes. Archer sent the 19th Georgia in pursuit and the Georgians hustled forward. They, as Archer described, "crossed the run and advanced about a half mile," gathering up wounded and left-behind Northerners.[20] The Tennesseans held the ground above Bull Run for the rest of the day, they were ordered back to Manassas Junction. The Tennesseans bivouacked and from their location watched the devastation of the Union supplies. Nearly all night long, huge flames arose above the depot as hundreds of tons of supplies were destroyed.

The Tennesseans marched again the next morning, moving through Centreville on the Warrenton turnpike and crossing Bull Run. They turned to the left and formed a battle line about a half mile from a railroad cut. Later that afternoon an artillery duel flared up and Archer moved his brigade forward, positioning them to assist the Southern artillery. The veterans kept their heads down until the shooting ceased. Once the sun set the 7th Tennessee was repositioned near the railroad cut.

On August 29, 1862, they found themselves on a sloping hill, about two hundred yards west of the railroad cut, not far from Sudley Springs. Their brigade sat safely behind the South Carolinians of Gregg's brigade. The morning went by quickly and without incident, though heavy fighting roared not more than a quarter mile away.

At 4:00 P.M., Archer moved his regiments into the railroad cut, and as they were filing into the defensive position Union infantry advanced. Major Shepard's riflemen thundered a volley into the charging Union soldiers, decimating their first rank. The 7th poured several more destructive volleys into the Northerners and the Yankee attack stalled. Determined officers attempted to rally their broken ranks but more Tennessee lead shattered any thought of continuing the assault. The Southerners howled triumphantly. They understood a valuable lesson — to charge across open ground meant to meet a horrible fate.

Archer's riflemen had just destroyed much of Maj. Gen. Philip Kearney's 2nd Brigade, commanded by Brig. Gen. David Birney, Northerners from Maine, New York, and Pennsylvania. By the time this battle ended, Birney's brigade suffered over 600 casualties.[21] Kearney was not content to just destroy one of his brigades. He sent a second forward to attack Archer's men. They passed through the shattered remains of the first wave. Tennessee bullets slammed into the Northerners, crushing this futile attempt. The Federals, men from Indiana and Pennsylvania, resisted, standing out in the open, taking massive losses and bravely shooting back.

Northern bullets began striking Tennesseans. First Lieutenant Rufus Doak (Co. H) went down, badly wounded in the chest. Private Joseph Anderson (Co. C) was struck in the hip, the bullet shattering the bone. Private Albert R. Hearn (Co. D) was seriously hit in the chest, and Pvt. William Johns (Co. G) was grievously injured when he was struck in the head. Second Lieutenant William Harkreader's (Co. I) right arm was shattered by a Minié bullet. The furious fight lasted no more than ten or fifteen minutes before the Yanks in Brig. Gen. John Robinson's brigade collapsed, having lost over 200 men.

Then, Kearney sent in a third brigade, men from New York, Pennsylvania and Michigan. They picked their way through the debris of two brigades and closed upon Archer's dangerous riflemen. The Confederates unleashed a sheet of fire into the blue ranks, dropping scores of bluecoats and halting their advance. This third wave of Union attackers inched closer to the Tennesseans, firing steadily, their marksmanship deadly. Surprisingly, a Yank force located a gap between Archer's brigade and the adjoining formation and the bluecoats worked their way around and behind the Tennesseans. They fired into the Southerners. Tennessean boys went down: Pvt. James H. Paty (Co. B), Sgt. Robert Irby (Co. D), Cpl. William Clendening (Co. E), Pvt. Eli Smith (Co. I), and Pvt. Preston Hill (Co. K).[22]

This flanking movement eroded the Southerners' defense until Stonewall Jackson responded by throwing in his reserves in and they stiffened Archer's lines. Major Shepard's men reformed and attacked along with Jackson's reinforcements. The Northerners resisted fiercely, downing more Tennesseans; wounding Sgt. Maj. John Carter (staff), killing Pvt. Edward Clark (Co. C), and wounding Pvt. Dan Riggans (Co. K).[23] The Yanks folded, but not before 2nd Lt. James Martin (Co. D) was slightly wounded, Pvt. Harris Berry (Co. D) was struck in the leg, and Cpl. William Lester (Co. K) was killed.[24] One relieved Southerner noted, "When reinforcements arrived a charge was made, and the enemy repulsed."[25] Corporal J. P. Bashaw (Co. H) simply remembered, "We held our own."[26]

This third Union brigade fell back, demolished, having lost over 150 troops. General Philip Kearney's division had been chopped to pieces by Archer's men; over 1,000 Federals, including Kearney, who now was dead, had been killed or wounded.[27] Later, a Southerner wrote of the attacks upon the railroad cut, "Three lines of battle, one after another in beautiful order with banners flying, hurled themselves against our men in the cut ... [and were] nearly annihilated."[28]

In the lull after the third Union brigade faded away Shepard's officers checked their men's ammunition supplies. The answer was frightening; many of the battle-weary Tennesseans' cartridge boxes held less than a handful of rounds. General Archer noted, "I did not average over two cartridges to the man."[29] Major Shepard ordered his men to go out onto the battlefield and take cartridges from the dead and wounded Yankees. Finishing this, the men hunkered down in the railroad cut, readying for the next Union onslaught.

But the Federals had suffered enough; there were no more attacks. General Jackson called for a massive Confederate assault. Later that evening thousands of gray-coats arose from behind the railroad defenses and surged forward. The Yanks fought back, shooting more of Major Shepard's boys; 1st Lt. Martin Baird (Co. K) was wounded, and Pvt. John New (Co. H) was struck in the hand. Also, both Chamberlain brothers, James and Foster (Co. D), were shot down.[30] The Northerners' defenses crumbled and an excited Cpl. J. P. Bashaw wrote, "Old Stonewall came down the line, with his hat in his hand, and his whole corps moved forward [and] Pope's army stampeded."[31]

Once darkness halted the killing the Tennesseans returned to the railroad cut. Shepard's surviving officers and sergeants counted heads, completed casualty reports and made sure everyone had something to eat. Sadly, the flag-saving hero of the Battle of Mechanicsville, Roger "Cu" Word (Co. H), had been captured. Fortunately for Pvt. Word, the 22-year-old from Lebanon would remain a prisoner of war for only two months before being exchanged and able to return to the regiment.[32]

With the battle over, it was time for the surgeons to go to work. The 7th Tennessee had nearly two dozen injured men in need of medical attention. One of these soldiers, 24-year-old 2nd Lt. William Harkreader (Co. I), had suffered a grievous wound to his left arm. There was nothing for the surgeons to do but amputate. Later one of Harkreader's comrades remarked, "I saw Billy Harkreader with his arm amputated lying under a bush arbor with the hand of death hanging close over him."[33] But the young officer from Silver Springs, Tennessee, survived. Harkreader eventually was sent to a hospital in Knoxville, where he remained until October 1863. By then, the hard-pressed Southern forces needed every available veteran they could employ — even one-armed men. He was transferred to Rome, Georgia, and assumed supply duties. Lieutenant Harkreader served in this capacity until May 1864, when he was captured by Sherman's army and sent to Johnson's Island prison. He remained there until the end of the war.

The worn-out soldiers slept, and as one Southerner remarked, "Nothing keeps the soldier from sleep after a hard fought battle. He may stand the strain like a man while fighting, but after it is over he will be as limp as a dish rag."[34] Their rest ended abruptly at sunrise the next morning, August 30, 1862, by rifle fire. Though the shooting was heavy, this time the Union forces did not send masses of soldiers to be slaughtered. Instead, the Yanks crept forward and fought against a screen of 130 Southern skirmishers from the 1st Tennessee. Archer, not understanding the fierceness of the struggle, noted, "The firing between my pickets and the enemy's skirmishers ... became so rapid and continuous that, fearing my men were wasting ammunition, I sent my aide-de-camp ... to ascertain what it meant."[35]

The day's heat mounted, searing the tinder-dry countryside. A soldier recalled, "Where the scorched grass caught [fire] it burned briskly and sent white smoke across the blue sky."[36] At 2:00 P.M., the Federals attacked again, driving in the 1st Tennessee skirmishers and pushing toward Archer's brigade. The Tennesseans were ordered to attack. The gray-uniformed soldiers swept toward the blue line and the Yanks opened fire, killing Pvt. Joseph Derickson (Co. B) and Pvt. William Watkins (Co. K), and wounding nearly a dozen more 7th Tennesseans.[37]

The Yankees, having suffered enough, withdrew. Private John Williams (Co. D) noted, "The earth was so covered [with dead] that a man could have walked upon them without touching the ground."[38] The Confederates scavenged among the Union casualties, taking ammunition and food, accoutrements, boots, and clothing. One thoughtful Southerner remarked, "Most of [the dead] had been robbed by someone. Some had nothing on but their underclothing. If they had on pants the pockets had been turned [out].... You can't find a [dead] man on the battlefield the next morning that ha[d] not been robbed."[39]

At 5:00 P.M., Maj. George Shepard's Tennesseans left their defenses and pushed through a stand of trees and out into the open. A six-gun battery could be seen, barely three hundred yards away. Shepard's men ducked into a hollow. Archer, seeing Brig. Gen. Pender urge his brigade to take the guns, ordered his own brigade to attack. The action proved swift and decisive. Archer proudly boasted, "I ... marched in double-quick directly on the battery.... The enemy stood to his guns and continued to fire upon us until we were within 75 yards, when he abandoned three of his pieces, which fell into the hands of my brigade."[40] Archer's competitor, Pender, captured the other three cannon.

Once the guns were secured, Archer's men continued their advance and took possession of a large Union hospital. Finally, darkness halted the Tennesseans' movements. Major Shepard's men lay down where they were; their part in the second Battle of Manassas over. The farm boys-turned-veteran soldiers knew which side of the battlefield they preferred — behind breastworks or in entrenchments. The Tennesseans shuddered at the memory of how easily they had destroyed an entire division. That night a tremendous thunderstorm pummeled the tired soldiers, but by morning the sky was clear and the temperature cooler. The Tennesseans were stunned by their losses: 45 out of 300 men. They buried their dead comrades and visited their wounded friends, glad to be safe, at least for the moment.

The 7th Tennessee moved on September 1, 1862, slogging along mud-choked roads, marching to Chantilly and from there to near Leesburg. The Tennesseans splashed across the shallow waters of the Potomac River and crossed into Maryland. This river divided the North from the South, and its importance impressed the boys from Wilson, Sumner, DeKalb, and Smith counties — they were taking the war to the North. One rifleman wrote, "The river where we crossed [was] about 400 yards wide, and not over four feet deep at any place. Everyone had his own ideas about fixing himself up for wading and acted accordingly." The soldier continued, "[I] don't think the picture would be suitable for the parlor."[41] The invading Confederates marched along the Furnace Road to Buckeystown and from there crossed the Monocacy River.[42]

As George Shepard's riflemen walked the dust-choked roads they were surprised to learn their division commander, General A. P. Hill, had been removed from command. General Hill, frustrated by Stonewall Jackson's unwillingness to share marching routes, had circumvented Jackson's authority and given his own orders. Hill's commands had resulted in chaos and huge numbers of straggling soldiers. Jackson immediately countermanded Hill's directives and did so in front of the frustrated general. Hill approached his superior and angrily shoved his sword into Jackson's face, shouting, "If you take command of my troops in my presence, take my sword also." Jackson refused to take the sword but answered, "Put up your sword and consider yourself in arrest."[43] He immediately turned command of the division over to Brig. Gen. Lawrence Branch. General Branch, a 42-year-old North Carolinian with a Princeton education, reluctantly took charge of the division.

Regardless of who led the division, the soldiers' conditions were dreadful. The fledgling Confederate supply department again failed in its responsibilities, leaving the Tennesseans in desperate shape. Their equipment was worn out, their uniforms were in tatters, and a number hobbled along on inadequate footwear. Corporal J. P. Bashaw (Co. H) wrote, "My feet [were] badly blistered, owning to wet feet and bad shoes."[44] Not only were their supplies lacking, since the regiment's wagons lagged far behind, most of Shepard's men had little to eat. The soldiers were "stealing everything eatable they could lay their hands on."[45] Farmers along the Confederates' route saw their fields and orchards stripped. A Tennessean recalled, "After entering Maryland, [our] ... supper was of green corn roasted on fires made from the rails of the fences that surrounded the fields."[46]

Major George Shepard's hungry Tennesseans bivouacked not far from Frederick and remained there until September 10, 1862. A Confederate wrote, "The men had little food. They added potatoes where they could ... but they had green corn, meal after meal, as their basal diet."[47] Then the Southerners marched west, crossing through South Mountain and ending up outside of Williamsport. From here the Seventh crossed back over the

Potomac and turned southward. On September 12, 1862, Archer's brigade marched cautiously into Martinsburg and "consumed an incredible quantity of food," and then hiked six miles toward Harper's Ferry.[48] The next day they closed in on Harper's Ferry and bivouacked, the men knowing a battle was brewing. The veterans could see the Yank earthworks on top of the heights around Harper's Ferry and shuddered. George Shepard's men realized they would have to attack, a prospect no one wanted.

On September 14, 1862, the Tennesseans waited for orders, calmly preparing for battle. Major Shepard, though feeling poorly, commanded the small regiment, now numbering less than 300. His second in command, the regiment's senior-most captain, was a 34-year-old lawyer from Lebanon, William Williamson, who nursed a wound he had received in June. Shepard's two wing commanders were Captains Asoph Hill and Archibald Norris, and his adjutant was 1st Lt. George Howard. Together, these leaders watched over an ever-shrinking number of friends and relatives who remained. Private David Phillips (Co. K) wrote, "Since our regiment has become so small, we have all become acquainted with each other and there is a genial spirit ... like a brotherhood."[49]

Fortunately, while the Tennesseans were preparing for the coming fight, General Robert E. Lee had skillfully handled the personality conflicts between Jackson and Hill averted a crisis and reinstated Hill to division command. That afternoon word came from General A. P. Hill instructing the Tennesseans to move. The Tennesseans shifted from their bivouac near a set of railroad tracks to a dirt path taking them toward Bolivar Heights. The popping of skirmishers' rifles could be heard. The 7th Tennessee took position in the brigade battle formation and slowly moved forward. When Shepard's troops reached the crest of a hill they came into full view of the Northern batteries occupying the

WILLIAM H. WILLIAMSON. William Williamson was born in 1828 and attended Cumberland University in Lebanon, Tennessee, and earned a law degree. He enlisted into Company H and was immediately elected captain. After being wounded at Gaines Mill (6/27/1862) he was wounded and lost an arm at Gettysburg (7/3/63) and captured. He remained a POW for the rest of the war. He married Martha Ready Morgan in 1873 and they had four children. He served as a Tennessee judge. William Williamson died in 1887 (Loewentheil Family Photographic Collection).

heights. Federal guns opened fire. Shepard's boys hustled to the protection of a stand of woods.

General Archer wanted the Tennesseans to sneak through the woods and flank the Union artillery positions. Having no desire for a head-on assault, Shepard's men gratefully took that route, but the Tennesseans discovered their path obstructed by a cleverly-fashioned abatis. The men became so entangled in this hazard that by darkness they were still four hundred yards from the batteries.[50] The Tennesseans could not build fires, nor could they move about; instead, the troops just shivered in the chilly night air. One sufferer wrote, "We had a cold night on the Mt."[51]

Confederate artillery broke the quiet early the next morning. Federal guns returned fire and the two sides dueled with each other until about 8:00 A.M., then the Northerners ceased fire.[52] The call came for the infantry to attack. The Tennesseans stood up and scrambled into the impeding obstructions. Union riflemen opened fire and within a few minutes their musketry took effect. Private John Nix (Co. A) was wounded, as were Pvt. George Carlisle (Co. B) and Pvt. Nelson Smith (Co. B). The entanglements proved impassable; the Tennesseans could neither advance nor retreat, so the men dropped to the ground and took shelter. Confederate artillery resumed its bombardment of the Yank guns. This hampered the Federal sharpshooters' aim, but still, over the next hour two more Tennesseans were injured: Pvt. Hugh McGuire (Co. E) and Pvt. Robert Ozment (Co. G).[53]

Then, to the Tennesseans' relief, the Federal shooting ceased and the bluecoats began waving white flags. The battlefield grew quiet and the Southerners learned the Yankees wanted to quit fighting. One Southerner noted, "[As we] began a forward movement upon the works of the enemy, the siege was terminated by the surrender of the enemy."[54] The dazed Tennesseans, whose fortunes had suddenly changed from a possible disaster to complete victory, promptly moved forward and took possession of the Union position, and rounded up prisoners. Private Preston Hill (Co. K) noted, the Federals "surrendered to us about 12,000."[55]

With the fight for Harper's Ferry over the men remained on the heights, bivouacking among the Federal gun emplacements. For Shepard's riflemen, the advance had cost five men. One of these casualties, Pvt. Robert Ozment (Co. G), had now suffered his second wounding in barely three weeks. But this time the 33-year-old blacksmith from Oak Point, Tennessee, was seriously hurt; there would be no return to Company G. Robert Ozment was sent to a hospital and eventually placed on a medical furlough. He would finally be medically discharged and sent home in April 1863.[56]

Early on September 16, 1862, curious Tennesseans descended from their hilltop bivouac and explored Harper's Ferry. Shepard's boys fanned out, exploring the famous little town and soon discovered stores filled with food and supplies. Quick-thinking officers immediately finagled orders to take charge of guarding the storehouses. A thrilled Confederate guard wrote, "[We] liberated the Yankee's sugar and coffee, blankets, shoes and all other captured equipment."[57] Another wrote, "[While] ... guarding the vast quantity of stores captured ... most of the men spent the time enhancing the contents of their haversacks with the captured Union goodies."[58] Many of George Shepard's Tennesseans threw away their bedraggled Confederate uniforms and replaced them with new, Yankee wardrobes. The men, now full of belly, their haversacks stuffed, and their equipment re-outfitted, lounged about, relaxing and congratulating themselves "on the prospect of several days' rest."[59]

But there was to be no respite. At 6:30 the next morning, September 17, 1862, the men in A. P. Hill's division received orders to hurry to Sharpsburg, a distance of seventeen miles. Archer's brigade took its place in the column and marched northward along the Baltimore and Ohio Railroad tracks. They turned off the railroad grade after several miles and picked up a dirt road heading toward Shepherdstown.

General Stonewall Jackson was in a hurry; Robert E. Lee needed his men immediately—a desperate crisis faced the Confederate army at Sharpsburg. Jackson pushed his men ruthlessly, even refusing them their customary hourly ten-minute breaks. A dust-caked Tennessean remarked, "We went down that 17-mile road like the dogs was after us."[60] The day turned hot and the men sweltered beneath the sun's force. One soldier noted, "[It was] a very warm day, and quite dusty; our soldiers are as dirty as the ground itself and are nearly of the same color."[61]

Jackson's hardnosed pace wore out his soldiers. At first, only the weaker men straggled, but soon, even some of the strong dropped behind. The heat, combined with the harsh marching, stripped away hundreds of men. Major George Shepard found he could not keep up the pace so he turned the regiment over to Captain William Williamson. Other Tennesseans did the same, falling out, calling to their comrades not to worry and promising they would catch up later. By the time the 7th Tennessee reached Moler's Crossroads the regiment had lost over fifty men.[62]

From Moler's Crossroads the column turned onto a lane leading northeasterly. Many of the soldiers had not been as fortunate as the Tennesseans and did not have new shoes; these men limped along painfully, either on worn-out shoe leather or barefoot. One sufferer noted these soldiers "could have been tracked by their blood, trying to march over rough turnpike roads."[63] Thus, with each mile of hurried marching toward Sharpsburg, the formation lost more men.

Captain William Williamson staggered on, relying on his surviving company leaders to keep their units together, but each mile proved costly, more Tennessee boys could not maintain the grueling pace. Even Gen. Archer collapsed and turned the brigade over to Colonel Peter Turney of the 1st Tennessee. Archer remarked, "Being too unwell for duty ... I followed in an ambulance."[64]

Later, the tired Confederates waded across the Potomac River at Boteler's Ford and reformed on Miller's Sawmill Road.[65] The soldiers could now hear the rumble of artillery coming from the Sharpsburg battle. At 3:30 P.M., the small band of 7th Tennessee survivors turned left at the intersection of Miller's Sawmill Road and the Harper's Ferry Road. Captain Williams was now gone, having also fallen behind. The command of the regiment now resided in the hands of Adjutant George Howard.[66] The 21-year-old first lieutenant marched in front of less than one hundred Tennesseans. Though Howard was an able regimental adjutant, many of the same qualities making him administratively competent also caused the men not to like him. Lieutenant Ferguson Harris (Co. H), who had just been promoted "for gallant conduct on the field," by Gen. Archer, recalled, "In camp of instruction with raw recruits he was unpopular."[67] This antipathy toward their leader would prove decisive later in the day.

General Archer rumbled by the staggering Tennesseans in his ambulance, reached the head of the brigade column and took over command of his shrunken formation. He recorded, "This was a long and fatiguing march; many of the men fell, exhausted from the march ... so that when ... my brigade reached the battlefield there were only 350 men."[68] The small Tennessee battalion followed the brigade northward, listening to the thunderous roar of artillery, and as they got closer, the continuous rattle of musketry. Lieutenant Jack Moore (Co. B) reported, "The Seventh ... had been reduced to less than one hundred men."[69]

When Archer's formation closed to within a half mile of Sharpsburg he moved his men in behind four Georgian regiments commanded by Colonel Henry Benning. Archer's troops now bordered the road, resting on the western edge of a cornfield.[70] When Benning's Georgians crashed into the corn and began shooting toward the east, Archer maneuvered his brigade north, past the Georgians and slipped in on their left flank. Heavy musketry could be heard off to the north toward Sharpsburg. Archer faced his small brigade eastward and his men scrambled over a stout fence. The Confederates reformed on the edge of a cornfield and then advanced.

The Tennesseans stomped through the tall corn, bullets zipping above their heads. However, before they had gone more than fifty yards into the cornfield, Adjutant George Howard believed he heard a command to fall back. Without consulting anyone for confirmation of the surprising order, Howard turned the 7th Tennessee around and backed them out of the corn. When the commanders of the 1st Tennessee and 19th Georgia saw the Seventh about-face they also reversed their units' direction. The three meager-sized regiments returned to the fence line beside the road in confusion, everyone puzzled by this order to retreat. Archer quickly realized three of his regiments were missing and sent an aide to find them. The staff officer located the errant formations and vehemently shouted orders for them to rejoin Archer. Later, Archer censured Adjutant Howard, writing, "[Howard] had called out, 'Fall back,' which was mistaken for an order from me."[71]

The Tennesseans hurried back through the cornfield and reformed into a battle line with the 14th Tennessee. The field in front of them had recently been plowed; it was an open field of fire with Yankees crouching behind a stone wall 250 yards away. The veteran Tennesseans looked at each other and gritted their teeth, knowing Archer would order another frontal assault.

General Archer shouted the command to attack and his stalwart men raced across the plowed field. Surprisingly, the Northerners did not fire and the Tennesseans covered much of the distance without injury. A Federal officer recalled, "I felt convinced that the advancing troops were our friends, and gave the order not to fire upon them." [72] The Yanks were confused because so many of Archer's men were decked out in blue uniforms. However, once the Confederate battle flags were unfurled, the Yanks knew who approached.

The Federals unleashed their first volley into Lt. Howard's small band of Tennesseans. A Federal officer wrote, "Soon after all doubt vanished ... [a] furious attack ... was made ... almost at feeling distance."[73] Private John Close's (Co. A) hand was shattered. First Lieutenant John Jennings (Co. F) fell, his leg shattered. Private John McDonald (Co. H) had his right thigh ripped open, and Pvt. John Shannon (Co. K) was shot in the head.[74]

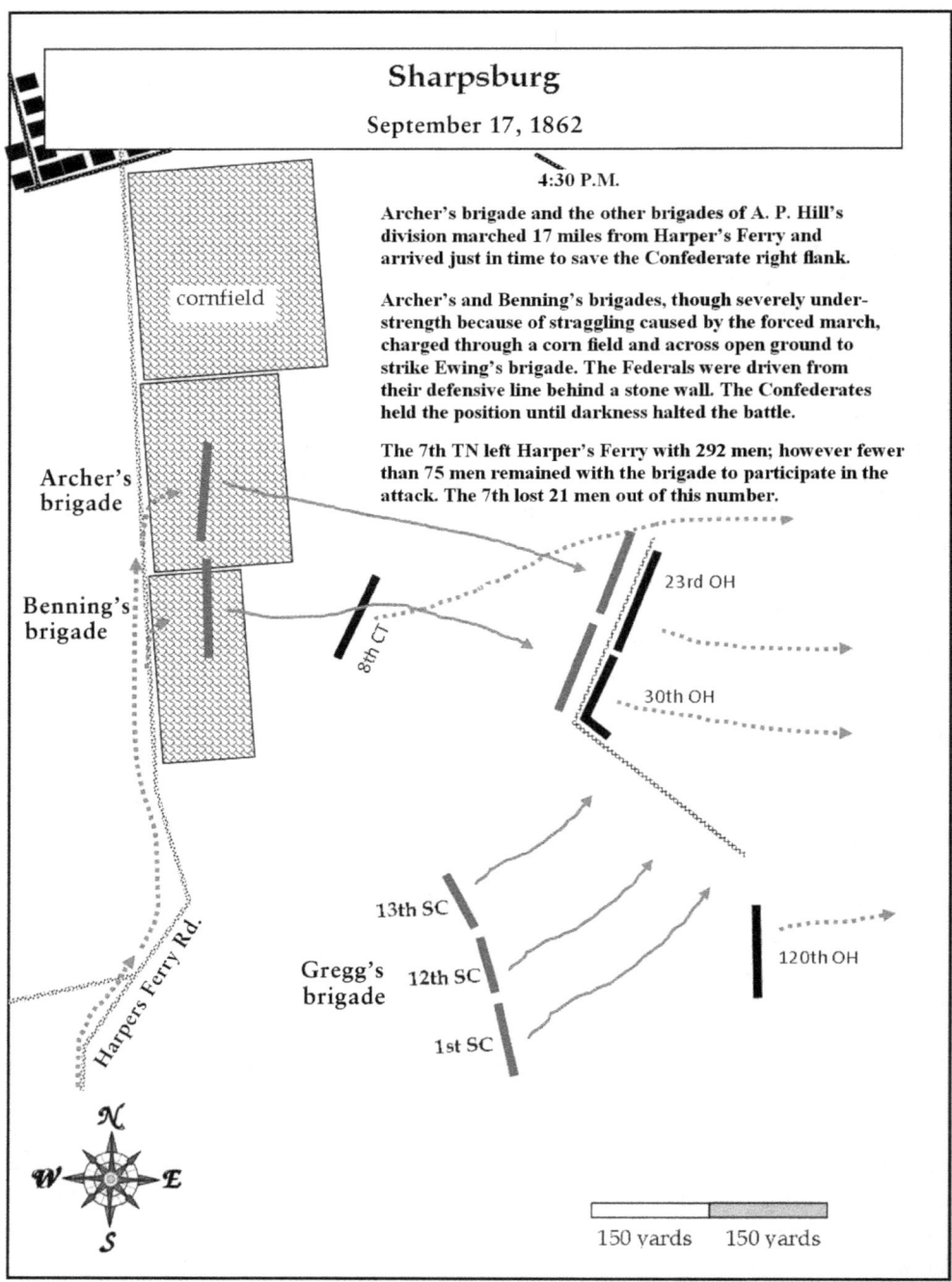

And Pvt. James Gray (Co. E) went down when a "ball entered left of [his] breastbone, [went] through his lungs to [his] right shoulder [and] out through [his] arm."[75]

The Tennesseans returned fire and pressed toward the stone wall. Some Yanks went down, but their shooting did not cease. Private Alex Bledsoe (Co. E) had his right arm shattered by a bullet, while Pvt. William Ricketts (Co. F) was shot through the head; the 25-year-old Ricketts died within minutes. Lieutenant William Vivrett's (Co. I) neck was sliced open by a bullet. Captain Asoph Hill (Co. F) took a flesh wound, and Pvt. John Parton (Co. I) was hit in the thigh.[76] And Lt. Robert Miller (Co. E) was shot through the chest.[77] But still, the defiant Tennesseans approached the stone fence.

Northerners began slipping away from their battle line and the Yanks' fire withered. At first this melting-away occurred only in small numbers, but soon entire squads quit shooting and fell back. An unhappy Union officer recorded, "Our men ... were forced to fall back ... this time out of the cornfield [and] beyond the fence."[78] Though the Federal battle line unraveled, some resolute riflemen remained on duty, firing at the Tennesseans. Sergeant Samuel Major (Co. H) fell, seriously wounded. Private Martin Drake (Co. K) had a bullet tear through his right leg, and Pvt. Jim Weaver's (Co. K) left thigh was mutilated.[79]

Ignoring their fallen brothers, the Tennesseans came on, firing and advancing, and eventually reached the stone wall. The Yankees had no stomach for resistance, their defense collapsed and they fled. The Northerners ran toward the east, their force reduced to a panicked mob. A few bellicose Confederates wanted to chase after the fleeing Yankees, but cooler heads prevailed. Archer's survivors scrunched down behind the rock defense and prepared for a counterattack. Later, Archer bragged, "In passing over the ... cornfield, I lost nearly one-third of my already greatly reduced command, but it rushed forward ... at [the] double-quick ... and drove him from his strong position."[80]

The exhausted Tennesseans kept their heads low and waited anxiously until darkness closed the day's fighting. Then, Lt. George Howard's tiny formation retrieved their fallen friends. The swift assault across 250 yards of open field had cost the regiment twenty-one Tennesseans. One of these wounded, Lt. William Vivrett, was carried off by stretcher bearers and taken to a field hospital. From there he rode in an ambulance to Jordan Springs, near Winchester. This once beautiful, pre-war vacation resort had been turned into a Confederate hospital. Here, as just one of hundreds of badly wounded soldiers, Vivrett struggled to recover. Unfortunately William Vivrett could not overcome an infection attacking his injury. The 26-year-old merchant's clerk from Lebanon died a month later.[81]

Most of the regiment's stragglers rejoined the regiment during the night, tripling the formation's strength to nearly two hundred. Early the next morning they hunkered down behind the stone wall, poised to fight off Federal counterattacks, but nothing happened. Instead, the Yankees sent out emissaries requesting a truce. Both sides quickly agreed and the morning was spent collecting and burying the dead. At times, Yanks and Rebs worked side by side tending to the fallen. It was at this time the Tennesseans learned they had badly damaged three Union regiments, the 8th Connecticut, the 23rd Ohio, and the 30th Ohio.[82]

The day passed quietly and ended with a noisy thunderstorm. During the night the Confederate army began its retreat, crossing back over the Potomac, but the Tennesseans did not move; they were assigned the rearguard duty. Finally, though, it was their turn and the Tennesseans crossed a pontoon bridge to Virginia soil. They marched about five miles beyond Shepherdstown and bivouacked. Division commander Gen. A. P. Hill reported, "My division crossed the Potomac into Virginia about 10 A.M. the next morning [September 19, 1862], every wagon and piece of artillery having been safely been put on the Virginia shore."[83]

The next morning Archer's brigade, plus five brigades in General A. P. Hill's division were ordered to return to the Boteler's Ford and attack the Union bridgehead on the south side of the Potomac. The Southerners moved northward four miles, toward the sounds of artillery and musketry. Archer's men inched in behind the first wave of Confederates, Tar Heels under Brig. Gen. William Pender. Not long afterward, orders were given to move up on the North Carolinians' left flank.

The Tennesseans obliqued to Pender's left and came onto the battle line. They immediately opened fire on the Union troops occupying an open hilltop not more than 150 yards away. A Federal officer wrote, "Springing as it were from the bushes and cornfield which had concealed them to this time, and ... within short musket range, a rapid and vigorous fire commenced immediately."[84] The bluecoats shot back, but ineffectively. A frustrated Union officer complained, "About the same time the right was fired on from a heavy force in front, and [we] commenced [shooting].... Owing to the worthlessness of our pieces (condemned Enfields), not more than 50 per cent of which could be discharged."[85] Even though the Federals had shoddy weapons, some of their bullets struck among the 7th Tennessee. Private Tom Copeland (Co. E) was killed instantly. Captain James Bond (Co. G) was struck down with a blow to the upper body, and Pvt. Bart Warford (Co. A) suffered a badly maimed left leg.[86]

The Confederates surged toward the Federals. The Yanks' resistance splintered and the bluecoats streamed down the steep slopes toward the Potomac River. The Tennessee boys pressed forward, firing as they came. The Yanks, veterans from Pennsylvania, reformed and turned on the Southerners. Federal bullets flew among the Tennesseans. Private Alex Taylor (Co. E) was severely wounded. Lieutenant John Ingram (Co. G) was disabled by a bullet tearing through his shoulder, and Cpl. Henry Williams (Co. E) was disfigured by a flesh wound. Archer's riflemen volleyed into the advancing Yanks, shooting down their colonel and pummeling his followers. The Northerners held briefly, firing a few minutes before disintegrating. But in that final exchange of gunfire, Pvt. Samuel Dorris (Co. E) was killed, and Pvt. Frank Jennings (Co. F) was mortally wounded.[87]

The Confederates continued shooting at the Federals until they splashed across the Potomac. The bluecoats had been routed and suffered heavy losses in this brief fight. A surviving officer of the 118th Pennsylvania counted his regiment's losses at "277 out of 737 men."[88]

Once the Yanks' infantry were out of the way, Union artillery unleashed a massive barrage on the Confederates. James Archer, shocked by the artillery's violence, quickly ordered his men back out of danger. He wrote, "The advance of my command was made under the heaviest artillery fire I have ever witnessed."[89] The Tennesseans quickly retreated beyond the ridge top and to safety.

The 7th Tennessee reformed its ranks and first sergeants took roll. Search parties went back and located all the missing; the wounded were turned over to the surgeons, and Tom Copeland and Sam Dorris were buried. One of the wounded, Cpt. James Bond, a 24-year-old from Ponderella, Tennessee, was sent to the hospital at Jordan Springs. Sadly for the young officer, though his wound healed, he soon took ill with disease. Finally, James Bond resigned his commission three weeks later, writing, "I hereby respectfully tender my resignation from the Army of the Confederate States. My reason for doing so is a physical inability to perform the duties of my office."⁹⁰ Company G would now be led by 1st Lt. Williams Graves.

Other Tennesseans snuck back onto the battlefield and relieved the dead Federals of their boots, because, no matter how many pairs of footwear were supplied, the men always seemed ill-shod. One of the Wilson County boys was caught in this act by General Lee. His story became a legend throughout the regiment. A Tennessean recalled, "All of us know how Lee hates stragglers. Soon after the Battle of Sharpsburg, he was riding through the woods and came upon a man detached from his company, sitting on the ground. Evidently Lee didn't see that the man was removing the shoes from a dead Federal's feet. Lee accosted the man with, 'What are you doing out here? Why aren't you with your company?' ... 'Oh yes?' said the man, without looking up. 'You hid in a hole all day yesterday, while I fought barefooted. So now, when the danger's over, you come out of your hole, do you? I'm just trying to get myself a pair of shoes. I'll be back with my men in a few minutes. You go on and tend to your own business.' The general rode away laughing. One of his fellow soldiers went to the man. 'Do you know to whom you were speaking?' he asked. 'No, some little old lieutenant. They're always sticking their noses into other folks' business.' 'That was General Robert E. Lee.' The man said, 'I'm a goner now!' He ran off and hid in the bushes."⁹¹

That night the battle weary veterans trekked to the west, toward Martinsburg. Here, they camped along the banks of the Opeqon Creek, and in the following days had the time to recover from the battles in August and September. One soldier observed, "The soldiers are ... washing off the dirt of our long marches and battles and washing their clothes [as] the vermin have become very numerous."⁹²

A week later the men moved to the Berryville area and remained there for the entire month of October. Lieutenant Colonel John Fite returned, though still hobbling about. He recalled, "I was still on crutches, but my leg was mighty near well."⁹³ Fite allowed the majority of the regiment's operations to be handled by Major George Shepard, who made sure the Tennesseans drilled every day. Combat had taught the Tennesseans the foolishness of fighting in close ranks, with the men standing shoulder to shoulder. Fite and Shepard ordered the unit's commanders to improve their companies' skills in fighting while spread out. One rifleman noted, "Drilling has been resumed, especially skirmish drill."⁹⁴

Besides drill, the men had plenty of the duties necessary to maintain an army camp; collecting firewood, cleaning up garbage, getting water, supplying food, and gathering livestock forage. However, an additional chore irritated the soldiers. One veteran complained, "Had a brigade skirmish drill ... for the special benefit of some young ladies, six in number, each escorted by a staff officer. They looked very nice on their fine horses with long flowing riding skirts and no doubt enjoyed the maneuvers, but I am pretty certain the men performing them did not."⁹⁵

At the end of each day's work the soldiers returned to their tents, tired and homesick. The lonely Tennessean boys read and reread precious letters from home. Since Union troops held Middle Tennessee communication with home was difficult. Each letter had to be hand-carried by someone slipping through the Federal lines. On occasion the couriers were caught and a batch of mail lost. Each note from home was priceless though often heartrending. Many of the boys received a note similar to this message: "The Yankees ...

have been very mean, taking everything that they want.... [W]e have looked for you and John until we have become discouraged.... Oh that you could come."[96] George Shepard's sister wrote, "[We] had to hide [our] meat, flour, sugar, meal, and other food in out-of-the-way places."[97]

As recovered wounded veterans returned to the formation the regiment's companies slowly rebuilt themselves. By the end of October 1862 the Seventh's numbers were over 300. Private Joseph Hamilton (Co. H) wrote, "Our army is in better condition now than it ever was."[98] The regiment was sent out to the picket line along the Shenandoah River and here the men brushed up against Federal advance guards near Snickers Gap on November 6, 1862. The Tennesseans deployed in their well-practiced skirmish lines and suffered no casualties. They came away from the fracas, excited and confident.

Winter came early, announcing itself on November 7, 1862, with a snowstorm. The soldiers celebrated the occasion with a massive snowball fight. A Southerner wrote, "Snow fell for the first time this winter. What a time the boys had snowballing each other."[99] Optimism spread throughout the camps; the coming of cold weather meant the war's suspension — after all, battles were seldom fought in winter. The soldiers relaxed, told stories, and shared the comradeship of soldiers away from home. Private David Phillips (Co. K) recalled they "talk[ed] of the golden days we have passed, of loves lost and wasted, of loves still living and burning on the tablets of our hearts, or of moments of golden opportunities miss-improved."[100] Another remembered, "We are having delightful weather, just cool enough to enjoy marching and our campfires at night when we cook our rations.... What is more jovial than a group of old soldiers telling war stories and smoking their pipes around the camp fires at night."[101]

Just as the Tennesseans settled in for the winter, rumors flooded their camp of a new Union offensive and that General Lee was going to put the army back in motion. Not long afterward, on November 21, 1862, the Confederates moved, heading toward Fredericksburg. The march to Fredericksburg was forced, as General Jackson ordered a series of long marches. The 7th Tennessee covered 120 miles in eight days. Meanwhile, the weather turned cold, chilled by rains and sleet. The soldiers plodded on, enduring their privations. One Southerner complained, "It was raining, then commenced sleeting, and afterward went to snowing, covering the ground about six inches."[102] Another shivering veteran wrote, "It rained, snowed, and hailed all day.... The mud was deep and partially frozen." Two days later he noted, "Ground frozen quite hard and it did not thaw."[103]

On December 12, 1862, Archer's brigade relieved the Texans in Hood's division and took up a defensive line near the edge of a stand of trees; their position was in a ditch overlooking some railroad tracks along the Bowling Green turnpike. The veterans were pleased with their expansive field of fire. James Archer wrote, "I found my brigade posted in the edge of a wood." The general also noted, "My left rest[s] where the wood extends forward to a point beyond the railroad."[104] Archer may have noticed the woods to his left, but he did not send out pickets to cover that region, a mistake which would hurt the Tennesseans.

John Fite and George Shepard placed the 7th Tennessee's ten companies on the line and the men bedded down for the night, confident. One rifleman boasted, "The men are cheerful almost to recklessness, used to hardship, veterans in action and in camp life."[105]

That night was cold and clear and the soldiers were treated to a display of the aurora borealis. Though this sight thrilled some, others were frightened, especially since many had observed a recent lunar eclipse. One veteran recalled, "There was a total eclipse of the moon this [early] morning. I was up in time to see about half of the eclipse."[106] Some of the soldiers believed these spectacles prophesied something horrible. Ferguson Harris (Co. H) remembered, "Some ... discussed it in connection with Armageddon, while those of us who knew little about Armageddon contented ourselves by prognosticating that the morrow would bring the bloodiest day the world ever saw."[107] Consequently, the Tennessean pickets peered into the silent darkness, worried what sunrise would bring.

The frigid cold forced many shivering Tennesseans to huddle around campfires. They kept looking toward the east, watchful for whatever the Federals had in mind, but the terrain was hidden by a thick layer of fog. The mist dissipated around 9:00 A.M., revealing the Yanks' massive army. General A. P. Hill wrote, "The lifting of the fog discovered to us the lines of the enemy drawn out in battle array on the low grounds between us and the river, covering the whole of my front and extending far to the left toward Fredericksburg."[108]

Around noon Federal artillery opened fire and shells came toward Archer's position. Lieutenant Colonel John Fite observed, "The Yankee artillery [opened] up with their artillery, shooting at us, but the shells would go way 40 or 50 feet above our heads.... The shells would come over ... making great noise."[109] The veteran Tennesseans waited out the artillery, guessing this was the precursor to an assault. The barrage went on for nearly two hours, but did no damage. The Yank infantry was not idle during this cannonade. The Tennesseans watched three brigades of bluecoats form up, a thousand yards away. Fite's officers and NCOs made sure their men were prepared, and the experienced Tennessee riflemen checked their weapons and cartridge boxes and bided their time. They knew what to do.

When the Northern infantry started across the open field, the Tennesseans saw one entire brigade aimed directly at them. The gray-clad soldiers gripped their muskets as their pickets scampered back to safely.[110] The Seventh waited until the Federal assault had swept over the railroad embankment and was about two hundreds away, and then, as Col. Goodner recorded, "When they came near enough of us to fire with effect, we did so."[111] Scores of bluecoats fell to the ground, but the Yanks continued rushing forward.

A Tennessean described the slaughter: "The firing along the line ... now became general, and had great effect upon the Union lines, killing and wounding a large number of men and officers."[112] The veteran continued, "The fighting with small-arms had only lasted about ten minutes when the enemy directly in front of our position took shelter in a railroad cut."[113] As the smoke cleared away the Tennesseans saw a field littered with hundreds of casualties, the closest of which were no nearer than fifty yards away. Lieutenant Jack Moore (Co. B) wrote, "We successfully met [the] assault ... without any or little loss.... We regarded the efforts of the Federals ... as futile in the extreme."[114]

Just as the Tennesseans began to relax from this easy victory the men began to sense something had gone wrong to their left. While Archer's brigade practically destroyed the brigade directly in front, another Federal brigade assaulted Lane's brigade, about six hundred yards to Archer's left. However, a third Union brigade had stormed into the swampy underbrush separating Lane's and Archer's formation. Once the Federals penetrated into

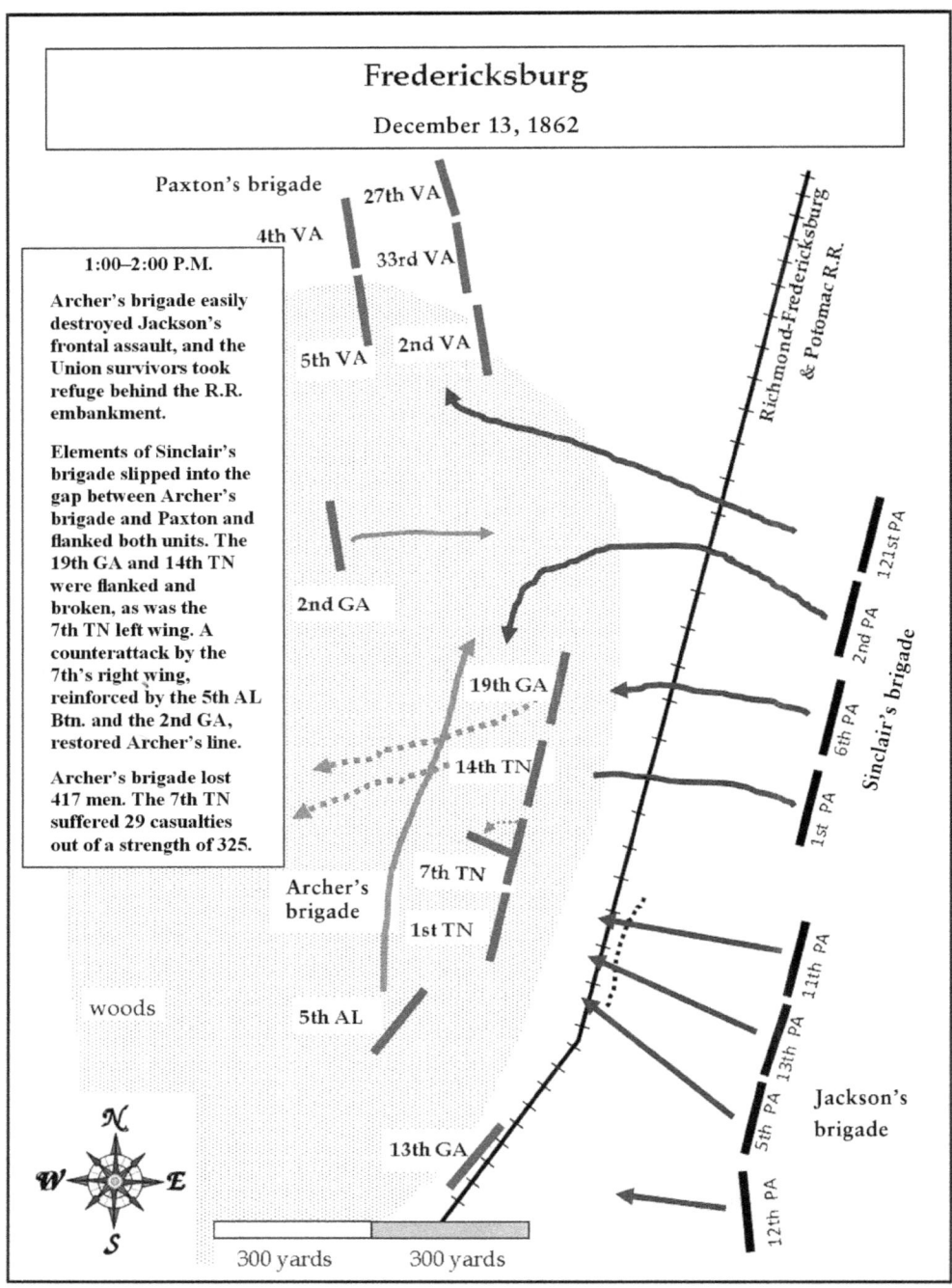

the woods and found themselves unopposed, their quick thinking commander sent his regiments sweeping toward Archer's left flank. They struck the 19th Georgia's, both from the left and from the rear. The Georgian regiment tried to fight back but soon broke, and its men streamed to the rear. The Georgian commander reported, "Through this wood they advanced, and succeeded in gaining our rear through a gap left open on our left. We held our position some fifteen or twenty minutes ... [but] we gave way."[115]

4. August 20, 1862: Before Dawn

Once the Federals enveloped the 19th Georgia they crashed into the next regiment, the 14th Tennessee. The results were the same. The 14th's colonel, James Lockert wrote, "[We] fell back in disorder."[116] Private Frank Goodall (Co. B), not understanding what had occurred, shouted, "Look yonder! See the cowardly Georgians running."[117] The jubilant Northerners surged forward, prepared to demolish the next Southern organization — the 7th Tennessee. Company B, commanded by 1st Lt. Frank Timberlake, held the Seventh's left flank. Though Timberlake's company was the largest formation in the regiment, with nearly fifty men, there was little these Tennesseans could do when the Federal onslaught reached them. The Yanks, hardened veterans from Pennsylvania, fired into Timberlake's formation, and then charged with fixed bayonets. Sergeant Blake Thackston was shot in the thigh, Pvt. Frank Goodall was hit in the hip, and Pvt. Elijah Knight was struck in the left breast.[118] Others went down quickly, and a handful surrendered. The rest of Lt. Timberlake's company broke and ran, taking with them nearby Tennesseans. Lieutenant William McCall (Co. E) noted, "I lit out, making about thirty miles an hour."[119]

The next companies suffered similar fates. Captain Bill Grave's Company G melted away once 1st Lt. Newborn Jennings was injured in the right shoulder, Pvt. Lafayette Hutchens was hit in the chest, Pvt. Peter Young was struck in the breast, and Pvt. Reuben Hagar was seriously wounded. Companies C and D did not do any better. First Sergeant Hart Harris (Co. D) was shot down, Pvt. Gilmore Eubanks (Co. C) was killed, and Pvt. Tom Brown (Co. D) had his thigh shattered. Private James Love (Co. C) was killed by a bullet through his head. Lieutenant Ferguson Harris (Co. H) recalled, "[Lt.] Oliver Foster coolly and calmly [wrote] his name on a piece of paper and pinn[ed] it on Love's breast."[120]

By now the Seventh's right flank knew what was coming and prepared. They wheeled around and delivered accurate volleys into the charging Yanks, forcing them to halt. But the Northerners did not quit; while some of their veterans tried to scoop up the scattered Tennesseans, others took shelter behind trees and maintained an unrelenting fire upon the Tennesseans. Lieutenant William Baird (Co. I) was killed, Pvt. Tom Holloway (Co. H) received a flesh wound, and Pvt. James Tate (Co. K) was struck by a bullet and mortally wounded.[121]

Fortunately, help arrived. General Archer had kept the 5th Alabama Battalion in reserve and he rushed them toward the broken position. The Alabamans, one hundred fifty men in all, raced across the rear of the brigade and reached the shattered left flank in time to provide a rallying point for the retreating Tennessee and Georgian veterans. At first, there was nothing but chaos, but soon the remaining officers regained control of their veterans. Two Virginia regiments joined Archer's counterattack and the Confederates surged forward with renewed vigor.[122] The Northerners were stunned by this assault. The shooting was at close quarters, and brutally violent for a few moments. Then, as one Pennsylvanian noted, the fighting caused "the whole line to break and fall to the rear."[123] The Union troops retreated out of the woods and onto the plain, fleeing to the protection of the railroad embankment.

Archer reformed his defensive line, his riflemen content to be back into their original positions, but disconcerted by the events which had taken place during the last forty-five minutes.[124] As the subdued veterans looked about and noticed how many comrades were missing, they fumed in anger, knowing their losses had been caused by leadership failure.

No one had an answer to the question, "Why was there a six hundred yard gap between Archer and Lane?"

When fresh brigades from Brigadier General Jubal Early's division moved forward and attacked the Federals hiding behind the railroad tracks, Archer's men joined the assault. This charge broke the Northerners' resolve and they fell back, leaving the ground to the Confederates. Following this success, the Tennesseans returned to their position at the edge of the woods. The tired soldiers looked out over a battlefield covered with bodies, and as one veteran noted, after examining the dead, "[I] have seen but few pleasant looking corpses."[125]

That night, the Tennesseans gathered around campfires and talked quietly about the day's fighting. Though they had been flanked and pushed back a few hundred yards the men had rallied, reformed, driven the Yankees from the field, and defeated the Northerners again. The Tennesseans mourned their missing comrades, knowing this fight had removed nearly three dozen more friends and relatives from among their ranks. Later that night, the shivering soldiers struggled to keep warm. One weary veteran complained, "The weather is extremely cold. The ground is hard frozen and we are without tents ... we [built] log-heap fires and all lie around them with our feet to the fire."[126]

CHAPTER 5

December 14, 1862: Early Morning

"By his gallant attack he secured the key to the enemy's position."

The Tennesseans awoke on December 14, 1862, ready to confront the Federals' next undertakings but the morning was quiet and the hours passed without incident. One Confederate wrote, "Everything was quiet save some occasional artillery."[1] The Tennesseans gazed over the field in front of them and surveyed the destruction. They counted nearly fifty dead lying among the clutter of hundreds of wounded. The corpses had been stripped. Private John Johnson (Co. A) summarized the situation, "[W]e captured most of [their] clothes."[2]

The day's only activity occurred when, as one Southerner noted, "the Federals asked for a truce ... for the removal of the dead who lay unburied nearer the Confederate lines than the Federal squads had been willing to venture at night."[3] Then, when the Southerners awoke the next morning, they found the Yankees had retreated across the Rappahannock River.

That afternoon A. P. Hill's division moved, heading southward to Hamilton Station. From there, the Confederates marched a dozen miles and encamped near Guinea Station. The men immediately received permission to build winter quarters, and a flurry of activity erupted as the veterans cut down trees and constructed huts.[4] A veteran described their constructions, writing, "In order to protect [ourselves] from the rain and snow the men ... built their quarters in the ground by digging holes [and] using pine poles covered with dirt for roofs."[5] The Tennesseans called their winter home site Camp Gregg, in honor of Brigadier General Maxcy Gregg, who had been killed at Fredericksburg when "a bullet tore through the brigadier's spine."[6]

The Tennesseans promptly adjusted to the winter schedule: work details, drill, time on the picket line, and waiting out the wintry weather. When they took their turn at picket duty the men swapped items with the Yankees on the other side of the Rappahannock. Private John Williams (Co. H) recorded, "[We] ... enjoyed ourselves by talking with the Yankees. Some of the boys got in a canoe and crossed the river and made some exchanges with the Yankees; tobacco for coffee."[7] A second veteran remembered "picket duty ... became an [opportunity to] exchange tobacco, newspapers, coffee, and sugar with the enemy across the river."[8] Other soldiers, though, did not get to trade with the bluecoats and remembered their time on the picket line as miserably cold. One noted they "made big log fires to sleep by [to] thaw ground around the fire to go to sleep. [The] fire would go down and clothes would freeze to the ground."[9]

Back in Camp Gregg, the men played cards and checkers, read books and sang to pass the time. For many Tennesseans though, lonely for home, boredom became the principle enemy. Regardless whether Colonel Goodner's boys were content or unhappy, the one item everyone desired was a letter from their families. The Tennesseans knew their home towns were occupied by Northern troops, a fact causing them great torment. Any communication from loved ones came from Tennesseans who crept in and out of Middle Tennessee. These travelers brought letters, as well as verbal messages and small packages. Private Jimmy Hale (Co. B) recorded, "Captain Norris has arrived ... he came late this evening ... he brought me some clothes and a lot of letters which I have hurriedly read."[10]

Unfortunately, even though the lonely soldiers craved news from home, often these tidings proved painful. Private John Williams (Co. H) lamented, "I ... have heard from home and that the Yankees had been through and taken everything they could set their hands on." The unhappy farmer-turned-rifleman continued, "It seems to be their object [to] commit rape on every negro woman they can find."[11] Another Tennessean, this one fearing the distance between himself and his sweetheart, wrote, "I am jealous of my best girl, and have a right to be, for an old widower with a spanking pair of horses and a light buggy is paying too much attention to her to suit me."[12]

Regardless of the Tennesseans' emotional needs the Confederate high command reorganized Hill's division. General Archer's brigade changed when the 19th Georgia was transferred to an all-Georgia brigade and the 13th Alabama added, giving Archer's formation a total strength of 1,600.[13] There were adjustments within the 7th Tennessee as well. Colonel John Goodner's illness lingered, preventing him from commanding the regiment. Finally, the 7th Tennessee's surgeon, James Fite, forced Goodner to a decision when he wrote to General Archer, "I find him [Goodner] incapable of performing his duties of his office because of ... chronic diarrhea and general debility."[14] Following this announcement John Goodner resigned, writing, "In consequence of protracted ill health, without any improvement ... to enable me to discharge the duties demanded of me, I am induced to tender this as my resignation of the office of Colonel of the 7th Regt. of Tennessee."[15] A week later on April 8, 1863, Lt. Col. John Fite was promoted to colonel, Maj. Sam Shepard to lieutenant colonel, and Cpt. William Williamson to major.

In late April 1863, the North's new commander, Maj. Gen. Joseph Hooker, began moving his ponderous army. Robert E. Lee immediately responded. On April 29, 1863, Archer's Tennesseans and Georgians abandoned their winter huts and marched north to Hamilton Crossing. The Tennesseans remained here for several days until Lee figured out where Hooker was planning to attack, and then the Confederates shifted their strength toward Chancellorsville.[16]

On May 1, 1863, the 7th Tennessee marched toward the west, covering eight miles before forming into a line of battle. The veterans fanned out to the right of the Plank Road and listened to gunfire for two hours before being told to return to the road and resume their march. They traveled two more miles before, once again, forming into line of battle. This halt did not last long before the Southerners continued along the Plank Road. Their next movement was another three-mile march, still heading west.

At 4:00 P.M. Archer's brigade moved off the road, heading north, tramping into the vegetation for about eight hundred yards. The Southerners swung around to the west and slogged through a "swamp covered with dense undergrowth" for about nine hundred yards.[17] Archer's men worked their way forward until they reached the rear of Brigadier General Alfred Iverson's North Carolina brigade. Here, Archer's brigade was told to bivouac for the night.

The next day, around 10:00 A.M., the Tennesseans moved forward and assumed Iverson's position as the North Carolinians moved away, off to their left.[18] Shooting erupted when the 1st Tennessee's skirmishers brushed up against their Federal counterparts. The sniping lasted for about an hour before Archer received word to move his brigade. The 7th Tennessee backed away from its defensive position and turned to the left, in a southwest direction. Colonel John Fite's troops followed a dirt road and marched past an iron foundry and away from the sounds of musketry. Then, after traveling about three miles, they received orders to turn around and hurry back to the foundry—to defend against a Yankee attack on a Southern supply train. The Tennesseans and Georgians hustled back to the foundry, only to discover a peaceful situation. General Archer reported, "[W]hen I arrived at the furnace I found that the enemy had already been repulsed."[19] Once they caught their breath, Archer's men turned around and journeyed for another four miles before reaching the intersection of two plank roads, one leading east-west, and the other heading north-south. Here, as one tired officer noted, "we bivouacked."[20]

Colonel John Fite's men did not sleep long; instead, as their commander recorded, "[T]hey were awakened sometime before one A. M. and instructed to begin marching."[21] The Tennesseans stumbled slowly in the darkness nearly all night, though covering only three miles until reaching Dowell's Tavern. Then, they were directed into thick underbrush, where the exhausted soldiers lay down in line of battle, facing toward the northeast. Colonel John Fite noted as the eastern sky began to lighten that the "men were very much fatigued."[22]

An hour later, a staff officer arrived and informed one of John Fite's lieutenants the regiment must readjust its position. The weary Tennessean misunderstood this order. Lieutenant Jack Moore (Co. B) recorded, "We reached our position just before day break…. So tired and exhausted were the men that a moment after being halted many … were asleep. Just after dawn the brigade on our left began to move slightly to correct its alignment. The officer on the extreme left of the Seventh, mistaking this for an advance, gave the order, 'Forward; the brigade on the left is advancing.' This order was immediately passed up the line and the Tennessee Brigade, by this mistake, moved forward at once."[23]

The brigade pushed forward and brushed aside a thin screen of Yank pickets and clamored up the slopes of a hillside. They burst out of the tangled undergrowth and found themselves on a hilltop, not far from a farmhouse, and very close to a four-gun Yankee battery.

The Confederate veterans moved quickly, wheeling and attacking the guns. The Southerners swarmed over the artillery pieces, sweeping the cannoneers away. Colonel

Fite proudly exclaimed, "The enemy retired in great confusion to their second line of defenses, leaving many killed and wounded on the field and [four] pieces of artillery and a considerable number of prisoners."[24] The excited Confederates crowded around the weapons, ecstatic with their quick victory and giddy from exhaustion. General Archer then gave the order to advance toward the Union battle lines, about 600 yards away.

Colonel John Fite urged his 300 men forward. Fite's Tennesseans were veterans and knew this attack would not be as easy as that quick dash which captured those four artillery pieces. The experienced Confederates could see the open field stretching before them, as well as the Yank-infested breastworks. The Tennesseans knew what Archer would demand of them — a frontal assault against a well-defended position. The farm boys-turned-veteran riflemen lowered their heads, gritted their teeth, and advanced.

The Federal infantry opened fire as soon as the Tennesseans were within range. Lieutenant George Gregston (Co. A) had his left arm mangled by a Minié bullet. Private William Carlisle's (Co. B) kneecap was splintered. Private Burchett Hunter (Co. D) was struck twice, once in the knee and a second time in the right leg. Private William Guthrie (Co. E) was shot in the chest and died within minutes. Private James McClain (Co. H) went down, his right leg shattered, and Pvt. Andrew Hall (Co. I) was killed.[25]

The Union musketry continued relentlessly, dropping Luke Robertson (Co. G) with a bullet through his left arm, Pvt. John Hale (Co. B) received a lead chunk against the side of his head, and Pvt. James Cheek (Co. E) was killed.[26] By now the Tennesseans had closed to within a hundred yards of the Yank breastworks and were deep within the Yank kill zone. The dauntless Southerners could go no farther. One Tennessean wrote, "Our ranks [were] thinned, regiments ill-formed, and with no support on the right or left. We ... halted, and engaged the enemy in a terrible fire of some minutes, [before] ... we were forced to retire."[27] The retreat back across the open field was pounded by distant artillery, knocking more Southerners to the ground. One such casualty recorded, "While falling back, a shell burst so near my person that I fell senseless, and was carried off the field."[28]

JAMES H. MCCLAIN. James McClain was born in 1838 and attended Cumberland University as a law student. He enlisted in Company H as a sergeant. He was reduced to a rifleman in April 1862 and severely wounded at Chancellorsville. He rejoined the regiment equipped with a wooden leg and served until 1864. James McClain died of fever in 1864 (Loewentheil Family Photographic Collection).

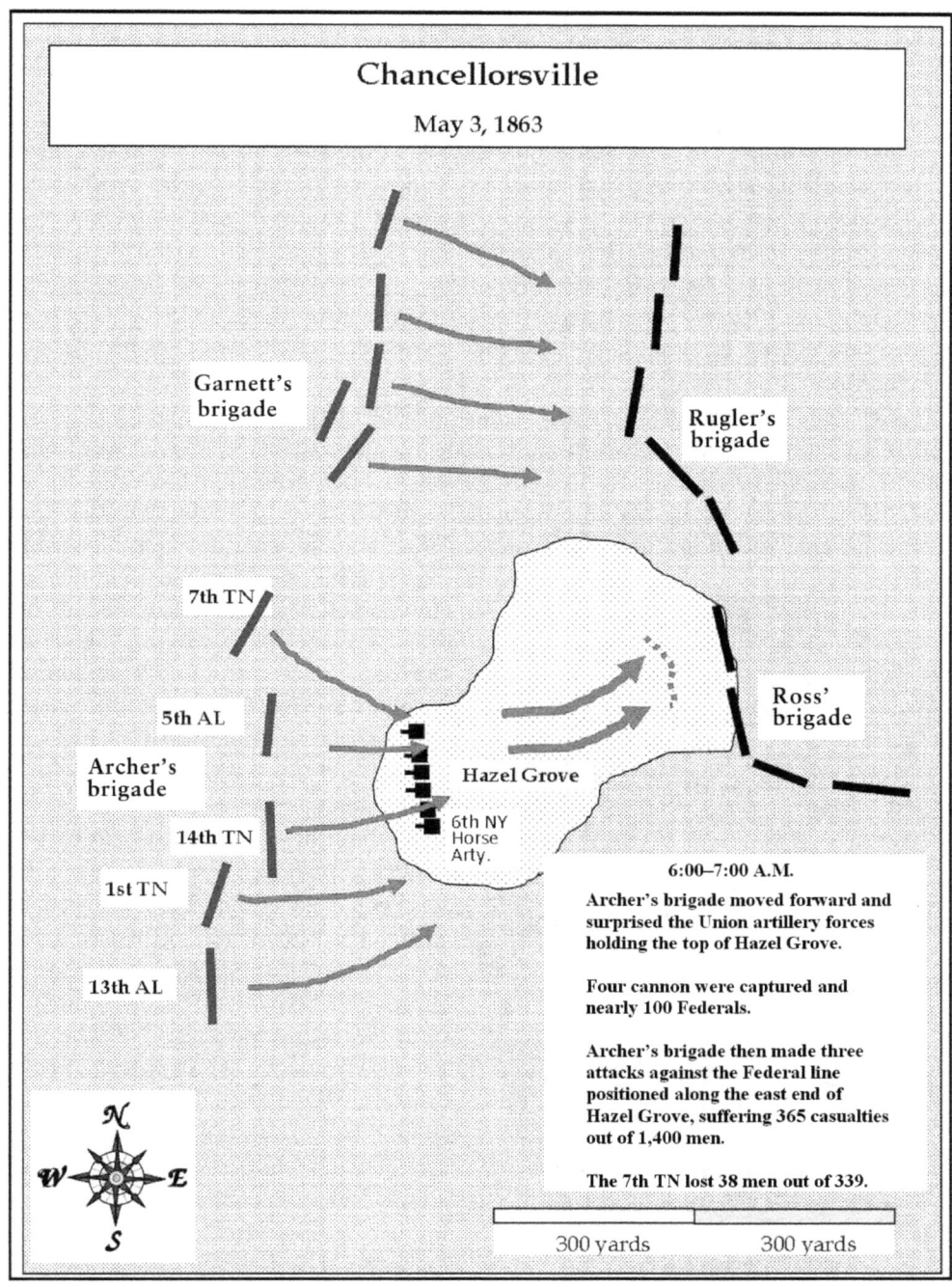

When the survivors reached the safety of the captured guns the regiment's harried officers gathered their shattered companies together. The assault had been a disaster, but General Archer would not give up. Indeed, he ordered his battle-worn soldiers to attack a second time. The Tennesseans shrugged their shoulders and went forward again, but their hearts were not in the attack. They halted just as soon as the Northerners opened fire, but not before Lt. Andrew Paul (Co. K) had been killed and Sgt. Tom Anderson

(Co. I) so seriously wounded that he would die a month later. One Tennessean wrote, "We ... made a second charge against the same position with less effect than the first."[29]

The men in the 7th Tennessee retreated back to the safety of the captured guns at Hazel Grove and were arranged back into their companies. Colonel John Fite had Adjutant George Howard get a quick count. Their losses were dreadful; over three dozen men were missing from the ranks. Meanwhile, Major William Pegram, the division's artillery commander, directed four batteries to the top of Hazel Grove. Pegram's guns began shelling the Union lines even as more batteries arrived. Soon, there were 25 Confederate guns massed on the crest of Hazel Grove and they bombarded the Yankee lines for the next sixty minutes.[30]

General Robert E. Lee arrived and saw 1st Lt. Oliver Foster (Co. C) and Lt. Ferguson Harris (Co. H) and, as Harris remembered, "Gen. Lee approached and asked whose troops these were. Capt. Foster answered that it was Archer's brigade, and pointed out the General." Lee got Archer's attention and the brigadier general hurried to him. The two lieutenants hovered within hearing. Harris noted, "With a soldier's curiosity we followed to hear what he would say to Gen. Archer. After salutations Archer [described] ... the strong entrenched line on the hill, which they could not carry. Gen. Lee looked steadily for some minutes at the strong line on the hill, then turning to Gen. Archer, said in a businesslike way: 'General, if you will move your brigade to the front about half way to that ravine, then make a left wheel move in that direction until your right is opposite that clump of trees, then right wheel again and strike those people in the front, you will drive them out. They will not bother you much until your last movement.'"[31] The two young Tennessean officers stared at each other in amazement; Lee's tactics were simple, but so very brilliant. Their next assault would not be a suicidal frontal attack, but rather a flanking movement hidden by a stand of trees! Lieutenants Oliver and Harris raced back to their regiment with the news.

General Archer, encouraged by Lee's advice, called his regimental commanders together and explained what Robert E. Lee wanted. Then Archer's brigade moved forward, buoyed by artillery support, Lee's directions, and the addition of three Geor-

ANDREW F. PAUL. Andrew Paul was born in 1840 in Georgia. He attended Cumberland University in Lebanon, Tennessee. He enlisted into Company K as a rifleman and was appointed lieutenant (8/30/1862). Andrew Paul was killed at Chancellorsville (5/3/1863) (Loewentheil Family Photographic Collection).

gian regiments. They moved forward, at first heading directly toward the Federal lines, but then wheeled to the left and into the safety of the trees. They covered almost 500 yards before the Georgian regiments halted, pleading with Archer for enough time to distribute ammunition.[32] After this pause, Archer moved his regiments again, holding to Lee's instructions. They bypassed the scene of their disastrous frontal assaults and came within a hundred yards of the Union line.

Lieutenant Harris (Co. H) wrote, "The Seventh Tennessee … went into the works 'on right into line.'"[33] At most, the Southerners had not much more than fifty yards to cover to reach the breastworks. They raced across this short distance, yelping the rebel yell. One of Archer's commanders reported, "When we had arrived within 40 paces of their breastwork, I allowed my regiment to return fire for about three minutes, which they did with spirit, and then ordered a charge. The men dashed forward with a cheer."[34] The fighting was quick, fierce, and deadly. First Sergeant Charles McClain (Co. B) was shot in the head. Captain John Fry (Co. C) was struck in the right hand and wrist. Sergeant John Ozment (Co. G) was mortally wounded. Private Frank Renfro (Co. E) had his left leg fractured. First Sergeant Henry Wingo (Co. I) was shot through the chest and killed, and 1st Sgt. Richard Moxley (Co. K) was hit in the shoulder.[35]

More Tennesseans went down as they closed to within almost hand-to-hand fighting distance. Private Littleton Parkinson (Co. A) was killed. Private William Wynne's (Co. C) right foot was shattered. Private Fred Gibbs (Co. B) had his right arm almost dismembered by a Minié bullet, and Pvt. James Oliver (Co. G) was struck in the hand.[36] Then, as the Tennesseans reached the earthworks, Colonel John Fite was knocked down, a bullet striking his stomach. Fite wrote, "The last regiment failed to run, most of them lay down, and one fellow, the bravest man I ever saw, stood up and kept firing at us, and one of his bullets hit me right in the stomach. It knocked the breath out of me.... The bullet didn't break the hide, but it bruised me, and I suffered more than a day or two with it than I did with any wound I got during the war."[37]

One of the first Tennesseans to jump into the Northern entrenchments was Sgt. Hal Manson (Co. H). Lieutenant Ferguson Harris (Co. H) noted, "Hal Manson … never stopped until he stood on top of their works on the other side, waving his hat to the boys to come on."[38] More Tennesseans and Georgians swarmed into the Federal breastworks and the Yanks fled in disorder. The Seventh's officers and NCOs hollered at their ebullient Tennesseans and shoved them back into ranks, preventing any from attempting to chase after the disappearing Union soldiers. Afterward, with a few minutes to gulp something to eat, Lieutenant Harris recalled seeing Pvt. Hal Morris "worrying John [Harlin (Co. H)] for some of his rations." Harris noted, "'Old Bones' knew who carried the biggest haversack."[39]

The Yankees reacted rapidly. A new brigade attacked and one of its officers reported, "A terrible enfilading fire now commenced, and a portion of the [Confederate] brigade gave way on the extreme left."[40] Part of the Seventh slithered back to the right, but most of the formation held, fighting to hold the breastworks they had just captured. Lieutenant Andrew Miller (Co. D) was wounded, Pvt. James Shoemaker (Co. B) was mortally injured, Pvt. Sterling Rucker (Co. G) was shot in the side, and Pvt. Henry McIntyre (Co. K) was killed.[41] The Tennesseans refused to budge. Colonel Fite recorded, "After a brisk fire of about ten minutes, the enemy retired again behind a hill."[42]

As the Tennesseans tried to catch their breath, Brig. Gen. Augustus Wright's Georgians slipped past them and fanned out as skirmishers. Wright's men moved forward and a scattering of gunfire erupted but soon tapered off. A few minutes later the Tennesseans saw a bluecoat officer approaching, carrying a white flag. A surrender was quickly negotiated and soon afterward, several hundred bluecoats shuffled past Archer's weary men.[43]

A lull in the activity allowed the Tennesseans to rest. A skirmish line went out in front of the breastworks and the exhausted soldiers slumped down within the earthworks. The rest of the day went by quietly. Later, General Henry Heth, now commanding A. P. Hill's corps, congratulated Archer, informing him that "by his gallant attack he had secured the key to the enemy's position."[44]

The price for Hazel Grove and the territory captured by Archer's brigade had proven extremely expensive; his 1,400-man brigade had been reduced to just about 1,000 men.[45] Colonel John Fite's 7th Tennessee had also been severely hurt. Along with Colonel Fite's injury, the Seventh lost 64 soldiers.[46] The survivors bedded down for the night, subdued by their losses, and by the devastating news; General Stonewall Jackson had been shot. Corporal J. P. Bashaw (Co. I) wrote, "The great general was lost to us, and we were in mourning."[47]

The next morning's sunrise, on May 4, 1863, came with orders to hold their position at all costs. Colonel John Fite's soldiers spent the morning cutting down trees and piling up dirt and branches in front of their breastworks. Then, once the Tennesseans were convinced their position was impregnable, Archer gave orders for the regiment to move. Fite's soldiers reluctantly filed out of their defenses and moved 900 yards to their left. A frustrated veteran complained, "After throwing up some strong works, we moved ... one-half mile ... and [again] prepared entrenchments."[48] They remained here, hidden for the rest of the day.

That evening, Colonel Birkett Fry was placed in control of the brigade when Archer had been given command of the division. Archer noted his promotion, "General Pender, in command of the division, being wounded in the evening, the command of the division devolved on me, and that of the brigade on Colonel Fry."[49] John Fite described Pender's wounding, writing, "We had a picket line not far in front of us. It was thick undergrowth there, and every time a fellow showed himself he would be shot at. General Pender came to where I was, and asked where the enemy was. I told him just in front there. He bounced up on top of our little breastworks. I said, 'General, you'll be picked off by a picket there.' He said, 'No, I guess not.' I hadn't more than said it until a Yankee ... shot him in the hand." John Fite also commented on Archer's reaction to Pender's injury, recording, "Archer asked, 'Wasn't that Pender up there just a while ago?' I said, 'Yes, and the Yankees shot him in the hand.' ... Archer said, 'I wish they had shot him in his damn head.'"[50]

May 5, 1863, was even quieter than the previous day. General Archer ordered Col. Fite to send out his troops and determine if the Yanks had left. John Fite wrote, "[I] ... led [my] men two or three hundred yards when we came to their [Federal] field hospital and captured a thousand prisoners.... They had laid down there to sleep and the whole Yankee army had gone back across the river."[51] The Tennesseans remained in their earthworks, waiting for what would happen next. They were dismayed by their losses and remarked that the war would kill them all. One despondent veteran wrote, "Our company looks like a platoon.... We have plenty of tents and room now that so many were killed and wounded.... Every time we form the company it makes me feel bad to see so many vacant places in the ranks."[52]

Rain fell the next morning as Colonel Birkett Fry led the brigade out of its entrenchments and eastward on the Orange Turnpike. Then, word was given to march back to Fredericksburg. The war-weary veterans returned to their winter home, feeling fortunate to be alive, and worried about their commanding general, Stonewall Jackson. Four days later, on May 10, 1863, Lieutenant General Thomas "Stonewall" Jackson died.

During the thirty days following Jackson's death Robert E. Lee re-organized his army. He created three corps out of his original two. General Lee promoted Ambrose P. Hill to command the new Third Corps. Lieutenant General A. P. Hill, known as "Little Powell" by his men, was a Virginian raised in the martial custom. He was a West Point alumnus who served in the Mexican War. Hill then battled Seminole Indians in the cypress swamps of Florida.[53] Then, when the war began Hill became a colonel of Virginia troops and quickly rose to brigadier general, and ultimately up to division command. Hill's division became known as the Light Division due to his aggressive tactics and ability to move troops rapidly. Thus, A. P. Hill was General Lee's choice for the command of three large divisions.

One of these divisions went to Maj. Gen. Henry Heth. Henry "Harry" Heth came from a military background. Harry, a Virginian whose grandfather had been a colonel during the Revolutionary War, had graduated from West Point and participated in the Mexican War. Heth then served out west, fighting against Sioux Indians and earning acclaim for leading a successful flanking maneuver against them in the battle of Ash Hollow in 1855. Harry Heth had written the army's first marksmanship manual, *A System of Target Practice*. With the coming of the war he distinguished himself and rose quickly from colonel to brigadier general. Some said Harry was a member of the tightly-knit "Old Boys Club" of professional officers known for their fighting tendencies.[54] But there was no one who would deny that Harry was always ready for a brawl. Harry Heth took command of four brigades, and James Archer's 1,000 riflemen became one of these formations.[55] With Heth in charge of the division, Archer returned to lead his brigade.

Colonel John Fite's boys were fairly healthy, in good spirits, and had, "the most implicit confidence in [General] Lee."[56] The 7th Tennessee remained in the Fredericksburg area until June 15, 1863.[57] The regiment's numbers were now below three hundred troops. They were rested and poised for action, and knowing General Robert E. Lee was planning something extraordinary. One overconfident Tennessean wrote, "It seems to be as soon as [the Yankees] hear us coming, it excites them to death ... [and] they skedaddle worse than a flock of scared sheep."[58]

Lee's Confederate forces headed west and reached Stevensburg, and from there, Culpeper Court House late in the afternoon of the eighteenth.[59] The Tennesseans trekked northwest to Sperryville, crossed over the Blue Ridge Mountains and descended into Front Royal, and marched on to Berryville with each mile coming at the expense of shoes, rations, and human energy. One soldier wrote home, "We have had a long hard march since I wrote you last and some very hot weather. It was severe on us soldiers ... hundreds of our boys fainted and fell in the road."[60]

The Tennesseans continued northward from Berryville to Shepherdstown and waded across the Potomac at Boteler's Ford, on June 25, 1863.[61] Then Colonel Fite's infantrymen hiked to Hagerstown, and from there, to Leitersburg. The Confederates crossed into Pennsylvania at Waynesborough, passed on to Quincy, and ended up not far from Cashtown on June 29, 1863. By now, the Tennesseans were dusty and tired, and their boots were in poor shape. Lieutenant John Ingram (Co. G) noted they "suffered for shoes more than any other article."[62]

The Tennessee farm boys were impressed by Pennsylvania, and they studied the surrounding farmlands in amazement. Never before had they experienced such astonishing richness. Endless fields of wheat, corn, and hay bordered fenced-off orchards, vegetable gardens, and animal pens. As one Confederate remarked, "I have never yet seen any country in such a high state of cultivation."[63] Another wrote, "The country is the most beautiful I ever beheld, and the wheat and corn crops are magnificent. All the fields are covered with beautiful green grass and clover, two and three feet high."[64]

Not only did the fecundity of Pennsylvania astound the Confederates, many were also astonished by the size of the barns. Pennsylvania's barns surpassed anything the Tennesseans had seen. These barns, as a farmer-turned-soldier exclaimed, "far excelled the dwelling places of the owners."[65] But the Southerners gave only passing notice to the barn qualities; they all were much more interested in what the barns contained. They went into those massive structures and filled their haversacks.

The Confederates were experts at "flanking," the word the soldiers used to mean foraging. They relished their evening meals, bragging, "We had not been many hours in bivouac until turkeys, ducks, chickens, crocks of milk, butter, apple butter and various delicacies began to make their appearance in almost every mess."[66] Another noted, the "cherries were getting ripe and we found them very delicious and filling, but not sustaining. We would have to fill up several times a day to keep the proper stomach dilation. They [grew] abundantly, however, and we never enjoyed fruit more."[67] Dinners now often included "confiscated chicken," along with a mélange of other stolen delectables, which were washed down with the hooch filling their canteens, because as one Confederate admitted, "We succeeded in getting our canteens filled with cherry wine."[68]

For the Pennsylvania residents though, these thousands of foraging Confederates were a disaster. The Pennsylvanians stared at the Confederates in alarm and tried to protect their farms, but they were helpless against the scavenging Southerners. One soldier recalled, "This whole country is frightened to death. They won't take our money, but for fear that our boys will kill them, they give away what they can spare." The veteran continued, "The most of the soldiers seem to harbor a terrific spirit of revenge and steal and pillage in the most sinful manner."[69]

One Tennessean who saw no problem with the Southerners' foraging was Captain Marcus "Lafayette" Walsh, the 7th Tennessee's quartermaster officer. The 29-year-old from Mt. Carmel, Tennessee, was tasked with making sure his boys were sufficiently fed, properly outfitted, and effectively armed; a difficult and frustrating task. Fortunately today, Walsh did not have to fret about insufficient supplies. Astonishingly, he struggled with a reverse challenge. The trek into Pennsylvania had been a godsend. No longer did the blue-eyed quartermaster captain have to beg for rations, equipment, or fodder. Penn-

5. December 14, 1862: Early Morning 79

sylvania's bountiful farms had furnished a lavish richness. Lafayette Walsh worked feverously, stuffing every one of his regiment's wagons with hay, corn, wheat, and oats, as well as clothing, footwear, and equipment. Walsh recorded; the 7th Tennessee possessed 3,729 pounds of hay, 1,115 pounds of corn, 33½ bushels of wheat, and 11 bushels of oats.[70] All of Cpt. Walsh's regimental vehicles, 18 in total, overflowed. Each company had a wagon, now loaded to the point of breakdown, as were the regiment's forage trucks, the quartermaster's cars, the blacksmith's carriage, the ordnance transport, and the commissary coach.[71] Walsh had even crammed extra larder into Colonel Fite's personal wagon and into the regiment's ambulance. Right now, Walsh was scheming to acquire more wagons.

Lafayette Walsh and the brigade's quartermaster, Captain Rufus McClain, were old friends. McClain, a Tennessean from Silver Springs, had enlisted into the 7th Tennessee along with Walsh. However, when the regiment's first colonel, Robert Hatton earned a promotion to brigade command, Hatton assigned Rufus McClain to run the brigade's quartermaster department. This was an arrangement advantageous for the 7th Tennessee. Rufus McClain often enabled his old regiment to be the first to get supplies. Therefore, Lafayette Walsh was confident McClain might be able to scrounge around and deliver more transports to supplement the 7th Tennessee's wagon train.

CHAPTER 6

July 1, 1863: Morning

"There are those damned black-hatted fellows again. It ain't the militia."

Colonel John Fite's 7th Tennessee remained just outside of Cashtown on June 30, 1863, manning the picket line three miles east of Cashtown.[1] His Tennesseans enjoyed plundering Pennsylvania farms. Though they were far from home, John Fite's boys were content with their situation. They knew if there were Union troops nearby General Lee would put together a battle plan that would win another victory. So, the men did not fret. They would enjoy Pennsylvania's farms today and let tomorrow come.

The Tennesseans were up before sunrise on July 1, 1863. They ate "confiscated chicken" for breakfast, kicked dirt onto their campfires, and then started marching eastward on the Chambersburg Pike.[2] The rising sun turned the early morning's showers into steam, cloaking the countryside in stifling humidity. The Southern boys endured the heat's miseries, buoyed by thoughts of relieving Gettysburg's merchants of foodstuffs, tobacco, and above all, shoes and boots. The soldiers moved quietly and without apprehension. After all, their commander, Brig. Gen. James Archer, had promised them there were no Yankees nearby. Archer, as well as the Third Corps commander, Lieutenant General Ambrose P. Hill, "did not believe that there was any force at Gettysburg and there was nothing to worry about."[3] For the riflemen, this day's excursion was but a simple reconnaissance in force.

Colonel John Fite, marching at the head of his regiment, fumed in agitation because of what had taken place between him and Gen. Archer. Yesterday John Fite had traveled to Hagerstown, Maryland, and while there spent time in a saloon with staff officers. Later and moving a little unsteadily, Fite left the saloon, only to meet Gen. James Archer. The two ended up "in a parlor filled with young ladies, and a table covered with champagne bottles." One thing led to another and Fite found himself with "one very handsome young lady [who] said, 'You'll take a glass with me?'" The 7th Tennessee's senior officer "couldn't resist the temptation, so [he] drank with her." Then, Fite drank "several more with other gals."[4] Later, when it was time to rejoin the brigade Fite could not stay atop his horse so he climbed into the regiment's ammunition wagon and slept the entire way back to the unit.

When Fite returned to the regiment he discovered his men were not moving with their brigade. Incredibly, they plodded along trapped behind a slow-moving battery of artillery pieces. Fite found his second-in-command, George Shepard, and asked, "Why in the thunder he wasn't with the brigade?" Shepard answered, "An artillery company had got in between it and the balance of the brigade."[5] Fuming with annoyance at this blunder by Shepard, Col. Fite immediately hustled the regiment around the artillery train and caught up with their brigade.

That evening Gen. Archer called Fite to brigade headquarters and criticized him because his unit had not maintained its position within the brigade. John Fite, though irritated by Shepard's lapse, was not about to be censured by Archer; after all, Archer also had not been with the brigade. Their dispute became heated and eventually Archer threatened to arrest Fite, finishing his accusations by declaring, "You've been drunk today." But Fite refused to give in and fought back, arguing, "Yes, and the only difference ... between you and me is that I've got sober, and you are still drunk."[6] Ultimately, the two men calmed down and no charges were pressed, but even so, John Fite's irritation lingered. The aggravated regimental commander remained incensed, an emotion leaving him with little thought about what lay ahead and unprepared for what was about to happen, just like his boss, Brig. Gen. James Archer.

A few dozen yards behind Col. John Fite, Sergeant William "Billy" Cato (Co. K) marched quietly. Sergeant Cato, a 23-year-old from Statesville, Tennessee, was two weeks away from his twenty-fourth birthday. Cato, like so many of the boys in the regiment, found celebrating a birthday far from home a hollow ceremony. Billy Cato missed his family, as well as his neighborhood friends, and a special, certain young lady — Helen "Hattie" Price. He even found himself craving the smell of his father's rich bottom-lands. The Cato farmstead consisted of nearly 600 acres of fertile, well-watered soil that produced bountiful corn, wheat, oats, and hay harvests. Billy longed to walk into his father's barn and inhale the fragrance of hay, silage, and livestock. He even missed the friendships he shared with his father's slaves.

Billy Cato had been with the 7th Tennessee from the start. He bore the scars of two wounds: a serious injury received in the fight at Cedar Run which landed him in a hospital for over two months; and a second one, just minor damage by soldier standards, received at Chancellorsville. Both brushes with mortality left the young man reflective. He had seen what a Minié bullet or an artillery shell could do to human flesh. Cato possessed no illusion about his chances for survival. He pondered his existence, and as many a reflective soldier had done, wondered if his "life had not been spent as ... it should be spent." The homesick farm boy-turned-sergeant took a deep breath and let out a soldiers' lament: "Oh, unhappy day that gave birth to this unhappy war."[7] His messmates nearby gave Cato a quick look, however they said nothing. They knew their sergeant. Cato may have stood only five feet five inches tall, but he was as solid and true as a Southern boy could be. Billy often said little; none the less, when he did speak, everyone leaned in to listen. He plodded eastward, saving his strength for the effort required to haul gear and stave off the rising morning's heat. He, like his Tennessean brothers, did not know they were not alone.

Around 7:30 A.M. the stillness ended; a shot rang out, punctuating the quiet morning air. Lieutenant Marcellus Jones (Co. E, 8th Ill Cavalry), the officer in command of the Union pickets west of Gettysburg, "vaulted from his saddle and asked Sgt. [Levi] Shafer for the loan of his carbine. Resting it on a fence rail, Jones shot at ... [a Confederate] officer on [a] gray horse." [8] Though this first shot was mostly symbolic, as the distance which Jones fired was between 600 and 700 yards and beyond the effective range of his cavalry carbine, it is claimed to be the first for the Battle of Gettysburg.

The rattle of more gunfire caused the entire column to stagger to a halt. Not far from Sgt. Cato, Private Tom Holloway (Co. H) carried his musket balanced on his shoulder. Holloway, a 24-year-old ex-teacher who also had written articles for *The Banner of Peace*, a Lebanon, Tennessee, newspaper, had enlisted, feeling as many did — excited about the prospects of becoming a war hero. Holloway, like a number of his comrades, believed he "went into this measure with the conviction that it was [his] imperative duty."[9] The young Tennessean had suffered a minor injury in the fight at Seven Pines, and a second, and more serious wound at Fredericksburg. Therefore he, like all the Tennessee veterans, understood the gravity of this war.

Private Tom Holloway was tired, having not gotten much sleep the previous night; it had been his company's turn for picket duty, and he had been caught out in the rain.[10] Also, Holloway's feet hurt; his shoes were still new to his feet. He had first put them on yesterday, in Cashtown, Pennsylvania. Holloway and a squad

JOSEPH P. (J.P.) BASHAW. Joseph Bashaw was born in 1842 and worked on the family farm near Rural Hill, Tennessee. He joined Company I and was promoted to corporal (12/31/1861). He was wounded twice, including at Gettysburg. He was captured and paroled twice before surrendering in the Petersburg trenches in March 1865. After the war he married Salura Cook and they had 4 children. Joseph Bashaw died in 1934 (Paula Kelsey Bashaw family collection).

from his company had searched the town, scouring it for footwear. Finally, they met a man who said, "Go across the street to that big house over there, and [you will] find all the shoes [you] want." The Confederates entered the house and went down into the cellar. Holloway and others, as one soldier noted, "unlocked the door and the cellar ... [and] got out as many shoes as [we] thought we had any use for."[11]

Not far from Tom Holloway, Corporal Joseph Peter Bashaw (Co. I) sweated in the morning's heat. "J. P.," as his messmates called him, was twenty years old, and hailed from Rural Hill, Tennessee. He was the youngest son of a prosperous corn and wheat farmer who had put away his farm tools and joined the 7th Tennessee's Company I. Though slightly wounded during the fight at Mechanicsville, in June 1862, he had been with the regiment almost without interruption, with the exception of a short period of time when he was excused from service because, as he proclaimed to his friends, "My feet were badly blistered, owning to wet feet and bad shoes."[12] But now J. P. had new footwear, though the leather was stiff and unyielding.

Bashaw, Holloway, Cato, Shepard, Fite, and the rest of the 7th Tennessee soon learned there was Federal cavalry in front of them. Then, Gen. Archer sent out his Alabamians to push the cavalry aside. The 13th Alabama and 5th Alabama Battalion left the column, moved into an apple orchard next to the Chambersburg Turnpike and loaded their weapons. The Alabama boys deployed as skirmishers and hurried over the top of the swale, disappearing down its other side, and immediately scattered popping from their rifled muskets shattered the quiet.

Colonel Fite called an officers meeting. As his officers gathered around him, Fite realized none of the regiment's original captains now served as company commanders. Indeed, the only remaining initial captains were himself, George Shepard, and Major William Williamson. The other seven were gone.

One had died — James Baber — and another, Thomas Bostick, had resigned because of his ill health. The other five, Robert Wright, Monroe Anderson, Dewitt Douglas, Nathan Oakley, and Joseph Anthony had been relieved of duty when the 7th Tennessee re-organized in late April 1862. These five officers lost elections and were replaced, and of their replacements, John Allen (Co. B), by virtue of his promotion date, was the regiment's senior line officer. Captains Jonathan Dowell (Co. A), Archibald Norris (Co. K), and Asoph Hill (Co. F) were next in line.

John Allen, a 26-year-old merchant from Carthage, Tennessee, stood five feet eight inches tall. Though he was shorter and considerably frailer than his fellow officers, his resolute and unyielding personality caused others to pause, step back a little, and regard him with respect. Allen was used to getting his way; after all, that was how he had been raised. His father, a Tennessee congressman and planter, owned a sizeable plantation. John Allen had grown up on the estate, working the fields and managing his father's sixty slaves. Now, Allen commanded the regiment's largest formation. While most of the regiment's companies numbered in the mid-twenties, Allen's unit had nearly twice that many. Allen faced the world square on, gravely and without merriment, and his boys were proud of their intense commander. There was no one, they bragged, who swore like Captain John Allen, because, as one succinctly noted, Allen was "not so choice in his language."[13] John Allen's profanity had only worsened following his nearly mortal wounding at the

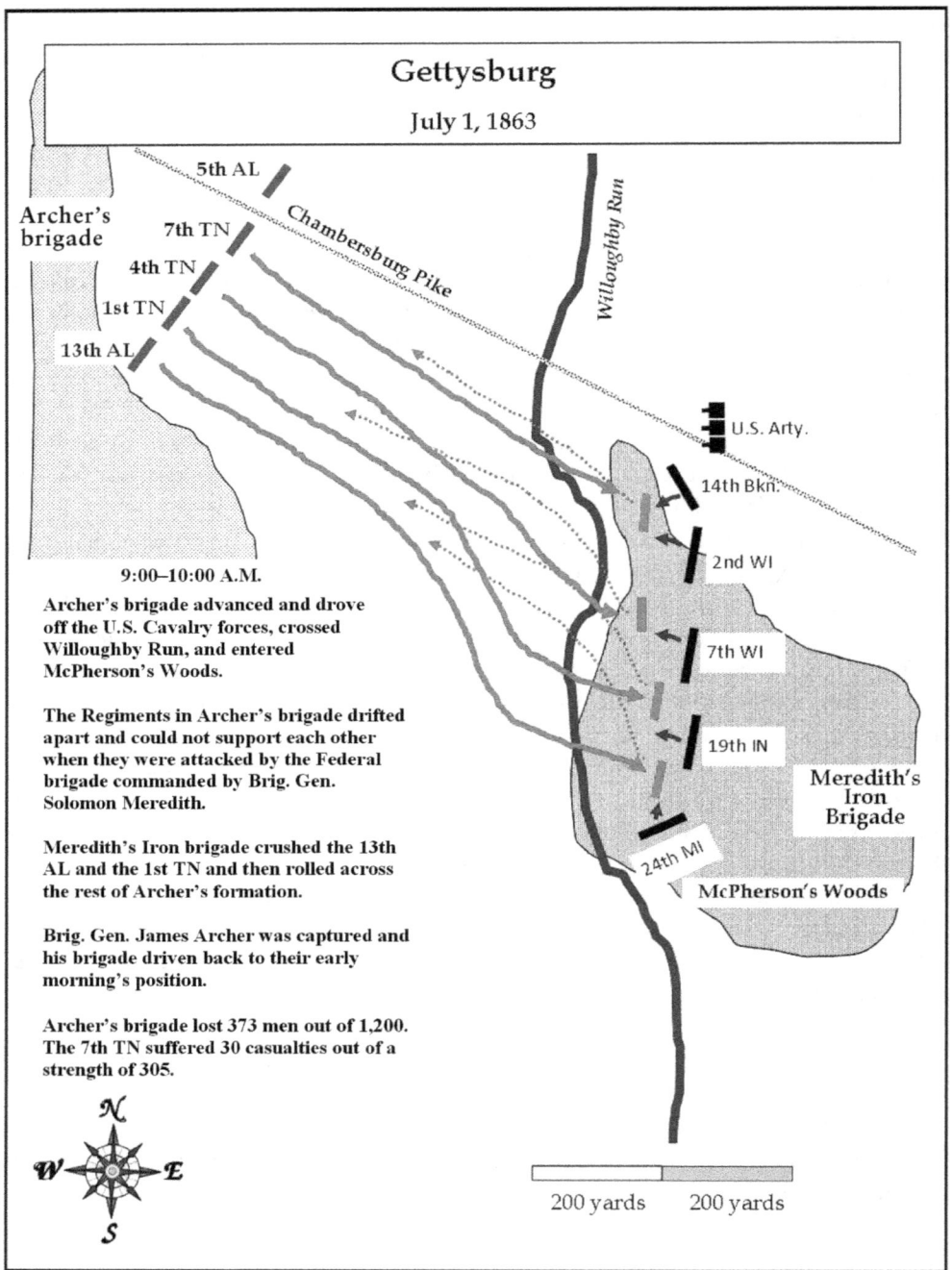

Battle of Seven Pines. The severity of his neck wounds forced the tenacious officer into a hospital bed for nearly four months. When he returned to the regiment he was gladly received by his fellow mates, because as one Tennessean remarked, John Allen "was conspicuously brave."[14]

Colonel John Fite gave his company commanders what little information he knew and dismissed them back to their units. There was nothing else to do at this time. Meanwhile, on the other side of the low ridge was a terrain favoring defenders — a shallow hollow choked with underbrush and swampy vegetation. Marsh Creek meandered sluggishly through the little valley's center. Archer's Alabamians moved cautiously forward in measured intervals, some soldiers shooting, others just darting from hiding place to hiding place. The Alabama skirmishers moved efficiently, each squad working forward independently, locating the Yanks' hiding spots, fixing the Federals in place with covering musketry, and then circling around against their flanks. The bluecoats sullenly gave ground, only to rally at another position and fire back upon the Alabamians. The Confederates reformed again and worked to get around the Yanks' next defensive location. The process was time-consuming, methodical, and well-practiced. One officer stated, "It was a slow, cautious drive."[15] Another recorded, "The enemy fell back slowly, resisting our approach."[16]

Directions filtered down from division to brigade thirty minutes later; they were to deploy in line of battle. The 7th Tennessee Regiment's orders were to form near Chambersburg Pike; the rest of the brigade, then, was to deploy to their right. The brigade fanned out, the 7th Tennessee on the left, then the 14th Tennessee, the 1st Tennessee, and finally the remainder of the 13th Alabama.[17] It took time to move all 1,200 men into proper position. Finally Archer's men were posted and ready for battle; having created a line anchored on Chambersburg Pike and extending south through woodlots and wheat fields for nearly 400 yards. North of the road, another one of Harry Heth's commanders, Brig. Gen. Joseph Davis, worked his 2,300 men into position, with his regiments extending northward for nearly 750 yards. This process was time-consuming; nearly an hour passed before the two brigades were properly arrayed and ready to advance.

Once the 7th Tennessee was correctly positioned, Col. Fite ordered his soldiers to load their muskets. Fite studied his veterans, boys from Wilson, Smith, Dekalb, and Sumner counties. They had mustered into the regiment two years earlier, eager to battle the Yankees, filled with patriotism and clamoring to set things right. They had been young and vibrant, nearly all of them toughened by years wielding an axe and muscling mules behind a plow. Fite's Tennesseans had set down their wheat cradles, slop buckets, and garden hoes and taken up rifles. His men had turned their backs on milking cows, feeding hogs, and endless farm chores and learned to march in step, drill by company, and deploy in battalion formation. And finally, these patriots had left behind, "fretful mothers, solemn-faced fathers, teary-eyed sweethearts, and anxious wives."[18]

Today though, Col. John Fite's veteran Confederates were not novices to battle. The farmers-turned-soldiers knew what a musket ball could do to a human body. They had all seen friends die, and many knew what it felt like to have been struck by a bullet; they knew the anguish and terror. Many had writhed in agony on the field of battle, only to enter the nightmare of a battlefield hospital. Then, they suffered as their damaged bodies slowly mended. Indeed, these men grasped the reality of what lay ahead, and yet they stood, prepared to move forward into the killing zone.

The Tennesseans watched as the Alabamian skirmishers withdrew. The Alabamians reformed behind the brigade's battle line and then deployed as skirmishers, creating a connecting link between Archer's brigade and the left flank of Davis' brigade, north of Chambersburg Pike. The veteran Tennesseans scanned the terrain before their regiment, studying the ground they would have to cross. It was open country; wheat fields, pasture, and marshland. There was no place to hide; there was nothing between them and the Yankees' positions. With the skirmishers gone, the brigade's battle front was completely unprotected. When the formation advanced, there would be no way to prevent an ambush. They would go forward, blind to what dangers existed before them. Someone looked at his timepiece and announced it was nine o'clock.[19]

Brig. Gen. James Archer gave the order for the brigade to advance. The Seventh stepped forward, nearly 300 experienced veterans. A slight breeze caught the regiment's battle flag and pushed the cotton-bunting folds out for everyone to see. The flag bearer, 30-year-old Pvt. Thomas Lownsborough (Co. C), had been carrying the colors for over a year, though the flag he now held aloft was barely a month old. It had been issued following the Chancellorsville campaign and as yet was without blemish.[20] The colors danced in the breeze. One rifleman recalled that "their battle-flags looked redder and bloodier in the strong July sun than [he] had ever seen them before."[21]

A Federal battery commanded by 2nd Lt. John Calef opened fire. Though the range was 1,000 yards, Calef's gunners aimed accurately.[22] An artillery shell knocked down Sgt. George Lamberson (Co. A), a 28-year-old from Liberty, Tennessee. He sat on the ground inspecting his rifle, and then pitched it aside. Lamberson recalled, "They commenced shooting ... at us and one [piece of shrapnel] hit the [breech] of my gun and tore it off and turned me around."[23] He struggled to his feet and staggered after the regiment. John Fite immediately ordered the command to "advance at the double-quick." One rifleman noted that they "moved somewhat faster, attempting to run from under the shells."[24] The Tennessean raced toward the safety of a low spot in the terrain, where, once out of the artillery's field of fire, the soldiers paused to realign their ranks and catch their breath.

Sergeant Billy Cato (Co. K) checked to make sure everyone was present—they were. He glanced over at their captain, Archibald Norris. It was easy to find "Archie," as everyone called the 25-year-old ex-teacher; Norris stood well over six feet tall, and his stride was unmistakable. Lieutenant Ferguson Harris (Co. B) described Norris' unique stature: "there [was] no duplicating them legs."[25] Norris had gone to college in Pennsylvania before the war, but he spoke little of his experiences in northwestern Pennsylvania.[26] The tall captain glanced back at his sergeant, checking to see if the company was all right. His boys had called themselves the Wilson Blues back in 1861 when they formed as a volunteer company in Lebanon. At that time they numbered nearly 100 strong and accepted Thomas Bostick as their leader. That was two years ago. Now the company consisted of 25 survivors, all battle-tested veterans, all very cognizant of war's dangers, and remaining only because of their forged-in-fire fellowship.[27]

The 7th Tennessee splashed across a small stream called Willoughby Run. The watercourse was not much to look at, just a shallow, rock-bottomed brook bordered by brush and tall grasses. One soldier described it as "knee-deep and [with] clear water and a pebble bottom."[28] The water got the Tennesseans' shoes wet and soaked the lower portions of their trousers. Some of the quick-thinking veterans refilled their canteens. The experienced soldiers knew the day would be hot, and there was no guarantee when they would get another opportunity to replenish their water supply.

Up ahead, 470 veterans from the 8th Illinois waited for the Tennesseans to come within range of their carbines.²⁹ The dismounted horsemen opened fire when Colonel Fite's riflemen were about 300 yards away. Lieutenant Harris reported, "After crossing the branch, we ascended the hill where the first volley struck us."³⁰ Though the distance was long for the cavalrymen's' carbines, the packed mass of Tennesseans made them an easy target. Private Henry Rison (Co. B) tumbled to the ground, his left thighbone fractured by a bullet. Henry Rison, a 23-year-old from Smith County, Tennessee, was left behind as the regiment closed upon the Yank cavalrymen. By battle's end Pvt. Rison ended up captured and in a Northern hospital in Chester, Pennsylvania. Eventually his shattered leg became infected and he died in August 1863.

Rison's injury was only just the first. Yank bullets impacted into the advancing Tennesseans. Captain Jonathan Dowell (Co. A) was knocked backward, having "receive[d] a bullet through his breast."³¹ Private Joab Bailiff (Co. A) dropped, a bullet slashing through his neck muscles. Bailiff, a 28-year-old father of three from Helton, Tennessee, had been severely wounded once before. However, this injury could not be treated. Bailiff died two weeks later.³²

Colonel Fite gave the command and his riflemen fired a volley toward the Yank cavalry. The fury released by the Tennesseans momentarily pinned the Northerners to the ground, enabling the Tennesseans to rush forward and take cover behind an embankment. One Southerner wrote, "[W]e were protected from the fire of the enemy by an abrupt rise ... in our front. We halted to reform, reload, catch our breath, and cool off a little."³³ The Tennesseans relished the security of this protection and returned fire. Private John McCall (Co. B) noted, "We opened fire, and the engagement soon became warm. The enemy made a stubborn resistance."³⁴ Lieutenant Colonel Shepard recalled, "We were not over 40 or 50 yards from the enemy when we opened fire. Our men fired with great coolness and deliberation, and with terrible effect."³⁵

As Cpt. John Allen (Co. B) urged his men to load and fire quickly he noticed one of his men cringing against the earthen bank. Allen knew about Isaac "Ike" Dawson's penchant for hiding during battle and being a loud-mouthed bully in camp. Allen called to Lt. Jack Moore (Co. B), and pointed with his sword. The two officers converged upon the reluctant man. Lieutenant Ferguson Harris (Co. B) wrote, "Jack Moore on one side and Capt. John Allen on the other [drove] old 'Bully Ike' into the fight."³⁶

The Tennesseans "were lying down, loading while on their backs and rolling to their bellies to aim and fire."³⁷ Heavy smoke billowed out in front of their position. Someone shouted, "Look at Lane!" and the Confederates saw a stalwart rifleman from Company K standing erect, oblivious to the Yankee bullets buzzing past him. A Tennessean described this bravery: "I remember how Jack Lane [Co. K] stood up while the balance of us were lying down [,] rapidly firing into the great mass of troops before him."³⁸

The murderous exchange of gunfire continued. One Tennessean wrote, "[F]or thirty minutes the firing was severe, and the smoke of battle hovered near the ground."³⁹ At times a soldier would drift backward, out of position and his shooting endangered those in front of him. The regiment's officers and NCOs worked to keep their men safely positioned. In Company C, Lt. William Baber "caught a fellow by the hair ... firing [from] behind the lines, and pulled him to the front."⁴⁰

Finally, the cavalrymen began to slink back away, retreating toward the east. The

Federal horsemen had been resisting for several hours now, fighting as they gave ground — trading territory for time. The weary soldiers dashed from tree to tree, fleeing. Private John McCall (Co. B) recalled, "The enemy fled in great disorder toward the town."[41] Once the shooting ceased Col. John Fite informed 1st Lt. George Cowen to take charge of Company A, now that Cpt. Dowell was wounded. Lieutenant George Washington Cowen, a 29 year old, hailed from Nashville, Tennessee. He was a lawyer who lived with his mother before the war. Cowen had joined Company A as a private but earned a promotion to second lieutenant when the regiment re-organized in April 1862.[42]

Though the situation in front of the 7th Tennessee was quiet, General Archer now dismounted and without any way to communicate with his commands had allowed his regiments to drift apart. The 7th and 14th Tennessee moved straight ahead, toward the east, while the 1st Tennessee and the 13th Alabama wandered toward the southeast. Then the 14th Tennessee and 13th Alabama separated when the 14th Tennessee's movements slowed and stopped. One Tennessean described their halt, saying they "went to the ground to avoid canister."[43] The 13th Alabama swung further south in a flanking effort of the guns shelling the 14th Tennessee. Thus, the brigade's regiments could no longer support each other, were without overall leadership, and then, at this precise moment of leadership breakdown, had come in contact with an aggressive and hard-fighting foe who was spoiling for a fight — the Iron Brigade of the I Corps.[44]

Even though Archer had lost control of his brigade he gave orders to advance. Fite, always leery of Archer's decisions, argued the brigade was too strung out for effective support, but his objections were brushed aside with the directive their new division commander, Maj. Gen. Henry Heth, was pressing for the advance. John Fite wrote, "Once the cavalry had been driven off ... Major General Henry Heth, aflame with his new authority as divisional commander pressed Archer to continue."[45] Fite gave the command and his regiment advanced. The Tennesseans climbed up from the embankment's protection and the men "rushed ... with a cheer."[46] They immediately received intense rifle fire. The Tennesseans halted and sought shelter. This time the weaponry striking them came from infantry muskets. The Southerners realized they no longer faced cavalry and when they saw their opponents, one shocked Confederate proclaimed, "There are those damned black-hatted fellows again! ... It ain't the militia. It's the Army of the Potomac!"[47] The 7th Tennessee took fire from rifles manned by the 2nd Wisconsin. These tough-minded Westerners were known for their distinctive black Hardee hats and a habit of inflicting severe punishment.[48] Wisconsin lead slammed into the Tennesseans. Private William H. Harrison (Co. G) was struck in the head. Harrison, a 24-year-old farm boy from Gladesville, Tennessee, had survived two years of service without even a scratch, until now. The blue-eyed young soldier dropped, killed instantly. Not far away, Pvt. Tom Sneed (Co. A) was seriously wounded, and Pvt. John Harlin (Co. H) took a Minié bullet to his arm. Harlin, like Sneed, had also never been hurt before.[49]

Then, sounds of gunfire erupted along the brigade's right flank, deep within the woods south of Fite's regiment. The roar of this combat increased and soon the Seventh began to receive fire from their right, as well as the hammering they were taking from the front. Col. John Fite surmised something bad was taking place along the brigade's right flank, and he was correct. The 13th Alabama had smacked into the black hatted soldiers of the 19th Indiana and 24th Michigan. These two Iron Brigade regiments struck the 13th Alabama head on, across their right flank, and also from the rear. One Indiana soldier recorded, "At our first volley the line in our front was broken."[50] The Alabamians cracked, losing almost half their strength in less than twenty minutes. One Alabamian recalled, "I had discharged my gun at them just before they got to us ... it seemed to me there were 20,000 ... of course I had to surrender."[51]

James Archer did not react as the 13th's left wing dissolved. He did not, as one Alabamian recorded, "grasp time by the forelock and [leave]."[52] Instead, Archer gathered a small mob of riflemen and attempted a fighting retreat. The Iron Brigade riflemen closed upon this small group. One Confederate noted, "What a deadly trap we were in."[53] An aggressive Irishman, Pvt. Patrick Maloney (2nd WI), jumped forward and wrestled Archer to the ground. When Maloney had Archer subdued he turned the general over to Lt. Daniel Dailey. The lieutenant approached Archer, saying, "I'll relieve you of that sword." And with those quick words Brig. Gen. James Archer became a prisoner of war.[54]

Moments later dozens of Archer's men ran through Fite's command. These panicked soldiers cried that "Yankees had surrounded them and everybody was being killed or captured." Some of Fite's Tennesseans drifted away from this pressure, easing toward the north and west. A massive volley swept across the 7th Tennessee. Private Robert Hughes (Co. D) was knocked to the ground, wounded.[55] More Tennesseans crept away from the battle line.

George Shepard noted, "We had encountered the enemy but a short time, when he made his appearance suddenly upon our right flank with a heavy force, and opened upon us a cross fire. Our position was at once rendered untenable, and the right of our line was forced back."[56] At 9:45 A.M., the Tennesseans eased backward. More panicked soldiers from Archer's other regiments stampeded through their line and the Federal pressure increased. Private Charles Lane (Co. I) was hit and dropped.[57] Another soldier was "blasted three feet high in the air when a bullet hit his cartridge box and exploded his rounds."[58] The Tennessean formation crumpled when a line of black-hatted Union soldiers approached, their bayonets fixed. It was time to skedaddle; Cpl. J. P. Bashaw (Co. I) described their retreat, writing, they ran "quicker than hell would scorch a feather!"[59] Fite recorded, "We fell back two or three hundred yards."[60]

A number of Tennesseans retreating toward the northwest came under fire from another Union regiment, veterans of the 14th Brooklyn. The Tennesseans ducked down into the safety of a gravel pit to escape. The Yanks — the "Red-legged devils," as they were called because of their red trousers — swarmed around the gravel pit. Other Federals, the black hatted fellows from the 2nd Wisconsin joined the Brooklyn boys clustered around the gravel pit's rim, aiming their weapons at the Southerners. One Confederate wrote, "We had Yankees on the front, Yankees on the flank, and soon Yankees behind us."[61] Over a dozen of the trapped Tennesseans threw down their rifles and surrendered.[62]

The survivors scampered to the west, fleeing across the wheat field and into the shelter of the woods on Herr Ridge. Here, beneath the shady branches of sheltering trees Confederates from Pettigrew's brigade watched in horror. They were not used to seeing an entire Confederate brigade collapse and run. And then their shock heightened when they recognized another Southern brigade, the one commanded by Brig. Gen. Joseph Davis, fall apart and flee from the battle front. A few minutes later, four regiments of black hatted soldiers (the 19th IN, 24th MI, 2nd WI, and 7th WI) appeared on McPherson's Ridge, aligned themselves in line of battle, and went about the business of preparing to defend their position.[63] A North Carolinian, astonished by what he saw, turned to another and asked, "[D]o you think that we will have to advance on the enemy as they are?"[64]

Later, amid the safety of the trees and behind the sheltering strength of the North Carolina brigade, Col. John Fite collected his riflemen around the regiment's sacred battle flag. Fite had already heard General Archer was missing and presumed captured, and that some of the other regiments had been badly hurt. It was 11:30; the Seventh had been engaged for less than two hours and now the men huddled behind a wall of North Carolina rifles, discouraged and jumbled. The 7th Tennessee was missing 30 men, including Cpt. John Dowell (Co. A), 3d Lt. William Robbins (Co. G), and 1st Sgt. Lewis Westbrook (Co. H).[65]

General Heth immediately chose Birkett Fry to replace Archer as brigade commander. Fry, a soft-spoken and slightly-statured man, was 41 years of age. He possessed a varied military history, including studying at both the Virginia Military Institute and West Point. Fry had served in the Mexican War as a first lieutenant before moving to California to assist in the struggle to make that territory a state. A few years later Fry traveled to Nicaragua in support of a private military expedition. When this force was defeated Fry returned to Alabama, to "engage in cotton manufacturing."[66] He took command of the 13th Alabama when the war commenced and by July 1, 1863, had been wounded three times. Fry's fellow regimental commanders respected him; he may have been a small-sized man, but everyone knew he had a "gunpowder reputation."[67] The new brigade leader checked his brigade for casualties: Maj. Felix Buchanan (1st TN) announced 109 casualties, Col. Fite reported 30, Cpt. Bruce Phillips (14th TN) stated 62, Maj. Algernon Reaves (13th AL) said 168, and Maj. Albert Van de Graaff (5th AL Battalion) declared just four — the brigade had lost 373 men.[68]

General Heth called for another assault. Heth turned to his remaining two brigade commanders, James Pettigrew and John Brockenbrough. James Pettigrew, an attorney from North Carolina, was the perfect example of a dashing Southern gentleman. Pettigrew, at age thirty-five, could speak six languages, including Hebrew and Arabic, and was a mathematical genius who had been President Polk's professor of astronomy at the National Observatory.[69] He was well read and had traveled through Europe, as well as having written a book on Spanish anthropology entitled *Notes on Spain and the Spaniards*.[70] James Pettigrew's life had always been directed in pursuit of knowledge and academics. When the war began he took command of the 12th South Carolina but soon was promoted to brigade leadership.

John Brockenbrough, a 33-year-old graduate of the Virginia Military Academy, had originally been the 30th Virginia's colonel. He assumed brigade command following the Second Manassas battle but struggled to lead the unit effectively. Lee eventually gave Brockenbrough's brigade to Harry Heth, but when Heth was promoted to division command, the brigade leadership fell back to Brockenbrough. He remained an ineffective leader and was as poor as Pettigrew was excellent.

Since Davis' brigade was shattered and far from returning to a fighting force, Gen.

Heth turned to Col. Fry and ordered him to take his brigade and cover Pettigrew and Brockenbrough's right flank. Then, with Heth's plans finalized, nothing happened. As everyone waited, Col. Fite shifted his Tennesseans into a body of woods and the Seventh "remained in the woods for ... three hours."[71] The signal to advance came around 3:00 P.M. General Heth's brigades moved forward in line of battle, nearly 3,000 Southerners.[72] The men moved as one in a massive formation over a half mile wide. They marched shoulder to shoulder, across the battleground of the morning, now vacant except for litter and trampled fields. The Iron Brigadiers held their fire, letting the Confederates approach. The Tennesseans hunched their shoulders in anticipation of that first terrible volley. Then, once the Confederates splashed across Willoughby Run the Union line disappeared behind an enormous cloud of smoke and the noise of massed musketry rolled across the small valley like the sound of a huge door slamming shut.

That first volley ripped into the North Carolina regiments, far off to the left of the Tennesseans. One soldier described the effects of this rifle fire upon the North Carolinian line, writing, the men "dropped like chopped wheat."[73] The veteran North Carolinians raised their weapons and within moments, as one of the Iron Brigade soldiers recorded, it was a "whirlwind of death."[74] The constant rattle of musketry filled the air; smoke billowed up above the battle lines, and the trampled ground began to clutter with fallen men. The formations, both gray and blue, melted away "like dew before the melting sun."[75]

For the boys in the 7th Tennessee, this "slaughter in [the] ranks" took place far away.[76] Colonel Fite's men faced a grassy pasture, some sturdy fences, and the solidly-constructed buildings of a small farm. General Heth's order had sent Fry's regiments to a location near the Old Mill Road and the Finnefrock buildings, along one of the main thoroughfares to Gettysburg, the Hagerstown Road—a location containing no Federal units.[77] The Tennesseans in Colonel Fite's formation moved forward slowly, keeping pace with the rest of the brigade's battle line, thankful it was not they who "fell like grass before the scythe."[78]

Then, a low cloud of dust boiled up in the east on the Hagerstown Road. The veteran Southerners knew what this swirl of airborne dirt meant—approaching cavalry. Colonel Fry responded immediately by deploying the Alabamians as skirmishers and wheeling the brigade. George Shepard recorded, "the enemy threw a body of cavalry upon our right flank. Seeing this, Colonel Fry changed the direction of his front so as to protect our flank."[79]

The Federal cavalrymen, seeing the stout line of Confederate riflemen waiting for them, yanked their horses to a stop. The Alabamians pushed toward the Yankee horsemen while the rest of the brigade followed along behind the skirmishers. The cavalrymen dismounted and scampered to a position behind a stone wall, maybe 500 yards south of the Alabama skirmishers. When the skirmishers came closer the bluecoats opened fire. The Alabamians immediately dropped into the tall grass and while lying on their bellies returned fire. The brigade halted and the Confederates took cover.

Meanwhile, north of the Tennesseans, the North Carolinians were locked in a death struggle with the Iron Brigade. Towering clouds of smoke arose above McPherson's Ridge. The musketry was continuous, a death rattle without end. One North Carolinian wrote, "Lots of men were ... throwing up their arms ... falling to the ground ... and clawing the earth."[80] Another noted, "The whole field was covered with gray suits soaked in blood."[81]

Later, the dismounted troopers advanced from beyond the protection of their stone wall. They moved forward in a ragged alignment, firing their carbines as they advanced. The Alabama boys returned fire, but as the Yankees closed upon them the Alabamians jumped up from the ground and darted backward toward the safety of the brigade battle line. One observer recorded this movement, writing, "[T]he 8th Illinois threatened an assault and Fry consolidated the brigade by ... calling in all the skirmishers."[82] Once the Alabama boys reached shelter behind the brigade's battle line Colonel Fry ordered his formation to advance. This sudden response extinguished any thoughts by the cavalrymen of glory and they turned tail and scuttled back to their stone wall. Fry pushed the line forward and the bluecoat defense behind the rock wall collapsed and the horsemen fled. Fry halted the line and ordered the men to lie down.

The Tennesseans remained near the Hagerstown Road for the remainder of the day. George Shepard noted, "The cavalry did not advance upon us, but hung around ... [and] we lay in position upon a road upon the right of the line."[83] The roar of combat behind them eventually ended, though more sounds of battle came to them from farther away, and closer to the town of Gettysburg. Rumors reached the Tennessee soldiers telling of a great victory. General A. P. Hill made note of "the almost total annihilation of the First Corps of the enemy ... [and the capture of] 2,300 prisoners."[84] Others though, learned the Yankees still held the hilltops east of Gettysburg and wondered "why we failed to push on and occupy the heights."[85] This breakdown, the experienced Confederates knew, meant there would be more fighting tomorrow.

After sunset a full moon arose above the battlefield. Beneath this moonlit darkness, the distant sounds of fighting melted away, and as quiet descended over the landscape the pitiful cries from the wounded floated over the Tennesseans. Some of John Fite's men slipped back over to the morning's battlefield, searching for lost comrades. It was easy to find the battlefield in the moonlit darkness; all one had to do was go toward the sounds of agony. The sight before them was dreadful. One soldier wrote, "The ranks ... had become thinned, a windrow of killed and wounded indicating the position[s]."[86] A second veteran recorded, "[Men's] arms and legs and head[s] shot off.... They were lying on won [sic] another. Some was shot all to peases [sic]."[87] A third recalled, "The poor wounded Federals were crying piteously for water in every direction ... it was horrible beyond description."[88] And sadly, the Tennesseans observed, "The enemy dead ... [and] our dead were lying where they had fallen, but the 'battlefield robbers' had been there plundering."[89] Another noted, "The dead's pockets were slit open.... The money was gone, as were watches, rings, and jewelry."[90]

Later, once historians had time to total up the "butcher's bill," the immensity of the losses would be known. Besides Archer's 300 casualties, Pettigrew's North Carolinians lost over 1,000 and Brockenbrough suffered another 100 lost. The Federal's Iron Brigade—those black hatted fellows who had tangled with these three Confederate units—lost nearly 1,100. Thus, in the small area of McPherson's Woods over 2,600 soldiers had been shot down, wounded, missing, or killed.[91] One soldier simply wrote, "It was a terrible sight to see."[92]

The Tennesseans returned to the Seventh, despondent over locating only one comrade, William Harrison (Co. G), whose body was then buried in a shallow grave. The evening's chill descended upon the unhappy men. One melancholic soldier wrote, "[A] gloom had settled over the entire regiment."[93] The men shared stories of the day's events and wrapped themselves in their blankets, but as one homesick farm boy noted, "It is a troubled and dreamy sleep ... that comes to the soldier on the battlefield."[94]

For the 7th Tennessee's missing comrades though, sleep was not possible. Those men shot down and wounded in the morning's fight had been captured by Iron Brigade soldiers and carried to makeshift field hospitals. There, they struggled to survive amid appalling conditions, lying on the ground, surrounded by hundreds of others. One such ill-fated man recalled, "[T]he air was heavy with the stench of decay, and ... clouds of flies attended to each man, the creatures feeding at their wounds."[95] What surgeons were present worked until they dropped from exhaustion, overwhelmed by the numbers. One such doctor wrote, "It was a gigantic task that confronted the willing hands that sought to alleviate the suffering."[96]

And for the Tennessean riflemen who were captured in the gravel pit—they spent the night marching away from the battlefield, guarded by Federals. They were hustled through the town, to the "jeers and laugh[ter]" of Yank soldiers and Gettysburg's citizens.[97] Then, after a short pause the prisoners were pushed "almost at a 'double-quick' toward Baltimore."[98] From there, they would ultimately end up at the prison at Ft. Delaware. Some would remain there until the end of the war.

For Brig. Gen. James Archer, his travails had only begun. He soon found himself at Ft. Delaware where he described his situation: "Am comfortable as could be expected in crowded quarters which receive all the odors of an extensive privy through windows where fresh air might have been expected to come."[99] From here, James Archer was transferred to Johnson's Island, near Ft. Sandusky, Ohio. At first, Archer accepted his situation, writing, "there are about 800 Confederate officers here—we spend our time visiting from one block of quarters to another."[100] However, his attitude changed. A month later he wrote his wife, "There is no pleasure in writing when letters must be read by strangers—it becomes a disagreeable and even difficult task."[101] And then homesickness set in. Archer, in February 1864 grumbled, "It is nearly three weeks since I have received a line from any one at home.... I cannot believe that no one has written." He also admitted, "I have had a slight attack of dysentery."[102]

James Archer's health worsened. He eventually wrote, worn out by illness, "Nannie ... sen[t] me medicines and medical advice."[103] Then, in June 1864 a Federal surgeon examined Archer and recommended the ailing general be released. James Archer was shipped to Ft. Delaware, and from there to Hilton Head, South Carolina, where he found himself penned up, aboard a ship in the harbor for over a month. He complained, "We have been here on board a prison ship three weeks and [are] still ignorant of what next."[104] Archer would remain a sea-bound prisoner until his exchange in August 1864.

But for Birkett Fry, with Archer gone from the brigade, the responsibilities now rested upon his shoulders. Fry got little rest that night as he worked to make sure his men were prepared for tomorrow. Then, all too soon, the summer sun lit up the Pennsylvania landscape and sleepy pickets began shooting at each other. But right now, with the situation quiet, the boys rested and ate, and stayed out of danger. Some remembered what Col. Goodner had said not too long ago: "We have a heavy task before us this summer and thousands who are living today will bite the dust before six months elapse."[105] Now, they wondered what would happen next. Soon, orders were given and the entire brigade moved forward, heading farther south, but just as the men got into the rhythm of marching, calls came to halt and deploy into a defensive formation. The brigade now occupied a position on the extreme southern point of Herr's Ridge.[106] The men were ordered to stand down and here they remained until sunset. George Shepard wrote, "We were not in the engagement of July 2."[107] Later, in the dark hours of night, the men were awakened and shoved into a marching column. They stumbled eastward, toward Gettysburg and by 4:00 A.M. on July 3, they arrived at a position on Seminary Ridge, in a stand of trees called Spangler's Woods.[108] Shepard recorded this movement, writing, "During the night of the 2nd we moved around, and took position in front of the enemy's works."[109] The Tennesseans waited for dawn, aware something momentous was going to happen.

CHAPTER 7

July 3, 1863: Morning

"Oh, if I could just come out of this charge safely."

That morning the officers in Fry's brigade learned they would be part of a nine-brigade assault. They were stunned by the news. There was to be a massive assault, composed of nine brigades, lined up with Kemper's Virginians on the extreme right, and to his left Garnett's Virginians, and on Garnett's left, the boys under Fry. Then, to their left, the North Carolinians of Pettigrew's brigade, the Mississippians of Davis, and finally on the far left, Brockenbrough's Tar Heels. Behind Kemper and Garnett would be Armistead's men, and on the left, behind Fry, Pettigrew, Davis, and Brockenbrough were Lane's and Scales' brigades. Plus, two more brigades, under Wilcox and Lang, were also to move forward in support.[1] This was a massive force, totaling over 12,500 men.[2]

Robert E. Lee had given the extreme honor to their brigade—Archer and Fry's—to be the very center of the Confederate line. All the assaulting brigades would be dressing on them! As one officer noted, "The Tennessee brigade (Archer's) was ... the brigade of direction ... the other brigades ... had orders to press on the Tennesseans."[3] Archer's boys had better be up to the task, because, "Theirs was the post of honor."[4] The brigade would be organized in the usual formation: the 1st Tennessee on the right, then the 13th Alabama, the 14th Tennessee, the 7th Tennessee, and the 5th Alabama Battalion.[5] Birkett Fry even called John Fite aside with brigade-command instructions should Fry fall.

Colonel John Fite met with his company commanders, and knowing the importance of the regiment's staying in correct formation, informed his officers he would station himself at the regiment's far right. He wanted to "keep an eye on the regiment to his right so that he could stay dressed."[6] Lieutenant Jack Moore (Co. B) wrote, "This was ominous and showed plainly how hazardous those officers regarded the undertaking."[7] John Fite laid out the company alignment as follows—from left to right—B, G, K, E, H, F, C, I, D, and A.[8] The senior company commanders were John Allen (Co. B), and Archibald Norris (Co. K). Company A, now commanded by 1st Lt. George Cowen, and John Allen's boys were the flanking companies, and the other eight units were to fit in between them. The regiment numbered about 250 officers and rank and file.

Colonel Fry told his company commanders, "Get across those fields as quick as you can, for in my opinion, you are going to catch hell."[9] That statement, along with the news Gen. Lee had ordered all of his senior officers not to mount their horses, left his Tennesseans feeling little optimism. One soldier wrote, "I could not believe General Lee would insist on such an assault ... [but] we had nothing to do but obey the order."[10] The men understood; it was up to the infantrymen to fulfill the General's bidding. Another rifleman looked out at the field Lee wanted them to cross and noted, "I would not give 25 cents for my life if that charge [was] made."[11]

The popping of musketry broke the morning's still. Lieutenant Ferguson Harris (Co. H) and his brigade sharpshooters had been ordered by Col. Fry to take his band of marksmen and investigate a farm in front of the Confederate lines. The 23-year-old from Tucker's Crossroads, Tennessee, assembled his soldiers and they advanced upon a farmstead, built around a barn, described as "almost a citadel in itself ... seventy-five feet long and thirty-three feet wide, its lower story ... ten feet high, constructed of stone, and its upper part, sixteen feet to the eves, of brick."[12] This property, the Tennesseans would eventually learn, belonged to William and Adeline Bliss.

Lieutenant Harris' sharpshooters explored the structures and in doing so roused out the farm's occupants. The Pennsylvanians stumbled about, confused, until being steered toward the Confederate lines.[13] Soon though, as the Tennesseans searched the buildings, a line of bluecoats raced toward them. Harris ordered his boys to pull back, and the Southerners raced away, some squeezing off shots at the Yanks. Several of the attackers were hit but the bluecoats, nearly 200 veterans from the 12th New Jersey, returned fire, and as one of their officers noted, "The rebs ... skedaddled."[14]

Later, once Harris' boys were settled, the order came to move. Birkett Fry marched his formation to the western slope of Seminary Ridge. Once Fry was content with the brigade's battle line, he ordered his man to stand at ease while the North Carolinians of Pettigrew's brigade formed up on their left. Brigadier General James Pettigrew no longer led his brigade; he had been promoted to temporary command of the division. Maj. Gen. Harry Heth had been injured in the battle on July 1, 1863. Heth wrote of this wound, "I was struck by a minie ball on the head which passed through my hat and the paper my clerk had placed there, broke the outer coating of my skull and cracked the inner lining, and I fell senseless."[15] It would be several days before Heth would recover enough to resume his duties, but in the meantime, Pettigrew shouldered his responsibilities.

The entire assault force was in position by 11:00 A.M., with everyone awaiting Lee's command. But Lee had more ideas; it would not be just an infantry assault across an open field. Lee had also given orders for nearly every Confederate artillery battery to move their pieces so they could aim their gun tubes at the anticipated attack's focal point, a copse of trees on Cemetery Ridge. By 11:00, the Southerners had nearly 100 cannon prepared to bombard the Union lines. The closest battery to the Tennesseans was a 4-Napoleon unit commanded by Cpt. Addison W. Utterback.[16]

Colonel John Fite and Lt. Jack Moore (Co. B) ventured beyond the woods to view the terrain they must cross; the scene was frightening. The Tennesseans would have to cross over a thousand yards of open ground, ever so slightly rising up toward a low ridgeline. Fields of straw-stalked, harvested wheat alternated with the lushness of green pasture in a patchwork of color. A series of post-and-rail fences crisscrossed the landscape, the barriers looking more like hedges because of their accompanying shrubbery.[17] The entire distant ridge line was dark with Union infantry. Gaps in the Union infantry were plugged by artillery, with each dangerous barrel pointed directly across the open field. Lieutenant Jack Moore noted, "We could distinctly see the formidable line of artillery."[18]

Lieutenant Moore noticed Robert E. Lee, surrounded by a covey of senior officers. The Tennessean watched their leaders. Though they were too far away to hear what was being spoken, the different generals' body language and movements spoke clearly. This was not an amicable discussion. Some of the officers paced back and forth while others shook their heads or waved their hands emphatically.[19] But through all the agitation Gen. Lee stood firm. It was obvious his decision would not be changed. Later, one of the officers would recall Lee's final words on the subject: "The enemy is there, and I am going to strike him."[20] In time, the meeting broke up and the officers went their different ways. Lieutenant Moore noted he "did not feel encouraged by the menacing sight."[21]

The landscape grew silent by 11:00 A.M., and a "tense stillness" left many Confederates with queasy stomachs. One soldier wrote, "Such a stillness I had never experienced before, nor since."[22] A few men, ignoring their circumstances horsed around—they found a tree laden with unripe apples, which they picked and threw at each other. A comrade watched his frolicking companions and penned, "So frivolous men can be in the hour of death."[23] But most of the men were quiet, because, as one Confederate noted, "This news has brought about an awful seriousness with our fellows."[24]

The hush continued, and by noon "the stillness lay heavy."[25] The July sun bore down on the uneasy men, punishing them. One sufferer grumbled, "The sun gave forth a heat almost stifling and not a breath of air came to cause the slightest quiver to the most delicate leaf or blade of grass."[26] Another Confederate recalled, "A soldier in the field rarely thought his time to die had exactly arrived—that is, it would be the other fellow's time.... Occasionally [though] a man was met who had made up his mind that the next battle would be his last."[27] When that happened, the morose soldier would go to his partner, saying, "I wish you would take my money and this little Journal and give it to my mother if I get killed."[28]

The quiet continued for another sixty minutes. Some soldiers passed the time by napping. An officer wrote, "The men were extremely tired ... [and] their nerves worn down. Many of them simply settled the matter of what to do by going to sleep."[29] Lieutenant Jack Moore (Co. B) simply noted, "Our suspense was intense."[30]

Finally, at 1:00 P.M., two artillery pieces banged, their dull booms echoing across the Pennsylvania landscape. Moments later, nearly every cannon along the Confederate line thundered. Gun after gun fired, and the noise became a continuous roar. One cool-headed Union officer recorded, the "Rebels were averaging seventy or eighty shots a minute."[31] These projectiles rained down upon the Federal lines causing pandemonium. The rifled shells "screamed through the air creating noticeable trails of hot air in their wake."[32] Other shells tumbled "end over end like misshapen minie balls."[33] And then they struck, exploding and hurling "fragments about in a most disagreeable and promiscuous manner."[34]

A Yank artilleryman wrote, "From the first shot they had our range and elevation exactly.... Guns were hit and knocked off their carriages, [and] ammunition chests were blown up."³⁵ Shells also came down among the horses corralled behind the Federal lines. One projectile "butchered two pack mules, spraying them and the[ir] contents ... all around." Another horse "dropped in a bloody heap."³⁶ A third "rolled in heaps ... tangled in [its] harness with[its] dying struggle."³⁷ Confederate shells also tore into human flesh. One such unfortunate soldier was struck "just below the left shoulder. Ripping his body to pieces, it left him in a gory puddle on the ground."³⁸ Another piece of shot hit a Yank in his legs, "rip[ping] both away below the knees ... [his] comrades drag[ged] him [away] on his back.... They left him lying there with his hands hooked together under his bleeding stumps and there he bled to death."³⁹ A third Federal soldier was part of a trio injured by the same artillery round; "A ... bolt ... struck [a soldier] in the side, it [also] slammed against ... [a] lieutenant['s] left hip ... and continued onward. [Then] it ripped the left hand away from [a] private at the wrist."⁴⁰

Federal artillery returned fire; their shells arched up from the Federal line and crashed down among the trees above the Confederate soldiers. A Tennessean wrote, "The limbs and trunks of trees were torn to pieces and sent crashing to the earth."⁴¹ One Confederate wrote, "A terrific explosion occurred, which for a moment deprived me of my breath ... I found myself lying off from my former position ... around me were brains, blood and skull bones." The stunned soldier continued, "[T]he shell had exploded almost directly over me, a little below my left shoulder ... the heads of the two men who lay on my left side had been blown off just over their ears."⁴² The Confederates clutched at the ground. A rifleman wrote, "We were all hugging the earth and we would have liked to get into it if we could."⁴³ Private John McCall (Co. B) noted, "The whole earth seemed to reel and totter."⁴⁴ Colonel John Fite wrote, "So intense were its vibrations that loose grass, leaves, and twigs arose from six to eight inches above the ground, hovered and quivered as birds about to drop."⁴⁵ Some soldiers scrambled to dig themselves protection. One wrote, "I got out ... my bayonet and began digging a hole and throwing the dirt in front of me."⁴⁶ Others huddled on the ground, praying. A soldier recalled, "Great big, bearded men prayed loud too, and were in earnest — it was really a praying time."⁴⁷

The Union guns, over 200 in all, thundered all along the Federal line, their concussions, "sen[ding] 'waves' across the grass field ... like gusts of wind."⁴⁸ Their shells shrieked as they dropped among the Confederates. A soldier recorded, "You could actually see the comparatively slow traveling, smooth-bore projectiles, but the disconcerting thing was that whenever you saw one it seemed to be coming directly at you."⁴⁹ Federal armament also exploded among the Confederates. Colonel Birkett Fry "received a painful wound on the right shoulder from a fragment of shell."⁵⁰ But the plucky officer refused to succumb to his wound and brushed away offers to take him to the safety of the rear. There were plenty enough casualties being hauled away. Surgeon James Fite assisted the brigade's physicians with the injured. One surgeon wrote, "The first to arrive, born on a litter ... [had] the lower abdomen torn from left to right by a cannon shot, largely carrying away the right half of the pelvis."⁵¹

A Confederate wrote, "It seemed that death was in every foot of space, and safety was only in flight; but none of the men did that."⁵² Private John McCall (Co. B) noted, "None but those who have experienced it have little conception how straining it is on the nerves under a heavy artillery fire."⁵³ Another penned, "The smoke soon darkened the

[sky] and the scene produced was similar to a gigantic thunderstorm, the screeching of shot and shell producing the sound of the whistling blast of winds."[54]

In the 7th Tennessee, good fortune continued to protect the men. Though men in regiments on each side of Col. Fite's soldiers died, the Tennesseans' position fortuitously sheltered them from disaster. Shells rained overhead, or bounced past, doing nothing more than battering the men with dust, bits of earth, and noise. The closest call came from an errant cannonball. Lieutenant Ferguson Harris (Co. H) described the event, writing, "A solid shot, traveling at a very slow speed, and losing altitude fast, dropped with a tremendous thud in front of the 7th Tennessee within inches of sutler Jim Bradley's head."[55] James Bradley, a 25-year-old assistant marshal from Dixon Springs, Tennessee, scurried away from the hot shell, much to the delight of nearby Tennesseans.

The artillery fire tapered off after ninety minutes. The soldiers, their ears ringing from the clamor, looked at each other in relief. Afterward, many remembered the artillery bombardment was, as Col. Birkett Fry noted, "the most terrible of the war."[56] The men staggered to their feet, thankful the danger had passed, but realized there were worse hazards to follow. One rifleman wrote, "This pandemonium ... as suddenly as it commenced, it ceased. For a few minutes all was quiet again. Then was to come — the work of death."[57] The veterans, knowing what was to come, prepared themselves. Birkett Fry, his shoulder now bandaged, wrote, "After lying inactive under that deadly storm of hissing and exploding missiles, it seemed a relief to go forward to the desperate assault."[58] The soldiers tended to their rifles. One wrote, "They knew what was coming, and they stood with a snapping, popping rattle as they fired percussion caps."[59] Lieutenant Jack Moore (Co. B) remembered, everyone "seemed to appreciate ... the impending carnage."[60] Another, a grim realist recalled, "When you rise to your feet as we did ... I tell you the enthusiasm of ardent breasts in many cases ain't there."[61]

The veterans lined up quietly, because as one rifleman remembered, "They felt the gravity of the situation, for they knew well the metal of the foe in their front.... None of the usual jokes, common on the eve of battle, were indulged in."[62] These men knew what their general wanted and they also understood what the price would be. A Southerner wrote, "It is not easy to be enthusiastic about going into battle again when you are aching with the memory of lost comrades and the shattering horror of devastating casualties [to come]."[63] Private John Johnson (Co. A) studied the distant objective and trembled. He believed "we could never get there."[64]

Colonel John Fite knew what was going to happen, just as his men did. Fite, as well as the other officers, understood what held the regiment together — the bond between the men. They had served together for two years, all suffering equally, their pain having forged a link between each man as strong as tempered steel. The Tennesseans knew if John Fite, their leader, went forward, they would follow, because if just one man stepped toward the enemy lines, his partner would go with him, and his partner, and his partner. One soldier wrote, "Officers and men knew at what cost and at what risk the advance was to be made, but they had deliberately made up their minds to attempt it."[65]

Colonel Fite spoke to his Tennesseans, reminding them to look out for their comrades and admonishing them to perform their duty. One Tennessean remembered his commander's speech: "Boys, if we have to go, it will be hot for us, and we will have to do our best."⁶⁶ The question was asked, "Are you ready to do your duty?" and the men answered, "We will." John Fite stood, humbled by his neighbors' devotion to each other, because as one officer remarked, "Every man felt his individual responsibility, and realized that he had the most stupendous work of his life before him."⁶⁷ However, they "did not relish going into the fight and many of them did not expect to survive."⁶⁸ Every man, regardless of rank, whispered the same plea, "Oh, if I could just come of out this charge safely how thankful I would be."⁶⁹

When Col. Birkett Fry gave the command to advance a young lieutenant call out daringly, "Turn us loose and we will take them."⁷⁰ The men marched forward, their double-ranked lines straight and exact as if on the parade ground. Lieutenant Jack Moore (Co. B) noted, "There was no turning back."⁷¹ Another Confederate added, "All knew that victory won ... was to be at a fearful cost."⁷² Their pace—they covered 85 yards a minute—would take about fifteen minutes to reach the Union position.⁷³ The Confederates were out in the open and the enemy behind defenses. They knew nothing good could come from this. One Tennessean proclaimed they were "going to be thrown into a very desperate situation."⁷⁴ A minute passed and the Union troops did nothing. The Tennessee formation descended into a slight depression, hiding them from the "frowning cannon-crowned heights far off held by the enemy."⁷⁵ A Confederate summed up their situation: "Never were men more conscious of the difficulty imposed on them by duty."⁷⁶

The 7th Tennessee covered nearly 300 yards and yet the battlefield remained quiet. The Confederate line was too far away for rifle fire, but the veterans knew the Yanks were waiting; they were letting the Confederates come to them. The 7th Tennessee marched out of the shallow hollow and crossed a higher piece of ground.⁷⁷ The men could now see the massive lines of Pickett's men who had emerged from behind a stand of trees. The Virginians were level with Col. Fry's formation, though 250 yards away.⁷⁸ General Pickett's Virginians moved as one, "their flags proudly held aloft, waving in the air, with polished muskets and [bayonets] gleaming ... in the sunlight."⁷⁹ An observer commented: "Did you ever see a more perfect line than that on dress parade? It was, indeed, a lance head of steel, whose metal had been tempered in the furnace of conflict."⁸⁰

Suddenly, portions of the Federal line vanished amid clouds of billowing white. Sharp crashes of sound, along with bursts of flame erupted among the Virginians. Gaps appeared among Pickett's lines and as the Virginians moved forward, they left behind clumps of broken men. Shell after shell blasted holes in the Virginian lines, "the men [closed] ... ranks and [went] forward ... leaving the dead and wounded in its track."⁸¹

The 7th Tennessee advanced another hundred yards and found themselves among the scraggly apple trees of some farmer's orchard.⁸² One of the Seventh's officers, 1st Lt. Robert Miller, sighed in relief; if he could not see the Yankee guns, they could not see him. Robert Miller, a 25-year-old from Gallatin, Tennessee, had served as Company E's commanding officer ever since the battle of Cedar Run. The unit's captain, James Franklin, had been wounded in that battle and never returned to the company. Nonetheless, Franklin remained in the regiment as one of the regiment's recruiting officers. Since Franklin was maintained on the muster rolls as captain of Company E, Robert Miller was blocked from promotion. Lieutenant Miller was frustrated by this situation. He was the son of a family familiar with success; his widowed mother was wealthy from her first marriage, and his new stepfather was the president of a bank. Here, in the 7th Tennessee, the young officer performed all the duties of captain, but he did not have the rank, nor did he draw captain's pay. Though Miller did not worry about the money, this obstruction to promotion proved annoying.[83] First Lieutenant Robert Miller could see the Federal artillery pounding the Virginians with "concentrated, accurate and fearful fire of shell and solid shot ... [that] plowed through or exploded in [their] ranks, making great havoc."[84] Pickett's men "seemed to sink into the earth under the tempest of fire."[85]

The 7th Tennessee advanced another hundred yards, now having covered 500. The Confederates worked their way through another orchard, this one larger and with more established trees that broke up their parade-ground-straight alignment.[86] An incoming shell exploded among the Alabamians. Several more artillery rounds detonated, both left of the 7th Tennessee and to their right. The Tennesseans stumbled through more trees and up onto higher ground. Now, all that protected Colonel Birkett Fry's brigade from the distant cannoneers was the drifting smoke arising from the Bliss barn. The smoke did not linger and the Northern artillerymen re-adjusted their gun tubes. An explosion cracked in front of the men of Company E. Lieutenant Robert Miller was tossed to the ground by the blast, his left leg broken, a foot lacerated, and his head clawed by pieces of metal.[87] Sergeant James Garrett (Co. E) also was injured, taking shrapnel in his groin and right knee.[88]

Colonel John Fite saw a shallow ravine just ahead. This depression would be a good place to stop and realign the unit. Another shell exploded, this time just in front of the regiment's right companies. First Lieutenant James Martin (Co. D) went down, struck in the right arm and foot.[89] Martin slowly arose and "[went] back with his arm all torn and bleeding."[90] Strangely, the first two artillery strikes to hit the 7th Tennessee had eliminated two company commanders.

John Fite's regiment closed in on a post-and-rail fence. In Company F, Sgt. John Lanier helped his platoon push the barrier down. The 22-year-old farmer from Statesville, Tennessee, though young, was married to a fine girl named Mary Craddock, and together they owned a small farm.[91] He never shirked responsibility, and that was why, he, a poor dirt farmer, had attained a position of authority. The fence collapsed and the barricade tumbled to the ground. Lanier's men hurried past, while Lanier lingered for just a moment, staring at the destroyed fence. John Lanier promised himself he would do what was necessary to come home to Mary.

Once everyone was within the safety of the gully's shelter Col. Fite ordered the regiment to reform. His veterans took only a minute to slide back into their assigned rank-and-file slots. John Fite estimated his Tennesseans were now 650 yards from their starting point, and they had about the same distance to go to reach their destination. Fite looked to his right and saw Pickett's men. They were still on an elevated hump of ground, exposed to every cannon in the Union army. Pickett's men were being slaughtered, and "men fell like ten-pins in a ten-strike."[92]

The 7th Tennessee advanced, rising up out of their sanctuary, their red Confederate battle flag floating above the regiment, its color bearer holding its staff tightly and marching five paces out in front.[93] Shepard briefly saw the battle names which had been painted on the banner before a breeze whipped the cloth in another direction. An artillery round exploded directly in front of Company H. Captain William Tate was blasted to the ground. Private Tom Holloway broke ranks and hurried to his captain, but 1st Sgt. Lewis Westbrook angrily gestured at him to get back in line. Holloway slunk into position. Captain Tate "was so stunned by the cannon shot ... that his comrades left him for dead."[94] Not far from Tate, Lt. Ferguson Harris (Co. H) was also downed, with shrapnel wounds to his head, leg, and foot.[95]

The 7th Tennessee marched forward another hundred yards, putting them a quarter mile from the Federal positions. More artillery rounds struck among the 7th Tennessee. Shrapnel ripped Pvt. Thomas Brashnahan's (Co. C) face and leg, and Sgt. John Williams' (Co. A) left knee and right leg.[96] Comrades immediately dropped out of the line and hurried their wounded comrades back to James Fite's surgery. The 7th Tennessee's strength dribbled away.

The regiment marched up onto a rise, exposing them to the Federal infantry just over 300 yards away.[97] The Southerners could see the Yankees crouching behind a stone wall, their bodies but shadows beneath their national flags. They waited for the Confederates to get closer. One of these Federals, a member of the 14th Connecticut, wrote, "Step by step they came; the music and rhythm of their tread resounding upon the rock-ribbed earth.... There is no swaying of the line, no faltering of the step. The advance seems as resistless as the incoming tide."[98] But the Northerners did not waver. They no longer panicked at the sight of Confederates coming at them. Drill, training, and experience had forged this bunch of civilians into deadly warriors. Plus, many of the riflemen in the 14th Connecticut were armed with breech-loading weapons, an advanced technology enabling them to load and fire much more quickly than a man with a standard musket.[99] These veterans knew how much damage they could inflict.

The Tennesseans were now only fifty yards from a stout-looking double-fence. These post-and-rail barriers bordered both sides of a highway. It created another barrier, but also provided shelter. Lieutenant Jack Moore (Co. B) noted, "This roadbed was perhaps some two feet below the level of the ground, and afforded protection to one lying down."[100] The Tennesseans moved eagerly toward the fence. The 14th Connecticut riflemen facing the Tennesseans numbered no more than a hundred. They stood behind a low stone wall, impatiently waiting the command to fire.[101] The boys from the Nutmeg State, commanded by Major Theodore Ellis, were veterans and refused to be shaken by the massive Confederate line closing upon them. They weren't alone; to their left several Pennsylvania regiments waited, and to their right, over 200 men of the 1st Delaware lined another section of the stone wall, also prepared to "pour a murderous fire into the rebel[s]."[102] The Delaware men had already tussled with the 7th Tennessee earlier this morning near the Bliss farm. Now, once again, they aimed their muskets upon Colonel Fite's men. Finally, as a Connecticut soldier remembered, "General Hays raised his stentorian voice above the din ... and shouted, 'Fire!' Up and down the Union line officers repeated his order, and the Union infantry responded."[103] George Shepard wrote, "The enemy held their fire until we were in fine range, and opened upon us a terrible and well-directed fire."[104]

A sheet of lead slammed into Colonel Fite's men, sweeping across the Tennesseans in a destructive wave rolling from left to right. The range was between 175 and 200 yards and the Union riflemen's aim proved true; Fite's men went down in droves. In the time it took the Tennesseans to take those last crucial steps to the fence line over twenty men were hit, including the flag bearer. Private John McCall (Co. B) recorded, "We were met by a heavy fire ... which told sadly upon our ranks."[105] On the far left, Sgt. John Cheek (Co. A) toppled backward, and Pvt. Benjamin Thackston (Co. B) was wounded in the neck. Captain Williams Graves (Co. G) dropped, as did Cpl. Thomas Sullivan (Co. G) and Sgt. Richard Vaughn (Co. G), who took a bullet to his right thigh.[106] Farther to the right, in Cpt. Archie Norris' Company K, several men had fallen to the ground when that first lethal wave ripped over them. Corporal William Lane and Pvt. John Lane were casualties, as was Lt. Mitchell Anderson. Private James Moxley did not appear to be moving, and Pvt. James Seat clutched at blood pouring from his face.[107] Archie Norris, whose long legs made him one of the regiment's fastest runners, reached the post-and-rail shelter and dove to the ground. Soon, the rest of the company crashed down beside their commander. They lay on their bellies or flat out on their backs, having reached this protection before the Federals' second volley savaged them.

Private Tom Holloway tumbled onto the ground behind the fence. He had seen Pvt. Milton Brown (Co. E) fall. Holloway had also watched as a Minié bullet slammed into Pvt. John Simmons' head (Co. H), splattering blood and brains over those around him. Behind Simmons, Sgt. John Williamson (Co. H) groaned when a ball ripped through his right thigh.[108] He staggered and fell to the ground. More Tennesseans sprawled on the ground, west of the Emmitsburg fences. Lieutenant Thomas Jennings (Co. F) crumpled to the earth, and Pvt. Alfred Brown (Co. C) spun completely around before falling, a chunk of lead slashing through his arm.[109]

Sergeant John Lanier dropped and rolled to a stop. Bullets from the second Federal volley hummed dangerously past or splintered pieces of fence timber. Not far from John Lanier, Cpl. J. P. Bashaw (Co. I) slowly recovered. Thankfully, they had reached the fence line. Sadly, others had not. Bashaw's sergeant, John Jennings (Co. I), lay quietly out in the open, bleeding. Private Albert Wilkerson (Co. I) thrashed about, grabbing at a mauled left thigh, while Pvt. John Sullivan (Co. I) struggled to crawl to safety, leaving behind a trail of blood. First Sergeant Hart Harris (Co. D) did not move, and a few yards from him, Pvt. William Hawkins (Co. D) screamed for help.[110] A large splinter flashed past Bashaw's face and gouged a hole in the ground, forcing him to forget the casualties and worry about his own situation. The Yankee bullets now ripped over his head in a continuous sheet of fire. Never before in the 7th Tennessee's first two years of war had so many men become casualties so quickly. Lieutenant Jack Moore (Co. B) wrote, "Volley after volley culled the ranks in large numbers before the regiment reached the road."[111] The surviving soldiers huddled on the ground behind the first of the two Emmitsburg fences, stunned. Then, calm-thinking officers and sergeants organized details to go back and retrieve the casualties and pull them to safety.

The Yank infantrymen loaded and fired their muskets and breech-loading rifles with such speed that the air above the Confederates constantly buzzed with death. Bullets whacked into the posts and rails, sounding, "Like hail upon a roof."[112] The Tennesseans did not shoot back at the Northerners; to rise up above the fence rails meant suicide. The veteran soldiers did not like their situation; they could not fight back, nor go forward, nor safely retreat.

Colonel John Fite knew General Lee depended upon the Tennessean brigade to anchor the entire assault. Lee would not want their advance to stall here, still over a hundred yards from pressing home the attack. John Fite shouted at his boys to knock the fence down. The Tennesseans frantically pushed and shoved at the posts and cross pieces. Corporal J. P. Bashaw (Co. I) noted, "Our men went against the fence and tried to push it down, but could not."[113] The mortise and post construction proved unyielding. John Fite saw no alternative; he gave the order to climb over the fence. But to mount the fence meant death. No one was anxious to be first, but, there was no other way. One of Fite's men stated it simply: "We had to climb these fences."[114]

Colonel John Fite led the way. He stood up, mounted the cross rails, jumped over, and landed with a thump in the sunken road on the other side. Fite sat up and faced his men. He shouted at them. Captain John Allen (Co. B) vaulted over the fence, falling to the ground near his colonel. Allen waved at the Tennesseans and shouted a stream of obscenities. Sergeant Billy Cato grabbed at the riflemen around them, yanking them to their feet and then leading them over the fence. Other sergeants did the same and more Tennesseans made the venture, spinning over the top rail and tumbling into the safety of the sunken Emmitsburg Road. A Tennessean wrote, "Our stay ... could not have been called a halt. In a moment the order to advance was given and on we pressed across the ... fence."[115] A steady stream of desperate men followed, rising up, but now the Union troops had targets to aim at. Their fire swept the top of the fence line and Northern lead thudded into Tennessean tissue.

One Yank observed, "The [Confederates] dropped from the fence as if swept by a gigantic sickle swung by some powerful force of nature."[116] Second Lieutenant John Ingram (Co. G) fell back from the fence, a bullet knocking him to the ground. Privates James Hale (Co. B), Luther Ralston (Co. D), and Joseph Love (Co. E) fell, hurt by Federal lead. Private Tom Holloway climbed to his feet and kicked his leg up over the top rail. Bullets hummed past him and splintered into the wood. He plummeted onto Emmitsburg Road's gravel and landed awkwardly, stunned by the fall. Jack Moore (Co. B) recalled, "The time it took to climb to the top of the fence seemed, to me, an age of suspense.... It was not a leaping over; it was rather an insensible tumbling to the ground, in the nervous hope of escaping the thickening missiles."[117]

More Tennesseans tried their luck, but Yank bullets caught them; Pvt. William Bradley (Co. B) was struck in the right leg, Pvt. Frank Frazer (Co. E) screamed when a ball shattered his left knee, Pvt. Andrew Foster (Co. G) went down with a splintered right arm, and Sgt. John Hamilton (Co. H) suffered a wound to his shin.[118] Lieutenant Moore (Co. B) wrote, "The 7th Tennessee hit the plank fence ... and spilled into [the road] like cattle falling off a precipice. What was left ... pressed itself on the packed dirt."[119]

Emmitsburg Road provided a refuge from the Federal fire, as the roadbed was below ground level. Tennesseans scurried about, traumatized by having survived the fence's crossing, or suffering from bullet wounds. Emmitsburg Road's dusty surface became a hectic ant hill, filled with screams, moans, cries, and shouts. Compassionate men worked to help their fallen brothers. Privates Henry Forbis (Co. K) and William Johnson (Co. K) lay bleeding, as did the mortally wounded 1st Sgt. James Winfrey (Co. A). Private William McGee (Co. B) clutched at a wound in his head, and Pvt. James Gray (Co. E) lay on the ground, watching blood drain from his shattered arm.[120] Another Tennessean, Pvt. Eli Smith (Co. I) rolled in pain, blood pouring from a gaping wound.

There were still scores of Tennesseans who had not made the crossing. Those who did shouted at the reluctant ones, challenging their courage. More men tried. Some made it while others didn't. Pvt. James Donnell (Co. A) and Pvt. Hartwell Bradshaw (Co. G) fell wounded. And still, more Tennesseans took their turn at crossing. They toppled over the fence and joined their brothers, either healthy, or wounded; 1st Sgt. John Puckett was paralyzed by a bullet passing through his left arm, and Cpl. Mead Anderson was struck "in the foot, knee, and hip."[121] The injured mingled among the unhurt, all bunching together in a cluster of cowering men. One wrote, "[The] troops who survived the scaling of the fence huddled in the roadbed, lying flat beneath the stream of deadly fire."[122]

Colonel John Fite estimated, "About half of my men never got over the first fence."[123] Fite shouted for his company commanders to join him. John Allen and Archie Norris crawled to Fite and joined the other surviving officers. Fite tried to speak but, as one man observed, "the concussions from the Federal guns ... had become so loud that the officers could not hear."[124] Colonel John Fite's desperate words were echoed by all the other regimental commanders in Fry's brigades. "That hill must fall!" was the order from General Lee — it was the soldiers' duty to carry out his directive.[125] Someone shouted over the musketry's racket, "It's ridiculous, Colonel, perfectly ridiculous."[126] Bullets continued to smack against the fence boards, sounding like "large raindrops pattering on a roof."[127] Someone else yelled, "[It's] a hell of an ugly place."[128] But John Fite remained firm, which surprised no one. He had demonstrated in two years of war that duty came first; fear was not allowed. And John Fite, like many other senior Confederate officers refused to contradict Robert E. Lee's mandate. As one officer remembered, "We [couldn't] stay here; we must go ... forward."[129] Fite, like other surviving regimental leaders, looked to his men and called out, "Who will follow me?"[130]

Only about 150 healthy Tennesseans remained who could be counted as present to make the attack. George Shepard clutched his sword and scanned his brothers, knowing many were near their limit. They could hear the bluecoats taunting them, hollering, "Come on, come on!"[131] John Fite's veterans knew death loomed imminent the moment they went forward. They would be throwing their lives away.

Timing a brief interlude of light Yank rifle fire, John Fite mounted the second fence, dropped down onto the eastern side, and hunkered down in a ditch. He turned to his regiment and charged them to accompany him. A flurry of officers and riflemen clamored over the fence and clustered around him. Tom Holloway (Co. H) followed his colonel. Holloway was joined by dozens more. Not far from Holloway, Cpl. J.P. Bashaw (Co. I) and two of his riflemen, John Eatherly and James Walpole, waited to follow their colonel. Maybe Tennesseans joined them, but so many didn't. Lieutenant Jack Moore (Co. B) recalled, "There seemed to remain a line of battle in the road ... the men who remained claimed it was impossible to push on."[132]

Sergeant Billy Cato knelt beside Cpt. Archie Norris and both Company K lieutenants, Martin Baird and David Phillips. There were a couple others from their company: Sgt. Henry Williams and Pvt. Robert Anderson. Captain John Allen (Co. B) found his lieutenants, Frank Timberlake and John Moore, and his first sergeant, Charles McClain. He had them round up Company B members, a task taking seconds; they only found a dozen. Allen hollered out a volley of curses so loud and vehement the men around him burst out laughing. This entire clump of Tennesseans supporting Colonel Fite was about the same size of John Allen's company strength two days ago. Later, Fite recorded, "Not more than [seventy] of us got across the last fence."[133] The small band of Tennesseans gazed up the gentle slope toward the stone wall and the mass of Yankees. One Tennessean noted, "It was one hundred and fifty yards of open field.[134] John Fite wrote there "was not a bush on it."[135] Colonel Fite then pointed to their Confederate flag being held by Pvt. William Oliver (Co. G) and admonished his Tennesseans to do their duty.

The Northerners, so impressed by this Tennessee valor, slowed their shooting and prepared for this Confederate assault. One Yank officer stated, "My men were directed to reserve their fire until the foe was within 50 yards."[136] They waited, watching as the veterans in each small Confederate regiment clustered around their battle flags. The entire Southern line, which at one point spanned a mile in width, had shrunk to barely a couple of hundred yards. Nonetheless, the Federals knew these Confederates forming in the ditch east of Emmitsburg Road were capable of inflicting horrible punishment.

A Confederate recalled, "Then the rebel yell sounded over the roar of the battle and [they] surged beyond the fences."[137] George Shepard recorded, "The men rushed ... as rapidly as they could, and advanced directly upon the enemy's works."[138] The Tennesseans pushed forward. One soldier described their formation; they "moved up the slope in [a] spearhead under [their] flag."[139] Another noted, "Many of the soldiers marched in a half stoop with their heads bowed, as if walking in a storm."[140] The Tennesseans crowded close to John Fite, who kept pace with William Oliver and their battle flag. The rest of the regiment remained back at the splintered and riddled Emmitsburg fences, many of the men tending to their wounded comrades. Private Andrew Bradley (Co. B) tried to staunch the bleeding of his wounded brother, William; and Pvt. Oren Anderson (Co. I) helped his injured cousin, Mead. But there were others who crouched in the sunken road's safety, having reached that point in which they could not move. One such soldier confessed, "I can't go forward. I know I am disgracing my family, but I can't go."[141] These men were not shirkers. Indeed, everyone here had served for two years and experienced his share of danger and anguish; but some had just reached the end of their endurance.

Birkett Fry's regiments desperately moved forward. John Fite's small band of Tennesseans was not alone, and Fry's brigade was not attacking the stone wall position by itself. Mobs of Confederates clustered around Virginia flags and North Carolina flags as well as other banners. The entire Confederacy was in on this frantic rush. The Confederates closed upon the Federal positions for another fifty yards, covering that distance in less than thirty seconds. But by now they were deep within the killing zone and the Northern riflemen resumed their destructive fire. A Southerner wrote, "Volley after volley of crashing musket balls swept through the line and mowed [the Confederates] down like wheat before the scythe."[142] Colonel John Fite went down, shot through the leg, and Captain John Allen (Co. B) was hit in the neck. Private James Paty (Co. B) was killed, Pvt. James Sutton (Co. F) killed, and Sgt. John Webster (Co. D) was severely wounded.[143]

The 7th Tennessee's flag went down when William Oliver was stunned by a blow to his leg. He remarked: "The ball struck a large pocket knife in my trousers pocket."[144] A

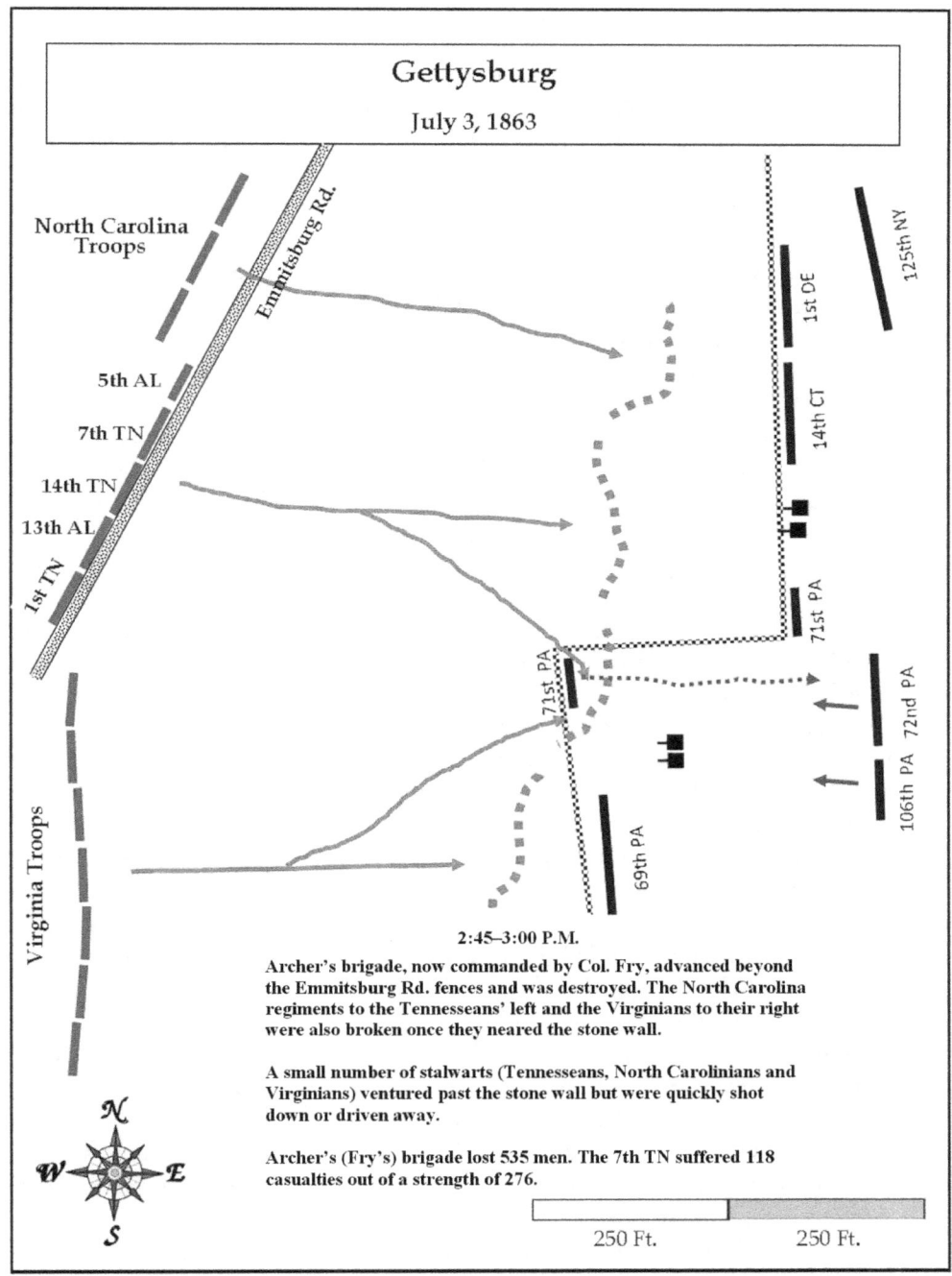

nearby Tennessean raised the flag, an action occurring all along the line. One Southerner wrote, "Half the flags went down.... Then the flags came up again."[145] The riflemen of the 14th Connecticut and 1st Delaware blazed away at the Tennesseans, slaughtering them. One Federal officer described their fire; it was "so effective and incessant ... that the advancing enemy was staggered."[146] Private John Luck (Co. A) fell with a wound to his right arm. Private Samuel King (Co. B) was struck, as were Privates James Walpole (Co.

I), William Wade (Co. H), George Hamilton (Co. E), Andrew Whitehead (Co. D), and Paleaman Dillard (Co. B).[147] The 7th Tennessee's flag went down again, only this time it was not raised; the staff had been shot in two. More Tennesseans fell; Lt. George Cowen (Co. A) was killed, Pvt. John Etson (Co. E) was wounded, and Sgt. William Baird (Co. G) was killed.[148] Major William Williamson and Pvt. Robert Wormack (Co. H) went down, "both having lost their good right arms."[149] Corporal J.P. Bashaw (Co. I) was hit. He wrote, "I was shot through the leg and knocked to my hands and knees."[150] And Lt. Frank Timberlake (Co. B) was struck by a Minié bullet in the side. Lieutenant Colonel George Shepard wrote, "The line ... seemed to melt away."[151]

The Southerners staggered forward, their formation now little more than a frenetic knot of men. An observer wrote, "The Southern brigades ... merged into one crowding, rushing line, many ranks deep."[152] They were barely 100 feet away from the stone wall. The Federal fire did not let up. One Confederate recalled, "Who can stand such a storm of hissing lead and iron?"[153] Private John Roberts (Co. G) had been killed, and so was Pvt. John Eatherly (Co. I). Private John Hall (Co. B) went down, as did Cpl. William Garrett (Co. E) and Pvt. James Hearn (Co. D).[154] George Shepard reported, "Our lines ... had become very much weakened."[155]

They were leaderless now, and many Tennesseans dropped to the ground, trying to escape the bullets ripping through Confederate flesh. There was nothing to hide behind, but being flat on the ground proved safer than standing. Incredibly, a small number continued forward, maybe two dozen or so, crowding around Cpt. Asoph Hill (Co. F), Lt. Jack Moore (Co. B) and Sgt. Billy Cato (Co. K). They merged with survivors from the other regiments, a tiny clump of reckless and valiant men, all charging forward, indifferent to their mortal fates. The Confederates kept coming and then, surprisingly, when this frantic mass of Southerners was barely twenty yards away, the Pennsylvanians to the left of the 14th Connecticut fell back. Fry's brigade, which numbered less than a couple companies, surged over the wall, having attained Robert E. Lee's goal of breaching the Angle. But, this magnificent Southern division had been so weakened one Tennessean wrote, "We were reduced to a mere skirmish line."[156]

These survivors halted and fired, and then dashed past the stone wall toward some cannons nearby. One Confederate wrote, "The 1st Tennessee, with [some] ... officers and men from the 7th Tennessee ... rush[ed] into a melee."[157] The Federals had strong reserves, veterans from the 72nd Pennsylvania, who counterattacked. Sergeant Billy Cato (Co. K) was wounded, as were Pvt. Thomas Hubbard (Co. B) and Pvt. David Lynch (Co. B), who fell with injuries to his arm and hip.[158] Captain Asoph Hill, who many believed to be "a fine specimen of Southern chivalry," went down with wounds to his breast.[159] The struggle ended suddenly; one Tennessean wrote, "It did not last five minutes longer."[160] A few Confederate survivors fled back across the stone wall.

For those Tennesseans who had not reached the stone wall at the Angle, the slope in front of the Connecticut soldiers was a death trap. These Federals fired their breech-loading weapons so fast "that the barrels became so hot that it was impossible to use them."[161] The Nutmeg State soldiers kept up a devastating level of fire, covering the field with a sheet of death. No Tennesseans remained standing. One Yank officer noted the Confederates "dropped on the ground to escape our destructive fire."[162] Many of the Tennesseans were casualties but others, having had the good fortune of being spared injury, stayed on the ground, some of them, "singly or in pairs ... plugging away at the Federals."[163]

Billy Cato (Co. K) painfully crawled back toward the Emmitsburg fences. He was not alone; Lt. Jack Moore (Co. B) cautiously worked his way away from the Federal line, as did a handful of others. Private John McCall (Co. B) wrote, "Now seeing we had a hopeless case. We began to fall back ... under a terrible fire."[164] Other soldiers also crawled slowly back toward the Emmitsburg fences. This was a dangerous process, scuttling toward the Emmitsburg Road for a few seconds, and then lying "dead" while bullets hissed past, above their heads.

The Connecticut riflemen created such a cloud of gun smoke in front of their position they no longer had a clear view of what lay before them. Nonetheless, they did not cease fire and wait for the smoke to clear, but were content to shoot, spraying the field and the Emmitsburg fences. Their shooting was rapid and frantic, but fortunately for the Tennesseans who lay prone on the open field, the Yanks' no longer shot accurately. One of the Federals, though, offered another reason why so many of their bullets went wide. He wrote, "We could have picked off many ... but we did not have much desire to [keep] kill[ing]."[165] Regardless of why the bluecoats' accuracy remained poor, for the Tennesseans, these feverish moments of terror seemed to last forever. Colonel John Fite, who was pinned down by the Yank shooting, remembered, "While I was lying there on the ground, the Yankees kept shooting ... I expected every minute to be shot."[166]

The Federals fired with such intensity few realized the Southerners no longer resisted. In fact, few of the Union soldiers understood the attack was finished. Colonel Birkett Fry, who lay bleeding among dozens of wounded, dead, or pretending-to-be-dead soldiers recalled, "The roll of musketry was incessant, and I believe the Federal troops — probably blinded by the smoke — continued a rapid fire for some minutes after none but dead and wounded remained on their front."[167]

Tom Holloway (Co. H) lay on his belly among a cluster of Tennesseans, some unhurt, while others were injured or dying. Not far from Halloway, Pvt. Jim Hale (Co. B) lay on his side in a growing pool of blood. Someone suggested they surrender but Holloway dis-

UNNAMED TENNESSEE YOUNG WOMAN. The Connecticut soldiers, once they had done their part to stop Pickett's Charge, went out among the dead and wounded Confederates. A Federal soldier found the daguerreotype of this young woman clasped in the hands of a dead soldier not far from where the 7th Tennessee flag had last been seen. This young woman would not know of her fellow's death for several weeks before his name was posted in a newspaper list. Who she is has never been determined (*Confederate Veteran* collection).

agreed. The call came to surrender again, but the ex-teacher replied, "Let's never surrender." Tom Holloway, "raised his head ... just then a bullet went crashing through his brain."[168] Not far from where Holloway, Sgt. Blackwell Dunn (Co. E) huddled. "Black," as everyone in his company called him, was a 20-year-old student from Hendersonville, Tennessee. Someone near him called out for surrender, but Dunn retorted, "They've got to get more blood out of me ... before I ever surrender." The defiant sergeant then crawled backward, but, "before he had gone twenty steps ... he was severely wounded."[169]

Seeing no alternative but death, the Confederates chose to surrender. At first it was only individual soldiers who grabbed something white and waved it above their heads, but then more joined in, frantically flapping white cloths.[170] Eventually all across the space between Emmitsburg Road and the stone wall, white bits fluttered in a moving carpet of capitulation. The Union riflemen realized what had happening and they set down their over-heated weapons. One Confederate chanced to take out his pocket watch and noted, "We [had] been just nineteen minutes coming."[171] The silence which followed the roar of musketry stunned everyone. Sadly, the quiet did not last long before it was overwhelmed by the groans and cries of wounded soldiers. One Yank remembered, "A wild cheer went up from the 14th Connecticut which was carried along a good bit of the II Corps line."[172] Following this, quick-thinking Federals leaped over the stone wall and hurried out among the fallen Southerners, rushing to capture Confederate battle flags. A few clear-headed Confederates saw this as an opportunity for escape; they guessed the Yankees would not shoot with their own men moving out among the dead and wounded. Lieutenant Jack Moore decided to make a break for it. He jumped up and sprinted toward the Emmitsburg Road. Moore wrote, "[I] feared death every second during the frenzied run across the body-strewn field."[173] Another Tennessean, Pvt. John Johnson (Co. A), recalled, "When I saw the white flags go up, I got to running."[174]

Lieutenant Colonel George Shepard slipped back toward the Emmitsburg Road fences. Captain Archie Norris (Co. K), his wits still with him, crawled over to the regiment's flag and stripped its remaining stays from the shattered flagstaff. Norris then stuffed the cotton emblem into his coat and took off, racing toward the rear. Shepard later would write, "Every flag in the brigade excepting [ours] was captured."[175] Both George Shepard and Archie Norris tumbled over the easternmost of the fences and rested in the security provided by the sunken highway. However, as Lt. Jack Moore (Co. B) noted, "It seemed almost death to retreat ... [but] it was surrender to remain."[176] Shepard, Moore, Cato, and a small contingent of Tennesseans "sped through the open field, expecting every moment to be shot," leaving behind "a roadbed littered with dead, wounded, and frightened and unhurt comrades."[177]

Moore, Norris, and Shepard were not alone in their successful getaways, though their flight proved easier than some. Corporal J.P. Bashaw (Co. I), though slowed by his badly bruised leg, limped toward freedom. He recalled, "I hobbled on a little distance and then I was hit by a ball in the middle of my back.... I was knocked some distance and fell.... I thought that the ball had passed through me and that I would die right there.... [But] I had laid there a while and had not died. I ventured to feel for the hole, but to my surprise, there was no hole, only a large knot on my back." Bashaw continued, "With much gladness I arose and continued my slow journey to the rear."[178]

As the disorganized soldiers retreated back across the ground some recognized wounded comrades. They lifted up their injured brothers and carried them to safety. One of the wounded, Lt. Ferguson Harris (Co. H), recalled, "I ... [was using] two guns as a pair of crutches, until rescued by ... John Lanier [Co. F]."[179] Another Tennessean, Pvt. James Grissom (Co. G), a 23-year-old from Lockport, Tennessee, slowly made his way toward the safety of the distant tree line; the young Tennessean saw 1st Lt. Robert Miller (Co. E) shuffling along. Grissom put his arm around Miller's shoulders and helped him toward safety. Once out in the open, hundreds of yards west of the Emmitsburg Road the two were out of infantry range. But they still were not safe; fresh Union batteries were rolled into position along a southern section of Cemetery Ridge and the gunners opened fire at the retreating Confederates. Lieutenant Harris (Co. H) described what happened: "One [shell] came screaming along and seemed as if it would hit us in spite of all we could do ... [Grissom] dropped [Lt.] Miller and jumped about ten feet to his left, close to the stump of a large tree.... Just as he stooped the shell struck him on the shoulder and ... exploded.... It literally tore him into a thousand pieces."[180]

Back among the wounded and trapped soldiers, Col. John Fite knew he could not escape. He watched Yank soldiers approach. His adjutant, George Howard, hovered at his side, bristling to protect him, but Fite told the young officer to relax; there was nothing they could do. John Fite recorded, "When they stopped shooting they jumped from the rock fence and came down to where we were ... a fellow came up to me.... He said, 'You are my prisoner.' I told him I recognized that fact. I asked him if he wanted my sword. He said, 'I will take you up and let you surrender to my officer.'" And with that, John Fite surrendered to Major Theodore Ellis (14th Connecticut).[181]

Colonel Fite, along with two dozen 7th Tennesseans, and hundreds of other Confederates in front of the stone wall were gathered up and sent to Union hospitals. Another three dozen Tennesseans were marched away, part of the throng of defeated Southerners trapped out in the open. Also, another thirty-six Tennesseans who had remained amid the bloody chaos along Emmitsburg Road were swept up by flanking Union riflemen and hauled away to hospitals or prison pens.

George Shepard stumbled back to the trees, accompanied by Lt. Jack Moore (Co. B) and the two found themselves near General Robert E. Lee. The gray-haired officer approached them and took Shepard's hand. "Colonel, rally your men and protect our artillery," Lee said quietly. And then he continued, "The fault is mine, but it will all be right in the end." Before Shepard could reply, General Pettigrew rode up and Lee shifted his attention to him, saying, "General, I am sorry to see you wounded; go to the rear."[182]

George Shepard now had a serious task to accomplish; gather together his Tennessean survivors, identify leaders to command companies, resupply the men with weapons and ammunition, make sure the wounded were directed to surgeon James Fite, and then build a defensive line to help hold off the expected Yankee counterattack. At first he only had Lt. Moore to assist him, but soon Captains Archie Norris (Co. K) and James Bass (Co. I) as well as Sgt. Maj. Samuel Jennings joined them. With these veterans, Shepard rallied the regiment's shattered ranks. He wrote, "[We] reformed upon the ground from which we advanced, and awaited the advance of the enemy."[183] The Yanks did not attack and sunset brought a conclusion to the day's fighting and an end to the Battle of Gettysburg.

CHAPTER 8

July 3, 1863: Sunset

"Bury these poor men and let us say no more about it."

Darkness on July 3, 1863, brought the Tennesseans little relief. Lieutenant Colonel George Shepard's night proved hectic; there was so much re-organization required. Fortunately, Cpt. Fayette Walsh and his workers found the 7th Tennessee's location and rushed in to help. Fayette Walsh moved among the exhausted men, making sure each Tennessean was supplied with weapons, bullets, caps, and any accoutrements missing. He also oversaw efforts to feed each man and make sure their haversacks were stuffed with rations. Shepard's boys may have been weary and disconsolate, but at least that night they had plenty of food.

Meanwhile, the regiment's surgeon, Dr. James Fite, and his assistants located nearly five dozen wounded 7th Tennesseans and worked on them throughout the night. One of these casualties, J. P. Bashaw (Co. I), wrote, "I went on back to the field hospital. My wound ... was dressed, [and] the pain became less and I fell asleep."[1] James Fite had set up his medical center not far from a tiny creek. Whenever he looked out from his surgical tent he saw wounded men crawling down to this little stream and "washing their wounds in [it] ... making its clear waters run red."[2] James Fite worked ceaselessly, all the while knowing his wounded brother was in Federal hands. Fite's brother, Col. John Fite, was now a prisoner of war and waited out the night in a field east of Gettysburg. Colonel Fite was accompanied by Lt. Col. Newton George (14th TN), both officers being too injured to travel. They would remain for another day before being loaded into boxcars and shipped to Baltimore and from there to the prison on Johnson's Island.[3]

With John Fite no longer in command, and with Col. Birkett Fry also gone, there was no one left to lead the brigade except George Shepard. He met with the surviving senior officer of each of the brigade's other regiments and passed along division orders. The brigade had instructions to maintain a presence along a fence line; their mission was to protect the 18 cannons of Lt. Col. William Poague's battalion battery.[4] Shepard's brigade strength was barely more than 300 men, and these exhausted survivors could do little besides slink down behind a split rail fence and hope the Yanks did not attack. The men dozed near their weapons or lay awake, haunted by the day's events. There was no real escape from the calamity, and though darkness hid the terrible sights out on the battlefield, the survivors were appalled by "the piteous cries of the wounded and dying."[5] The soldiers were miserable; so many of their relatives and friends had fallen, and for what? One despondent Confederate summarized the attack: "It was simply waste."[6]

Sunrise came with the fear of a Yankee assault. Captains Archie Norris (Co. K) and James Bass (Co. I) set their Tennesseans to digging rifle pits and piling up dirt, rocks, and timbers. The Confederates then rested behind their works, hopeful they could give a good account of themselves when the bluecoats advanced. But even as the men added an extra stone or two to their defenses they heard rumors the army was going to retreat. That news was stoically accepted; the Tennesseans no longer wanted to look out across the huge field they crossed yesterday. Too many bodies littered the ground, a testimony to so many lost comrades. One Confederate wrote, "It struck horror to us all."[7] Small details were sent out, the men armed with shovels, and as one Tennessean noted, "July 4th was spent ... burying the dead."[8]

The Federals looked out over the corpse-strewn field and had no incentive to repeat what Lee's man had attempted. Small units crept forward cautiously, but no one attacked the Confederate defenses. Instead, the Yanks spent the day collecting the wounded, dealing with the prisoners, and burying the dead. This responsibility proved to be a monumental task. The slaughter near the stone wall and the area called the Angle was so heavy one Northerner reported, "Five hundred and twenty-two dead Confederates ... [were] buried in a mass grave in the field that extended from the angle area to the Emmitsburg Road."[9]

General Robert E. Lee did not have the luxury of dealing with the dead; instead he met with his staff and fashioned plans to save his army. The morning's muster and hospital reports provided Lee with a ghastly truth, he had nearly 19,000 wounded. He needed to protect them when the army retreated. Lee planned to load his wounded on 1,200 wagons and transport them back to Virginia.[10] This venture went into motion immediately after sunrise, but without the speed Lee desired. By the time the orders reached the 7th Tennessee several hours had been wasted and there was little time to make arrangements. Shepard contacted Cpt. Fayette Walsh and the regiment's quartermaster officer hastily shifted supplies and cleared wagons. It pained Walsh to dump supplies, but the wounded had first priority. Then, once the wagons were empty, Surgeon Fite filled the vehicles with the 7th Tennessee's casualties. The wounded J. P. Bashaw wrote, "About noon ... [we] were ... loaded in wagons."[11]

Before the first wagon could move onto the Cashtown Pike, nature stepped in and complicated the situation with rain, lightning, and strong winds. One Confederate noted, "The very windows of heaven seem to have opened."[12] The downpour turned the pike into a quagmire, the lightning and thunder terrorized the horses and mules, and the winds ripped at the canvas protecting the injured. Consequently, by the time the wagon train was ready to move, nearly all the wounded passengers were wet, cold, and miserable.

The wagon train was huge, and even though each of the 1,200 wagons was loaded with up to ten men there were not enough vehicles to transport all the wounded. Nearly 7,000 Confederates were left behind. Lieutenant Ferguson Harris (Co. H) noted, "Dr. Fite had secured his wounded ... [others, though] could not [and] they made them as comfortable as possible, placing water, food and medicine ... for them and leaving an attendant to look after them until they were taken in by the Federals."[13]

Lee, though pained by the loss of thousands of men he was leaving behind, gave the order for the wagons to move. This immense convoy of wagons, once in motion, stretched out in a procession nearly 17 miles in length. Brigadier General John Imboden, the Confederate cavalry officer tasked with protecting the wagon train, wrote, "By 4 P.M. ... the wagon train was in motion ... [but] it was well after dark when the last wagons rolled out." Imboden continued, "I was never out of the hearing of the groans and cries of the wounded and dying."[14] General Imboden ordered the teamsters not to stop and the wagons rolled throughout the night, hauling their wretched passengers, who lay helplessly, crying out in pain. Imboden recalled, "Inside each wagon lay men with shattered bones and open wounds, lying on bare boards in spring-less wagons jolting over badly rutted roads."[15]

The vanguard of the wagon train reached Greencastle, Pennsylvania, on the morning of July 5, and the tail arrived by early afternoon. Greencastle's citizens watched in horror as this never-ending stream of agony-filled wagons rumbled through their town. One resident wrote, "No one, with any feelings of pity, will ever want to see such a sight even once in a lifetime."[16] The caravan turned south, aiming for Hagerstown, Maryland, inching slowly, the weary teamsters fighting to keep their exhausted mules and horses moving.

Union cavalry had been sent out to determine where Lee was heading, and these horsemen descended upon the wagon train like packs of wolves. Swarms of company-sized cavalry units wrecked wagons, killing drays, and nabbing able-bodied wounded. General Imboden's Southern cavalry troops reacted as quickly as possible, but the train stretched for 17 miles; it could not be defended. Eventually, one of these Federal strikes hit a portion of the train containing some of the 7th Tennessee's wounded. The raid was swift and effective, wounding Pvt. William Conditt (Co. B) before nabbing several dozen vehicles, including at least two 7th Tennessee wagons. The Yanks hauled away to captivity two 7th Tennessee teamsters, John Canary (Co. D) and Tom Hatcher (Co. D), and six wounded.[17] One of these captured soldiers, Cpl. J. P. Bashaw (Co. I), recorded; "About four o'clock in the afternoon the Yankee's cavalry captured about 30 or 40 wagons with our wounded, I among them."[18]

The captured wagons were driven to Mercersburg, Pennsylvania, ten miles away, and the wounded confined inside the brick buildings of Marshall College. Corporal Bashaw wrote, "We spent that night in an [old] college.... The next morning they paroled those of us who could not walk, the rest they took to prison. We, that were paroled, stayed there for about a week without any rations and the citizens fed us.... The Yankees came back ... and carried us to Chester, Pa.... We remained here for about six weeks."[19] Bashaw described his hospital stay, writing, "We faired just like their soldiers did: We had the best treatment ... and [were] furnished clean underwear once a week, and were required to bathe when we changed clothing. Each ward had a bath room, with hot and cold water, soap and towels." Bashaw concluded his description, stating, "I [got] completely well."[20]

For the rest of the wounded Confederate passengers, their travails continued. The massive wagon train reached Williamsport only to discover the continuous rains had swollen the Potomac River to the point none of the fords were passable. Quick-thinking wagon masters commandeered a small fleet of water craft and began ferrying the wounded across the river, but the helpless thousands who waited their turn to cross, they needed food, water, and medical attention. A Confederate surgeon wrote, "Rather than have the sick and wounded men in the ambulances ... [they] moved them into houses and barns, and out of the pouring rains."[21] Plus, harassing swarms of Union cavalry threatened to capture the entire lot, as well as the Confederates' valuable wagon train. There was much to be done if General Lee was ever again going to see his veteran soldiers, as well as his entire supply of wagons. General Imboden's 3,000 horsemen stood in the way of what could become another Confederate disaster.

On July 6, 1863, Imboden rounded up every teamster, quartermaster, commissary officer, and anyone else who could hold a shovel and ordered them to dig fortifications on the hills overlooking Williamsport. Then, Imboden's dismounted cavalry, supported by a wretched force of wounded soldiers and non-combat troops desperately held off nearly 4,000 Federal cavalry troops commanded by Brig. Gen. John Buford long enough for the first of Lee's retreating infantry brigades to arrive. The Yank cavalry, knowing the power of Lee's veterans, withdrew, leaving the huge train of wounded men to cross the Potomac.

General Lee's engineers constructed a long line of entrenchments extending for nearly seven miles. Later, when one of the Federal cavalry officers examined the fortifications he wrote, "[they] were the strongest [he had] seen yet, built as if they were meant to stand a month's siege."[22] Fortunately for the Confederates, the Yanks did not realize most of the works were unmanned, as the main body of Lee's army had not as yet arrived.

Lieutenant Colonel George Shepard received orders to pull the brigade off the line during the night of July 4, 1863. The tired Tennesseans slogged through the mud. They reached Fairfield, Pennsylvania, turned south and entered Maryland. For the Tennesseans, the march was a nightmare; the men were exhausted, wet, cold, miserable, and hungry. Lieutenant Harris (Co. H) wrote, "Woe unto a chicken that impeded our march."[23] What most bothered the survivors was a sense of catastrophe. They had left friends and relatives out on Gettysburg's fields, good men lost in a failed gamble. One Southerner noted, "There was a feeling among the men that somebody had blundered." Another miserable rifleman looked about at the remaining survivors and declared, "In my opinion our Army will never be ... [the same] again."[24]

The Tennesseans were directed into a position toward the southern end of the Williamsport entrenchments. By now, all of Robert E. Lee's remaining soldiers had reached the earthworks. The men were exhausted and hungry but still capable of inflicting grievous injury. The Federals lacked the aggression to assault, so the two sides stared at each other. Meanwhile, pontoon bridges were constructed over the Potomac and the Confederate army began to slip across those fragile lines to safety. Lee sent Ewell's corps across the river at Williamsport and Longstreet's men farther south to a crossing called Falling Waters. Hill's corps was the last to leave the entrenchments, with General Heth's division of about 800 men the rear guard.[25] And then finally, on July 13, 1863, it was the Tennesseans' turn to move.

The Tennesseans moved ever so slowly. One wrote, "The night was entirely dark and the roads in a dreadful condition, the entire distance between our breastworks and Falling

Waters being ankle-deep in mud."[26] George Shepard's boys covered seven miles in twelve hours, before halting within two miles of the river. One tired Confederate remembered, "This was the most uncomfortable night I passed during the war; it rained incessantly [and] the roads were eight or nine inches deep in mud and water."[27] For some of the Tennesseans, fatigue, hunger, and despair, combined with this grueling passage, proved to be too much. A Southerner recorded, "While the column was [delayed] on the road, a number of men ... lay down in barns by the roadside, and many were ... left behind."[28] George Shepard's regiment lost a few more of its precious veterans.

Union cavalry pressed up against Heth's feeble division, forcing the general to order his men to turn around and prepare to fight off this Federal attack. The blue cavalrymen, though, would have nothing to do with the gray infantry and backed off, but they did not go away. Instead, the Union cavalry lingered, just out of range, their leaders waiting for an opportunity to strike. George Shepard's men found some rifle pits near a location the locals called Falling Waters. The worn-out Tennesseans stacked their arms, lay down and many went to sleep.[29]

After a two hours' pause a small Union force consisting of less than 100 cavalrymen approached the Confederate line. At first, the sleepy men in Shepard's formation could not determine if the horsemen were friend or foe. General Heth, positioned not far away, recalled; "They galloped up the road and halted some 175 yards from my line of battle. From their maneuvering and the smallness of their numbers, I concluded it was a party of our own cavalry."[30] Then, while the puzzled Southerners watched, the Northerners, men from the 4th Michigan Cavalry, pulled out their sabers and attacked. Shepard described what followed: "Their first charge was upon the 1st Tennessee.... Our men, unfortunately did not have their guns all loaded, and were forced to fight with clubbed guns. The enemy ... moved down the line upon the 13th Alabama, [and] 7th and 14th Tennessee, who by this time had succeeded in getting many of their guns loaded."[31] The attack lasted less than five minutes and nearly the entire Michigan squadron was wiped out. Sadly, in this brief moment of savagery Brig. Gen. James Pettigrew was shot in the groin. Pettigrew died three days later.

Following the Michigan cavalry unit's destruction, the other nearby Yank formations lost all thought of attacking. This lack of aggression gave the Southerners the time they needed to move the last of their wagons and cannon across the pontoon bridges. Finally, Heth's men were given the order to fall back. Lieutenant Colonel George Shepard wrote, "Our route to the river was ... through a dense and tangled copse of undergrowth, with deep ravines running up from the river. We kept our line pretty well organized ... and passed beyond the river."[32] The last of the men raced across the pontoons as engineers stood ready to cut the ropes holding the temporary bridge in place. Lieutenant Jack Moore (Co. B) described this final moment: "We ... barely reached the pontoons as they were cut loose and swung rapidly around to the opposite shore."[33]

Once safely across the Potomac, and free of Federal threat, the battered Confederate army had an opportunity to rest. The Southern infantrymen, many of whom had been separated from their commands, located their formations and muster rolls were recorded. The retreat from Gettysburg had cost George Shepard's tiny regiment the loss of 18 more Tennesseans. The unit's strength now barely topped 80 officers and men.[34] These few survivors clung together, shocked by their losses. Joseph Bashaw (Co. I) succinctly summarized their situation: "We lost a good many."[35]

General Robert E. Lee shifted his army to the Orange Court House area and began the difficult chore of rebuilding. Lee, because many so brigades were diminished in size, and due to a serious loss in experienced leaders, combined units and consolidated commands. The Tennessee men, along with their Alabama brothers, were lumped together into a single brigade with the Virginians led by Col. John Brockenbrough. General Lee had not been satisfied with Brockenbrough's performance during the Gettysburg campaign and removed him from brigade command. Lee promoted Col. Henry Walker to lead the consolidated brigade. Henry Walker, a 31-year-old Virginian, was a West Point graduate who first saw hostilities in Kansas in its bloody enmities before the Civil War. Walker had served the 40th Virginia with distinction and had been wounded twice.[36] The new brigade commander immediately set upon a plan to improve his combined brigade, numbering less than 1,200 veterans.

Lieutenant Colonel George Shepard sent recruiting officers to Knoxville, instructing them to find replacements. Shepard let his recruiters know they could sign up volunteers or invoke the Confederate Conscription Law and draft individuals. The recruiters spread out and collected three dozen men, all of whom signed for the $50.00 bounty.[37] George Shepard was elated by this news and buoyed by a steady return of now-healed wounded veterans and envisioned the 7th Tennessee regaining its pre–Gettysburg numbers.

Unfortunately Shepard was more optimistic than realistic. The Knoxville area of eastern Tennessee was not a good place to collect volunteers to join the Confederate army, as Northern sentiments were strong here. The East Tennessee recruits arrived in camp with anti-war opinions and pro-Yankee attitudes. These feelings, along with their lack of respect for the sacrifices the Confederate veterans had made, created rifts between the two groups. The veterans deepened this animosity by disparaging these new fellows, calling them "conscripts" and belittling their $50.00 bounties. The result was mass desertions by the new recruits. In fact, in August 1863, over half of the entire Knoxville group deserted. One night, August 30, seven men slipped away.[38] September 1863 proved to be equally bad as another eight vanished from the rolls, taking with them equipment, weapons, and morale.

Dismayed by the failure to strengthen the regiment with East Tennesseans, George Shepard turned to Cpt. Fayette Walsh and together the two reduced the number of regimental non-combat positions. They then shunted the Tennesseans holding those positions back to their original companies. These returnees, along with the few conscripts remaining and the additional men coming back from hospital stays bolstered the 7th Tennessee's numbers to 175.[39]

With his army partially mended Robert E. Lee went on the offensive in early October 1863. Lee sent his Second and Third Corps northward. The Tennesseans in Henry Walker's brigade shouldered their bedrolls and with Shepard leading, and Cpt. Archie Norris his second in command, marched toward the Union camps centered north of Culpepper.

The Tennesseans casually moved forward until receiving news Federal troops were retreating. Then, Henry Heth urged the Confederates to hurry after the fleeing Yankees, and as the Tennesseans hustled forward, they saw evidences of an army in flight. One jubilant Southerner wrote, "The road toward Bristoe was strewn with the articles retreating soldiers throw away."[40] General Henry Heth's men, their eyes glowing with the prospect of rich plunder and an easy victory, raced northward. They did not get far; instead, on October 14, 1863, Heth's division ran into a well-defended set of Federal positions along the Orange and Appomattox Railroad tracks. Heth, following orders from his ambitious superior, General Ambrose P. Hill, immediately shifted two brigades to strike this position. He also sent Walker's brigade to guard the division's left flank.

Heth's two brigades, Cooke's and Kirkland's, assaulted the Yank position near Bristoe Station before probing to determine their opponents' strength. The Confederates learned the Yankees were well protected and ready to fight. One rifleman noted, "We received a terrific fire ... and were driven back with considerable loss."[41] In less than thirty minutes Cooke's and Kirkland's brigades lost over 1,300 men.[42] Meanwhile, in Walker's brigade, George Shepard's Tennesseans worked their way through "dense woods ... [for] half a mile," along Broad Run, searching for the bluecoats.[43]

As Cooke's and Kirkland's survivors fell back the quick-thinking Gen. Walker slid his troops in between them and the Federals to cover the disorganized retreat. The Yanks did not advance, so Walker "deployed [his men] as skirmishers ... and remained until ... night [fall]."[44] Fortunately for the 7th Tennessee, this had been another soldiers' fight; only Pvt. Elisha Blackburn (Co. E) was wounded.[45] However, for the men in Heth's division the advance upon the Union position had been a disaster. General Heth, writing in frustration and anger at the orders he had received from A. P. Hill, and the losses he had taken, concluded his report, "We inflicted little loss upon the enemy."[46] Later the next day, once the Federals abandoned their battle line, Robert E. Lee inspected the body-strewn ground and sadly remarked, "Bury these poor men and let us say no more about it."[47]

The Confederate army was pulled back south of the Rappahannock River, and the 7th Tennessee camped without incident for nearly two months. For George Shepard, though, this was a time of hardship; his health failed, forcing him to be hospitalized in Richmond.[48] Captain Archie Norris took over leadership of the regiment with Cpt. James Bass (Co. I) his second in command. Their Tennesseans built shelters and eased into another winter's inactivity.[49]

The Confederates had barely settled down for the winter when, in late November, their stay was interrupted. The Union army pressed southward, and Robert E. Lee responded. He rushed men of his Second Corps forward and they encountered Northern troops on November 27, 1863, in the fields around Payne's farm. The odds were uneven; one Southern division against an entire Federal corps. Repeated assaults and counterattacks by both sides slowly pushed Maj. Gen. Edward Johnson's Southern division backward. One Confederate described the fighting as "a stubborn and confused action."[50] Johnson's men suffered serious losses, but inflicted heavier casualties and gave General Lee time to get the rest of his troops into position.

The Confederate Third Corps, including Heth's division, marched toward the sounds of the fighting. Late that afternoon Brig. Gen. Henry Walker and his brigade reached a tangle of woods just a mile or so south of the battle. Henry Heth assigned Walker the task of deploying his men as skirmishers in front of the division and told them to find the enemy.[51]

Captain Archie Norris fanned out the small 7th Tennessee regiment, his 175 men covering their allotment of the division front. The Tennesseans crept forward through the heavy underbrush as darkness shrouded the landscape. Then, just as vision was obscured by nightfall, the Tennesseans stumbled into a Yank line and rifle fire erupted. The growing darkness only made this inadvertent exchange even more terrifying. Sergeant Robert Irby (Co. D) was seriously wounded. His comrades hauled him out of the line of fire and back to Surgeon James Fite. Unfortunately there was little Dr. Fite could do for the 24-year-old farm boy from Shop Springs, Tennessee; he died soon afterward. The shooting lasted for some time, though it was much more a hide and seek affair with frantic men hunkered down behind trees and aiming at the musket flashes of other men veiled among the foliage. More Tennesseans were hit; James Turnage (Co. C) and Charles Windham (Co. C) were struck down, injured, and David Jennett (Co. C) was killed. Then, the exhausted men were pulled back, the small regiment having lost seven.[52] Later, a Southerner would write, "Heth's division ... was engaged for a while in skirmishing ... but with trifling damage."[53]

Norris' boys were instructed to dig in, an activity the Tennesseans took to immediately. Some men dug deeply while others took axes and cut down the trees and underbrush in front of their position. They created a defensive line which became part of a massive set of entrenchments that "reach[ed] from the Rapidan across some six or seven miles."[54]

The next morning, November 28, 1863, once the Federals realized what the Confederates had constructed, the blue-coated soldiers became reluctant to advance. Instead, the Northerners put out a thin line of skirmishers who immediately found hiding spots. The weather changed and a cold winter rain soaked the men, further disposing the Yanks to inactivity. The Confederates, on the other hand, were anxious to have their enemy attack. They had visions of Fredericksburg in their minds. General Henry Heth even noted, "I was hoping [they] would attack."[55]

November 29, 1863, remained quiet, save for artillery duels. For the boys in Cpt. Norris' command, the highlight of the day came when they observed a Yank run out into the open and try to catch a wild turkey. The bluecoat darted back and forth, chasing the panicky bird, much to the Tennesseans' merriment. Finally though, the persistent soldier caught his quarry and began to carry it away. At this point the Southerners took up their muskets and opened fire. The scavenger dropped his prize and fled, chased away by the Confederates bullets. Then, to everyone's surprise, a Federal general (later identified as Maj. Gen. Gouverneur Warren, commander of the VI Corps) dismounted from his horse and calmly walked out, snatched up the bird and made off with it. The soldiers watched in amazement, and one wrote, "This is the first time on record that a Major General has been known to indulge in a foraging expedition."[56]

The two forces faced each other for another forty-eight hours and yet the Northerners did not attack. Finally, the Union commanders concluded an attack here would be a repeat of Fredericksburg. General Warren, the hero of the turkey catch, noted, "The [Confederate] breastworks ... [were] formidable [with] epaulements and abatis.... [Plus] a run of eight minutes would be required for our lines to close up the distance between them and those of the enemy, during which our entire advancing lines would be subject to every description of fire."[57] On the night of December 2, 1863, the Federal army retreated, ending the Mine Run campaign.

The Tennesseans returned to their winter quarters but soon received orders to travel to the Shenandoah Valley, where they were to join forces with General Early's troops. The Tennesseans reached Staunton, Virginia, on December 15, 1863, and settled in for the winter.[58] The men in Norris' command rested, regrouped, and the regiment slowly increased in strength. One Tennessean wrote, "Fatigue duty was light as the weather was cold ... [and] food was plentiful, even if clothing was not."[59]

Since the Tennesseans' home towns remained under Union control, communications with loved ones was difficult and achieved at great peril; yet, resolute Tennesseans slipped into Wilson, Dekalb, Sumner, and Smith counties and delivered messages to their families. A homesick Thomas Capehart (Co. K) wrote his mother, "I want to hear from you as often as possible. I would like to see you all and be with you all tonight but I will have to wait awhile yet."[60] Capehart continued, writing; "Tell little Hatton [his son, named after Robert Hatton] that he must be a good boy till I come home," and finally Capehart finished the note to his son with, "ask him if he has forgotten me."[61]

Those resourceful Tennesseans who slipped home and then returned to the regiment brought back letters to the homesick boys; the words were treasured, even if the news often was not pleasant. One 16-year-old Tennessean young woman wrote her brother, "All the stores are closed ... [and] I suppose [the Yankees] have killed every rebel within twenty miles of Gallatin and burned every town."[62] She later penned, "Yesterday [the Federals] went up the country a few miles to a Mr. Dalton's, whose son came home from the Southern Army the day before, and had the same day taken the Amnesty Oath.... [They] carried his son a half

DICK R. HAWKINS. Dick Hawkins was born in 1831 in Wilson County, Tennessee. He attended Cumberland University in Lebanon, Tennessee. He enlisted into Company H as a rifleman and was transferred to the commissary department. He vanishes from the military record in December 1862. Dick Hawkins married and settled in Wilson County after the war. His date of death is not known (Loewentheil Family Photographic Collection).

mile away and shot him six times."⁶³ The Tennesseans knew General Lee would not let their regiment go home to Tennessee, a fact difficult to accept. There was nothing they could do except desert, and they were not ready to turn their backs upon their brothers.

Lieutenant Colonel George Shepard returned from his convalescence and resumed command of the regiment. Also, a few more recovering wounded veterans were welcomed back into the ranks. The Seventh Tennessee's recruiters continued to feed new replacements into the regiment, sending three dozen more men to bolster the regiment's numbers. Many of these fellows proved to be able-bodied recruits who remained within the fold. Shepard and Norris looked over the healing regiment and awarded promotions to men who had earned accolades. Captain Archie Norris wrote of William Oliver's (Co. G) advancement, "[William Oliver] has carried the colors of my regiment since the 20th of July 1863 ... [and] on account of gallant and meritorious conduct in the battles of Fredericksburg, Chancellorsville, Gettysburg, and other engagements ... [he] be appointed 'ensign.'"⁶⁴ Oliver would serve as the regiment's adjutant in the upcoming battles.

Winter gave way to spring and with the budding of plants came the knowledge the Yanks would advance again, only this time the Southerners knew the conditions would be different. President Abraham Lincoln had assigned a new general to lead the army facing Lee's, and this commander assembled a huge force with numbers some said tripled what the Confederates possessed. This latest general, Ulysses S. Grant, seemed different; he was a leader pulled from the Western theater, and a chief with claims to many victories, including capturing a Southern army at Vicksburg. The Tennesseans feared this man. Shepard's boys knew he would be different and they dreaded the coming of the warm weather. This coming season of battle was faced with apprehension.

CHAPTER 9

May 4, 1864: Morning

"I can see horrors insurmountable through the summer months."

Lieutenant Colonel George Shepard led the regiment as it marched along the Orange Plank Road, his Tennesseans part of a long column moving toward an imminent collision with the Union army. Shepard, along with the rest of the unit commanders in what now was known as Walker's brigade, knew it was again time for battle. Shepard was worried; the Yankees had a new general, this fellow who seemed different from all the others Lincoln chose in the past. This new commander, Grant, had changed the Union army. Many veteran officers believed this coming meeting with Grant's bluecoats could not come out well. One such officer wrote, "I dread the approaching campaign. I can see horrors insurmountable through the summer months."[1]

Harry Heth's division marched all day on May 4, 1864, covering 12 miles before ending up near Mine Run.[2] The next morning, the men in gray moved out beneath skies choked by a low hanging fog. General Heth's dictates placed Walker's brigade third in line, behind Kirkland's and Cooke's North Carolinians. Trailing behind Walker's men, Heth's final brigade followed: the Mississippians of Davis. Farther behind them, another division followed, that of Maj. Gen. Cadmus Wilcox.[3] These two divisions totaled around 14,000, an impressive amount, but only a fraction of what the bluecoats possessed.

George Shepard's Tennesseans numbered fewer than 200, the smallest they had ever been at the commencement of a summer's campaigning. The regiment had seven captains with the most senior being Archie Norris, who acted as Shepard's second-in-command. The other six led their companies, and most of these formations numbered a dozen rifles or so. And to make matters worse, each of the companies had been weakened by division orders to maintain a division sharpshooter unit (commanded by Lt. Ferguson Harris of Co. H), and a brigade skirmish force (led by Lt. Burgess Wilmouth of Co. A).[4]

The Tennesseans' march was interrupted when word flashed down the column, "The Federals are ahead." Shepard leaned forward, as did each veteran in his formation, because that "message always made hearts beat faster."[5] Then, the ugly, rumbling noises of combat floated down upon them, seeping in from the north. Their column hurried forward, the men no longer chilled by the early morning's dew.

At 1:00 P.M. the Confederate line stumbled to a halt and the leading units deployed skirmishers. The popping of muskets quickly informed everyone the Tennesseans the Yankees had been located. General Heth gave orders to position the division in battle formation. Davis' brigade shifted off the Orange Plank Road, sliding to the north; Cooke's men formed their battle line directly across the road, and Walker's Confederates obliqued to the right and moved south of the highway. Kirkland's brigade inched up behind Cooke's fellows, the division's reserve unit.

Lieutenant Colonel Shepard gave his Tennesseans permission to construct temporary rifle works and within an hour they had worthwhile defenses.[6] One Confederate wrote, "Reaching a slight swell, [we] placed logs on top of the swell ... as shields ... from the Union fire."[7] George Shepard no longer had any qualms about his boys expending this extra effort, though it was possible orders would come to move away, making their exertions for naught. Shepard realized his survivors were different from the ones who filled the ranks a year ago. So many good men were absent. Now, the remaining Tennesseans possessed little inclination to stand unprotected when they had the opportunity to shelter themselves. Every surviving veteran was courageous, but each man understood what a Minié bullet could do. Shepard knew his Tennesseans would perform as required, but few had any proclivity for unnecessary risk. George Shepard appreciated the tenor of his men; they had remarkable mettle, but they would never again make the kind of assault the regiment had at Gettysburg. That type of fortitude had been ripped out of their hearts by Yankee lead.

Not far from the brooding Shepard, Captain Archie Norris conferred with Lt. Burgess (everyone called him "Byrd") Wilmouth. Norris wanted Wilmouth to keep a vigilant watch on the woods in front of the 7th Tennessee's defenses. Burgess, a 33-year-old from Alexandria, Tennessee, was older than most of the fellows. He had owned a blacksmith shop before the war, managed a small number of assistants, and understood the elements of leadership.[8] Byrd Burgess had been the only Company A officer to survive Gettysburg. Then, once Gen. Walker noticed his abilities, Burgess was pulled from his responsibilities as Company A's commander and assigned the duty of commanding the brigade's skirmishers. Thus, this morning the ex-blacksmith led a collection of veterans from each of the brigade's regiments.

Lieutenant Wilmouth motioned to his troops and they climbed over the defenses, deployed into a spread-out skirmish formation, and slipped forward, cautiously searching for the bluecoats. One Southerner noted, "Skirmishers were thrown out on a wide front. Soon the pop-pop of rifles announced they had found the Union skirmish line."[9] The rest of the regiment hunkered down behind the defenses and waited for whatever would happen.

Sergeant Billy Cato moved among the new soldiers making sure they were calm. These fellows had been conscripted in the early months of 1864 and Lt. Col. Shepard assigned most of them to Companies D and E. These new men were important, as they totaled thirty, making them a fifth of the entire regiment's present strength, so it was critical they fit into the organization.[10] These men, none having seen combat before, shifted about nervously, poking their heads up and down, uneasy about the coming moments. Since these men were untested, Sgt. Cato wondered how they would perform once the lead started to fly. These men were older than the original volunteers; many were married and with farms or small businesses in the eastern Tennessee area. Cato figured these fellows would not make a frontal assault, but he believed they would do ok as long as protected by defenses.

Billy Cato watched one of the new fellows, a conscript who seemed to have adjusted to the martial world — Private Sterling Rhea. Sergeant Cato had spoken with Rhea and came away impressed. Sterling Rhea was 35 years old, married and the father of five children. He hailed from Brier Creek, Tennessee, where he owned a blacksmith shop. Rhea had several assistants working for him, including a slave. Sterling Rhea was not a happy conscript, but had vowed to those who could hear that he would serve dutifully.[11] Sergeant Billy Cato hoped this second batch of new replacements were more like Pvt. Rhea than last fall's bunch of misfits.

Suddenly a flurry of rifle fire erupted in front of the defensive line and within moments Lt. Wilmouth and his skirmishers came scampering back. The Tennesseans grabbed their weapons and took position behind the works, knowing Wilmouth's skirmishers were fleeing an advancing body of Federals. Soon, a wall of bluecoats emerged from the trees and, hollering loudly, attacked. General Heth reported, "My line was assailed at 3:30 by a strong line of battle ... the enemy came within 90 yards of my line."[12] The Tennesseans opened fire on the closely packed ranks and slaughtered the advancing Yanks. The attackers did not persist long before turning tail and bolting back to the safety of the trees. However, even before the Confederates' musket barrels had time to cool, another Union formation appeared and marched forward across the body-littered field. General Heth wrote, "The enemy attacked me again, and met with the same fate."[13]

The Federals, Northerners from Brig. Gen. George Getty's division continued to push toward the Confederates, attacking with wave after wave of soldiers; Gen. Heth claimed they made seven separate assaults. But the end result remained the same; the vastly outnumbered Southerners did not budge. They stopped each attack with a sheet of fire. Finally, the Union commander, having squandered his entire division, called off the slaughter and the survivors slunk back into the woods, leaving behind them a field covered with hundreds of casualties.

George Shepard's Tennesseans had weathered each successive attack, protected by their defensive works, and suffered only a few minor injuries, at most, only a handful. The Tennesseans looked out beyond their earthworks and surveyed the destruction. One Southerner simply wrote, "[Our] defense was stern."[14]

Before the Tennesseans could relax, General Henry Heth decided to go onto the offensive. Bolstered by the arrival of men from Wilcox's division, Heth gave the command to counterattack. The Tennesseans, as well as the rest of the men in Walker's brigade, climbed out of their works, hurried across the body-covered field and slammed into the Union division's scattered remnants. The Yanks fled deeper into the thick underbrush. Heth ordered his men to pursue, however as the Confederates pushed farther into this almost-impenetrable wilderness they ran into four new Union brigades, veterans from Maj. Gen. David Birney's division and Brig. Gen. Gershom Mott's division. General Heth recorded, "This proved to be a mistake ... I should have left well enough alone."[15]

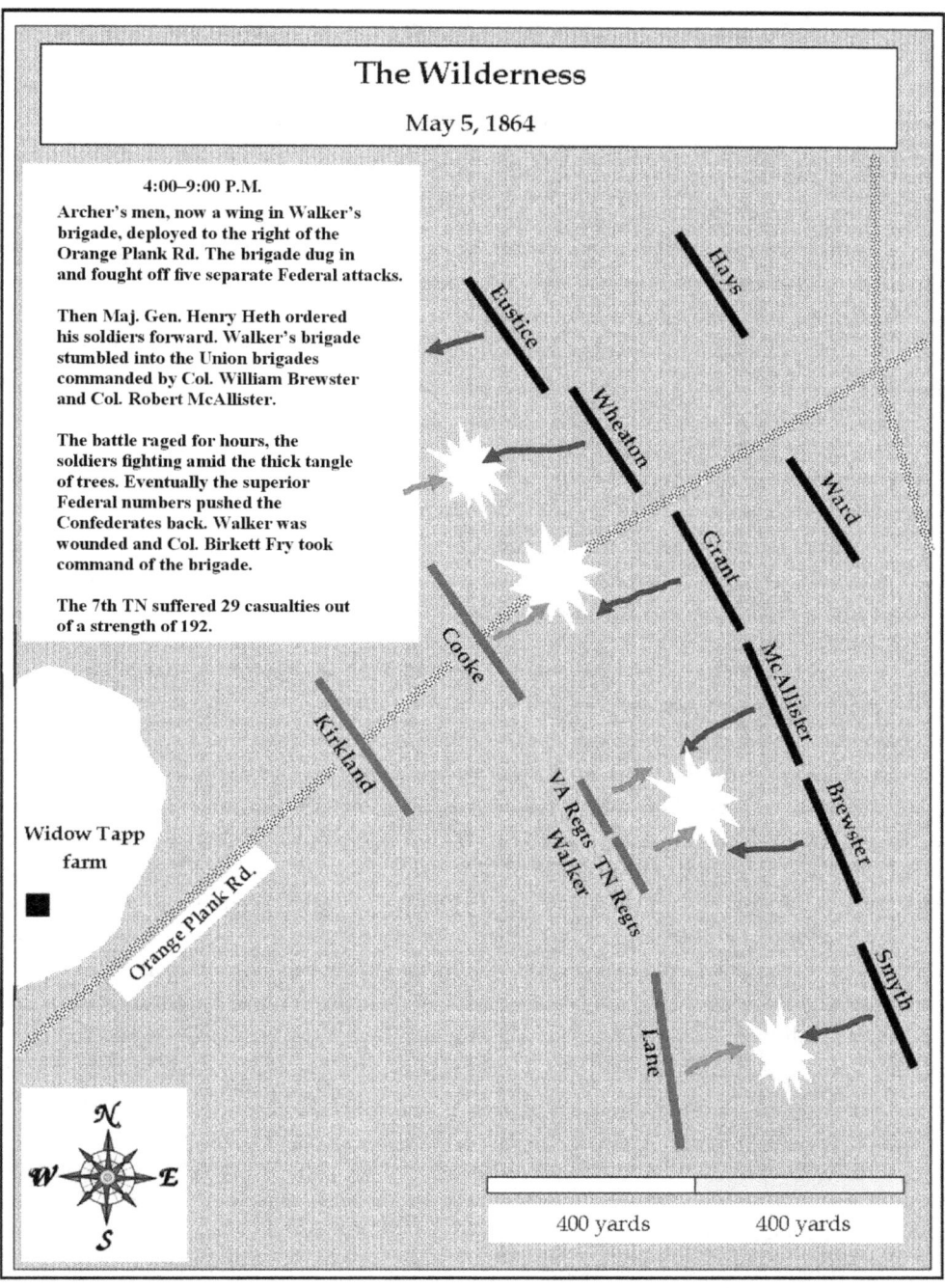

Federal volleys punched through the underbrush, battering trees, fallen logs, and human flesh. Tennesseans began to fall. Pvt. John Hale (Co. B) was killed, Sgt. Thomas Hearn (Co. D) went down wounded, and Cpt. William Graves (Co. G) was struck in the leg. Sergeant John Cheek (Co. A) was killed, Cpt. William Tate (Co. H) fell, hurt by a Minié bullet, and Sgt. John Jennings (Co. I) was wounded.[16] The Tennesseans dropped to the ground and the next series of volleys swept over their heads. The regiment's leaders spurred their riflemen to return fire, but more Yankee bullets struck Shepard's men, and sadly, it was the experienced veterans — men who had survived Gettysburg — who were being struck; Sgt. Alphonso Emerique (Co. A) was killed, 1st Lt. Newborn Jennings (Co. G) was seriously injured, and Sgt. Jesse Cage (Co. E) was wounded.[17]

George Shepard's regiment suffered so many losses among its NCOs and line officers the formation was rendered nearly helpless. Then, another force of Yanks pushed through the thick foliage and smacked into the 7th Tennessee's flank, crushing the regiment. The survivors fell back, leaving behind nearly a dozen men to be captured.[18]

But the 7th Tennessee was not the only regiment in trouble; the entire brigade had crumbled, and men from every regiment streamed toward the rear, fleeing the Yankees pushing toward them. A Confederate noted, "The enemy ... turned on [us] and drove [us] back to the open fields of the Tapp farm."[19] Here, the remnants of Heth's and Wilcox's divisions scratched together a defensive line and held off the Northerners until darkness halted the fighting.

The exhausted and battered Confederates were completely disorganized; companies were scattered, regiments fragmented, and the men of different brigades so intermingled neither General Heth nor Wilcox controlled their men. Both generals wrestled with this chaos, but in the darkness and almost impassable underbrush, little could be done to sort out the confusion. That night a worried General Heth recorded, "A skirmish line could drive both my division and Wilcox's."[20]

For Lt. Col. George Shepard, the afternoon had been nightmarish. His remaining officers and NCOs rounded up as many Tennesseans as they could find and spread them out in a defensive line. The Confederates could not see the bluecoats, as the night was dark and the underbrush frighteningly thick, but the sounds of shovels and axes told them the Yankees were hardly more than fifty yards away. Lieutenant Wilmouth inched forward a skirmish line and these vigilant pickets lay down and stared into the darkness, relying on their ears more than eyes.[21] There would be little sleep for the weary soldiers. Corporal J. P. Bashaw (Co. I) recorded, "That night we rested on our arms."[22]

George Shepard now directed fewer than 150 men. Even more important, this afternoon's fight thrashed his leadership; half of the regiment's companies possessed sergeants as their senior officers. Shepard's riflemen were nearly out of ammunition, had little food, scant water, and no one to turn to for help — Cpt. Fayette Walsh and the regiment's supply wagons were lost in a traffic jam miles away. So, all night long, the lieutenant colonel and his second, Cpt. Archie Norris, moved among their fatigued comrades, apportioning out rounds, and preparing for tomorrow, because they both knew, "We shall certainly be attacked early in the morning."[23]

Much later that night a courier arrived from Gen. Walker ordering Shepard to pull his regiment back to an area where the brigade was being rebuilt. Shepard and Norris woke their men and the tired force followed a guide away from the Union positions and into a thick scrum of vegetation where remnants of Walker's regiments congregated. Shepard's exhausted men lay down with their rifles nearby and quickly fell asleep.

At 5:00 A.M., on May 6, 1864, a single cannon boomed. Then, the Tennesseans heard the sounds of the Union army crashing toward them through the dense foliage. Shepard's tired riflemen gripped their muskets and waited, knowing Confederate troops were between them and the bluecoats. The sounds of gunfire increased as Maj. Gen. Winfield Hancock's five divisions struck the Confederates.[24] There was nothing the Southerners could do to resist this massive tide of Northern steel. General Heth gave the order to "fight in retreat" but the Federal pressure broke the gray line and the Confederates fled in disarray.[25] Corporal Bashaw noted, "They came with such a rush that ... we were all in confusion ... [and] stampeded."[26]

George Shepard, seeing the panicked Confederates fleeing toward them, realized "the crisis was instant and desperate."[27] He immediately ordered the 7th Tennessee to march toward the rear, and in doing so kept the regiment together. The Tennesseans moved back nearly a thousand yards before Shepard turned them around and reformed the line. Shepard's small formation appeared like rock about which hundreds and hundreds of fleeing Confederates scurried past. J. P. Bashaw (Co. I) wrote, "[They] were all in confusion and the officers were trying to rally the men but ... they could not be rallied."[28]

Fortunately, just as Heth's and Wilcox's divisions dissolved into chaos, the leading division of Lt. Gen. James Longstreet's First Corps arrived, men from Texas. They pushed through the tide of broken regiments and headed straight for the blue lines. The Texans were angry at Heth's and Wilcox's rattled men and yelled out, "Do you belong to Lee's Army? ... You don't look like the men we left here ... you're worse than Bragg's men."[29] The Texans, though, saw the 7th Tennessee regiment standing solidly and one Lone Star State officer singled them out, recording, "The Tennesseans came out of the Wilderness in good order."[30]

Longstreet's brigades charged past the Tennesseans and crashed into the Federal divisions, stopping the Yanks' assault. Meanwhile Brig. Gen. Walker struggled to reform his broken formation. By 10 A.M., Walker had reorganized his brigade, though many of his men were badly shaken. General Heth, understanding Walker's brigade's condition, ordered him to move his men to the north of the Plank Road and entrench.[31] Walker's Confederates immediately dug in and within a couple of hours fashioned powerful earthworks. Later, Shepard's riflemen rested inside their fortifications and listened to the dreadful racket of the close-by conflict. The anxious soldiers ate their meager rations, restocked their cartridge boxes, and tended to cuts and bruises, while just a half mile away thousands of men, blue and gray, were locked in a death grip.

That evening the Tennesseans heard James Longstreet had been shot. The veterans moped about, knowing they had lost one of their best generals. They were shocked by the similarities between Longstreet's and Jackson's shootings — both generals had been struck down by friendly fire and both on nearly the same date — just a year apart. Rumors floated along the entrenched formations, some declaring Longstreet was dead, and while others contended he still lived. James Longstreet's condition was serious; "A Minié bullet had entered near the throat and had crashed into his right shoulder."[32]

The evening's nightmare continued; the battle's intensities had been so scorching forest fires erupted in many places. One Southerner wrote, "The reflection of the fire gave the clouds a sickening yellow cast," and even more upsetting, "the nearer men ventured to the fire, the louder were the frantic cries of the wounded."[33] The Tennesseans huddled within their entrenchments, alarmed by the flames spreading near their position. Mercifully, May 7, 1864, dawned quietly and Lt. Wilmouth's pickets reported no activity to their front; news which gladdened the red-eyed and fatigued Tennesseans. The landscape before them had been transformed by the last two days' fighting. Large swaths of blackened forest smoldered and no attempts had been made by either side to bury the dead or to collect the weapons and materials of war strewn about. One Southerner proclaimed it was "a hideous temple of Mars."[34]

The hours trickled by with no renewed fighting, though the danger did not diminish. Snipers popped away, forcing the Tennesseans to hide within their entrenchments. No one wanted to die, and to be shot needlessly was beyond comprehension. So, Shepard's boys huddled quietly, and tried to catch some sleep when not on duty. That afternoon one rumor floating about proved to be accurate; the Yankees were moving away. The Tennesseans hoped the Federals had taken enough of a beating and were retreating, but soon new stories filtered down the line — the Yanks were not retreating; instead they were shifting farther to the south, and the fighting was not over.

May 8, 1864, arrived peacefully. Wilmouth's pickets scoured the front before them and announced it vacated. Captain Walsh brought up rations, and many Tennesseans had slipped out over the battlefield to garner coffee and other amenities from Federal haversacks and packs. The day went by quickly. One veteran wrote, "[We] remained behind [our] breastworks and did not leave."[35] Later that evening George Shepard and Archie Norris attended an officers' call and learned the division would soon be marching southward; General Lee wanted to get his riflemen to another location before Grant arrived. Not long before midnight, the brigade got its orders and the Tennesseans filed out of their entrenchments and marched southward.

Shepard's men stumbled through the dark until reaching a little village called Shady Grove, where they bivouacked. Early the next morning, May 9, 1864, they resumed their trek and reached Spotsylvania Court House. The temperature soared, punishing everyone, but no fighting occurred. Heat may have been tough to endure, but it was much better than the fire from Federal weapons. The sweating Tennesseans grabbed their shovels and dug in, spending the hot afternoon building breastworks. At first there were no bluecoats opposite their positions, but later a Union brigade arrived and quickly put up its own barricades. The two forces glared at each other across an area of several hundred yards, but the soldiers on both sides refrained from shooting. A couple more hours passed quietly, and Gen. Heth reported, "My division lay in front of Spotsylvania Court House and held the extreme right of our army."[36]

Around 3:00 P.M., the Union army stirred, but not where the Tennesseans held their portion of the line. Instead, the Federals, using three divisions in Hancock's II Corps, moved against the Confederates' far left flank, three miles away. General Lee, having only a brigade in that area to hold off nearly an entire corps, ordered Heth to get his division to that location. General Walker's men hustled to cover the southern left flank and reformed with Heth's other brigades near a collection of houses called Waite's Shop. The bluecoats backed off and quickly dug in. Heth ordered his division to move to a position near Glad Run, and the Tennesseans scratched out a defensive line. Corporal Bashaw (Co. I) wrote, "Our boys were lying down behind some little protection that they made with their bayonets by digging up the earth and piling it with their hands."[37]

The next morning, May 10, 1864, General Heth gave the order for his veterans to move against the Northerners. Confederate skirmishers crept forward and easily pushed the Yanks for a quarter mile, back to Waite's Shop. The Union troops resisted but without much determination. It almost seemed as if they had no stomach for a fight, so Heth ordered an all-out assault.

General Hancock's veterans stopped retreating and a fierce fight erupted in the open fields north of the Shady Grove Church Road. One Confederate wrote, "[We] hit them at 2:30 P.M.... The Union Brigade repulsed two attacks before ... [we] enveloped the Union soldiers, pushing them across the [Po] river."[38] Fortunately for Shepard's boys they served as part of a reserve formation, but even so, two more Tennesseans were lost; Pvt. William Rabeck (Co. D) and Pvt. John Nettles (Co. K).[39] Brigadier General Henry Walker also went down, his foot so shattered by a bullet the injury required the amputation of his foot and part of the leg. The shooting tapered off and the Confederates and Federals separated from each other. Then, new orders came from General Lee, directing Heth to get his brigades back to the entrenchments on the army's far right flank. The worn out Tennesseans gathered up their equipment and trudged the four miles back to where they had been just 24 hours ago.

General Heth met with the brigade's senior officers and appointed Colonel Robert Mayo as the new commander. Mayo, a 27-year-old Virginian, had attended William and Mary and the Virginia Military Academy. Following his graduation Mayo taught mathematics at a school in New York. When the war began he joined the 47th Virginia as its major. Robert Mayo assumed command of the regiment in 1862 and led his Virginians from then on. He was a hard drinker and fearless and had been wounded at the Second Battle of Manassas. Thus, when he accepted the congratulations from his fellow officers, they knew their new leader was a war-tested veteran. Mayo immediately let his commanders know he would divide the brigade into two wings, one composed of the Virginians and the second made up of the boys from Archer's brigade.

That evening the veteran Tennesseans set about improving their entrenchments. Their portion of the line protruded out about fifty yards onto a spur of land, forcing the construction of earthworks running at right angles to the main trench line. Shepard's boys fortified this position, making allowances for this difficult slant, and the fact there was only about 50 yards of open ground between them and a stand of pine trees. Lieutenant Jack Moore, who now commanded Company B, wrote, "Our line ... jutted out ... and so abrupt was the apex that traverses had to be constructed to protect our men from enfilading fire."[40]

The next morning, May 11, 1864, began quietly and the Tennesseans took advantage of this lull by improving their entrenchment. Then Lt. Col. Shepard and Cpt. Norris allowed their riflemen to rest and wash. Lieutenant Moore noted, "After ten days of constant service ... not a single soldier ... had time to take his shoes off or wash his face ... [nor] to take time to remove or change his scanty clothes."[41] The Tennesseans napped, grateful the Yankees before them were quiet. Jack Moore recorded, "A deep stillness pervaded, broken only by the incessant and monotonous chirping of the summer beetle."[42]

A shower interrupted the Tennesseans' slumbers, which was followed by a drizzle that increased into a steady rain. The Confederates huddled beneath their ponchos and shelter-halves as the sounds of fighting erupted north of them. The Tennesseans looked to their weapons, wondering when they would be pulled from their works and thrown into the fray. The call to relocate did not come and the Tennesseans battled only the weather. One Confederate noted, "A torrential rain soaked the men and their ammunition."[43]

George Shepard sent Lt. Wilmouth and his skirmishers out in front of their line and they crouched in shallow rifle pits all night, soaked and cold. Then, in the dark, early hours of May 12, 1864, Wilmouth sent back reports of Yankees massing in the woods in front of them. At 4:30 A.M., flashes from muskets lit up the low-lying clouds as Federals rushed toward the Confederate positions, a half mile north of the Tennesseans. The first volleys were followed by a continuous rattle of rifle fire, a noise which would last without stopping for the next twenty hours — the attack upon the Mule Shoe had begun.

The Tennesseans waited for the call sending them into the "Bloody Angle," as well as watching their own field of fire. Finally, as Lt. Jack Moore (Co. B) described, "an ominous sight was presented in the pines ... flocks of small birds and owls ... [flew into] the open space in our front, their flight rapid, low, and meaningless, save their efforts to flee."[44] Shepard's riflemen hardly had time to digest the implications of this spooked flock of birds when Wilmouth's skirmishers opened fire. Wilmouth's pickets dueled with their Yankee counterparts for several hours. At 9:00 A.M., George Shepard could see the Federals forming in the woods. He called in his skirmishers. Lieutenant Byrd Wilmouth, once his riflemen were all safely within the entrenchments, jumped up onto the earthworks and strutted about. Ignoring the calls from his comrades to get down he hollered, "Get ready boys, there are three lines of coffee coming!"[45] Union sharpshooters fired at the reckless officer and he quickly jumped down into the trenches.

Moments later the Federals attacked. General Heth wrote, "My breastworks [were] vigorously assailed by General Burnside."[46] Lieutenant Moore described the assault: "The enemy approached, marching in splendid order, in three lines of battle.... Undaunted they advanced ... and received without wavering, volley after volley, but at length our well-directed fire told on their ranks ... and they retreated to the cover of the pines."[47] Then, a second formation emerged from the woods and advanced. The Confederates poured a sheet of lead into these bluecoats and their ranks fell apart. Jack Moore (Co. B) wrote, "This ended the ... two assaults.... Our loss was ... small, that of the enemy terrible."[48] George Shepard identified one Tennessean killed, Pvt. Isaac Griffin (Co. I), and a small number wounded.[49] General Heth reported, "Their assaults [were] repulsed with great loss ... we counted 300 odd dead in front of our works."[50]

Once this second thrust failed George Shepard noticed Robert E. Lee approach and stop within fifty yards of the Tennessee regiment's position. Lee met with Generals Wilcox and Heth, and a collection of brigade commanders and with great animation pointed toward the fighting to the brigade's north. Lee also faced in the direction of the pine woods from which the Federals had just attacked. Lee made sweeping motions and ordered, "Move your men ... and attack the left flank of the enemy."[51]

Colonel Mayo sent word for the brigade skirmishers and the division sharpshooters to advance. Lieutenants Ferguson Harris (Co. H) and Byrd Wilmouth (Co. A) immediately led their men out of the earthworks and onto the body-littered field. They advanced cautiously, in short leaps and bounds, and crossing the open field and pushing into the edge of the pine woods.

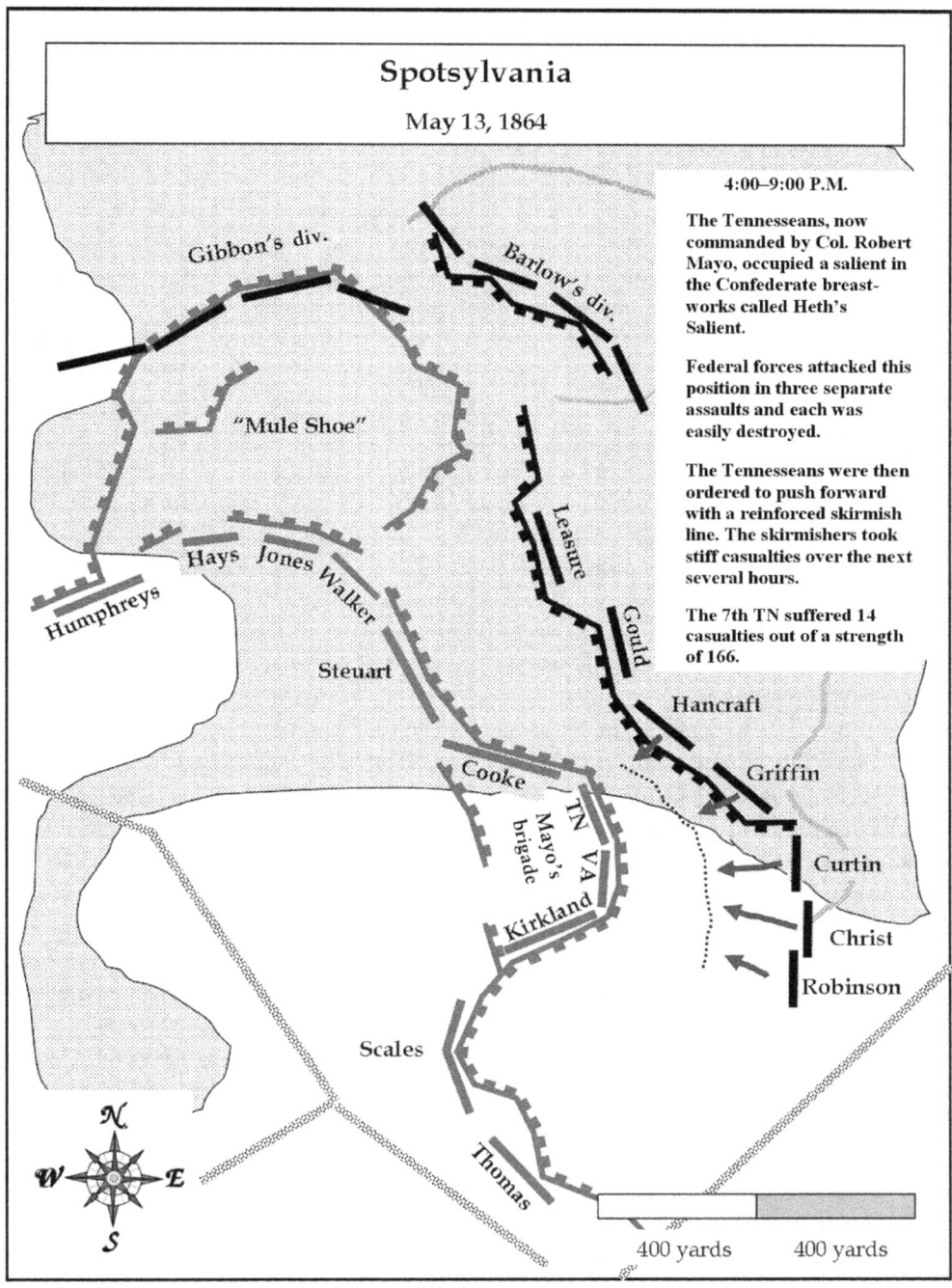

It was at this time that Lt. Ferguson Harris distinguished himself. Years later, Cpt. William Jones (18th VT) wrote, "It was my misfortune to be fearfully wounded ... on that terrible 12th of May 1864, in a charge against a Tennessee brigade.... We were ordered to charge [and] ... a terrible battle ensued. The Tennesseans refused to be driven from their position ... we retired again to our position ... [but] I was left wounded ... the Confederate sharp-shooters ... [were then] thrown to the front under [Lt. Ferguson

Harris] ... his line behaved splendidly under the galling fire that our brigade poured into them.... When the officer reached me I called out to him, 'in God's name give me some water.' He dropped to his knees and raised my head with his left arm and put a canteen to my mouth. I had hardly finished the draught when a bullet ... passed through my throat, and blood spurted from my mouth into his canteen.... He laid my head down gently, saying to himself, 'Poor fellow! He has fought his last battle!' I remember nothing else after he placed his own blanket under my head ... I can say for him that he was the bravest, the coolest, and the [most] kind-hearted man I ever saw."[52]

Lieutenants Ferguson Harris and Byrd Wilmouth and their units were supported by additional troops Colonel Mayo selected, including several companies of 7th Tennesseans. This force advanced into the woods and pushed at the retreating Northerners. Eventually they ran into fresh Yanks and a fierce fight erupted. The Federals attacked the Tennesseans, firing as they closed the range between the two forces, striking some of George Shepard's boys. Private John Close (Co. A) was wounded, Cpl. Oliver Stroud (Co. F) was killed, and Sgt. William Young (Co. I) was injured.[53]

The battle raged beneath the tall pine trees, the soldiers soaked by the falling rain and blinded by the choking smoke. Private George Kittrell (Co. K) was killed, while Privates Frank Goodall (Co. B) and Sgt. John Clemens (Co. I) were wounded. The Yank formation slowly pushed the Tennesseans backward. Lieutenant Byrd Wilmouth went down, a Minié bullet crushing his thigh and severing his main artery. Though his men tried a tourniquet to staunch the bleeding, the 33-year-old Tennessean bled to death.[54] Lieutenant Harris, now commanding the Confederates by himself, and realizing they could not hold back the Union onslaught, ordered a retreat. The Southerners scampered out of the pine woods and back to the entrenchments. The Union troops chased the Tennesseans only as far as the edge of the pine woods. Once the Confederates were safely within their breastworks the shooting tapered off to little more than an occasional sniper shot. Nightfall darkened the battlefield but did not stop the rain's relentless assault. The wet and chilled Tennesseans wrapped their soaked blankets around themselves and tried to sleep, but for those remaining on duty, all throughout the night, they could hear the terrible racket of musketry coming from the Mule Shoe.

The rain finally quit and by sunrise on May 13, 1864, the battlefield was quiet. George Shepard and Archie Norris moved among the regiment, its strength barely more than an early-war company. The two tried to raise their men's morale. The weary Tennesseans all agreed a day of sunshine and no fighting would certainly help, but Mother Nature did not approve. A grumbling Southerner recorded, "Heavy rain began on the morning of the 13th and lasted for [two] full days."[55]

George Shepard sent out a thin screen of skirmishers and they hunched down, enduring the night's discomfort. Corporal William Clendening (Co. E) wrote, "[The] firing ceased during the night, and a picket line was established across the field of carnage. The post assigned me was in the midst of the dead and dying ... the groans of the wounded could be heard all along the line. I groped my way over the field in search of something to eat. I stumbled over what I supposed to be a log, but it proved to be a dead man whose haversack was well filled with bacon and hardtack. Availing myself of this treasure, it was immediately transferred to my shoulders, and in a short time my hunger was appeased."[56]

The rain finally ceased and the soldiers had a chance to dry. On May 17, 1864, the sun burned with unusual heat, hastening the drying process. Corporal J. P. Bashaw (Co. I) noted, "The rain stopped.... Two other men and I ... were detailed to go back to the wagon train about a mile back and cook up rations. Between getting the fire started, finding the meal, skillets, and water, we had quite a time ... [cooking] our cornbread."[57] The next day the Confederate army again went into motion, though the Tennesseans remained, leaning against their earthworks and watching thousands of soldiers file past, all heading south.

The Tennesseans left their entrenchments on May 21, 1864, and marched eleven miles. The next day they covered fifteen more before camping two miles south of the North Anna River. From there they hiked along the Virginia Central railway tracks to Jericho Mills. The brigade caught up with the two armies, who now battled for possession of the North Anna River crossings. The Tennesseans raced to support General Wilcox's division, but before they could reach the battlefield the fight between Wilcox's men and General Warren's V Corps ended.

That evening while George Shepard's boys bivouacked along the railroad tracks he and Archie Norris were called to a brigade officer's meeting. Shepard and Norris were surprised to find Gen. Harry Heth joining the Tennessee and Virginian officers crowding around their commander, Robert Mayo. Heth informed the officers he was replacing Mayo and elevating Birkett Fry to brigade command. General Heth was unhappy with Robert Mayo and still smarted from criticism he had received because of actions taken by some of his brigades during Pickett's Charge. Heth also used Mayo's early-war drinking conviction as a reason to reduce his responsibilities.[58]

George Shepard was familiar with Birkett Fry and greatly respected the gritty officer. Fry, though wounded and captured near the stone wall at Gettysburg, had been exchanged and returned to the Confederate Army. He now assumed command of the combined brigade, now numbering less than 800 muskets. Once Heth left the meeting, Fry gave instructions for the regiments to dig rifle pits and prepare for a Yankee attack. Later, a Tennessean noted, "The Tennessee brigade ... built a fortified line [a half mile] from Oxford Mill."[59] The brigade remained along this line until May 27, 1864. The Tennesseans relished those days of quietness, though they were surprised by the Northern hostilities at night. One such nocturnal raid struck the Confederate picket posts and five Tennesseans were captured.[60] When orders came for the brigade to march, George Shepard's formation now totaled only 145.

The 7th Tennessee trekked eight miles on May 27, 1864, and eight more the next day. They reached a position along Totopotomoy Creek and immediately "commended digging entrenchments and fortifications."[61] Meanwhile, both Lee's and Grant's armies jockeyed into position, facing each other along a line extending nearly seven miles. Again, Lee's men had arrived to the scene before Grant's, and in the critical hours before the Union divisions took up positions the Southerners amplified their strength by digging breastworks. George Shepard and Archie Norris liked their regiment's new position. Their Tennesseans had become expert at quickly turning an open field into a highly defensible position. The two officers agreed; it only took their men a few hours. They were becoming "kings with spades."

On May 31, 1864, heavy Union attacks against Confederate positions about a mile to the left of their brigade forced Heth to send Birkett Fry and his Tennesseans and Virginians to assist Maj. Gen. John Breckinridge's troops. Fry's riflemen arrived, but by the time they pressed up behind the embattled Confederates the Union resolve had withered. Breckinridge, with Fry's support, pushed the bluecoats back to their lines. Sadly, even as the Federals retreated, their rifle fire struck with accuracy; Cpl. Benjamin Curry (Co. G) was killed and Sgt. John Lanier (Co. F) was wounded in the right hand.[62] Once the crisis ended Birkett Fry led his men back to their entrenchments. They arrived at sunrise, exhausted. However, after only a couple hours of sleep the tired men were awakened and ordered to march. Birkett Fry led his small force out of their works and to Hundley's Corner, near the far left end of the Confederate line. That evening Union cavalry probed the brigade's skirmish line, and Pvt. William Steed (Co. K) was severely injured.[63]

On June 2, 1864, two hours before sunset, orders came to advance. George Shepard and Archie Norris directed their small collection of veterans forward, part of a Confederate strike against Gen. Ambrose Burnsides' bluecoats. The Southerners raced forward and surprised the Yanks as they ate their dinner. The shocked Federals scrambled to their weapons and fought back. Yankee lead took its toll among the Tennesseans; Pvt. William Lindsey (Co. K) and Pvt. James Smart (Co. K) were knocked down, wounded.[64] The fighting lasting only a few minutes before Burnside's men spilled out of their rifle pits and fled. One Confederate wrote triumphantly, "[We] swept over Burnside's forces ... and captured hundreds of prisoners."[65]

By now the Confederate defensive line had become impenetrable. Lee's engineers, his soldiers, and hired crews with slave gangs had constructed works one Southerner described as "a maze and labyrinth of works within works ... [with] intricate, zig-zagged lines within lines [and] lines protecting flanks of lines [and] lines built to enfilade an opposing line."[66] The writer also noted, "Artillery [was] posted with converging fields of fire ... and stakes were driven into the ground to aid gunners' range estimates."[67] Any attempt by Grant to attack this formidable line could only result in a terrible slaughter. This fact emboldened the Confederates. They were confident no fighting would occur — Grant would not be that stupid.

The next morning, June 3, 1864, dawned with a thick ground fog, and the Union commanders facing the defenses occupied by the Tennesseans chose this opportunity to strike. Moving quickly, men from Brig. Gen. Robert Potter's division rushed forward and attacked the Confederate's forward rifle pits. George Shepard's men occupied many of those rifle pits, and they were quickly overrun. Private Sion Peek (Co. I) was mortally wounded in the right breast, Cpt. John Sloan (Co. F) was shot through the thigh, Sgt. James Watkins (Co. D) was struck in the forehead, and Lt. John Lapsley (Co. B) was wounded in both legs.[68] Then, a group of Northerners raced forward, silenced a battery of artillery, and succeeded in blowing up two caissons before a Southern counterattack drove them away. The men in Birkett Fry's brigade did not know of the tremendous slaughter occurring several miles south of them. There, not far from the little community called Cold Harbor, Grant launched a massive force of nearly 20,000 soldiers against the heavily defended Confederate entrenchments. The brave Union troops were butchered, suffering over 7,000 casualties.

Later that afternoon, once most of the fighting tapered off, a force of Union cavalry advanced against Fry's outposts, and in a brief but costly fight several Tennesseans were lost. Sergeant George Washington Huddleston's (Co. G) left foot was mangled by a cavalryman's carbine bullet, Pvt. Ira Royster (Co. B) was shot through both legs, and Pvt. William Munsley (Co. E) suffered a scalp wound.[69] Moore (Co. B) wrote, "Lieut. [William] Baber [Co. C] was shot ... while standing by my side, when a bullet passed through his shoulder and grazed my coat."[70] Thus, by the time the sun set that evening, the 7th Tennessee had lost another ten veterans, including Sgt. Huddleston, whose leg needed amputation. Unfortunately Huddleston's leg became infected. He died a few days later.[71]

June 4, 1864's sunrise came with the prospect of more Union attacks; but the men from the North had suffered enough. A Confederate wrote, "Nothing happened except some light skirmishing."[72] George Shepard now had only 130 boys from Wilson, Smith, Dekalb and Sumner counties remaining. His Tennesseans kept their heads down, and for the next week, as one noted, it was "seven days of stench and sharpshooting, thirst and heat."[73]

On June 13, 1864, Shepard's pickets reported the Union forces gone. The Tennessean sent out an exploratory force and they returned, confirming their pickets' accounts — the Yankees had slipped away during the night. This news did not delight the Confederates, who now realized General Grant was not going to quit; they guessed the bluecoats had just shifted their forces farther south. Orders from General Heth verified what Shepard's veterans surmised; they were to march southward. The Tennesseans filed out of their entrenchments and headed toward the James River.

On June 18, 1864, the 7th Tennessee crossed the James River on a pontoon bridge near Chafin's farm and journeyed on to Petersburg. As the battle-weary Confederates trekked through the city one citizen observed: "But oh! So worn with travel and fighting, so dusty and ragged, their faces so thin and drawn by privation that we scarcely knew them."[74] The men were not allowed to stop in the city and soon found themselves a mile south, along the Boydton Plank Road. They immediately began digging trenches, not even taking time to eat. Once darkness set in a soldier recorded, "The men were tired and hungry."[75]

Union troops approached the Southerners' partially completed earthworks the next day and the popping of skirmishers forced a halt to the digging. Shepard's men remained on the alert and did not continue working on their defenses until nightfall. Corporal J. P. Bashaw (Co. I) wrote, "The battle lines were [close] ... and at night under the cover of darkness each side threw up breastworks."[76] The next morning, June 20, 1864, the Confederates prepared for the Union attack, but the Yanks did not venture out of their works. The two sides stared at each other, 750 yards apart. Bashaw recorded, "The breastworks were worked on each night until raised to a height above our heads and we fired through portholes."[77]

On June 25, 1864, the brigade was ordered out of their works, back through Petersburg, across the Appomattox River and north of the city to a location where Swift Creek joined the Appomattox River. Here, the Confederates manned Fort Clinton, a post overlooking the Appomattox River. The tired Tennesseans quickly realized they had been assigned light duty and relished the next week rotating through details of picket duty and watching the river for enemy gunboats. Alas, just as Shepard's boys were getting used to this easy routine orders came bringing them back to the trenches south of Petersburg.

On July 4, 1864, the brigade moved into rifle pits on the far right of the Confederate line, near the Weldon and Petersburg tracks.[78] Here, the Tennesseans remained, digging entrenchments. Corporal J. P. Bashaw (Co. I) wrote, "The company was divided into thirds and one third of the men were at the portholes firing all the time, one third strengthening the fortifications, while the others were supposed to be asleep."[79] Their defenses were soon so strong any attempt to take their works would produce devastating losses, so the Federal troops settled in, satisfied to pin the Confederates to this position west of Petersburg. The Union forces then began artillery attacks using a new weapon, one the Tennesseans quickly grew to hate — mortars. Bashaw recorded, "We had pens built and covered with logs and dirt to protect us from mortar fire ... when the mortar fire began we would get in the pens for protection."[80]

Mortar shells rained down upon the Confederate works intermittently, forcing Shepard's men to scurry to their bombproofs for protection. Though few soldiers were hurt, the stress of uncertainty began to take its toll. The mortar fire also destroyed parts of the walls, compelling the riflemen to rebuild the damaged portions. Union snipers then focused on these sections of wall. Corporal Bashaw noted, "We worked on the fortifications at night so that the Yankees could not see us, however, they kept firing all the time so as to hinder our work."[81] This work was dangerous business, and Bashaw described a close call: "The detail I was with was given shovels and told to go to work. We were placed out in front of the fortifications on the open ground. We went at it for dear life, while the bullets were flying. As I was working a bullet hit the dirt as I threw it out of the shovel."[82] Other Tennesseans were not so fortunate; Pvt. Germain Shoemaker (Co. B), a 20-year-old farm boy from Carthage, Tennessee, was struck and killed by a sniper on July 10, 1864.[83]

The summer sun bore down on the war-weary soldiers. Bashaw lamented, "The troops had to contend with the hot sunshine and the bite of the dog flies during the day and through the night, with mosquitoes and mortar fire.... It was almost impossible to get any sleep."[84] The Tennesseans went through the motions of manning the lines and keeping themselves out of danger but their growing exhaustion made them prone to accident and danger. General Heth began rotating his brigades in and out of the line, enabling the weary men an opportunity to get away from the front lines, clean up, eat a hot meal or two, and sleep through the night without interruption. Birkett Fry's brigade alternated with William Kirkland's North Carolinians. An appreciative Tennessean wrote, "No troops could endure the hardships on the front line duty but a week or so. [We] were given frequent periods of rest."[85]

Birkett Fry's brigade rotated in and out of the trenches throughout the month of July 1864. The brigade's strength numbered around 700 men until the 2nd Maryland battalion was added, giving the formation another 150 rifles. The 2nd Maryland consisted of five consolidated companies and was commanded by Captain James Crane. The regiment came to the brigade possessing a tough reputation and was known for its resilient morale.[86] These veterans were readily accepted by the Tennesseans and Virginians.

When it was Fry's brigade's turn to switch out with Kirkland's boys, his soldiers moved away from the horrors of the trenches. A thankful veteran wrote, "[We] bivouacked in a little valley about one hundred yards wide, the hills on either side crowned with a few stately pines, and a bold stream coursing through the center."[87] This was a perfect location for battle-weary soldiers to rest.

On July 30, 1864, while the 7th Tennessee was away from the line, Grant tried a new tactic: exploding a mass of gunpowder beneath the Confederate lines. This gamble occurred several miles from the Tennesseans' position. Birkett Fry ordered his soldiers to form up and rushed them toward the fight taking place around the crater, but by the time Fry's men arrived they were not needed. Fry turned his men around and sent them back. Corporal Bashaw (Co. B) wrote, "We rushed back to the [Battle of the Crater] but got there too late for the fun."[88] Other Southerners saw nothing positive about the fight; instead, one wrote, "The explosion of a mine was a mean trick ... [and] the use of Negro soldiers an infamy."[89]

A few days later the Tennesseans returned to the lines for another week of "mortar fire, hot sun and dog flies in the daytime, and rebuilding breastworks at night."[90] Eventually, as the summer slowly passed, these afflictions were not all the Confederates had to worry about. Another concern grew among the entrenched Southerners — food — as their rations had become undependable and often paltry. One Confederate complained he was "without shelter from the weather, half-starved ... [and] subjected to a steady fire from the enemy."[91] The homesick Tennesseans' morale began to slip. They still manned the rifle ports when it was their turn, but fewer fellows volunteered for picket duty, and almost none wanted to be out when the mortar shells dropped down into the trenches. A soldier noted, "The wane in morale [increased] ... there was no great battle any day but a small battle [to stay alive] every day."[92]

On August 13, 1864, Brig. Gen. James Archer resumed command of the brigade. The tenacious Archer had returned to the Army of Northern Virginia, eager to fight, though still in poor health. Archer had convinced the Confederate high command he was able, and Robert E. Lee, desperate for experienced senior leadership, returned him to command of his old brigade. Birkett Fry, now relieved of brigade command, and because he possessed the rank of brigadier general, could not go back to his old regiment. Instead, General Fry was dispatched to oversee operations in a South Carolina and Georgia district.[93] Then, as the Tennesseans despondently bid Birkett Fry good-bye, James Archer ordered the brigade back to the trenches.

Days later, as the tired Southerners moved back to their recovery camp, they were "so drenched with rain that the fields were well-night impassable."[94] Then, even before the wet troops could start their much-needed rest, the heavy sounds of artillery floated toward them, followed by frantic orders to march. General Archer hustled his brigade into formation and his men joined the boys commanded by Brig. Gen. Joseph Davis, and they raced south to a point near the Vaughan Road, where it intersected with the Weldon and Petersburg Railroad tracks. They formed up, Davis's brigade to the west of the tracks, and Archer's unit just east. Then they advanced.

Lieutenant Colonel George Shepard's 140 veterans moved forward cautiously, passing through a stand of woods before coming out onto an open pasture. A rifleman wrote, "As we emerged from the woods the view that presented itself was an open space, nearly level, about half a mile wide, with a forest on the southern side."[95] The Tennesseans could see a Yank formation forming a battle line amid a belt of distant trees. The command was given and the stubborn Southerners rushed across the field, hollering the rebel yell.

The Confederates got about halfway across the field before the bluecoats opened fire. Private James Patton (Co. H) went down, struck by a Minié bullet. Sergeant John Powell's (Co. K) left wrist was broken, and Pvt. William Barner (Co. D) also was injured.[96] The Tennesseans closed upon the Federals, firing as they moved. One Confederate recalled, "Onward we moved, our line being bent like a bow."[97] Parts of the Union line collapsed, while other Yank companies held firm. These stubborn formations continued to pour lethal fire into the Confederates. Private Lafayette Parvine (Co. B) went down, his left thigh shattered. Parvine had been a regimental teamster for most of the war and had just recently been returned to the ranks when Shepard and Norris tried to refill the organization with more combat troops. He was carried back to Surgeon James Fite, who was forced to amputate his leg. Lafayette Parvine's stump did not heal well and infection set in. The 25-year-old Tennessean died in late September 1864.[98]

The Tennesseans climbed over a fence and pushed closer. The remnants of the Yank line dissolved and the bluecoats fled. A rifleman noted, "As we entered the woods ... we drove the enemy back easily."[99] George Shepard and Archie Norris collected their veterans and reformed the regiment. They continued this advance for several hundred yards through the woods. The Confederates halted at the woodlot's edge as another force of Federals appeared. The Tennesseans held a strong position amid the trees, and as the Union line approached, the Tennesseans poured a devastating fire into them. The Northerners were staggered by the Confederate fire and withdrew. One Southerner wrote, "[We] ... formed [our] line at the edge of the woods and fought off an attack."[100] Another wrote, "The enemy attempted to charge us, but a few well-directed volleys drove them back."[101]

Another Yank unit formed a battle line but did not move forward. The two forces stared at each other. Darkness settled the conflict; Gen. Archer pulled the brigade back, and the tired soldiers quickly dug rifle pits. An exhausted rifleman wrote, "The night was dark and damp. We kindled our fires, roasted our corn, and lay down on our wet wrappings."[102]

Sunrise on August 19, 1864, revealed an unwanted fact—more Union troops had arrived during the night. General Archer met with his regimental commanders and explained the Confederates' dire situation; the Yanks had taken possession of a portion of the Weldon Railroad. If the Federals were not driven from this position, a major supply route into Petersburg would be cut. The Southerners already were feeling pinched by their nation's weak logistical network; if they lost this supply route, rations would be even more difficult to acquire. The brigade's officers returned to their commands, anxious to explain the situation to their wary riflemen.

George Shepard addressed his brother Tennesseans; there were only 135 left, standing close by in the drenching rain. The Tennesseans listened to their commander respectfully, while gazing out at the strong Union formations. The Tennesseans looked to each other, their faces grim. To fail in this upcoming assault meant even tighter food supplies. But

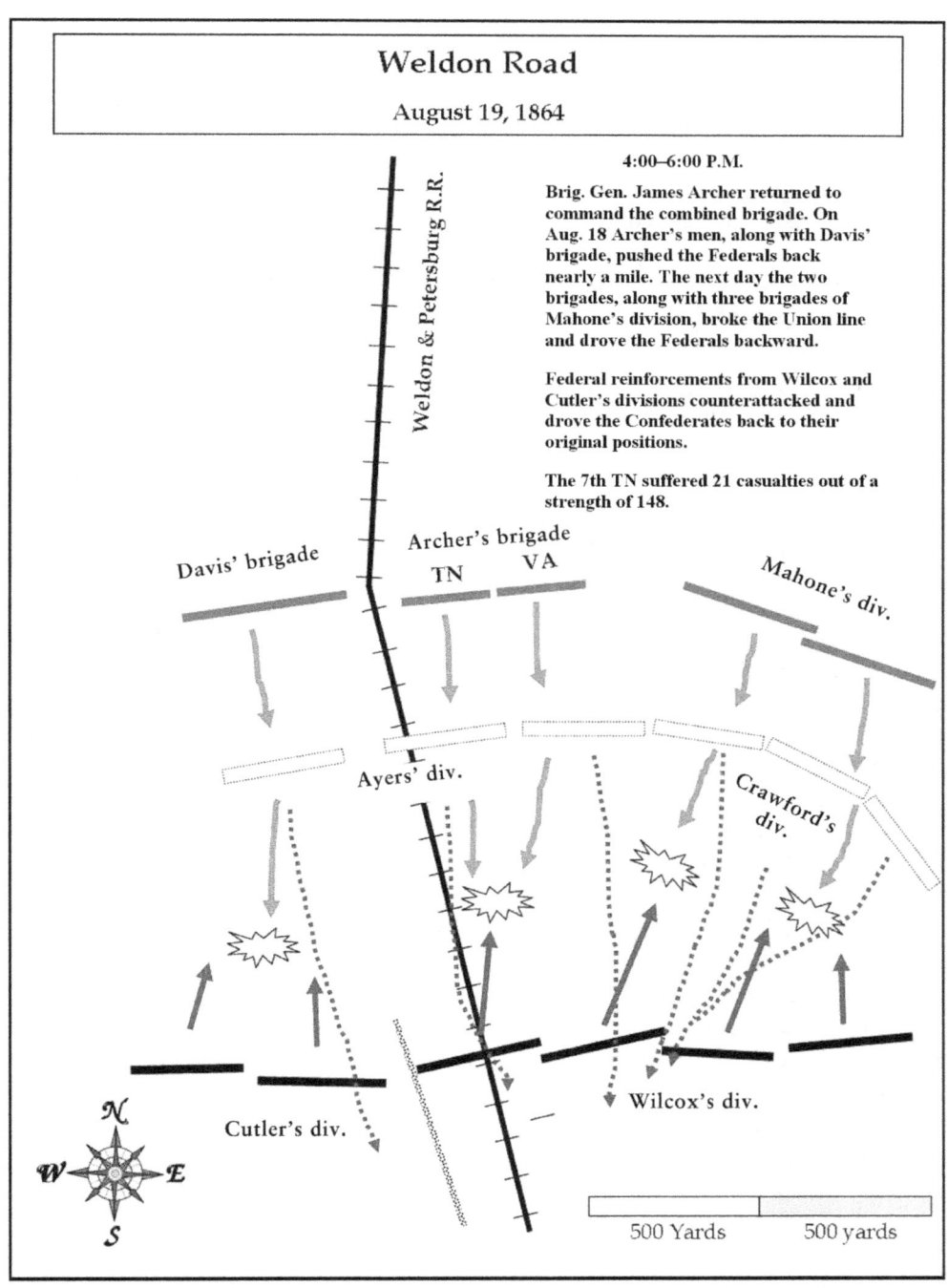

the veterans also knew what they faced — tough, veteran Yankees, well equipped, rested, and with full haversacks. Those Northerners occupied a strong position along the tracks, protected by the railroad's berm. The Tennesseans shook their heads in dismay; this was like Pickett's Charge all over again. This attack today could produce the same results. No one wanted to be the next person killed. No one wanted to be the next person lying on the ground, screaming in agony — plainly, no one wanted to make this attack. But they all listened to Shepard's aching words and knew they would go forward when the call came. Shepard ordered his veterans to spread apart, hoping this would make them harder to hit. The Tennesseans did as their commander ordered; after all, they stood by each other, and had done so for a long time.

At 4:00 P.M. General Heth gave the order to attack. Shepard's men advanced "through the drenching rain ... upon nearly the same ground."[103] The Yanks facing the Confederates were from the division commanded by Brig. Gen. Romeyn Ayers. Their first volleys crashed into the Confederate line. Private John Sullivan (Co. I) was struck in the left arm, Pvt. David Hamilton (Co. H) was hit in the leg, and Pvt. Thomas Davis (Co. A) went down, hit twice, in the right thigh and in the head.[104]

Strangely, the Yanks' initial volleys seemed feeble and misdirected, enabling the desperate Confederates to advance without suffering the horrible losses they expected. The Tennesseans did not know three other Confederate brigades, men from Maj. Gen. William Mahone's division, had swept down upon the Yanks' far right brigade, flanking the entire Federal battle line. The distracted Federals firing at the Tennesseans were much more concerned by this threat. A Union officer recorded, "Mahone, who was best acquainted with the woods, burst in on Ayer's right and swept down on [them] ... and seizing parts of the main line."[105]

The Yanks resisted only briefly once Archer's men reached their earthworks. A Southerner recalled, "The enemy was driven back, and the first line of works were soon in [our] hands."[106] George Shepard and Archie Norris rallied their small band of veterans together, grateful in having lost only a handful. Orders came to advance, and the 7th Tennessee moved forward, aligned with the other units in the brigade. Union troops from deep within the woods fired into the Tennesseans, knocking down, Pvt. William Rogers (Co. D) and Pvt. John Kennedy (Co. G).[107]

Archer's men captured the Yankees' second and third line of works before their advance stalled. Hundreds of frightened Federals milled around, surrendering or just cowering in their rifle pits. Quick thinking Federals held up haversacks and offered them to their captors. Others scampered about, forcing Confederates to chase them down. The resulting chaos ended the Southerners' advance. One Confederate wrote, "After driving the Yanks a considerable distance [we took many] ... prisoners."[108]

The hungry Southerners emptied captured packs and haversacks, snatching up rations and coffee. Archer's officers frantically struggled to maintain control over their excited men, knowing the day's fighting was not over yet. Two Union brigades advanced and obliquely struck Archer's disorganized men. The Confederates, standing amid piles of captured supplies, fought back. One Southern rifleman noted, "[Our] little brigade was battling with an overwhelming force ... for over an hour this unequal contest was waged."[109] Sergeant John Williamson (Co. H) was wounded; Pvt. Charles Robison (Co. I) went down, as did Pvt. David Sweet (Co. E) and Pvt. Winfield Eatherly (Co. H).[110] The entire Confederate line dissolved into bedlam and the Tennesseans' resistance crumbled. They fell back through the woods, the Yankees close behind, catching up scores of Confederates. One of these captured veterans, Corporal Joseph Bashaw (Co. I), simply noted, "I was taken prisoner."[111]

Archer's men were driven from the woods and onto a pasture, and from there into a field of corn. Here, amid the safety of the cornstalks, the Southerners' officers reassembled their formations. Brigadier General James Archer was adamant they retake those lost earthworks. If the Confederates could recapture those trenches they could continue to protect the Weldon railroad tracks; otherwise the railroad was lost, as well as the provisions which traveled those rails. Archer called for another assault, a desperate bid to save the railway.

George Shepard, anxious to keep his small command together, shouted at them to follow as he moved forward and out of the cornfield. Again, he spread his small force out in skirmish formation. The Southerners double-quicked forward toward the Union riflemen. The Federals immediately responded. One Federal officer recorded, "The enemy, collecting in a cornfield, came forward ... [and] Hartranft['s] brigade ... [struck] them under a terrific fire of musketry."[112] Private James Williams (Co. E) was killed, Pvt. John Lane (Co. K) took a Minié ball in his left side, and Pvt. James Craft's (Co. F) right leg was shattered.[113] The attack collapsed and the survivors scurried back to the cornfield, leaving behind them a field littered with casualties.

James Archer screamed at his regimental commanders to get their units back together. He demanded they retake those trenches, regardless of the cost. Davis's brigade formed up besides Archer's and both generals goaded their men to make one more assault. Everyone was exhausted. No one relished the idea of another attack; everyone knew the results. But when the call came to advance, the Tennesseans, once again, stepped forward with their Confederate brothers.

Federal musketry ripped through the Southerners, but the Confederates kept coming. A Union officer wrote in admiration of this Tennessee valor: "The stubborn Heth made his third, last, and most desperate attack."[114] In George Shepard's scruffy little formation, Pvt. Richard Gibbs (Co. B) fell, struck in the right leg, and Pvt. William Elliott (Co. C) suffered a slight injury.[115] The gray formation closed upon the Yank battle line, moving to nearly seventy-five yards distance. The Federal fire increased as the Southerners got closer. Private Benjamin Sullivan (Co. I) was wounded, and Pvt. Hugh Baird (Co. F) went down, hit in the foot.[116] The assault fell apart. A Federal wrote, "[My men] were stronger, both in troops and position.... Heth ... made a gallant charge [and] was repulsed."[117] General Henry Heth wrote with disappointment, "Another attack was made on the enemy but failed to accomplish anything."[118]

George Shepard and Archie Norris collected their survivors and led the miserable Tennesseans from the battlefield. Their attacks had failed, nearly two dozen more Tennesseans were gone, and they knew the railroad had been lost. The Confederate supply situation would now be extremely difficult. Every Tennessean knew hunger faced them with even a tighter clamp than before. They shook their heads in dismay, both at this battlefield defeat and at their terrible loss of comrades. Nothing good was coming of this war.

General James Archer sent word to Shepard to take his men back to the Petersburg trenches. They were to occupy a position in the lines near Battery 37, just south of the city. Here, the brigade remained for several weeks, "constantly engaged on the fortifications and in manning the trenches."[119] Then the weary men were shifted several miles west and ordered to commence the construction of fortifications parallel to the Boydton Plank

Road. The Tennesseans had nothing left; they were completely spent. No one looked forward to what the future would bring. There were too many Yankees, and the enemy had so many cannons, and plenty of everything the Confederates lacked. The coming months could bring only misery. Regardless of this situation, the Tennesseans remained, following orders, manning the trenches, and attempting to hold the line.

Chapter 10

October 20, 1864: Afternoon

"Who will be the last of us to go?"

General Heth's division now protected four miles of the Confederate defenses, with each of the four brigades charged with an equal distance.[1] This meant Brig. Gen. James Archer's brigade protected a mile's length of trenches. Archer's formation possessed about 800 officers and men, and the veterans knew there no longer would be brigade exchanges; all relief would occur within each individual unit. At best, Archer believed half the brigade could man the trench positions while the other half rested—400 men guarded nearly 6,000 feet of works—that was a man every five yards.

George Shepard had eight captains and four lieutenants. Of these, Archie Norris was the regiment's most senior captain. Captain Norris had been serving as second in command since Gettysburg and led the formation whenever Shepard was away. The next ranking line officer was Cpt. Lafayette Walsh. Captain Walsh had directed all of the regiment's logistical needs since the Fredericksburg campaign but no longer had any supply task duties, so he now led Company D.

The Seventh's other senior captain was John Allen, who had been severely wounded at Gettysburg and left for dead. A Southerner noted John Allen's "strong vitality pulled him through ... and after a long time in prison he secured an exchange [and] returned."[2] But Allen was no longer with the regiment; instead he served as Brig. Gen. Archer's brigade adjutant. Allen's company duties were handled by 1st Lt. Jack Moore. George Shepard's remaining captains, Robert Miller (Co. E), John Sloan (Co. F), William Graves (Co. G), William Tate (Co. H), and James Bass (Co. I), all led their companies.

George Shepard's regiment had nearly 150 officers and rifles, and another thirty who performed noncombat roles. That fall Shepard had instructed Cpt. Walsh to strip all the non-combat soldiers from their duties and return them to their companies. The 7th Tennessee was not going anywhere; there no longer was any need for teamsters or for wagon guards or extra quartermasters. Fayette Walsh had kept only the essential support people: an ordnance sergeant, a commissary NCO, and a quartermaster sergeant. Of course, Doctor James Fite had his staff, including assistant surgeon Thomas Webb, a hospital steward, and one male nurse. The 7th Tennessee's remaining support personnel were its two sutlers, James Bradley and James Corder, and the regimental chaplain, James Harris. Everyone else was handed a musket and reported back to their original companies.

The Tennesseans moved into the Confederate defenses, three miles west of Petersburg, and as one rifleman noted, "Work details were busy extending the fortifications."[3] They dug trenches four to five feet deep, and six to eight feet wide, and heaped the unearthed dirt in front to further heighten the shielding walls. Sandbags and timbers were used to shore up the walls. A small ledge was added to be used as a fire-step by the defenders, as were head logs for protection. Small, two-man rifle pits were scooped out in front of the entrenchments to be used as outposts to prevent against sneak attacks. All in all, their defenses were virtually impregnable, providing they had enough riflemen.[4]

Shepard's Tennesseans had barely settled into their entrenchments when James Archer realized his illness prevented him from successfully leading the brigade. He relinquished command in mid–October 1864, writing he was "still ... too unwell to perform any duty requiring physical exertion."[5] James Archer traveled to Richmond in hopes of regaining his strength but instead died on October 24, 1864.

General Harry Heth turned to the brigade's senior colonel, William McComb, and placed him in command. William McComb, a 35-year-old Pennsylvanian, had moved to Clarksville, Tennessee, at the age of 26. He had engaged in a variety of manufacturing pursuits, including the construction of a flour mill on the Cumberland River. When the war started McComb enlisted in the 14th Tennessee Infantry as a private and quickly became a second lieutenant. In 1862 he was promoted to major and after the Battle of Cedar Mountain to lieutenant colonel. His colonel's rank came after the Second Battle of Manassas. William McComb was not one to remain in the rear and had been wounded at Sharpsburg and at Chancellorsville. McComb was a well-tested veteran, respected by his officers and men.[6] He immediately instructed each of the brigade's regimental commanders to take great effort to rest as many soldiers as possible while at the same time vigilantly defending their trench sector.

George Shepard rotated his Tennesseans in and out of the trenches, working to keep his worn-out veterans as fresh as conditions allowed. For the most part, his soldiers dealt with their privations with a minimum of complaint, and at times even had brief opportunities to laugh. One such occasion occurred out on the skirmish line. Shepard sent Company D out beyond the work, commanded by 1st Lt. James Martin and 3rd Lt. Andy Miller. The Federals assembled a force and began pushing toward Martin's skirmishers. The 25-year-old realized his troops were in danger of being overwhelmed and gave the order to fall back. The skirmishers scampered back to the entrenchments. Once safely inside, Lt. Martin realized one Tennessean was missing — Pvt. Ben Ferrill, a well-liked 25-year-old farm boy from Rural Hill, Tennessee. Lieutenant Ferguson Harris (Co. H) recalled: "Martin crossed the works to go after him while Andy Miller mounted on top [and] called him in a loud voice ... as dangerous as it was ... [with] bullets and shells flying as thick as hail." Harris continued, "[Ferrill] got over that undergrowth, bushes, logs and stumps at a [rapid] rate ... his head thrown back and his legs working like a bundle of snakes ... [and] Dick Palmer [Co. D] and Babe [George] Freeman [Co. E] pulled him over [the wall] unhurt." The reminiscence finished, "[Ferrill] looked around

10. October 20, 1864: Afternoon

for a few minutes and ... asked, 'I wonder if old Shep (Col. Shepard) expected me to whip all those Yankees just by myself.'"[7]

Regrettably there were very few jovial moments; life in the trenches tested every Confederate. The summer's suffocating heat and humidity punished the soldiers. The Confederates scratched together primitive shades made from pine boughs brought up from the rear, or blankets and shelter halves. Nonetheless, whenever they wrote about the weather their description were always the same: "hot," "hot and hazy," or "the humidity is high."[8]

While the heat ruthlessly afflicted the Tennesseans, vermin such as lice tormented them almost to insanity. Since the men could not bathe while in the trenches, lice permeated their clothing. The soldiers scratched incessantly at their bites and whenever they had time tried to remove the insects from their clothing. George Shepard often found squads of soldiers clustered together, picking lice off each other. The harassed Southerners joked about their situation and carried on a lively debate about how to rid themselves of these creatures: "If you kill the old ones, the young ones will die of grief, but ... the young ones are easier to kill and you can catch the old ones when they come to the funeral."[9]

The Tennesseans may have been plagued by the lice, but at least those pests were not lethal. George Shepard's veterans also had to protect themselves from Federal sharpshooters. Yank marksmen preyed upon any Confederate sticking his head above the trenches. They also preyed upon the Southerners who slipped out of the works to take up forward picket duties. A slow but steady number of Tennesseans were picked off by accurate Yank shooting. Lieutenant Ferguson Harris recalled, "Frequently when gathered in a group one man would fall from the unerring aim of a concealed sharp shooter."[10] Another Confederate wrote, "[An officer] wanted to get a better look at the enemy works but heavy sniper fire prevented him from sticking his head over the parapet. Instead ... [he] held up a mirror and angled it so that he could view the enemy lines without exposing himself. In an instant, the mirror was shattered ... by a sniper's bullet, and the officer ... heard someone shout from the Federal trenches, 'Set it up again Johnny.'"[11]

Shepard and Norris selected their own best shots and used them to combat the bluecoats' marksmen. In one such incident, Pvt. Fran Bass (Co. I) and Pvt. Jack Lane (Co. K), two of the 7th Tennessee's crack shots, engaged in a duel with a Federal sniper. Lieutenant Ferguson Harris (Co. H) reported: "A Federal sharpshooter had wounded several of our men.... Lane and I were behind an impromptu breastwork at an exposed point ... [and he] discovered us [and] in a very few minutes his bullets were scraping the top of our pile of dirt. Lane held up his hat and Mr. Yank promptly put a bullet through it. His handkerchief on a stick caused a like result.... Bass ... loading his Enfield carefully [and] ... with the aid of glasses, located him about 500 yards off ... protected ... by a dense tree.... At the crack of Bass' gun, he fell from the tree."[12]

As the relentless strain took its toll on the Confederate and Yank infantrymen, both sides' soldiers tired of the killing and quietly arranged informal truces. These moments of peace lasted for short periods of time but gave the war-weary men brief interludes of refuge from danger. One Confederate wrote, "Fortunately for us, we found that an agreement had been entered into by the pickets not to fire unless it was necessary."[13] Another soldier noted, "We can see them plain in their rifle pits and [we] can walk about, as if there ain't no body in front. [We] make it up not to fire on each other until [we] get orders and then [we] would fire up in the air to [give] ... notice."[14]

These unofficial truces worked as long as the Confederates and the Yankees knew each other. However, when a new Federal unit rotated into the trenches the fresh soldiers were not as apt to honor these informal cease-fires. Lieutenant Harris remembered, "Tom Jackson [Co. G], George McKinney [Co. B] and myself were down one morning whistling for a Yankee to come out for our usual trade. Jackson was some distance to the right of McKinney and myself when a burly Negro soldier rose up behind us and we found ourselves looking into the muzzle of an ugly gun pointed directly at us, and [he] ordered us to move over to the Yankee lines. Tom Jackson ... presented a gun to the back of the [Yank's] head and ordered him to drop his. Tom and McKinney started with him to the rear to turn him over as a prisoner."[15]

The Tennesseans in the front lines dreamed of the intervals when they could escape the trenches. Surgeon James Fite had set up a relief camp several hundred yards behind the last line of entrenchments. Here, safe from the hazards caused by snipers and mortar fire, the Tennesseans had a chance to wash, boil their uniforms in an effort to eradicate their lice infestations, eat hot meals, and sleep. The camp was not much, but it provided a refuge. One Confederate wrote, "The accommodations ... were meager indeed. Our shelter consisted of old, dilapidated tents, with bunks made of pine poles covered with pine [needles], on which [to] lay."[16]

Unfortunately, even while the Tennesseans rested at the relief camp, there was no escape from the fact the Confederate army's logistical system was on the verge of collapse. Food rations, though never good at the very best of times, worsened. The loss of the Weldon Railroad line meant a forfeiture of nearly a third of the foodstuffs available to the troops. As the winter of 1864-65 deepened, the soldiers' daily rations seldom consisted of much more than a pint of corn meal and an ounce or two of bacon. One Southerner complained, "What we had was corn pone cooked three days before and raw Nassau bacon (sometimes called 'Mule' by the boys)."[17] Then, in December 1864 an acute meat shortage hampered the commissary officials, forcing them to scramble for any meat supplies, regardless of quality. A soldier moaned, "Canned beef ... was issued a few times, and at other times small bits of poor, blue beef." He also added, "Sometimes we had coffee, and now and then a spoonful of sugar ... once we had half a gill of whiskey."[18]

The Confederate high command, knowing hunger was worsening the soldiers' morale, announced a New Years' feast. The Southern soldiers looked forward to this banquet with great anticipation. Sadly, everyone was greatly disheartened when the meal arrived. A famished rifleman wrote, "But oh what a disappointment when the squad returned and issued to each man only one small sandwich made up of two tiny slices of bread and a thin piece of ham."[19] Of course, once the soldiers learned the citizens of Petersburg had scraped up this meal from their own trifling stores, their attitude changed dramatically. A chastened Confederate declared, "God bless our noble women! It was all they could do." The soldier admitted, "Every man in [our] ... tent indulged in a good cry. We couldn't help it."[20] And as the hungry soldiers consumed this meager meal they all knew "the enemy drank coffee, ate fat, fresh beef and good bread, and drank quantities of whiskey."[21]

While the hungry Tennesseans struggled to survive everyone prayed for a letter from home. Any word from their loved ones, no matter how short, was treasured beyond measure by the homesick and lonesome men. The situation in central Tennessee had not changed; their families were all under the control of Federal troops. Getting a note from home remained incredibly difficult. So many letters began with, "More than three months has elapsed since we have received a letter from you."[22] Other messages started in similar fashion: "I [last] received a letter from you in May [four months ago].... I am very anxious to get a letter from you."[23] An angst-ridden wife wrote, "If I could only get one line from [my husband] to know that he was alive it would do me so good.... I am afraid he is killed, and oh ... if he is, what will become of me and my two children? ... I am almost crazy. I don't see how I can stand it much longer if I don't hear from him pretty soon.... If John is killed I don't want to live any longer."[24]

Even when letters did arrive, they often contained disturbing news. One such message brought tears to a melancholy Smith County boy: "The Yankees done bad this time.... They killed some of our sheep and one hog, and ... killed two of our cattle; while at other places they killed all the sheep, hogs, cattle, chickens, geese and ducks, and what they did not kill they drove off."[25] Another letter recorded: "The damage done to the railroad, salt works, and lead mines ... can be repaired pretty soon. [The Yanks] can however, repeat the destruction again anytime they want to if more troops are not sent to the district."[26] And another message recorded, "The Yanks are forcing citizens to pay three years [taxes] ... and if a man is not able to pay it immediately ... their lands are ... sold."[27]

Many letters ate at the lonely young men's emotions, especially when they learned their sweethearts had given up waiting for them and married fellows who had not gone off to war. One such note informed the Tennessean boys, "Both of [Harrison] H. Stallings' daughters are married. Puss [Lydia] to Vince Taylor [and] Cat [Catherine] to Bark Stuart."[28] An additional missive from a lonesome girl declared, "Persons going to and coming from the army have to pass through [here], we necessarily got acquainted with a good many gentlemen ... we have enjoyed ourselves very much."[29] And another young lady who no longer waited for her beau to return, wrote, "Saturday evening six girls and six gentlemen left here to take a ride."[30]

Fortunately not all the messages coming from home sapped at the young soldiers' morale. Patient and faithful lady friends bolstered their distant suitors' spirits with notes such as "Lizzie requests me to present her love, double and twisted. She is a lively girl."[31] Another wrote, "Your lady friends are all well."[32] And another reported, "Tell Jack that ... Miss Eddie is not married as we once heard she was."[33] These messages kindled the lonely soldiers' hearts, occasioning one to write, "I shall dream of those women all night."[34]

For the far-away husbands-turned-soldier, the toughest letters to receive were those written by forlorn wives. One frank letter from a desolate wife described her wretched Christmas: "We are all sad.... I have nothing even to put in Sadie's stocking, which hangs so invitingly for Santa Claus.... [On Christmas] Sadie jumped out of bed very early ... to feel her stocking. She could not believe that there would be [nothing].... Finding nothing, she crept back into bed, pulled the cover over her face, and soon I heard her sobbing."[35] Another distressed wife wrote to her husband, informing him "his third child had died in infancy."[36] These messages forced some men to decide between their duty as a soldier in a war that could not be won, and supporting their wives and families. Some soldiers, such as Pvt. Peter Stiner (Co. E), made his decision and slipped away from the trenches. He deserted while on picket duty on January 1, 1865, two weeks after learning of his daughter's death.[37]

Private Peter Stiner's disappearance from the 7th Tennessee was but a single loss to the regiment, he was part of a steady dwindling of strength. The men did not believe the war could be won, and no one wanted to die. Plus, the war updates and political news were all negative. An increasing number of embattled Confederates reached the conclusion there was no point in remaining.

Word reached the Confederates of a failed peace conference. On February 3, 1865, President Abraham Lincoln and Secretary of State William Steward met with Confederate vice president Alexander Stevens and two others on the ship *River Queen* near Hampton Roads, Virginia. The Confederate delegation proposed an armistice and Lincoln refused. Then the Confederates suggested the independence of their nation and again Lincoln rejected their offer, and instead, demanded that reunion was the only option. After four hours of fruitless negotiations the meeting fell apart and the two sides separated, the conference a failure. The war would continue.[38]

More bad news battered the besieged soldiers in George Shepard's regiment; they learned the Confederate Congress wanted to conscript slaves, arm them, and use them in the fight against the Federals. The Southern soldiers were dumbfounded by this information; they knew the slaves would not fight. Instead, the veterans were convinced the slaves would immediately desert and join the Northern armies. This legislation fell apart, but the soldiers understood what this desperate news really meant to the Confederates; no one, not even President Jefferson Davis, believed the war could be won.[39]

Once the Southern soldiers realized just how hopeless their situation had become, their morale plummeted. A rifleman penned, "We drilled very little.... The truth is, the men were worn out in mind and in body, and every effort became painfully irksome."[40] One member of McComb's brigade summed up their condition, writing: "Men were starving, and were naked in the trenches. The sufferings of the poor fellows were beyond endurance. Their families were appealing to them for relief; their wives and children were at home reduced to gaunt specters, and these appeals caused many a brave man to leave his comrades and wend his way to his desolate home.... Hundreds of desertions were occurring every day, and the inevitable was not far off."[41]

The 7th Tennessee's strength melted away during the early months of 1865. Fourteen veterans were lost in January, nine in February, and another four more in March.[42] George Shepard and Archie Norris resorted to assembling "so-called picked men to guard the picket lines to keep the men from going over to the Yankees."[43] These men, as one veteran noted, "were required to keep on their accoutrements and remain in the pits all the time."[44] But this forlorn attempt did not stop the desertions. One of these worn-out veterans considering leaving was Corporal J. P. Bashaw (Co. I). He wrote, "We all knew that when the campaign opened up in the spring, General Lee would be compelled to surrender, and the men were very badly discouraged, low spirited [and] they did not care to be killed for no purpose."[45] Then, when Bashaw experienced a close call he recorded, "I got shot.... The ball missed me but struck my knapsack on my back. My blanket was folded in the knapsack and nine holes were cut in the blanket and the ball lodged in the middle of it. The force knocked me down."[46] Following this piece of good fortune, J. P. Bashaw concluded, "This was [my] last battle." He "surrendered near Petersburg, Virginia on the 1st day of March 1865, about 9 o'clock A.M."[47]

General Heth's regiments shrank at such a rapid rate he was forced to consolidate his formations. He took the remainder of the units in Bushrod Johnson's brigade, Tennesseans from 17th, 23rd, 25th, 37th and 44th Tennessee Infantry regiments, and added them to William McComb's command, pushing the consolidated brigade's strength to 87 officers and 860 rifles. The 7th Tennessee numbered 145 on March 31, 1865, and every man knew the end was close at hand. The Confederate lines were stretched to the breaking point. General A. P. Hill's entire Third Corps, now consisting of about 12,000 men, had eleven miles of trenches to defend, and everywhere "the morning reports became a sickening and bewildering story of new desertion."[48]

And sadly, the killing did not stop. Twenty-nine-year-old Pvt. Frank Bass (Co. I) "lost his valuable life ... by a long range shot."[49] The Tennesseans, distraught by the loss of this popular comrade from Silver Springs, Tennessee, despondently watching the unremitting thinning of their ranks and pondered, "[Why] I am spared; for what purpose, God in His Wisdom only knows."[50] Others wrote of their futures, "I do not expect to see my native land again."[51] Lieutenant Ferguson Harris wrote, "I wonder who will be the last of us to go?"[52]

On April 1, 1865, Grant moved to stretch the Confederate line even further. He sent Maj. Gen. Gouverneur Warren's V Corps, along with two divisions of cavalry commanded by Brigadier Generals Thomas Devin and George Custer, beyond the west end of the Confederate trenches. General Lee was forced to respond and dispatched three brigades led by Maj. Gen. George Pickett and two brigades from Maj. Gen. Bushrod Johnson's division, with the order of "Hold Five Forks at all costs."[53] The two forces collided at the Five Forks highway intersection and the battle proved to be a horrible disaster for the Confederates. By the time nightfall ended the fighting more than 3,000 Confederates were lost, of which nearly 2,400 had surrendered. One shocked Southerner reported, "Every Federal division ... that day overran the Confederates at their front."[54]

Word of this catastrophe reached the besieged soldiers and did nothing to sustain their determination. Pickett's men had been outnumbered two or three to one, and the Yankees attacked with such aggression the embattled rebs were simply overwhelmed. In the 7th Tennessee, three veterans slipped over the walls and deserted that night. For George Shepard's remaining comrades, as they guarded their 400 yards of trench line with 17 officers and 135 rifles, everyone knew there was no way they could hold back any type of Yankee assault. They all understood the end would come when the Yankees came. One noted, "Our front was so much extended that we could not keep a continuous line of battle."[55] General Grant also figured out what the Tennesseans knew: attack and the rebel defenses would crumble. He gave three corps, the VI, the XXIV, and the III, orders to strike against Heth's and Wilcox's divisions on April 2, 1865.

Guessing the assault would come before sunrise, George Shepard and Archie Norris kept everyone on the fire-steps, vigilantly watching for the expected assault. One combatant described the night: "A heavy mist made the moonless night more dark and gloomy."[56] The tiny band of Tennesseans huddled in the chilly air, tensed and waiting. One recalled, "The men listened ... and, although they said little, seemed to feel that the end was drawing near."[57] Then, around 1:00 A.M., rifle fire erupted from the picket line, a half mile to their left. Those fellows poking their heads above the trenches could see the rifle flashes popping like angry fireflies. One wrote, "The night was extremely dark ... we could see the flashes of musketry for a great distance."[58]

The shooting continued for several hours, though never shifting to the Tennesseans' position. At 4:30 A.M., a thunderous roar exploded, followed by the clash of thousands of weapons. Three divisions from Maj. Gen. Horatio Wright's VI Corps surged forward and struck the trenches occupied by the brigades of William MacRae and Joseph Davis. Fierce hand-to-hand fighting erupted in the early morning's darkness, the struggles frantic and fierce. A Union officer reported, "There was a desperate resistance and in 15 minutes ... Wright had lost 1,100 men."[59] Regardless of these initial losses, the outcome was never in doubt. The greatly outnumbered Southern defenders were crushed.[60] The Northerners were exuberant; in little more than a quarter of an hour they destroyed two entire Confederate brigades and captured almost two miles of trench.

By 5:00 A.M. there was enough light to see. William McComb's brigade had been missed by the slightest of margins. Only the brigade's far left flank position, the trenches covered by the 17th and 23rd Tennessee, had been affected. Colonel Horace Ready, who commanded this combined formation, wheeled his veterans to the left so they could face the hordes of Yanks bearing down upon them. But Ready's small unit could do little to stave off the massive breakthrough occurring east of them. The Federal brigades flooded through MacRae's and Davis's trenches and surged beyond the Confederate line, cutting the gray line in two.

As Shepard's and Norris's Tennesseans watched the disaster unfolding a half mile away, orders arrived. McComb's brigade was to plug the hole created by MacRae's and Davis's destruction. They also were to retake a small Confederate artillery fortress. When this word came to prepare to attack one Tennessean, Pvt. James Turnage (Co. C), heard the generals discussing this assault to retake the artillery position. A Southerner wrote, "General McComb gave specific ... instructions, winding up with, 'We must take that battery.'" Turnage, not wanting to leave the safety of their trenches, asked, "General, don't you think we have got artillery enough?"[61]

Regardless of Pvt. James Turnage's reservations about the need for artillery, another Tennessean noted, "We were immediately formed in line of battle, and although our brigade ... did not number more than 600, we were ordered to charge and retake the works."[62] The Tennesseans clustered around their leaders and crept forward, darting from traverse trench to rifle pit. They struck the flank of a Federal brigade. The veteran Yanks fell back several hundred yards, shooting as they retreated. First Sergeant Jesse Cage (Co. E) went down, his femur crushed by a Minié bullet, and a few moments later, 1st Sgt. Richard Moxley (Co. K) was struck in the face.[63]

The Tennesseans pushed forward, firing as they moved, until nearing the artillery position called Fort Archer. The Confederates rushed the defenses and chased the Federals out of the fort. Shepard's veterans entered Fort Archer's stout, earthen walls, short of breath, and anxious about the overall situation. They had driven the Federals before them backward, but their efforts had done little to salvage the massive Confederate disaster. A rifleman remembered, "We double-quicked to the rescue ... but the lines ... had been carried."[64] The Tennesseans gulped water from their canteens, shifted bullets around in their cartridge boxes, and waited for whatever happened next. Someone glanced at his pocket watch — it was 7:00 A.M.

The Federals reacted quickly and worked regiments around the fort. One Yank officer wrote, "A large part of Wright's soldiers moved down the reverse of the captured lines [toward] Hatcher's Run."[65] The bluecoats moved slowly, cautiously inching forward and skirmishing against small pockets of isolated Southerners. A Federal noted, "Turning to the left, the entrenchments [were] found to be heavily traversed, and the fighting went on from traverse to traverse."[66] The Tennesseans watched in horror, realizing the Yanks could soon cut them off and trap them here, amid the cannons of Archer's Fort.

Captain John Allen (Co. B), General McComb's brigade adjutant, arrived and informed George Shepard the 7th needed to withdraw. Shepard gave the orders and some of his riflemen sprinted out a western gate and raced for safety. Captain Archie Norris hollered at more of the regiment to follow, and squad after squad squeezed out the narrow opening and stampeded after their retreating brothers. Union troops pressed closer to the fort's defenses, advancing against the northern and eastern sides while another force slipped around and approached the western walls. A number of Tennesseans along the eastern and northern walls remained to fight off this Federal attack. These fellows were pinned down and could not extract themselves from the tightening net. A Southerner recalled, "Capt. John Allen, of [McComb's] staff, not so choice in his language, was making the air blue as he dashed among those [along the wall], urging them to [escape]."[67]

A few more Tennesseans turned from their firing posts and fled, but the rest could not break away. A shell struck nearby, knocking Cpt. John Allen to the ground, causing severe contusions to his thighs.[68] A couple of quick-thinking Tennesseans snatched Allen up from the ground, threw him over their shoulders and hustled out of the fort. Then, Union soldiers flooded into the fort from the west, catching the remaining Tennesseans from the rear. They called to the Confederates to surrender and the Southerners realized there was nothing they could do. A Yank officer recorded, "The enemy resisted stoutly from a fort ... but soon being outflanked and enveloped, the work was taken."[69] Thirty-three Tennesseans set down their weapons and raised their arms, including Sgt. Billy Cato (Co. K), Pvt. James Turnage (Co. C), and Pvt. Richard Gibbs (Co. B). Corporal David Hamilton (Co. H) was also captured, though not without trying one last attempt to get away. He jumped over the earthworks and broke his foot before being apprehended.

Lieutenant Colonel George Shepard and Cpt. Archie Norris worked feverishly to reform their disorganized regiment. The 7th Tennessee now numbered 100 officers and riflemen. These men hunkered down in a traversing trench, their weapons pointed toward the east. The Tennesseans watched in dismay as Union regiments aligned themselves in preparation to advance. At 7:30 A.M. a courier from General McComb arrived and informed Shepard the Confederate brigades of McGowen and Scales were retreating to the northwest. Shepard realized with McGowen and Scales gone, there no longer were any Confederate troops in the trenches behind the Tennessee brigade. The courier

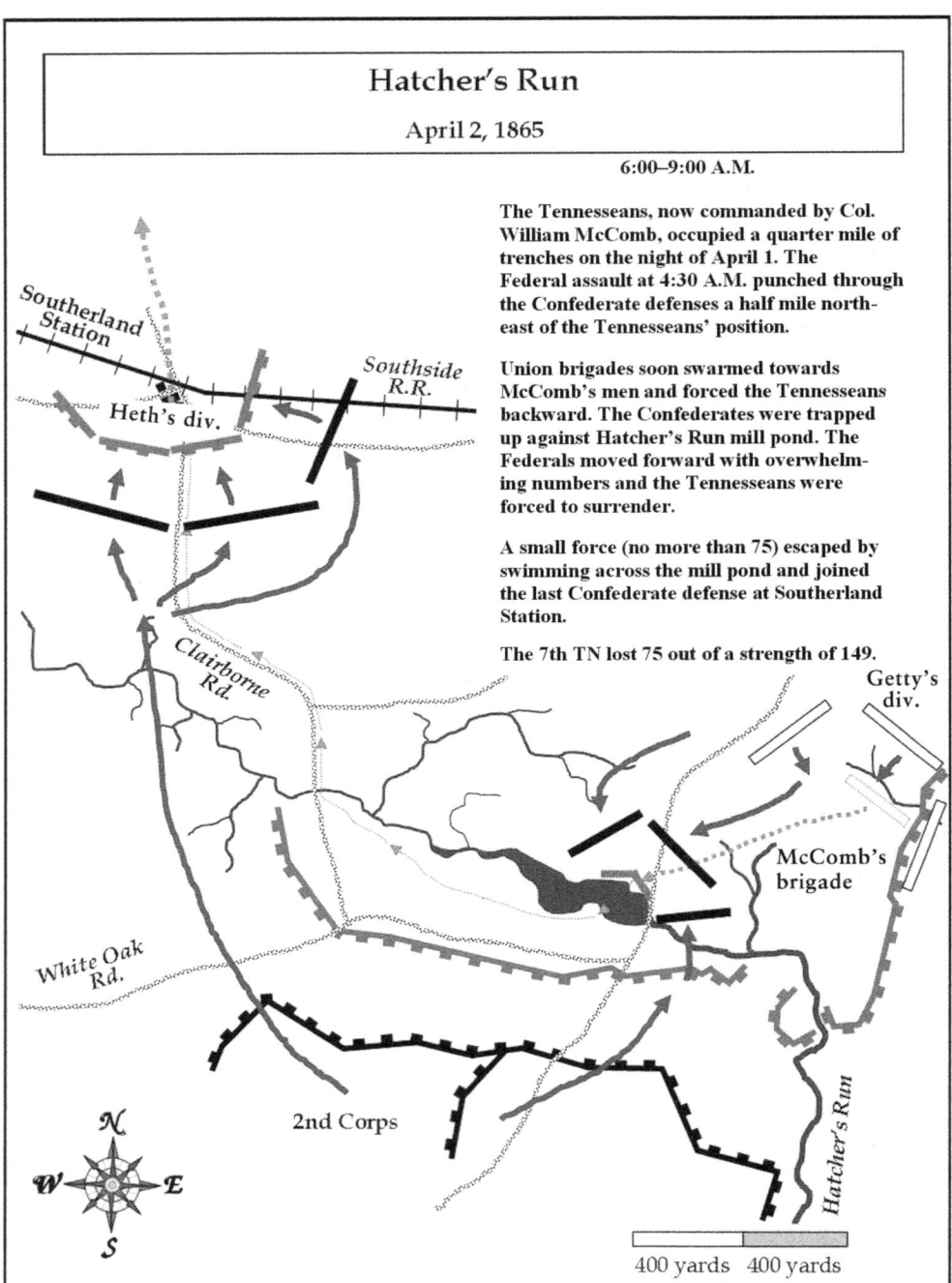

informed Lt. Col. Shepard he was to pull his troops back and try to rejoin the brigade as it retreated toward the northwest.[70]

Shepard gave the orders and his little band of Tennesseans fell back slowly, the entire regiment spread out in a skirmish line. The riflemen moved in little bursts of speed and then dropped to the ground for safety. Suddenly a volley of rifle fire raked through the Tennesseans, striking them from behind, from Federals who now pushed through the trenches abandoned by McGowen and Scales. Shepard's veterans could no longer fall back; Yanks were behind them, as well as to their front. The battle-weary Tennesseans dropped to the ground, pinned between two massive fists.

The beleaguered lieutenant colonel called to his officers and they huddled together in a small depression. A panicky officer called out, "The men are badly demoralized."[71] Someone suggested surrender, but this was argued down as others maintained escape was possible; all that was necessary was to create a diversion to hold off the Yanks long enough for the regiment to slip away. If they could get to a bridge spanning Hatcher's Run they would have the safety of a body of water called the Burgess Mill Pond between them and the Yankees.

First Lieutenant Ferguson Harris (Co. H) got everyone's attention and offered to attack the Yankees with his sharpshooter contingent. Harris said, "These men will fight.... Let me lead them."[72] One of the officers in the Tennessee brigade declared, "Harris knew those men would fight and go wherever he ... dare lead."[73] The officers gazed at Harris in admiration; there was little chance he and the men who went with them would return. This was truly Tennessee valor.

Lieutenant Ferguson Harris called to his sharpshooters; they loaded their weapons and gritted their teeth. Then Harris leaped forward, giving the rebel yell. His sharpshooters rose and followed him, screaming wildly and firing as they advanced. The Union troops were stunned by this ferocious attack and fell back a hundred yards. George Shepard and Archie Norris called to the regiment and the Tennesseans jumped up and ran through this open space, racing toward the bridge.

The Yanks discovered the size of Harris' attacking force and halted their retreat. They poured several volleys into the Confederates, knocking many down. Lieutenant Ferguson Harris fell, the flesh of his arm sliced by a bullet.[74] General Heth recalled, "I remember well the desperate charge ... I also remember General McComb ... telling me that [Harris] was fatally wounded; [and] that he had promoted [Harris] to Captain on the field that day."[75] As Harris lay wounded, he watched as the rest of his sharpshooters were shot down, putting an end to their valiant attack.

Ferguson Harris's valiant charge did not secure the Tennesseans enough time to escape. More Union troops had passed through the empty Confederate trenches and reached the critical bridge spanning Hatcher's Run. The Yanks formed up and opened fire upon the approaching Tennesseans, driving them away. General McComb quickly directed his frantic veterans to follow him around the mill pond toward the north but soon, more Union troops approached from that direction. The Tennesseans were trapped.

George Shepard's small band of survivors formed up with their backs to the mill pond's deep waters, the entire regiment covering a front of no more than twenty-five yards. A Tennessean noted, "Our command was ordered to form a strong skirmish line and hold the position."[76] The rest of the Tennessee units in McComb's brigade formed up to the right and left of the 7th Tennessee. All the veterans knew — this was it — this was where they would make their last stand. The bluecoats massed before them, just out of musket range, their numerous flags demonstrating just how many units were getting ready to attack the cornered Tennesseans.

The Federals stepped forward at 8:30 A.M., closing cautiously. Once the two forces;

one small, the other huge came within rifle range the shooting began. The Tennesseans poured volley after volley into the Yanks but for each bluecoat who was hit, another stepped forward to plug the gap. And in turn, the Northerners sprayed the Confederates with devastating accuracy. A rifleman recalled, "It was [here] that we lost most of our men ... forced back [against] Hatcher's Run ... against a force double our number in front and overlapping both flanks."[77] Private Benjamin Thackston (Co. B) was struck in the left leg, Captain Fayette Walsh (Co. D) was hit in the right heel, and 1st Lt. Thomas Clemens (Co. I) took a slug in his abdomen. The Yanks pressed closer, firing as they advanced. In the next few terrible minutes more Tennessean veterans were injured. Sergeant Henry Manson (Co. H) was downed by a Minié bullet to his leg, Pvt. William Bradley (Co. B) took wounds to his leg and his face, and Pvt. George McKinney (Co. B) also stopped a bullet.[78] Lieutenant Andy Miller (Co. D) was struck in the chest and "saved from death only through the fact that his folded blanket stopped much of the force of the bullet."[79]

By now many of the Tennesseans had no ammunition and could do little to protect themselves. Their defense collapsed. An officer suggested to Shepard that it might be possible to escape by swimming across the pond. George Shepard gave the order "for every man to save himself," and those closest to the water tossed their weapons and accouterments to the ground and jumped into the water and began swimming across the pond.[80] The Yank avalanche surged closer to the broken Confederate line, encouraged by their weakening fire. Most of the remaining Southerners milled around, some still shooting, but many having dropped their rifles and waving white rags. The Federals neared the beaten Southerners, no longer firing, just inching forward, bayonets at the ready. One Yank, Pvt. Milton Mathews (61st PA), darted forward and ripped the 7th Tennessee flag out of the stunned Tennessean holding it. A Federal officer recorded the feat: "[Mathews] ... dashed into a squad of Rebels who had gathered round a beautiful stand of colors, and ... knocked down the color bearer, seized the colors as they fell, and rushed on to another portion of the field."[81] This auspicious action would earn Pvt. Mathews the Medal of Honor and a thirty-day furlough.

Then, with their flag stolen from them, and many of their leaders frantically swimming across the mill pond, the remaining Tennesseans surrendered. A Union officer noted, "About 9:00 [we] captured a large number of men."[82] Another Federal officer reported, "The enemy, who being pressed so closely that they could scarcely fire a shot, and appeared to have given up all idea of resistance, and were only desirous to be taken prisoner."[83] One of the Tennesseans, the wounded Lt. Andy Miller (Co. D), simply noted, "When our lines ... were broken, I with ... [my] comrade[s] were cut off."[84] Captain Archie Norris, who had volunteered to remain with those who could not escape, formed up the defeated formation, including 1st Lt. Jim Martin (Co. D), Cpt. Fayette Walsh (Co. D), 1st Sgt George Murray (Co. A), and Pvt. Jeremiah Turner (Co. F). In all, forty veteran Tennesseans surrendered, their war now ended.[85]

George Shepard and about five dozen Tennesseans succeeded in swimming across the mill pond and escaping toward the northwest. The wet and devastated survivors drifted northward, following a stream of other veterans toward where rumors said General Heth was forming a defensive line. The 7th Tennessee was no longer a fighting force. Most men did not have weapons, few had their blanket rolls, and nobody had any food.

Therefore, when the fleeing men encountered a store of supplies, they crowded around it. One soldier wrote, "[We] found parties in charge of the stores distributing provisions to those who wished them. A large country ham attracted my attention, and soon found a resting-place on my bayonet."[86]

The Tennesseans reached Sutherland Station and joined the mass of men from Heth's surviving brigades, the soldiers furiously digging breastworks. George Shepard led his sixty survivors and found their brigade's part of the entrenchments. He reported to Brig. Gen. William McComb, informing him of the regiment's strength, and learned at least half of the brigade's surviving 400 men lacked muskets.[87] McComb informed Shepard there were no extra weapons; the unarmed men would just have to wait to retrieve a musket from a casualty.

General Heth had selected a position on a summit overlooking 800 yards of pasture. He had the remnants of five brigades; McGowen, Scales, Cooke, and what was left from MacRae and McComb. This force soon attracted Yankee attention. The Confederates could see Union formations moving into position to attack, a force consisting of several brigades from Brig. Gen. Nelson Miles' division (II Corps). Miles sent a brigade forward at 12:30 and the Confederates repulsed it rather quickly. One Southerner noted, "We rolled a perfect sheet of lead across the open interval, striking down scores of the enemy, [and] opening great gaps in their lines."[88]

This defense consumed much of the ammunition the riflemen had in their cartridge boxes. Then, with General A. P. Hill's death Gen. Harry Heth was ordered to leave his division and assume command of the entire Third Corps. The Confederate riflemen looked out across the battlefield and saw nothing but disaster. The fortifications which they had held since June of last year had been easily defeated. Regiments and brigades were destroyed and scattered everywhere, and masses of bluecoats could be seen crushing any point of resistance. Nothing looked good for the Confederates and some began to debate the merits of continuing the fight. One Confederate summed up the arguments spreading among the ranks: "Some were for resisting to the last, some advised immediate flight, [and] some gave up the cause and counseled unconditional surrender."[89]

Amid this rumbling of Confederate uncertainty General Miles reformed his lines and maneuvered his brigades. He sent a strong skirmish line against Heth's center and right, forcing the Southern units to stay in position. At 3:00 P.M., Miles attacked the left with two fresh brigades and easily rolled across the Confederate position. A jubilant Union officer reported, "[We] ... attacked his left ... with complete success, sweeping down inside the breastworks, capturing 600 prisoners."[90]

The Confederate defense disintegrated into chaos as the Southerners fled from the bluecoats' onslaught. One shaken rifleman proclaimed, "The Confederacy was considered as 'gave up,' and every man felt it his duty, as well as his privilege to save himself."[91] The survivors fled northward toward the Appomattox River. Once the frantic men reached the river they discovered it was too deep to cross without a boat. They milled about in terror. A few were able to find boats and cross, including General McComb, who with about 75 men got to safety late that evening.[92] Eventually, most of George Shepard's boys crossed, a survivor writing, "[We] made for the north bank of the Appomattox River, which ... [we] attain[ed] by means of two flat-bottomed boats."[93]

On the morning of April 3, 1865, the shocked Confederates headed west, following rumors of large ration stores waiting for them at Amelia Court House, some thirty miles away. There was little military bearing in the column straggling west. As one stunned enlisted man recalled, "When a solder became weary, he fell out, ate his scanty rations — if indeed he had any — rested, rose and resumed the march when his inclination dictated."[94] George Shepard's little band clustered together around their leader, laboring under the weight of "an indescribable sadness."[95] Over the next few days nearly half would find they could go no farther and would be left behind.[96] They would join those already captured by the Union forces.

The next morning, April 4, 1865, the Tennesseans stumbled into Amelia Court House and a few fortunate fellows drew rations. One proclaimed happily, "I procured some bacon and bread."[97] The rest though, we ordered to form a battle line outside of the town. The veterans quickly threw up some light works from nearby rails, and then they waited for the Yanks to attack. The Union cavalry did not have infantry support so the Confederates spent an undisturbed night.

On April 5, 1865, the Southerners resumed their westward trek until Federal cavalry massed before them, forcing the gray column northward. As Shepard's tired and hungry Tennesseans shuffled along they could see dark clouds of smoke boiling up into the sky, and word soon floated through the files; Yankee cavalry had destroyed the Confederate supply train. Then, Union cavalry struck the head of the Confederate column and heavy skirmishing could be heard. The procession halted and the men fell to the roadside, footsore and famished.

Once the sun went down strict orders came for an absolutely silent march. The Confederates staggered to their feet and quietly trudged forward. The Tennesseans saw why an edict for no noise had been demanded; as one Confederate wrote: "We soon came into sight of the bivouac fires of the enemy ... [and] we went by a wide detour around them."[98] The column of exhausted Confederates marched all night and did not halt until just before sunrise on April 6, 1865.

After only a couple of hours' rest word came to the worn out Tennesseans to continue the march. Union cavalry attacked the Confederates up ahead and a line of battle was assembled. The weary men doggedly fixed rudimentary breastworks, sent out a thin screen of skirmishers, and then the rest slumped down behind their defenses and slept. The Yanks probed but did not press their attack. A Confederate recalled, "Our skirmish line was felt ... but they did not come up to the main line ... most of us snatched some [sleep]."[99]

That evening the Tennesseans received news the Confederate army had been badly defeated in a fight near Saylor's Creek and that much of Lieutenant General Richard Ewell's corps had surrendered. The gravity of their condition wore heavily on Shepard's veterans as they again received orders for a night march. They moved slowly through the darkness and arrived in Farmville on April 7, 1865. The played-out men could hear fighting and soon orders came to form into line of battle. The weary veterans fixed breastworks, almost without thinking, and collapsed behind them. Many no longer even cared if the Federals attacked.

The march resumed. A tired Confederate noted, "We toiled on wearily, and almost hopelessly forward."[100] By evening, of April 8, 1865, the column bivouacked about four miles northeast of Appomattox Court House. Just before dawn on the morning of April 9, 1865, the drained and starving Confederates were ordered to take up their weapons and move to within two miles of Appomattox. Here, the men found themselves in a shallow basin, surrounded by a low circle of hills, with the countryside generally cleared of trees. The Confederates could see an immense muddle of confusion. Wagons, caissons, and artillery pieces clogged every road, and mobs of unarmed men roamed about, shifting one way, and then in another. One disheartened officer recorded, "The confusion in this place exceeded anything I had ever witnessed in the entire war."[101]

George Shepard's Tennesseans looked about at the pandemonium and said little. As one Southerner noted, "A horrible calm brooded over us ... [our] faces were haggard, [and our] steps slow and unsteady."[102] Everyone seemed to know the end had come. But then, around 11:00 A.M., orders came to move. The Confederates formed into a battle line and pushed across an open field, aiming toward a hillcrest a mile away. Skirmishing erupted just over the ridge's crest and the veterans checked their weapons.

A halt was called when the Tennessee battle line reached a hundred yards from the ridge's crest. The men stood in line anxiously, ready to fight whatever came over the hill top. The front rank was filled with soldiers with muskets, while often the rear rank men were not armed. Every Tennessean stood resolutely in the ranks; the entire unit clustered closely around George Shepard and the last remaining captain, 27-year-old Robert Miller (Co. E). The two senior Tennessean officers had done a count that morning; the 7th Tennessee had two lieutenants, Jack Moore (Co. B) and John Hamilton (Co. H), and 24 riflemen.[103] One soldier stood in the second rank, not having a musket, and with both of his arms bandaged. When someone asked him what good he could do, he replied, "I can still yell!"

A clump of horsemen appeared over the ridge line and road at an angle toward the battle line. The veterans recognized General George Custer and a small collection of Confederate officers. This odd procession rumbled past the Confederates without stopping. Then, the sounds of gunfire stuttered to a stop and a peculiar silence suffocated the landscape. The soldiers stood in formation for a few more minutes before drifting apart and congregating around their officers. No one had given the order to break ranks, but soon there was little military organization remaining.

After waiting an hour George Shepard searched out General McComb. The brigade commander, as well as a number of regimental leaders, stood about, talking solemnly. No one knew what was transpiring. Another hour passed and then an officer rode up, "bowed his head, murmuring that it was all over."[104] Shepard took this astounding information back to his Tennesseans but they already knew by the time he arrived. The Tennesseans stood, or sat, each man silent and deep within himself, the shock numbing. No one could believe the war had ended. One cried out, "My God! That I should have lived to see this!"[105]

The 7th Tennessee stacked what few muskets they had remaining during the surrender ceremony on April 12, 1865, amid the mud and rain. By then Lt. Col. George Shepard had rounded up 46 of his Tennesseans for the formality. One wrote, "We stacked arms ... and then returned to make ready for our departure."[106] Another noted, "When paroled, we filled our haversacks with cheese and crackers and turned our faces [toward home]."[107]

Next morning they would strike out toward Tennessee and a future they had dreamed about for the past four years. Private James Hale (Co. B) best summed up how the eager young men felt when he wrote to his sweetheart, "You must prepare for a jolly time when I come home.... I am anticipating a nice time with you!"[108] It had taken Tennessee valor to fight this war; it would now require another type of Tennessee valor to rebuild the peace.

PART II : 7TH TENNESSEE INFANTRY ROSTER

All names in bold died during their service as a member of the 7th Tennessee Infantry. Farmer indicates ownership of a farm. Farm labor indicates working on someone's farm (usually family).

When Appomattox is cited under "Comments," this individual was present for the surrender ceremony at Appomattox Court House.

Regimental Staff

Name	Initial Rank	D.O.B.	Home	Prewar Occupation	Comments
Hatton, Robert	Colonel	1826	Lebanon, Wilson Co.	Lawyer/ Politician	Brig. Gen. 5/23/62. **Killed — 5/31/62 (Seven Pines).**
Goodner, John F.	Lt. Col.	1823	Alexandria, Dekalb Co.	Farmer	Col. 5/23/62. WIA 6/27/62. Sick since 2/22/63. Resigned 4/8/63.
Howard, John K.	Major	1827	Lebanon, Wilson Co.	Clerk of Court	Lt. Col. 5/23/62. WIA 6/27/62. **Died of wounds, 7/9/62.**
Howard, George A.	Adjutant	1842	Lebanon, Wilson Co.	Student — U.S. Naval Acad.	Captured 7/3/63. Sent to Johnson Is. POW rest of war.
Hill, Asoph	Sgt. Maj.	—	—	—	Capt. 4/27/62. WIA 9/17/62. WIA & captured 7/3/63. **Died of wounds, 7/8/62.**
Robinson, Gutheridge L.	Surgeon	—	—	Physician	Resigned 5/20/62.
Fite, James L.	Asst. Surgeon	1832	Lebanon, Wilson Co.	Physician	Surgeon 2/63. Paroled — Appomattox, 4/9/65.
Jones, David C.	Asst. Surgeon	—	—	—	Sick since 7/62. Resigned 11/30/62.
Tuckett, J. H.	Asst. Surgeon	—	—	Physician	Enlisted 10/1/62. **Died of disease, 7/29/63.**
Allen, John D.	Capt. Com'sary	—	—	—	Commissary Capt. Resigned 6/7/62.
Vick, Alexander	Capt. Qtr. Mstr.	1834	Lebanon, Wilson Co.	Lawyer	Resigned 4/30/62.
McClain, Rufus	Qtr Mstr Sgt.	1836	Silver Spr., Wilson Co.	Student	Capt. of Qtr. Mstr. (brigade) 3/62. Paymaster (III Corps) 11/64. Surrendered 4/9/65.
Armstrong, William	Chaplain	—	Wilson Co.	—	Sick since 12/61. Resigned 8/26/62.
Bradley, James S.	Sutler	1838	Dixon Spr., Wilson Co.	Assistant Marshall	Sutler entire war. Paroled — Appomattox, 4/9/65.

Company A

Name	Initial Rank	D.O.B.	Home	Prewar Occupation	Comments
Wright, Robert V.	Captain	1828	Alexandria, Dekalb Co.	Farmer	Discharged, 4/27/62 (Term expired).
Dowell, Jonathan S.	1st Lt.	1837	Smith Co.	—	Capt. 4/26/62. WIA 5/31/62. WIA (throat) & captured 7/3/63. Exchanged 2/24/65. Surrendered Jonesboro, TN, 5/7/65.
Hobson, Francis Wade	2nd Lt.	1837	Alexandria, Dekalb Co.	Teacher	1st Lt. 4/26/62. Resigned (sickness) 9/17/62.
Bone, Robert	3rd Lt.	1839	Alexandria, Dekalb Co.	Farm labor	Resigned (sickness) 11/30/61.
Wilmouth, Burgess "Byrd"	1st Sgt.	1830	Alexandria, Dekalb Co.	Blacksmith	3rd Lt. 12/19/61. 2nd Lt. 9/17/62. 1st Lt. 4/28/64. WIA (groin) 5/12/64. **Died of wounds, 5/21/64.**
Vanatta, James	2nd Sgt.	1824	Alexandria, Dekalb Co.	Farmer	Reduced (Pvt.) 4/30/62. **Killed, 5/31/62 (Seven Pines).**
Donnell, James A.	3rd Sgt.	1834	Commerce, Wilson Co.	Farm labor	Reduced (Pvt.) 4/30/62. WIA & captured 7/3/63. POW rest of war.
Barber, James	4th Sgt.	1837	—	Farm labor	Discharged (disability) 11/30/61.
Newsom, James R.	1st Cpl.	1826	—	Shoemaker	Reduced (Pvt.) 4/30/62. Discharged (seniority) 8/19/62.
Robinson, Andrew M.	2nd Cpl.	1836	Alexandria, Dekalb Co.	Carpenter	Reduced (Pvt.) 4/30/62. Deserted 3/14/63.
Warford, Bartlett	3rd Cpl.	1831	Alexandria, Dekalb Co.	Farmer	Reduced (Pvt.) 4/30/62. WIA (left leg amputated) 9/20/62.
Allison, John H.	Private	1845	Alexandria, Dekalb Co.	Farm labor	Transferred to Tenn. Cavalry, 8/17/63.
Allison, Robert L.	Private	1846	Alexandria, Dekalb Co.	Farm labor	Discharged (minority) 8/19/62.
Anderson, William	Private	1837	—	Phys. asst.	**Died of disease, 11/30/61.**
Atwell, William	Private	1839	Smithville, Dekalb Co.	Clerk	Appointed Commissary Capt. 6/15/62. Last entry, 10/63.
Bailiff, Joab	Private	1836	Helton, Dekalb Co.	Farm labor	WIA 5/31/62. WIA (neck) & captured 7/3/63. **Died of wounds, 7/16/63.**
Bailiff, William	Private	1844	Wolfcreek, Dekalb Co.	Farm labor	Discharged (disability) 7/16/62.
Bartlett, William	Private	1826	—	Shoemaker	Discharged (non-conscript) 8/19/62.
Chapman, Chesley	Private	1838	—	Farm labor	**Killed, 6/26/62 (Mechanicsville).**
Cheek, John	Private	1835	New Middleton, Smith Co.	Farm labor	5th Sgt. 4/30/62. WIA 7/3/63. 4th Sgt. 12/63. **Killed, 5/5/64 (Wilderness).**
Close, John S.	Private	1833	Wolf Creek, Dekalb Co.	Boot salesman	WIA 5/12/64. Captured 4/3–9/65.
Coe, Martin Van Buren	Private	1841	Trucker's Crossroads, Wilson Co.	Farm labor	**Died of disease, 9/25/61.**
Compton, Jasper, N.	Private	1838	Alexandria, Dekalb Co.	Clerk	**Died of disease, 9/15/61.**

7th Tennessee Infantry Company A

Name	Initial Rank	D.O.B.	Home	Prewar Occupation	Comments
Cosby, John W.	Private	1838	—	Coach trimmer	Discharged (eye problems) 11/21/61.
Cowen, George W.	Private	1829	Nashville, Davidson Co.	Lawyer	2nd Lt. 4/26/62. 1st Lt. 9/17/62. **Killed, 7/3/63 (Gettysburg).**
Curtis, Hiram	Private	1843	Helton, Dekalb Co.	Farm labor	WIA 8/9/62. No other records after this date.
Davis, Thomas	Private	1838	Helton, Dekalb Co.	Farm labor	WIA (left hand) 5/31/62. WIA (head & right thigh) 8/19/64. Discharged (wounds) 12/13/64.
Driver, George W.	Private	1841	Smith Co.	—	3rd Cpl. 4/30/62. **Killed, 5/31/62 (Seven Pines).**
Emerique, Alphonso	Private	1841	Tucker's Crossroads, Wilson Co.	Clerk	WIA 6/26/62. 4th Sgt. 4/11/64. **Killed, 5/5/64 (Wilderness).**
Floyd, Robert D.	Private	1837	Alexandria, Dekalb Co.	Student	5th Sgt. 10/31/61. Reduced (Pvt.) 4/30/62. Commissary Sgt. 7/1/63. Captured 4/2/65.
Floyd, William T.	Private	1837	Alexandria, Dekalb Co.	Student (law)	Discharged (disability) 5/1/62.
Foster, William J.	Private	1845	Alexandria, Dekalb Co.	Stage driver	Discharged (minority) 8/19/62.
Foutch, Dixon A.	Private	1839	Helton, Dekalb Co.	Teacher	Discharged (disability) 11/7/61.
Foutch, Elijah A.	Private	1843	Helton, Dekalb Co.	Farm labor	Discharged (disability) 11/7/61.
Foutch, Francis "Frank" L.	Private	1834	Helton, Dekalb Co.	Farm labor	4th Sgt. 11/19/61. Reduced (Pvt.) 4/30/62. Captured 7/3/63. POW rest of war.
Foutch, Levi D.	Private	1839	Helton, Dekalb Co.	Farm labor	Deserted 9/17/63.
Garrison, John B.	Private	1838	Alexandria, Dekalb Co.	Farm labor	**Killed, 5/31/62 (Seven Pines).**
Goodner, Thomas W.	Private	1841	Alexandria, Dekalb Co.	Farm labor	3rd Cpl. 5/31/62. Captured 7/3/63. Released, 2/18/65.
Gregston, George W.	Private	1834	Smithville, Dekalb Co.	Wagoneer	2nd Sgt. 4/30/62. 3rd Lt. 7/17/62. WIA (left arm amputated) 5/3/63. Retired, 9/18/64.
Griffin, William C.	Private	1836	Rutledge, Grainger Co.	Carpenter	4th Cpl. 4/26/62. Captured 5/31/62. Exchanged. Captured 4/2/65.
Harris, James A.	Private	1836	Liberty, Dekalb Co.	Minister	Chaplain 8/24/63. Surrendered 4/9/65 (Appomattox).
Hendrickson, Abram H.	Private	1841	Forks of Pike, Dekalb Co.	Farm labor	Deserted 6/13/62.
Hinsley, William	Private	1827	Alexandria, Dekalb Co.	Farm labor	Discharged (disability) 6/19/62.
Hullett, William	Private	1841	Helton, Dekalb Co.	Farm labor	Discharged (disability) 8/15/63.
Johnson, John	Private	1839	Smithville, Dekalb Co.	Day laborer	WIA 5/31/62. Deserted 3/65.

Name	Initial Rank	D.O.B.	Home	Prewar Occupation	Comments
Lamberson, George W.	Private	1835	Liberty, Dekalb Co.	Farmer	3rd Sgt. 4/30/62. WIA 7/1/63. Captured 7/3/63. POW rest of war.
Lamberson, William R.	Private	1841	Walker's Cr., Dekalb Co.	Farm labor	2nd Cpl. 4/30/62. Captured 7/1/63. POW rest of war.
Lincoln, Lewis C.	Private	1845	Alexandria, Dekalb Co.	Student	Discharged (minority) 8/19/62.
Luck, John L.	Private	1838	Cherry Valley, Wilson Co.	Blacksmith	WIA (right arm) & captured 7/3/63. Exchanged 8/17/63. Discharged (wounds) 1/15/64.
Malone, Robert David	Private	1841	Helton, Dekalb Co.	Farm labor	Discharged (disability) 12/7/61.
Martin, John D.	Private	1837	Dry Creek, Dekalb Co.	Farm labor	1st Cpl. 4/30/62. Deserted 8/30/62
Martin, Joseph J.	Private	1839	—	—	Captured 5/31/62. Exchanged 9/62. Deserted 3/1/64.
Mason, Phillip J.	Private	1838	—	Farm labor	**Killed, 5/31/62 (Seven Pines).**
McGuffey, Levi D.	Private	1828	—	Farmer	**Died of disease, 9/15/62.**
Moore, Theodore	Private	1841	Alexandria, Dekalb Co.	Day laborer	WIA 5/31/62. Captured 4/2/65.
Murfee, Ervin V.	Private	1826	Helton, Dekalb Co.	Farmer	1st Cpl. 12/31/61. Reduced (Pvt.) 4/30/62. Discharged (seniority) 8/19/62.
Murray, George W.	Private	1838	Wilson Co.	—	2nd Sgt. 8/31/63. 1st Sgt. 4/27/64. Captured 4/2/65.
Newby, Thomas A.	Private	1838	—	Farm labor	Discharged (disability) 11/7/61.
Newsom, Horace "Harrison"	Private	1842	Alexandria, Dekalb Co.	Shoemaker	Discharged (disability) 7/22/62.
Newsom, Richard H.	Private	1839	—	Farm labor	Discharged (disability) 7/25/62.
Nix, John G.	Private	1843	Wilson Co.	—	Captured 5/31/62. Paroled. WIA 9/14/62. Captured 7/3/63. Paroled. Captured 5/5/64. POW rest of war.
Parkinson, Littleton	Private	1841	Helton, Dekalb Co.	Day laborer	**Killed, 5/3/63 (Chancellorsville).**
Paty, Burr	Private	1840	—	Merchant	Discharged (disability) 11/7/61.
Pendleton, John W.	Private	1842	Wilson Co.	Farm labor	Discharged (disability) 1/7/62.
Read, John	Private	1828	—	Farmer	Discharged (disability) 12/7/61.
Reasonover, George	Private	1840	Alexandria, Dekalb Co.	Day laborer	2nd Sgt. 9/18/62. 1st Sgt. 8/31/63. Deserted 3/1/64.
Sandlin, Isaac	Private	1836	Alexandria, Dekalb Co.	Farmer	4th Cpl. 4/30/62. WIA 5/31/62. Deserted 7/1/62.
Sewell, Daniel W. "Watts"	Private	1839	Dekalb Co.	Farm labor	**Killed, 5/31/62 (Seven Pines).**
Sewell, William	Private	1845	Walker's Cr., Dekalb Co.	Farm labor	Discharged (minority) 8/19/62.
Shanks, John W.	Private	1826	—	Carpenter	Discharged (disability) 2/14/62.
Shaver, Charles P.	Private	1839	—	Farm labor	Discharged (disability) 2/11/62.
Sims, William R.	Private	1840	—	Farm labor	**Died of disease, 1/5/62.**

Name	Initial Rank	D.O.B.	Home	Prewar Occupation	Comments
Sneed, Thomas J.	Private	1836	Alexandria, Dekalb Co.	Student	WIA 8/20/62. WIA & captured 7/1/63. POW rest of war.
Snyder, Daniel W.	Private	1839	Dekalb Co.	—	Captured 7/1/63.
Sullins, Walter	Private	1845	—	Farm labor	Discharged (minority) 8/19/62.
Terry, William	Private	1840	—	—	Deserted 2/8/63.
Tracy, Andrew	Private	1837	Wilson Co.	Farm labor	Discharged (disability) 6/20/62.
Trousdale, William W.	Private	1838	—	Farm labor	**Died of disease, 9/4/61.**
Webb, Thomas J.	Private	1836	Lebanon, Wilson Co.	Student (medical)	Hospital Steward 4/20/62. Asst. Surg. 5/1/63. Captured 4/6/65.
Williams, John	Private	1833	Temperance Hall, Dekalb Co.	Farmer	4th Sgt. 9/17/62. WIA (left knee & right leg) 7/3/63. **Died of wounds, 9/7/63.**
Williams, Owen J.	Private	1825	—	Farmer	Discharged (seniority) 8/19/62.
Willoughby, William	Private	1840	Buchanan, Henry Co.	Farm labor	Captured 7/14/63. **POW—Died of disease, 12/5/63.**
Wilson, R. M.	Private	1838	—	—	Discharged (disability) 4/15/62.
Winfrey, James A.	Private	1837	Dekalb Co.	—	4th Sgt. 4/30/62. 1st Sgt. 9/17/62. **Killed, 7/3/63 (Gettysburg).**
Yeargin, Thomas W.	Private	1826	—	—	1st Sgt. 12/19/61. Discharged (seniority) 8/19/62.
Yeargin, Wesley C.	Private	1837	Davidson Co.	—	Deserted 3/4/64.
Ashby, Samuel	Conscript	1814	Sullivan Co.	Farmer	Drafted 7/12/63. Deserted 8/30/63.
Batts, A. W.	Conscript	—	—	—	Drafted 7/63. Captured 1/12/64.
Cheek, Andrew J.	Recruit	1840	Dekalb Co.	Farm labor	Enlisted 8/2/62. **Died of disease, 10/6/62.**
Davis, S. L.	Conscript	1836	—	—	Drafted 4/1/64. Discharged (disability) 6/1/64.
Hood, Benjamin F.	Conscript	—	—	—	Drafted 7/8/63. Deserted 8/30/63.
Hood, Henry H.	Conscript	—	—	—	Drafted 7/8/63. Deserted 8/30/63.
Jones, Elyah	Conscript	1836	Hawkins Co.	—	Drafted 7/14/63. Deserted 9/5/63.
Light, Thomas	Conscript	1828	—	Farmer	Drafted 7/10/63. Deserted 8/2/63.
Pratt, Andrew J.	Conscript	1832	Green Co.	Farmer	Drafted 7/15/63. Deserted 8/10/63.
Risden, James	Conscript	—	—	—	Drafted 7/20/63. Deserted 8/30/63.

Company B. "Moore's Guards"

Name	Initial Rank	D.O.B.	Home	Prewar Occupation	Comments
Fite, John B	Captain	1832	Dixon Spr., Smith Co.	Lawyer	Maj. 5/23/62. Lt. Col. 7/9/62. WIA (chest) 8/9/62. Col. 4/8/63. WIA (leg) & captured 7/3/63. POW, Johnson's Is. rest of war.
Allen, John D.	1st Lt.	1837	Carthage, Smith Co.	Merchant	Capt. 5/23/62. WIA 5/31/62. WIA (neck) & captured 7/3/63. Exchanged 4/27/64. WIA 4/2/65. Surrendered 4/9/65 (Appomattox).

Name	Initial Rank	D.O.B.	Home	Prewar Occupation	Comments
Greer, Joseph "Joe"	2nd Lt.	1833	—	—	Relieved of duty, 4/25/62.
Moore, John H. "Jack"	3rd Lt.	1843	Carthage, Smith Co.	Student	2nd Lt. 4/26/62. 1st Lt. 11/18/64. Surrendered 4/9/65 (Appomattox).
Corder, James H.	1st Sgt.	1824	Carthage, Smith Co.	Merchant	Reduced (Pvt.) 5/1/62. Discharged (seniority) 8/22/62. Reg't. Sutler 1/63. Sutler rest of war. Paroled 4/9/65.
Allen, Armstrong	2nd Sgt.	1839	—	—	Discharged (disability) 7/1/61.
Lapsley, John D.	3rd Sgt.	1827	Carthage, Smith Co.	Merchant	3rd Lt. 4/30/62. WIA 9/17/62. WIA (both legs) 6/3/64. In hospital rest of war.
McDonald, William H. "Mac"	4th Sgt.	1839	Carthage, Smith Co.	Student (law)	Reduced (Pvt.) 4/26/62. Discharged (disability) 7/29/62.
Timberlake, Francis A. "Frank"	5th Sgt.	1832	Carthage, Smith Co.	Merchant	2nd Lt. 4/26/62. 1st Lt. 8/31/62. WIA (side) & captured 7/3/63. Exchanged 4/22/64. Retired (wounds) 11/18/64.
Mann, Stephen S.	1st Cpl.	1831	Carthage, Smith Co.	Merchant	Discharged (disability) 7/1/61.
Ferrill, Andrew Somers	2nd Cpl.	1825	—	Farmer	Reduced (Pvt.) 4/30/62. Discharged (seniority) 8/22/62.
Phelps, Silas M.	3rd Cpl.	1835	—	Farmer	Discharged (disability) 2/10/62.
Boulton, John D.	4th Cpl.	1834	Rome, Smith Co.	Farm labor	Reduced (Pvt.) 4/30/62. Captured 7/3/63. POW rest of war.
Thompson, Robert A.	5th Cpl.	1837	Smith Co.	—	Reduced (Pvt.) 4/30/62. Captured 7/14/63. Exchanged 3/3/64. Captured 4/2/65.
Reeves, Francis M. "Frank"	Musician	1842	Carthage	Student	Captured 4/2/65.
Abner, James	Private	1845	Smith Co.	—	Captured 4/2/65.
Anderson, Overton B.	Private	1824	—	Farmer	Discharged (seniority) 8/22/62.
Apple, Anthony	Private	1840	Smith Co.	Farm labor	4th Sgt. 4/30/62. WIA 8/9/62. Captured 7/3/63. POW until exchanged 2/27/65. Captured 4/5/62.
Apple, Henderson	Private	1843	—	Farm labor	Discharged (not a citizen of CSA) 8/19/62.
Beasley, Henry	Private	1845	Pleasant Shade, Smith Co.	Farm labor	Discharged (minority) 8/19/62. Re-enlisted 1/1/63. WIA & captured 7/3/63. POW rest of war.
Beasley, John H.	Private	1839	Dixon Spr., Smith Co.	Farm labor	Deserted 6/15/62.
Beck, Armstrong	Private	1840	—	—	Discharged (disability) 7/1/61.
Black, David	Private	1840	Dixon Spr., Smith Co.	Farm labor	Captured 4/2/65.
Boulton, James John	Private	1824	Rome, Smith Co.	Tenant Farmer	Discharged (disability) 11/23/61.
Boze, William C "Billie"	Private	1840	Gordonsville, Smith Co.	Farm labor	2nd Cpl. 4/30/62. WIA 8/9/62. TDY (hospital guard) 3/63 to end of war.
Bradley, Andrew Jack	Private	1841	Dixon Spr., Smith Co.	Student	WIA (head) 6/27/62. Captured 7/3/63. Paroled 10/10/64. Surrendered 4/9/65 (Appomattox)

7th Tennessee Infantry Company B

Name	Initial Rank	D.O.B.	Home	Prewar Occupation	Comments
Bradley, James A. "Jim"	Private	1837	Dixon Spr., Smith Co.	Asst. Marshall	4th Cpl. 8/15/62. Surrendered 4/9/65 (Appomattox)
Bradley, Leonard Keeling	Private	1833	—	Carpenter	Wounded (knee) 4/15/62. Discharged (wounds) 6/20/62.
Bradley, William T.	Private	1839	Dixon Spr., Smith Co.	Student	Captured 12/13/62. Paroled. WIA (right leg) & captured 7/3/63. Exchanged 7/20/63. WIA (face & leg) 4/2/65. Captured 4/3–8/65.
Brown, Enoch	Private	1810	—	Farm labor	Discharged (seniority) 8/19/72.
Burnett, David L.	Private	1838	Carthage, Smith Co.	Farm labor	**Died of disease, 5/17/63.**
Campbell, John H.	Private	1832	New Middleton, Smith Co.	Farm labor	Transferred to 20th Tenn. 7/1/61.
Carlisle, George C.	Private	1838	—	—	WIA 9/12/62. Deserted 11/12/62.
Carlisle, William Floyd	Private	1835	—	—	WIA (knee) 5/3/63. **Died of wounds, 6/10/63.**
Chambers, Peter L.	Private	1840	Carthage, Smith Co.	Clerk	Discharged (disability) 7/29/62.
Conditt, William H. "Billy"	Private	1837	Chestnut Mound, Smith Co.	Farm labor	WIA 7/8/63. Captured 5/8/64. POW rest of war.
Corley, Daniel B.	Private	1837	—	Mechanic	**Died of disease, 9/17/61.**
Dawson, Henry J.	Private	1828	Smith Co.	Farmer	Sick in hospital most of war. Discharged (disability) 1/15/65.
Dawson, Isaac "Ike" or "Bully Ike"	Private	1835	Smith Co.	Farm labor	Captured 7/20/63. No records for rest of war.
Dawson, James	Private	1840	Lebanon, Wilson Co.	Stage driver	Discharged (disability) 6/2/61.
Dawson, John	Private	1840	—	Farm labor	**Killed, 5/31/62 (Seven Pines).**
Dillard, Palaeman G.	Private	1836	Dixon Spr., Smith Co.	Lawyer	Captured 12/13/62. Exchanged. WIA & captured 7/3/63. Exchanged 10/20/63. TDY — Qtr. Mstr. 7/64. Captured 4/2/65.
Duke, Felix G.	Private	1833	—	—	Sick since 7/15/61. Discharged (disability) 10/3/62.
Duke, Samuel J.	Private	1838	Dixon Spr., Smith Co.	Farm labor	Deserted 9/18/63.
Duke, Wesley H.	Private	1839	—	Farm labor	Discharged (disability) 2/10/62.
Ferguson, Benjamin "Ben"	Private	1835	Granville, Jackson Co.	Farmer	Discharged (disability) 11/27/61.
Ferrell, James Walker	Private	1832	Elmwood, Smith Co.	Farm labor	WIA (knees & hips) 8/9/62. Deserted 9/15/62.
Fields, James	Private	1844	Club Springs, Smith Co.	Farm labor	Discharged (minority) 8/19/62.
Gibbs, Frederick "Fred"	Private	1834	Rome, Smith Co.	Tinner	WIA (right arm amputated) 5/3/63. Discharged (wounds) 8/63.
Gibbs, Richard C.	Private	1843	Smith Co.	—	WIA (knee) 8/9/62. TDY (nurse) 9/62 to 6/64. WIA (right leg) 8/20/64. Captured 4/2/65.

Name	Initial Rank	D.O.B.	Home	Prewar Occupation	Comments
Gillespie, James	Private	1835	Dixon Spr., Smith Co.	Farmer	Discharged (disability) 11/8/61. Re-enlisted 12/62. TDY (teamster) 5/63 to 9/64. Deserted 9/25/64.
Goodall, Francis M. "Frank"	Private	1844	Carthage, Smith Co.	Student	WIA (hip) 12/13/62. WIA (left foot) 5/12/64. Captured 4/2/65.
Hall, John	Private	1836	Carthage, Smith Co.	Farmer	WIA & captured 7/3/63. **POW — Died of disease, 10/17/63.**
Haney, Martin C.	Private	1839	Pleasant Shade, Smith Co.	Farm labor	Discharged (disability) 6/2/61.
Haynie, James	Private	1837	—	Farm labor	Discharged (disability) 12/14/61.
Hays, Henry C.	Private	1845	—	Farm labor	Discharged (minority) 8/19/62.
High, Branch N.	Private	1840	Carthage, Smith Co.	Farm labor	Captured 7/14/63. Exchanged 3/3/64. 5th Sgt. 8/64. Surrendered 4/9/65 (Appomattox).
Hopkins, Joseph H.	Private	1845	Elmwood, Smith Co.	Farm labor	Captured 7/3/63. POW rest of war.
Horn, James M. "Jim"	Private	1843	Chestnut Mound, Smith Co.	Farm labor	Captured 12/13/62. Exchanged. Captured 7/1/63. Paroled to Tennessee, 8/63.
Hughes, George W.	Private	1841	Rome, Smith Co.	Farm labor	Captured 5/25/64. Joined U.S. army 6/15/64.
James, William "Bill"	Private	1835	Carthage, Smith Co.	Farmer	Deserted 6/15/62.
Jarred, William C.	Private	1837	—	—	WIA 8/9/62. In hospital until 6/63. No other records.
Johnson, James H.	Private	1840	Dixon Spr., Smith Co.	Clerk	1st Sgt. 4/30/62. WIA (arm & lung) 6/27/62. **Died of wounds, 7/7/62.**
Johnson, Richard "Dick"	Private	1842	Smith Co.	—	2nd Sgt. 4/30/62. Captured 7/14/63. POW until exchanged 3/3/64. 1st Sgt. 9/1/64. Surrendered 4/9/65 (Appomattox).
Jones, Henry	Private	1840	—	Farm labor	Discharged (disability) 5/20/62.
Key, George M.	Private	1836	Pleasant Shade, Smith Co.	Farmer	Discharged (disability) 11/8/61.
King, Samuel H. "Sam"	Private	1841	Carthage, Smith Co.	Student	WIA & captured 7/3/63. POW rest of war.
Knight, Elijah H.	Private	1841	Elmwood, Smith Co.	Farm labor	WIA (left breast) 12/13/62. Deserted 6/1/63.
Knight, James H.	Private	1839	Elmwood, Smith Co.	Farm labor	4th Cpl. 4/30/62. WIA 6/27/62. **Died of wounds, 8/11/62.**
Lapsey, Norvell A.	Private	1831	Carthage, Smith Co.	Physician	Discharged (disability) 11/8/61.
Lynch, David J.	Private	1838	Dixon Spr., Smith Co.	Student	WIA (arm & hip) & captured 7/3/63. Exchanged 11/20/63. Furloughed to Tennessee.
McCall, John T.	Private	1842	Carthage, Smith Co.	Merchant's asst.	Captured 4/2/65.
McClain, Charles M.	Private	1840	Gordonsville, Smith Co.	Farm labor	1st Sgt. 7/10/62. WIA (head) 5/3/63. Captured 7/3/63. POW rest of war.

Name	Initial Rank	D.O.B.	Home	Prewar Occupation	Comments
McDonald, Henry C.	Private	1835	Carthage, Smith Co.	Physician	Transferred to 8th Tennessee, 6/10/61.
McGee, William H.	Private	1841	Smith Co.	—	WIA (head) & captured 7/3/63. Paroled 8/63. Deserted 2/1/64.
McKinney, George	Private	1842	Elmwood, Smith Co.	Farm labor	Captured 12/13/62. Exchanged. WIA 10/15/64. Captured 4/3–8/65.
Mitchell, Henry A.	Private	1836	Pleasant Shade, Smith Co.	Farmer	Captured 4/9/65 (Appomattox).
Oliver, Andrew	Private	1839	—	Merchant	Discharged (disability) 7/29/62.
Parvine, Lafayette	Private	1839	—	—	TDY (teamster) 8/13/62 to 4/64. WIA (left thigh amputated) 8/18/64. **Died of wounds, 9/25/64.**
Patterson, John W.	Private	1837	New Middleton, Smith Co.	Carpenter	Captured 7/1/63. Paroled. Deserted 9/15/63.
Paty, James H.	Private	1841	Gordonsville, Smith Co.	Farm labor	WIA 8/29/62. **Killed, 7/3/63 (Gettysburg).**
Paty, James M.	Private	1841	Rome, Smith Co.	Farm labor	Discharged (disability) 12/14/61.
Paty, John R.	Private	1843	Rome, Smith Co.	Farm labor	2nd Cpl. 4/30/62. WIA 8/30/62. TDY (nurse) until 10/63. 1st Cpl. 11/63. Captured 4/2/65.
Paty, Oren T.	Private	1843	—	Farm labor	**Died of disease, 12/1/61.**
Perry, Benjamin	Private	1843	Chestnut Mound, Smith Co.	Farm labor	4th Cpl. 10/31/63. Captured 4/2/65.
Phillips, William H.	Private	1843	Pleasant Shade, Smith Co.	Farm labor	**Died of disease, 11/5/61.**
Piper, Alexander	Private	1835	Pleasant Shade, Smith Co.	Farmer	5th Sgt. 9/30/61. Reduced (Pvt.) 4/30/62. WIA (thigh) 6/29/62. Reg't. Ordnance Sgt. 12/10/62. Surrendered 4/9/65 (Appomattox).
Piper, James	Private	1842	Carthage, Smith Co.	Clerk	Discharged (disability) 2/18/62.
Porter, Alexander "Alex"	Private	1834	Dixon Spr., Smith Co.	Farmer	Discharged (disability) 2/10/62.
Richards, Bailey P.	Private	1844	Carthage, Smith Co.	Farm labor	1st Cpl. 4/30/62. WIA (neck) 8/9/62. **Died of wounds, 8/12/62.**
Rison, Henry C.	Private	1840	Smith Co.	—	WIA (left leg) & captured 7/3/63. **POW—Died of wounds, 8/15/63.**
Robison, James M.	Private	—	—	—	Deserted 10/3/62.
Royster, Ira E. "Ike"	Private	1837	Dixon Spr., Smith Co.	Farm labor	Captured 7/14/63. POW until exchanged 3/3/64. WIA (left arm) 6/3/64. Captured 4/9/65 (Appomattox).
Sexton, James M.	Private	1841	Carthage, Smith Co.	Farm labor	Captured 12/13/62. Exchanged. Deserted 8/4/63.
Shoemaker, Germain	Private	1843	Carthage, Smith Co.	—	**Killed, 7/10/64 (Petersburg trenches).**

Name	Initial Rank	D.O.B.	Home	Prewar Occupation	Comments
Shoemaker, John	Private	1839	Carthage, Smith Co.	Carpenter	WIA 8/9/62. Put on medical leave. No other records.
Smith, Elezear "Ale"	Private	1830	Carthage, Smith Co.	Constable	Deserted 8/1/63.
Smith, Nelson E.	Private	1842	—	—	WIA 9/14/62. Put on medical leave. Deserted 10/10/62.
Stanfield, Joseph W.	Private	1818	—	Farmer	Discharged (disability) 7/29/62.
Stott, William A.	Private	1840	Rome, Smith Co.	Teacher	Discharged (disability) 2/22/62.
Thackston, Benjamin F.	Private	1842	Chestnut Mound, Smith Co.	Farm labor	WIA 8/30/62. WIA (neck) 7/3/63. WIA (left leg) & captured 4/2/65.
Thackston, Blake B.	Private	1840	Chestnut Mound, Smith Co.	Farm labor	5th Sgt. 4/30/62. WIA 8/9/62. WIA (thigh) 12/13/62. TDY (guard) 9/63 to end of war.
Thompson, Leonidas	Private	1839	Smith Co.	—	3rd Sgt. 4/30/62. Captured 7/14/63. POW rest of war.
Timberlake, Fountain	Private	1842	Carthage, Smith Co.	—	Captured 7/3/63. POW rest of war.
Trimble, Nathaniel W. "Nat"	Private	1841	Gallatin, Sumner Co.	Farm labor	Captured 7/3/63. POW rest of war.
Tubb, William R.	Private	1839	Chestnut Mound, Smith Co.	Carpenter	Discharged (disability) 6/20/62.
Tumlin, George H.	Private	1845	—	Student	Discharged (minority) 8/19/62.
Ward, William W.	Private	1832	Carthage, Smith Co.	Lawyer	Discharged (disability) 5/20/62.
Warmack, Albert G.	Private	1842	Smith Co.	—	WIA 5/5/64. Captured 4/3/65.
Washam, William A.	Private	1843	—	Farm labor	Discharged (disability) 6/20/62.
Yeaman, Robert H. "Bob"	Private	1844	—	Carpenter	Discharged (disability) 2/20/62.
Blair, Andrew	Recruit	1839	Carthage, Smith Co.	—	Enlisted 11/8/62. WIA 5/5/64. Captured 4/2/65.
Bonner, John J.	Conscript	—	—	—	Drafted 7/22/63. Deserted 9/14/63.
Boulton, Edward B.	Recruit	1842	—	—	Enlisted 2/23/63. WIA 5/3/63. Deserted 7/15/63.
Boulton, William T.	Recruit	1826	Elmwood, Smith Co.	Farmer	Enlisted 11/8/62. Deserted 7/20/63.
Derickson, Joseph "Seth"	Transfer— Co. K	1840	—	Farm labor	Transferred from Co. K, 5/1/62. **Killed, 8/30/62 (2nd Manassas).**
Derickson, Samuel W. "Sam"	Transfer— Co. K	1839	Wilson Co.	—	Transferred from Co. K, 5/1/62. WIA 12/13/62. Captured 7/14/63. POW until taking Oath 4/11/64.
Gann, George C.	Transfer— Co. K	1840	—	—	Transferred from Co. K, 5/1/62. **Died of disease, 6/19/63.**
Griffin, Charles T.	Transfer— Co. K	1833	—	—	Transferred from Co. K, 5/1/62. Deserted 8/15/63.

Name	Initial Rank	D.O.B.	Home	Prewar Occupation	Comments
Hale, James B. "Jimmy"	Transfer—Co. K	1833	Rainy, Smith Co.	Carpenter	Transferred from Co. K, 5/1/62. WIA 12/13/62. WIA & captured 7/3/63. Paroled. Captured 4/2/65.
Hale, John C.	Transfer—Co. K	1836	Wilson Co.	—	Transferred from Co. K, 5/1/62. WIA (head) 5/3/63. **Killed, 5/5/64 (Wilderness).**
Hubbard, Thomas J.	Transfer—Co. K	1839	Dixon Spr., Smith Co.	Farm labor	Transferred from Co. K, 5/1/62. WIA & captured 7/3/63. **Died of wounds, 8/2/63.**
Johnson, John W.	Recruit	1845	Spencer, Van Buren Co.	Farm labor	Enlisted 3/4/63. Captured 4/3–8/65.
Lang, John	Recruit	—	—	—	Enlisted 11/8/62. TDY (nurse) in Tennessee, 12/62. No other records.
Lynch, John	Recruit	1840	—	—	Enlisted 11/8/62. TDY (nurse) 5/1/63 to 6/64. Captured 4/2/65.
Rucks, Howell T.	Transfer—Co. K	1839	Rainy, Smith Co.	Farm labor	Transferred from Co. K 5/1/62. 1st Cpl. 8/15/62. Sick since 10/24/62. Transferred to 3rd Tenn. Cavalry, 4/1/63.
Sexton, Robert	Recruit	1844	—	Farm labor	Enlisted 11/8/62. **Died of disease, 12/28/62.**
Shoemaker, James H.	Recruit	1842	Carthage, Smith Co.	Farm labor	Enlisted 11/8/62. WIA (right foot) 5/3/63. **Died of wounds, 5/14/63.**

Company C. "Sumner Minutemen"

Name	Initial Rank	D.O.B.	Home	Prewar Occupation	Comments
Baber, James	Captain	1838	Gallatin, Sumner Co.	Farm labor	**Died of disease, 12/15/61.**
Fry, John D.	1st Lt.	1832	—	—	Capt. 12/23/61. WIA 5/31/62. WIA (right wrist) 5/3/63. Resigned (wounds) 9/11/63.
Wallace, Jehu C.	2nd Lt.	1826	—	—	Relieved of duty, 4/26/62.
Boddy, Elijah	3rd Lt.	1843	Gallatin, Sumner Co.	Farm labor	2nd Lt. 6/1/62. 1st Lt. 9/11/63. Captured 5/5/64. **POW—Died of disease, 3/15/65.**
Foster, Oliver H.	1st Sgt.	1836	Gallatin, Sumner Co.	Tailor	1st Lt. 12/23/61. Capt. 9/11/63. Captured 5/5/64. POW rest of war.
Franklin, John A.	2nd Sgt.	1840	—	—	Reduced (Pvt.) 4/26/62. WIA 12/13/62. TDY (Div. Qtr Mstr.) 11/30 63. Transferred to 13th VA. Cav., 12/5/64.
Phillips, William H.	3rd Sgt.	1826	—	Painter	1st Sgt. 12/23/61. Discharged (disability) 2/9/62.
Ingram, Cassius V.	4th Sgt.	1839	—	Druggist	2nd Lt. 4/26/62. **Killed—5/31/62 (Seven Pines).**
Castleman, Gad	1st Cpl.	1832	Nashville, Davidson Co.	Clerk	1st Sgt. 2/9/62. Reduced (Pvt.) 4/26/62. TDY (commissary Dept.) 5/62. Paroled 4/10/65 (Appomattox)

Name	Initial Rank	D.O.B.	Home	Prewar Occupation	Comments
Lucas, John	2nd Cpl.	1839	—	—	Deserted 3/5/63.
Searcy, Reuben T.	3rd Cpl.	1838	Green Hill, Wilson Co.	Student (literary)	Reduced (Pvt.) 4/26/62. Deserted 1/7/65.
Cleney, Henry	4th Cpl.	1836	—	Carpenter	Discharged (disability) 12/1/61.
Abbott, Henry	Private	1845	—	Saddler	3rd Cpl. 4/26/62. Discharged (minority) 8/22/62.
Anderson, Joseph	Private	1839	—	Farm labor	WIA (hip) 8/29/62. **Died of wounds, 9/5/62.**
Baber, John	Private	1834	—	—	WIA 5/31/62. Deserted 3/25/63.
Baber, Joseph G.	Private	1836	—	—	WIA 5/31/62. Deserted 8/9/62.
Baber, William	Private	1841	Gallatin, Sumner Co.	Farm labor	3rd Lt. 6/1/62. 2nd Lt. 9/11/63. WIA (right shoulder) 6/3/64. Retired (wounds) 12/9/64.
Branhan, Daniel	Private	1839	Gallatin, Sumner Co.	Day laborer	Captured 7/3/63. No other records.
Brasnahan, Thomas	Private	1835	Gallatin, Sumner Co.	—	WIA (leg & face) 7/3/63. Captured 7/5/63. POW until 3/15/64 (escaped). No other records
Brown, Alfred D.	Private	1839	Laguardo, Wilson Co.	Farm labor	WIA (arm) 7/3/63. Captured 3/9/65 (Appomattox).
Brown, John J.	Private	1835	—	Saddler	Discharged (alienage) 9/5/62.
Buck, Calvin E. "Cal"	Private	1840	Gallatin, Sumner Co.	Printer	Captured 7/3/63. POW rest of war.
Buck, James K. "Jim"	Private	1841	Gallatin, Sumner Co.	Blacksmith	WIA (leg) 5/31/62. Captured 7/1/63. No other records.
Buck, Madison	Private	1839	—	—	WIA (arm) & captured 5/31/62. Exchanged 12/1/62. Deserted 12/1/62.
Burke, James	Private	—	—	—	WIA & captured 7/3/63. No other records.
Busby, John	Private	1815	—	Machinist	Discharged (seniority) 9/5/62.
Campbell, George C.	Private	1835	—	—	WIA 5/31/62. Deserted 8/9/62.
Cantrell, Stephen O.	Private	1836	Gallatin, Sumner Co.	Farm labor	Captured 3/9/65 (Appomattox).
Clark, Reuben D.	Private	1837	—	Physician	TDY (Clerk in General's office) 8/24/61. Discharged (sent to Gen. Donelson HQ) 5/20/62.
Clarke, Edward G. "Ned"	Private	1842	—	—	**Killed, 8/29/62 (2nd Manassas).**
Clendening, James	Private	1837	Hendersonville, Sumner Co.	Farmer	Captured 7/3/63. POW until 11/64. Captured 3/5/65.
Cochran, Joshua R.	Private	1836	—	Farm labor	**Died of disease, 11/17/61.**
Collier, James R.	Private	1845	—	—	Deserted 12/17/61.
Crump, John A	Private	1840	—	Farm labor	4th Cpl. 11/30/61. Reduced (Pvt.) 4/26/62. WIA (thigh) 6/27/62. Discharged (wounds) 6/22/63.
Crump, William R.	Private	1838	Gallatin, Sumner Co.	Carpenter	Discharged (disability) 12/1/61.

Name	Initial Rank	D.O.B.	Home	Prewar Occupation	Comments
Davis, John W.	Private	1831	—	—	Discharged (disability) 1/27/62.
Douglas, James E.	Private	1841	—	—	4th Sgt. 8/1/62. 1st Sgt. 11/30/63. Sick on furlough since 2/18/65.
Edwards, Julius C.	Private	1841	Gallatin, Sumner Co.	Farm labor	2nd Cpl. 4/26/62. Sgt. 8/31/63. Captured 3/2/65.
Elkin, Colby	Private	1842	—	Farm labor	Discharged (disability) 1/25/62.
Elliott, James K.	Private	1845	—	—	Discharged (minority) 8/24/62.
Elliott, William S.	Private	1844	Gallatin, Sumner Co.	Blacksmith	WIA (hand) 5/31/62. Captured 7/3/63. Released. Captured 3/3/65.
Eubanks, Gilmore	Private	1838	—	Farm labor	**Killed, 12/13/62 (Fredericksburg).**
Faidley, Edward "Ed"	Private	1849	—	—	Deserted 8/26/62.
Foley, Edward	Private	1822	—	Painter	Discharged (seniority) 8/20/62.
Forbiss, John A.	Private	1826	—	Shoemaker	Discharged (disability) 2/9/62.
Forrester, Thomas N. "Tom"	Private	1842	—	Farm labor	WIA 8/9/62. **Died of wounds, 8/21/62.**
Gillespie, Foster C.	Private	1841	—	Farm labor	Discharged (disability) 2/2/62.
Goostree, Malkijah	Private	1840	—	Printer	Discharged (disability) 2/11/62.
Guthrie, Nathan L.	Private	1841	—	Farm labor	4th Sgt. 4/26/62. Discharged (disability) 6/22/62.
Hendricks, Mac	Private	1833	—	—	Deserted 7/10/61.
Henry, Jacob "Jake"	Private	1843	—	—	Discharged (disability) 9/30/61.
Herne, James W.	Private	1838	Shop Spr., Wilson Co.	Farm labor	Transferred to Co. D, 11/30/62.
Hester, Rufus	Private	1839	Gallatin, Sumner Co.	Farm labor	WIA 6/27/62. Captured 7/3/63. **POW—Died of disease, 12/27/63.**
Hill, John R.	Private	—	—	—	Captured 9/13/61. Exchanged 8/25/62. No other record.
Hope, Samuel R.	Private	1838	Sweetwater, Monroe Co.	Farmer	WIA (side) & captured 9/13/61. Exchanged 8/25/62. Sick in hospital until. **Died of disease, 9/20/64.**
Hubbard, James C.	Private	1845	—	Student	4th Cpl. 4/26/62. **Killed, 5/31/62 (Seven Pines).**
Jackson, Bailey P.	Private	1835	Sumner Co.	—	4th Cpl. 2/9/62. 2nd Sgt. 4/26/62. Captured 7/3/63. POW rest of war.
Jennett, David	Private	1838	—	Farm labor	1st Cpl. 7/1/63. **Killed, 11/27/63 (Mine Run).**
Kelly, John	Private	1835	—	Farm labor	**Died of disease, 1/12/62.**
Kirkpatrick, William "Buster"	Private	1839	Wilson Co.	—	WIA 5/3/63. Captured 4/2/65.
Leddy, Andrew J.	Private	1838	—	Farm labor	Discharged (disability) 8/15/62.
Lewis, John C.	Private	1839	—	—	WIA 5/31/62. Deserted 7/1/62.
Love, James .	Private	1840	—	Farm labor	**Killed, 12/13/62 (Fredericksburg).**
Loveall, Joseph M.	Private	1840	—	Farm labor	WIA & captured 5/31/62. **POW—Died of wounds, 9/1/62.**
Lownsborough, Thomas "Tom"	Private	1833	—	Shoemaker	Enlisted into CSA Navy, 3/31/64.

Name	Initial Rank	D.O.B.	Home	Prewar Occupation	Comments
Lowry, Jefferson H. "Jeff"	Private	1836	—	—	5th Sgt. 4/26/62. TDY (teamster/baggage guard) 8/20/62. Deserted 7/11/63.
Lum, Nathan	Private	1828	—	Day laborer	**WIA 5/3/63. Died of wounds, 5/19/63.**
Malone, David	Private	1843	—	—	Discharged (disability) 6/25/61.
Malone, Edward	Private	—	—	—	Discharged (disability) 7/2/61.
McKinley, William	Private	1837	—	Harness maker	Discharged (alienage) 8/24/62.
Prewett, Silas B.	Private	1836	—	—	Discharged (disability) 10/14/62.
Reed, Thomas "Tom"	Private	1839	Gallatin, Sumner Co.	Day laborer	4th Cpl. 8/1/62. Captured 4/2/65.
Roland, James N.	Private	1839	—	—	Deserted 8/25/61.
Roney, Elmore	Private	1837	Gallatin, Sumner Co.	Farm labor	TDY (commissary) 11/20/62, until 9/64. Captured 4/2/65.
Rose, Thomas "Tom"	Private	1845	Gallatin, Sumner Co.	Blacksmith apprentice	Discharged (minority) 8/24/62.
Rutledge, Richard J.	Private	1843	Gallatin, Sumner Co.	—	5th Sgt. 4/26/62. Missing, 5/5/64. No other record.
Shaub, Charles	Private	1840	Mitchellville, Robertson Co.	Carpenter	Cpl. 4/30/62. Captured 7/15/63. POW until exchange, 2/14/65. Captured 4/2/65.
Short, James	Private	1814	—	Farmer	TDY (teamster) 2/62. Discharged (seniority) 11/17/62.
Taylor, William	Private	1836	Gladesville, Wilson Co.	Farm labor	TDY (teamster) 2/62 to 10/64. Captured 4/3–8/65.
Turnage, James W.	Private	1837	Wilson Co.	—	WIA (leg) 5/31/62. Captured 4/2/65.
Tyree, George	Private	1831	—	—	Discharged (disability) 1/20/62.
Walker, William W.	Private	1843	—	Day laborer	**Killed, 5/31/62 (Seven Pines).**
Warren, Joshua	Private	1836	—	—	Sick from 11/16/61 to 9/64. **Drowned 10/31/64.**
Watkins, Charles W.	Private	1842	Gallatin, Sumner Co.	Student	Captured 7/3/63. POW rest of war.
Wells, Joseph	Private	1844	—	—	Discharged (disability) 11/20/61.
White, Henry	Private	1835	Gallatin, Sumner Co.	Weaver	Deserted 7/10/63.
Windham, Charles	Private	1839	—	—	WIA (right shoulder) 11/27/63. Hospitalized to end of war.
Windham, James	Private	1842	—	Day laborer	Discharged (disability) 9/30/61.
Woodall, Thomas C.	Private	1841	Gallatin, Sumner Co.	Farm labor	3rd Sgt. 12/23/61. Captured 4/2/65.
Wynne, William T.	Private	1836	—	—	WIA (right foot) 5/3/63. Medical leave until transferred to 2nd Tennessee Cavalry 4/64.
Young, James K.	Private	1824	—	—	Deserted 8/24/61.
Atchley, David	Conscript	1832	—	—	Drafted 7/22/63. Deserted 1/17/64.
Cheek, Joseph M.	Conscript	1826	—	—	Drafted 7/10/63. Deserted 8/13/63.
Crawford, John W.	Conscript	1838	—	—	Drafted 7/31/63. Deserted 8/12/63.

Name	Initial Rank	D.O.B.	Home	Prewar Occupation	Comments
Hale, Armstead	Conscript	1826	—	—	Drafted 7/31/63. Deserted 8/12/63.
Hale, George	Conscript	1843	—	—	Drafted 7/29/63. Deserted 9/16/62.
Loveall, James E.	Recruit	—	—	—	Enlisted 11/10/64. Captured 4/2/65.
Rutherford, Benjamin "Ben"	Recruit	1836	Hendersville, Sumner Co.	Merchant	Transferred from Co. E, 2/15/62. WIA (arm) 5/31/62. Captured 7/3/63. POW rest of war.
Smith, John	Conscript	1842	—	—	Drafted 7/63. Deserted 8/13/63.
Spencer, Noah N.	Recruit	1846	—	—	Enlisted 12/20/64. Deserted 1/27/65.
Tallant, William	Recruit	1837	—	—	Drafted 6/22/63. Deserted 9/16/63.

Company D. "Harris Rifles"

Name	Initial Rank	D.O.B.	Home	Prewar Occupation	Comments
Anderson, James Monroe	Captain	1839	—	—	Relieved of duty, 4/26/62.
Wharton, Joseph P.	1st Lt.	1836	—	—	Resigned (disability) 9/1/62.
Martin, William D.	2nd Lt.	1837	—	—	**Died of disease, 8/19/61.**
Walsh, Marcus Lafayette	3rd Lt.	1834	Mt. Carmel, Wilson Co.	Farm labor	2nd Lt. 9/25/61. Capt. 4/26/62. WIA 6/27/62. TDY (Reg'tal Qtr. Mstr.) 9/62, until 1/65. WIA (right heel) & captured 4/2/65.
Ralston, William T.	1st Sgt.	1838	Wilson Co.	Farm labor	Reduced (Pvt.) 4/26/62. 3rd Sgt. 9/1/62. Captured 7/3/63. POW rest of war.
Harris, Hart	2nd Sgt.	1834	Wilson Co.	—	1st Sgt. 4/26/62. WIA 12/13/62. WIA 7/3/63. Deserted 12/24/63.
Martin, James H.	3rd Sgt.	1839	Lebanon, Wilson Co.	Day laborer	2nd Lt. 4/26/62. 1st Lt. 8/31/62. WIA (right arm & right foot) 7/3/63. Captured 4/2/65.
Stratton, James E.	4th Sgt.	1839	—	—	Transferred to Co. H, 10/1/61.
Ralston, Luther W.	5th Sgt.	1840	Lebanon, Wilson Co.	Student	Reduced (Pvt.) 4/26/62. WIA & captured 7/3/63. POW rest of war.
Lester, Henry D.	1st Cpl.	1842	—	Student	4th Sgt. 10/1/61. **Died of disease, 12/17/61.**
Chambers, William L.	2nd Cpl.	1837	—	Farm labor	**Died of disease, 2/7/62.**
Hearn, George F.	3rd Cpl.	1840	Statesville, Wilson Co.	Farm labor	**Died of disease, 11/21/61.**
Wharton, Jesse	4th Cpl.	1839	—	Farm labor	Discharged (disability) 2/15/62.
Dailey, John	Teamster	1840	—	—	Deserted 6/1/62.
Alexander, George	Private	1845	—	Blacksmith	Discharged (minority) 8/19/62.
Allen, Frank Richard	Private	1846	Wilson Co.	Farm labor	Discharged (minority) 8/19/62.
Anderson, Dewitt	Private	1845	—	—	Discharged (surgeon's certificate) 9/25/61.
Bailey, Thomas	Private	1839	—	Farm labor	WIA 8/9/62. **Died of wounds, 8/12/62.**
Baker, Samuel	Private	1832	—	Farm labor	**Killed, 5/31/62 (Seven Pines).**

Name	Initial Rank	D.O.B.	Home	Prewar Occupation	Comments
Barkley, Joseph	Private	1817	—	Mill wright	Discharged (seniority) 8/19/62.
Berry, Harris	Private	1837	—	—	WIA (leg amputated) 8/29/62. No other records.
Bowers, Joseph C.	Private	1825	—	Carpenter	Discharged (seniority) 8/19/62.
Bradshaw, William M.	Private	1842	—	Farm labor	**Killed, 6/27/62 (Mechanicsville).**
Brown, Thomas E.	Private	1836	—	Tinner	WIA (thigh amputated) 12/13/62. **Died of wounds, 6/7/63.**
Bruce, William J.	Private	1839	Rainy, Smith Co.	Clerk	**Accidently killed by gunshot, 8/17/61.**
Bullard, Thomas W.	Private	1830	—	Mason	Discharged (disability) 10/10/62.
Calhoun, Samuel L.	Private	1826	—	Farmer	Discharged (seniority) 8/19/62.
Carson, Benjamin	Private	1838	Lebanon, Wilson Co.	Farm labor	TDY (teamster) 11/17/62 until 6/63. Sick on furlough since 1/27/65.
Carter, Henry C.	Private	1844	—	Farm labor	Discharged (minority) 8/19/62.
Carter, John S.	Private	1834	Lebanon, Wilson Co.	Merchant	Sgt. Maj. 6/27/62. 2nd Lt. 8/30/62. Captured 7/3/63. POW rest of war.
Chamberlain, Foster F.	Private	1838	—	—	WIA 8/29/62. Captured 5/4/63. POW rest of war.
Chamberlain, James M.	Private	1840	—	—	WIA 8/29/62. Deserted 8/10/63.
Chastin, John A.	Private	1836	—	—	Discharged (disability) 7/1/62.
Clary, James D.	Private	1838	—	—	WIA 6/30/62. In hospital until deserted 4/1/63.
Coe, Andrew D.	Private	1838	Tucker's Crossroads, Wilson Co.	Farm labor	**Killed, 6/27/62 (Mechanicsville).**
Dias, Jesse	Private	1844	—	Farm labor	Discharged (minority) 8/19/62.
Dillard, Pleasant	Private	1836	—	Farm labor	Discharged (disability) 6/20/62.
Donnell, John T.	Private	1841	Mt. Carmel, Wilson Co.	Farm labor	1st Cpl. 8/31/62. Captured 7/14/63. POW until taking the Oath, 1/24/64.
Donnell, Stephen M.	Private	1839	—	Farm labor	Discharged (disability) 5/12/62.
Evitts, Samuel P.	Private	1836	Dixon Spr., Smith Co.	Farm labor	Captured 4/2/65.
Evitts, William F.	Private	1838	Wilson Co.	—	4th Cpl. 11/1/64. Captured 4/2/65.
Ferrill, Benjamin B. "Shanks"	Private	1839	Rural Hill, Wilson Co.	Farm labor	Cpl. 4/11/64. Sick since 9/15/64 to end of war.
Freeman, James C.	Private	1841	Lebanon, Wilson Co.	Harness maker	4th Cpl. 4/26/62. Captured 7/3/63. POW rest of war.
Freeman, Robert B.	Private	1840	—	Carriage maker	**Died of disease, 10/24/61.**
Graves, James P.	Private	1838	—	Farm labor	WIA (shoulder joint) 5/31/62. Discharged (wounds) 10/18/62.
Graves, John F.	Private	1825	—	Farmer	Discharged (seniority) 8/19/62.
Graves, Samuel W.	Private	1837	Mt. Carmel, Wilson Co.	Blacksmith	WIA 8/29/62. TDY (blacksmith) from 9/62 to end of war. Paroled 4/9/65.

Name	Initial Rank	D.O.B.	Home	Prewar Occupation	Comments
Griffin, Charles. B.	Private	1845	—	Farm labor	Discharged (minority) 8/19/62.
Hatcher, Thomas W.	Private	1834	—	Farmer	TDY (teamster) 4/62 to, Captured 7/5/63. **POW — died of disease, 2/11/64.**
Hawkins, John A.	Private	1842	New Middleton, Smith Co.	Day laborer	Captured 4/2/65.
Hawkins, William T.	Private	1837	Lebanon, Wilson Co.	Blacksmith	WIA 12/13/62. WIA 7/3/63. Discharged (wounds) 1/18/64.
Hearn, Albert R.	Private	1839	—	Stone cutter	WIA 8/29/62. **Died of wounds, 9/16/62.**
Hearn, Albert W.	Private	1839	Lebanon, Wilson Co.	Clerk	3rd Sgt. 4/26/62. WIA 8/30/62. **Died of wounds, 9/20/62.**
Hearn, Hardy M.	Private	1825	Shop Spr., Wilson Co.	Farmer	**Died of disease, 10/5/61.**
Hearn, James D.	Private	1841	Shop Spr., Wilson Co.	Farm labor	WIA 5/31/62. WIA & captured 7/3/63. **Died of wounds, 8/16/63.**
Hearn, James E.	Private	1842	Shop Spr., Wilson Co.	Student	Discharged (disability) 11/9/61.
Hearn, James L.	Private	1841	Lebanon, Wilson Co.	—	WIA 5/31/62. In hospital until TDY (supply) 1/64 to 2/65. No other records.
Hearn, Mathew T.	Private	1840	—	Farm labor	**Died of disease, 9/11/61.**
Hearn, Richard A.	Private	1837	Shop Spr., Wilson Co.	Farm labor	Captured 7/3/63. POW rest of war.
Hearn, Thomas N.	Private	1835	Shop Spr., Wilson Co.	Farm labor	Sgt. 12/30/63. WIA (right hand) 5/5/64. 1st Sgt. 12/31/64. Surrendered 4/9/65 (Appomattox).
Helleman, George H.	Private	1841	—	Printer	**Killed, 5/31/62 (Seven Pines).**
Holloman, Coon	Private	—	—	—	Deserted 12/31/61.
Hughes, Robert C.	Private	1840	Lebanon, Wilson Co.	Farm labor	WIA & captured 7/1/63. Paroled 7/5/63. Sgt. 11/1/64. Captured 4/3–8/65.
Hunter, Burchett R.	Private	1834	—	Farm labor	WIA 5/31/62. WIA (right knee & leg) 5/3/63. In hospital until discharged (wounds) 9/25/64.
Irby, Robert J.	Private	1839	Shop Spr., Wilson Co.	Farmer	1st Cpl. 12/20/61. 2nd Sgt. 4/26/62. WIA 11/27/63. **Died of wounds, 11/29/63.**
Jaco, Andrew Jack	Private	1834	McMinnville, Warren Co.	—	Deserted 6/27/62.
Jennings, Samuel K.	Private	1844	Laguardo, Wilson Co.	Farm labor	3rd Cpl. 10/31/61. 2nd Cpl. 12/31/61. WIA (scalp) 5/31/62. Sgt. Maj. 8/30/62. Surrendered 4/9/65 (Appomattox).
Jennings, Thomas O.	Private	1843	—	—	Discharged (disability) 12/13/61.
Johnson, Thomas	Private	1838	White Co.	Farm labor	Captured 7/3/63. POW rest of war.
Johnson, Thomas H.	Private	1839	Lebanon, Wilson Co.	—	WIA 6/27/62. 2nd Cpl. 8/31/62. WIA 12/13/62. TDY (teamster) 8/17/62 to end of war.
Jones, Lorenzo R.	Private	1834	—	Farm labor	Discharged (disability) 6/19/62.

Name	Initial Rank	D.O.B.	Home	Prewar Occupation	Comments
Kavanaugh, John W.	Private	1841	Lebanon, Wilson Co.	Farm labor	Discharged (disability) 8/5/61.
Lamkins, William P.	Private	1835	Wilson Co.	—	Captured 4/2/65.
Lester, James R.	Private	1837	Lebanon, Wilson Co.	Physician's asst.	TDY (hospital steward) 9/61 until discharged (furnished a substitute) 6/11/62.
Lester, Joshua	Private	1840	Lebanon, Wilson Co.	Student	Discharged (disability) 2/11/62.
Little, Romanzoff	Private	1838	Wilson Co.	—	4th Sgt. 4/26/62. Deserted 12/24/63.
McClendenon, William	Private	1834	Davidson Co.	—	WIA 5/5/64. In hospital to end of war.
Miller, Andrew K.	Private	1842	Lebanon, Wilson Co.	Farm labor	5th Sgt. 4/26/62. 3rd Lt. 7/16/62. WIA 5/3/63. Captured 7/3/63. Released, 7/63. TDY (baggage train) to 1/65. Captured 4/3–8/65.
Miller, James P.	Private	1845	Lebanon, Wilson Co.	Shoe maker	Discharged (minority) 8/19/62.
Nettles, Joseph S.	Private	1845	—	Farm labor	Discharged (minority) 8/19/62.
Palmer, Richard H.	Private	1836	Lebanon, Wilson Co.	Farm labor	Surrendered 4/9/65 (Appomattox).
Parrow, William	Private	1828	Lebanon, Wilson Co.	Publisher	3rd Lt. 9/25/61. Relieved of duty, 4/26/62.
Ragland, Samuel	Private	1838	—	Farm labor	**Killed, 5/31/62 (Seven Pines).**
Ramsey, Thomas H.	Private	1835	Wilson Co.	Farm labor	Discharged (disability) 2/11/62.
Rogers, John M.	Private	1821	—	Stone cutter	Discharged (seniority) 8/19/62.
Seat, Hiram H.	Private	1826	Wilson Co.	Farmer	Discharged (seniority) 8/19/62.
Seat, John	Private	1843	Lebanon, Wilson Co.	Day laborer	**Died of disease, 4/15/62.**
Shaw, James M.	Private	1835	Lebanon, Wilson Co.	Farm labor	**Died of disease, 2/8/62.**
Shoemaker, William	Private	1837	Wilson Co.	Day laborer	WIA 7/27/62. **Died of wounds, 7/1/62.**
Shutt, George M.	Private	1838	Lebanon, Wilson Co.	Farm labor	Discharged (disability) 5/20/62.
Smith, William A.	Private	1836	—	—	Discharged (disability) 7/10/61.
Stevens, Bartholomew	Private	1831	Wilson Co.	Farmer	3rd Cpl. 8/31/62. Deserted 12/24/63.
Stiles, Allen B.	Private	1842	—	—	Deserted 6/1/62.
Tatum, Frank M.	Private	1835	—	—	3rd Lt. 4/26/62. Resigned (disability) 7/16/62.
Tribble, Haney	Private	1840	—	Farm labor	**Killed, 5/31/62 (Seven Pines).**
Walsh, Shelby	Private	1841	Wilson Co.	Farm labor	Discharged (disability) 11/9/61.
Walton, Robert J.	Private	1838	Wilson Co.	Farmer	Discharged (disability) 2/11/62.
Watkins, James T.	Private	1841	Lebanon, Wilson Co.	Wheel wright	WIA (foot) 8/9/62. Sgt. 12/31/63. WIA (forehead) 6/3/64. Captured 4/2/65.
Watkins, Zarah	Private	1840	—	—	Captured 5/3/63. Exchanged. Sick since 6/15/63, until deserted 7/24/63.

Name	Initial Rank	D.O.B.	Home	Prewar Occupation	Comments
Webster, John H.	Private	1840	Lockport, Wilson Co.	Farm labor	3rd Cpl. 4/26/62. 5th Sgt. 8/31/62. WIA & captured 7/3/63. Exchanged 3/3/64. Medical furlough since 9/15/64 for rest of war.
Whitehead, Andrew J.	Private	1843	Lebanon, Wilson Co.	Farm labor	Deserted 8/4/62. Court martialed, 2/18/63. Re-enlisted 6/63. WIA & captured 7/3/63. POW rest of war.
Williams, David T.	Private	1839	—	—	Sick off and on entire war.
Williams, John D.	Private	1841	—	—	WIA 9/17/62. In hospital until deserted 8/10/63.
Williams, Solomon S.	Private	1839	Shop Spr., Wilson Co.	Farm labor	TDY (teamster) 10/62, for entire war.
Wormack, John A.	Private	1841	—	Farm labor	**Killed, 5/31/62 (Seven Pines).**
Baldwin, Nicholas	Conscript	1828	Hawkins Co.	Farmer	Drafted 3/10/64. Discharged — 4/7/64.
Barnard, Robert	Conscript	—	Clairborn Co.	—	Drafted 3/28/64. Deserted 12/26/64.
Barner, William	Conscript	1836	Hancock Co.	—	Drafted 3/31/64. Deserted 10/10/64.
Beals, Amos	Conscript	1821	Green Co.	—	Drafted 3/64. Captured 5/5/64. **POW — Died of disease, 8/13/64.**
Bolen, Milem	Conscript	1817	Hancock Co.	—	Drafted 3/64. Captured 4/2/65. **Died of disease, 6/8/65.**
Brady, Alven	Conscript	1814	Locke Co.	—	Drafted 3/64. Captured 5/5/64. POW until 11/14/64 when he took the Oath.
Browning, Robert M.	Conscript	—	Green Co.	—	Drafted 4/25/64. WIA 6/12/64. Captured 4/4/65.
Canary, John	Recruit	1841	Richmond, VA.	—	Enlisted 6/11/62. TDY (teamster) 4/63. Captured 7/5/63. POW rest of war.
Conley, Patrick	Recruit	1838	Harrisburg, VA.	—	Enlisted 1/23/64. **Died of disease, 6/19/64.**
Fairchild, Jesse	Conscript	1819	Sneedville, Hancock Co.	Farmer	Drafted 3/10/64. **Died of disease, 6/21/64.**
Fish, John	Recruit	1846	—	—	Enlisted 2/12/65. **Died of disease, 6/18/65.**
Gibson, Jesse	Conscript	1817	Hancock Co.	—	Drafted 3/10/64. Captured 4/3/65.
Gibson, Uriah	Conscript	1817	Hancock Co.	—	Drafted 3/10/64. Deserted 4/11/64.
Green, Thomas	Recruit	1840	Huntersville, VA	Farm labor	Enlisted 8/2/61. **Died of disease, 9/14/61.**
Herne, James W	Transfer — Co. C	1838	Shop Spr., Wilson Co.	Farm labor	Transferred from Co. C, 11/30/62. Surrendered 4/9/65 (Appomattox).
Johnson, William A.	Recruit	1842	Staunton, VA	Farm labor	Enlisted 12/14/61. Discharged (disability) 6/19/62.
Knight, John	Recruit	—	Bristol, VA	—	Enlisted 4/4/64. Captured 5/26/64. POW rest of war.
Miller, Samuel	Conscript	1841	Greenville, Green Co.	—	Drafted 3/25/64. Captured 6/3/64. POW rest of war.
Miser, Thomas	Conscript	1826	Hancock Co.	Farmer	Drafted 3/10/64. Discharged (disability) 2/18/65.

Name	Initial Rank	D.O.B.	Home	Prewar Occupation	Comments
Pardon, Benjamin	Conscript	—	Greenville, Green Co.	—	Drafted 3/25/64. Captured 5/23/64. POW rest of war.
Phillips, John	Conscript	—	Greenville, Green Co.	—	Drafted 3/25/64. Captured 5/12/64. POW rest of war.
Phillips, Nelson	Conscript	—	Greenville, Green Co.	—	Drafted 3/25/64. Captured 5/12/64. **POW — Died of disease, 12/21/64.**
Rabeck, William M.	Conscript	1817	Hancock Co.	—	Drafted 3/10/64. Captured 5/10/64. POW rest of war.
Rhea, Starlin	Conscript	1828	Brier Creek, Hancock Co.	Blacksmith	Drafted 3/15/64. WIA (mouth) 9/30/64. Surrendered 4/9/65 (Appomattox).
Robertson, John	Conscript	1816	Green Co.	—	Drafted 3/10/64. Captured 5/5/64. POW rest of war.
Rogers, William F.	Conscript	1846	Green Co.	—	Drafted 3/10/64. WIA 5/5/64. WIA 8/19/64. No other records.
Snider, George	Conscript	1816	Green Co.	Farmer	Drafted 3/25/64. Discharged (disability) 9/7/64.
Spurgeon, Thomas C.	Recruit	1826	Sullivan Co.	Farmer	Enlisted 4/9/64. TDY (carding factory) 8/23/64 to end of war.
Winkler, Abraham	Conscript	1824	Hancock Co.	—	Drafted 3/64. Captured 5/6/64. **POW — died of disease, 3/5/65.**

Company E

Name	Initial Rank	D.O.B.	Home	Prewar Occupation	Comments
Douglas, Dewitt C.	Captain	1824	—	—	Relieved of duty, 4/30/62.
Hutchinson, James R. "Jim"	1st Lt.	1826	—	—	Relieved of duty, 4/30/62.
Donelson, James B.	2nd Lt.	1843	Hendersonville, Sumner Co.	Student	Relieved of duty, 4/30/62
Wise, John	3rd Lt.	1835	Sandersville, Sumner Co.	Constable	**Killed, 8/9/62 (Cedar Run).**
Taylor, Robert	1st Sgt.	1832	Sumner Co.	Farmer	**Died of disease, 9/1/61.**
McGuire, William J.	2nd Sgt.	1838	—	—	Discharged (disability) 12/1/61.
Kirkpatrick, William A.	3rd Sgt.	1834	Gallatin, Sumner Co.	Farm labor	Reduced (Pvt.) 4/26/62. WIA 5/31/62. Captured 7/3/63. POW rest of war.
Hurst, Marcus L.	1st Cpl.	1844	Gallatin, Sumner Co.	Farm labor	Reduced (Pvt.) 4/26/62. Captured 7/3/63. **POW — Died of disease, 7/16/64.**
Bartholomew, Thomas	2nd Cpl.	1837	Sandersville, Sumner Co.	Harness maker	Reduced (Pvt.) 4/26/62. TDY (harness maker) 8/17/62 to end of war.
Dugger, Andrew J.	3rd Cpl.	1844	Hendersonville, Sumner Co.	Day laborer	**Died of disease, 9/16/61.**
Clendening, John S.	4th Cpl.	1839	Sumner Co.	Farm labor	Discharged (disability) 1/1/62.
Alexander, Charles	Private	1841	Sumner Co.	Farm labor	Discharged (disability) 3/15/62.

Name	Initial Rank	D.O.B.	Home	Prewar Occupation	Comments
Blackburn, Elisha	Private	1838	Gallatin, Sumner Co.	Farm labor	Captured 9/17/62. Paroled. WIA (right leg) 5/3/63. WIA 10/14/53. Captured 4/2/65.
Bledsoe, Alexander	Private	1840	Sandersville, Sumner Co.	Farm labor	WIA (right arm amputated) & captured 9/17/62. No other records.
Brandon, Thomas J.	Private	1836	—	—	Discharged, 12/24/61.
Brown, Milton E.	Private	1815	Nashville, Davidson Co.	Carpenter	Discharged (seniority) 8/20/62. Re-enlisted as a substitute, 3/9/63. WIA 7/3/63. In hospital until Deserted 1/64.
Bruce, James F.	Private	1834	—	—	Discharged (disability) 2/10/62.
Cage, Jesse	Private	1841	Gallatin, Sumner Co.	Farm labor	3rd Sgt. 8/9/62. 2nd Sgt. 2/64. WIA 5/5/64. 1st Sgt. 2/24/65. WIA (leg amputated) & captured 4/2/62.
Cage, John F.	Private	1835	Gallatin, Sumner Co.	Farm labor	3rd Cpl. 9/17/61. Reduced (Pvt.) 4/26/62. TDY (teamster) 5/62 to —. Capt. (wagonmaster) 10/16/64. Last record, 12/64.
Callis, John C.	Private	1842	—	—	Deserted 7/12/61.
Cheek, James F.	Private	1833	—	—	**Killed, 5/3/63 (Chancellorsville).**
Clendening, William A.	Private	1837	—	Farm labor	4th Cpl. 4/26/62. WIA 8/29/62. In hospital until 4/64. 4th Sgt. 10/31/64. Surrendered 4/9/65 (Appomattox).
Coe, William A.	Private	1827	Mouth of Wolf, Overton Co.	Farmer	Captured 4/2/65.
Cooley, Joseph	Private	1840	—	—	WIA 8/9/62. In hospital until Deserted 3/15/63.
Copeland, Thomas	Private	1839	—	—	**Killed, 9/20/62 (Shepherdstown).**
Craig, N. S.	Private	1826	—	—	Deserted 6/6/61.
Cuffman, Benjamin F.	Private	1842	—	—	Discharged (disability) 7/4/61.
Dillon, George	Private	1823	Gallatin, Sumner Co.	Farmer	**Died of disease, 9/27/61.**
Dorris, Samuel M.	Private	1835	Gallatin, Sumner Co.	Farm labor	**Killed, 9/20/62 (Shepherdstown).**
Dorris, Thomsberry	Private	1839	Sumner Co.	—	Last record, 8/64.
Douglas, George W.	Private	1825	Sumner Co.	Farmer	Discharged (seniority) 8/20/62.
Dunavin, James M.	Private	1824	Sumner Co.	Saddler	Discharged (seniority) 8/20/62.
Dunn, Blackman H. "Black"	Private	1843	Hendersonville, Sumner Co.	Student	2nd Sgt. 4/26/62. WIA & captured 7/3/63. POW until 1/1/64. Escaped — no other records.
Elam, Daniel W.	Private	1838	—	—	Deserted 3/1/64.
Elston, John	Private	1840	Walker, Hancock Co.	Farm labor	WIA & captured 7/3/63. POW rest of war.
Franklin, James	Private	1841	Gallatin, Sumner Co.	Farm labor	1st Sgt. 9/18/61. Capt. 4/26/62. WIA (foot) 8/9/62. Disabled until Retired (wounds) 4/23/64.

Name	Initial Rank	D.O.B.	Home	Prewar Occupation	Comments
Frazer, Francis M. "Frank"	Private	1838	—	—	WIA (left knee) & captured 7/3/63. **Died of wounds, 7/11/63.**
Frazer, George W.	Private	1836	Sumner Co.	—	WIA & captured 5/5/64. Exchanged 10/11/64. Deserted 3/1/65.
Freeman, George W.	Private	1840	Somerville, Fayette Co.	Farm labor	Enlisted 8/14/61. Last record, 11/63.
Garrett, Allen M.	Private	1833	Sumner Co.	Farmer	**Died of disease, 10/22/61.**
Garrett, James B.	Private	1834	Hendersonville, Sumner Co.	Day laborer	4th Sgt. 8/1/62. WIA (right knee & groin) 7/3/63. In hospital. Last record, 1/1/64.
Garrett, William A.	Private	1841	Hendersonville, Sumner Co.	Day laborer	1st Cpl. 4/26/62. WIA 8/9/62. WIA & captured 7/3/63. **POW—Died of disease, 5/12/64.**
Gillespie, Jesse C.	Private	1835	—	—	TDY (wagon master) 3/62 to 2/64. Surrendered 4/9/65 (Appomattox).
Graves, Henry H.	Private	1837	Gallatin, Sumner Co.	Farm labor	3rd Sgt. 2/1/64. Captured 4/3–8/65.
Graves, William D.	Private	1826	Sumner Co.	—	**Died of disease, 10/1/61.**
Gray, James W.	Private	1844	Hendersonville, Sumner Co.	Stone mason's asst.	WIA (chest) & captured 9/17/62. Released. WIA (right arm) & captured 7/3/63. Exchanged 8/64. Hospitalized to end of war.
Gray, William M.	Private	1842	—	—	WIA 6/27/62. In hospital until. Deserted 6/18/63.
Guthrie, William D.	Private	1840	Gallatin, Sumner Co.	Farm labor	WIA 8/30/62. **Killed, 5/3/63 (Chancellorsville).**
Hamilton, George H.	Private	1841	Gallatin, Sumner Co.	Farm labor	TDY (teamster) 4/62 to 6/63. WIA (right leg) & captured 7/3/63. POW until escaped, 2/10/64. No other records.
Hogan, Alexander	Private	1837	Hendersonville, Sumner Co.	—	4th Sgt. 12/31/61. 2nd Lt. 4/26/62. Captured 7/14/63. POW rest of war.
Honeycutt, Thomas J.	Private	1826	Sumner Co.	Farmer	Discharged (seniority) 8/20/62.
Hughes, Faustulus	Private	1830	—	—	WIA 8/30/62. 2nd Cpl. 6/30/64. Sick since 10/15/64. **Died of disease, 2/17/65.**
Hughes, Joseph Q.	Private	1833	—	—	Deserted 6/27/61.
Idson, John E.	Private	1840	—	—	Captured 7/3/63. POW rest of war.
Idson, Joseph R.	Private	1844	—	Farm labor	Discharged (minority) 8/20/62.
Idson, Josiah R.	Private	1820	—	Farmer	Discharged (seniority) 8/20/62.
Jones, James P.	Private	1834	—	—	TDY (teamster) 8/13/62 to 3/64. **Killed, 5/3/63 (Chancellorsville).**
Jones, William T.	Private	1836	—	Day laborer	Discharged (disability) 1/1/62.
Kirkpatrick, Hugh A., Jr.	Private	1841	Hendersonville, Sumner Co.	Farm labor	Sick since 6/15/63. In hospital until. Deserted 7/2/63.

Name	Initial Rank	D.O.B.	Home	Prewar Occupation	Comments
Kirkpatrick, Hugh A., Sr.	Private	1806	Hendersonville, Sumner Co.	Farmer	Captured 7/14/63. POW rest of war.
Kirkpatrick, Peterfield	Private	1834	Hendersonville, Sumner Co.	Farm labor	**Died of disease, 12/21/61.**
Kirkpatrick, William B.	Private	1841	Gallatin, Sumner Co.	Student	2nd Cpl. 4/26/62. TDY (currier for Gen. Archer) 10/5/62. Currier for Gen. A.P. Hill for rest of war). Captured 4/9/65.
Koeph, William G.	Private	1838	Hendersonville, Sumner Co.	Day laborer	Captured 7/1/63. POW rest of war.
Lewis, William Albert	Private	1838	Gallatin, Sumner Co.	Carpenter	Captured 7/14/63. POW rest of war.
Love, Joseph A.	Private	1833	Sumner Co.	—	WIA & captured 7/3/63. **Died of wounds, 7/15/63.**
Matherly, Daniel F.	Private	1844	Sumner Co.	Mechanic	Discharged (disability) 8/20/62.
Matherly, William T.	Private	1840	Gallatin, Sumner Co.	Chair maker	Captured 7/1/63. **POW — Died of disease, 9/10/63.**
McCall, William H.	Private	1840	Rainy, Smith Co.	Farm labor	3rd Lt. 8/9/62. Captured 7/3/63. POW rest of war.
McGuire, Hugh	Private	1840	—	—	WIA 7/14/62. In hospital until captured in Davidson Co. TN., 2/8/63.
McMurtry, Daniel J.	Private	1840	—	—	TDY (Qtr. Mstr.) 8/61 to 10/64. Deserted 11/18/64.
McMurtry, Thomas J.	Private	1825	Sumner Co	Carpenter	Discharged (seniority) 8/20/62.
Miller, Robert G.	Private	1838	Gallatin, Sumner Co.	Clerk	2nd Sgt. 10/31/61. 1st Lt. 4/26/62. WIA (chest) 9/17/62. WIA (left leg & head) 7/3/63. Capt. 4/27/64. Surrendered 4/9/65 (Appomattox).
Montgomery, James M.	Private	1841	Sumner Co.	—	3rd Cpl. 10/31/64. Captured 4/3/65.
Payne, Greenwood B.	Private	1825	Gallatin, Sumner Co.	Cooper	Sick since 8/17/62. In hospital until Deserted 11/26/62.
Pierce, G. L.	Private	1837	—	—	Deserted 12/10/61.
Puckett, John E.	Private	1838	Cainsville, Wilson Co.	Farm labor	5th Sgt. 9/8/61. 1st Sgt. 4/30/62. WIA 8/30/62. WIA (left arm) & captured 7/3/63. Exchanged. Medical furlough until discharged (wounds) 2/24/65.
Purcell, Francis M.	Private	—	—	—	Sgt. 4/26/62. Captured 8/8/62. Exchanged. WIA 5/3/63. 1st Sgt. 8/31/63. TDY (mail carrier) 4/11/64 to end of war.
Purcell, Henry White	Private	1824	—	Salesman	WIA (left hand amputated) 5/31/62. Discharged (wounds).
Renfro, Francis M.	Private	1833	—	—	WIA (left leg) 5/3/63. In hospital until. Discharged (wounds) 4/64.

Name	Initial Rank	D.O.B.	Home	Prewar Occupation	Comments
Rutherford, Benjamin "Ben"	Private	1836	Hendersonville, Sumner Co.	Merchant	TDY (Qtr. Mstr.) 8/61. Transferred to Co. C, 2/15/62.
Sanders, James S.	Private	1842	—	—	Deserted 7/15/61.
Scott, Thomas	Private	1844	Gallatin, Sumner Co.	Student	**Died of disease, 1/16/62.**
Taylor, Alexander S.	Private	1841	—	Student	WIA 9/20/63. **Died of wounds, 9/30/63.**
Turpin, Thomas	Private	1826	—	—	Deserted 12/10/61.
White, Joseph L.	Private	1829	—	—	Sick most of war. Discharged (disability) 12/23/64.
Williams, Andrew J.	Private	1843	—	Farm labor	Discharged (disability) 1/1/62.
Williams, Francis M.	Private	1839	—	—	4th Sgt. 8/31/64. Deserted 10/18/64.
Williams, George W.	Private	1823	—	Farmer	Discharged (seniority) 8/20/62.
Williams, Henry T.	Private	1833	Wilson Co.	—	3rd Cpl. 9/20/62. WIA 9/20/62. Sick since, 1/20/63 to 3/64. WIA (left arm) 5/5/64. 1st Cpl. 10/64. Captured 4/3–8/65.
Williams, James P.	Private	1837	Castalian Spr., Sumner Co.	Farm labor	Captured 7/3/63. Exchanged 11/63. **Killed, 8/19/64 (Weldon Rd.).**
Williams, Joseph F.	Private	1837	Hendersonville, Sumner Co.	Farmer	Captured 7/3/63. POW rest of war.
Williams, William H.	Private	1823	—	Mechanic	Discharged (seniority) 8/20/62.
Wilson, Charles H.	Private	1834	Sumner Co.	—	Captured 7/3/63. POW rest of war.
Allen, Elden	Recruit	—	Shelby Co.	—	Enlisted 12/64. Captured 4/2/65.
Blackburn, William	Recruit	1834	Tazewell, Clairborne Co.	Clerk	Enlisted 1/65. Captured 4/2/65.
Conke, Higgins	Recruit	—	Sullivan Co.	—	Enlisted 11/30/64. Surrendered 4/9/65 (Appomattox).
Dockey, Oliver	Recruit	—	Bristol, Sullivan Co.	—	Enlisted 11/23/64. Captured 4/3–8/65.
Dorris, Isaiah	Recruit	1810	Gallatin, Sumner Co.	Farmer	Enlisted 1/23/64. 4th Cpl. 10/31/64. Deserted 2/22/65.
Fish, Jonas	Conscript	1818	New Canton, Hawkins Co.	Farmer	Drafted 2/12/65. Captured 4/2/65.
Goin, Leroy	Conscript	—	Sullivan Co.	—	Drafted 4/18/64. Captured 5/25/64. No other records.
Lindsey, Charles	Conscript	1843	Sevier Co.	Farm labor	Drafted 7/23/63. Surrendered 4/9/65 (Appomattox).
McKeehan, John G.	Conscript	1846	Happy Valley, Carter Co.	Farm labor	Drafted 2/12/65. Deserted 4/1/65.
McKeehan, Robert	Conscript	—	—	—	Drafted 2/12/65. Deserted 4/1/65.
McKeehan, Samuel	Conscript	1833	Happy Valley, Carter Co.	Farmer	Drafted 2/12/65. Deserted 4/1/65.
Munsey, William	Recruit	—	Sullivan Co.	—	Enlisted 2/18/64. WIA (scalp) 6/3/64. Deserted 1/3/65.

Name	Initial Rank	D.O.B.	Home	Prewar Occupation	Comments
Myers, James	Recruit	—	Sullivan Co.	—	Enlisted 11/29/64. Captured 4/3–8/65.
Pearce, Richard H.	Conscript	—	Sullivan Co.	—	Drafted 2/7/65. Captured 4/3–8/65.
Roark, Jesse L.	Recruit	—	Johnson Co.	—	Enlisted 1/13/65. Captured 4/3–8/65.
Saunders, William	Recruit	—	Sullivan Co.	—	Enlisted 11/30/64. Captured 4/3–8/65.
Sharp, William C.	Conscript	1820	Sullivan Co.	—	Drafted 4/18/64. Deserted 8/31/64.
Shelton, Lewis	Conscript	—	Knoxville, Knox Co.	—	Drafted 7/10/63. Deserted 8/30/63.
Shelton, Solomon	Conscript	—	Knoxville, Knox Co.	—	Drafted 7/10/63. Deserted 8/30/64.
Stiner, Peter	Conscript	1831	Loss Creek, Union Co.	Farmer	Drafted 4/18/64. Deserted 1/3/65.
Sweet, David B.	Conscript	—	Sullivan Co.	—	Drafted 3/64. WIA 8/18/64. Captured 4/3/65.
Wagoner, Daniel	Conscript	—	Sullivan Co.	—	Drafted 2/6/65. Captured 4/2/65.
Walker, Daniel W.	Conscript	—	Sullivan Co.	—	Drafted 4/18/64. Deserted 6/1/64.
Walker, John W.	Conscript	—	Sullivan Co.	—	Drafted 4/18/64. Deserted 9/5/64.
Williams, Thomas	Conscript	—	Green Co.	—	Drafted 2/65. Captured 4/2/65.
Wooten, John T.	Conscript	—	Hancock Co.	—	Drafted 12/64. Captured 4/2/65.
Yoakum, Robert G.	Conscript	1836	Clairborne Co.	Day laborer	Drafted 4/64. Captured 5/25/64. POW rest of war.

Company F. "Statesville Tigers"

Name	Initial Rank	D.O.B.	Home	Prewar Occupation	Comments
Oakley, Nathan	Captain	1828	Round Gap, Wilson Co.	Farmer	Relieved of duty, 4/30/62.
Kennedy, Elijah A.	1st Lt.	1824	Statesville, Wilson Co.	Merchant	Relieved of duty, 4/26/62.
Knox, William C.	2nd. Lt.	1836	Statesville, Wilson Co.	Merchant	Relieved of duty, 4/26/62.
Stroud, Andrew	3rd Lt.	1819	Statesville, Wilson Co.	Farmer	Relieved of duty, 4/26/62.
Jennings, John S.	1st Sgt.	1842	Statesville, Wilson Co.	Farm labor	1st Lt. 4/26/62. WIA (leg) 9/17/62. In hospital until. Resigned (wounds) 5/16/63.
James, Alvy	2nd Sgt.	—	—	—	Reduced (Pvt.) 4/26/62. Discharged (seniority) 8/20/62.
Porterfield, John W.	3rd Sgt.	—	—	—	Reduced (Pvt.) 4/26/62. Discharged (seniority) 8/20/62.
Webb, William J.	4th Sgt.	1833	—	Farm labor	Discharged (disability) 1/1/62.
Simpson, Charles	1st Cpl.	1825	Cainsville, Wilson Co.	Farmer	Reduced (Pvt.) 2/26/62. Discharged (seniority) 8/20/62.
Stroud, Lester D.	2nd Cpl.	1842	Statesville, Wilson Co.	Teacher	Reduced (Pvt.) 4/26/62. WIA (right shoulder) 8/9/62. Medical furlough until. Discharged (wounds) 4/27/63

Name	Initial Rank	D.O.B.	Home	Prewar Occupation	Comments
Stroud, Oliver B.	3rd Cpl.	1836	Statesville, Wilson Co.	Farm labor	Reduced (Pvt.) 4/26/62. 4th Cpl. 8/10/62. TDY—2/23/63 to 12/63. 2nd Cpl. 12/63. **Killed, 5/12/64 (Spotsylvania).**
Hill, Henry H.	4th Cpl.	1840	Lebanon, Wilson Co.	Farm labor	Reduced (Pvt.) 4/26/62. Discharged (disability) 6/25/62.
Adams, James W.	Private	1837	Wilson Co.	Farm labor	TDY (teamster) 9/20/61 to 2/63. WIA 5/3/63. **Died of wounds, 5/7/63.**
Alsup, Henry	Private	1841	Statesville, Wilson Co.	Teacher	Discharged (furnished a substitute) 7/5/62.
Anderson, Stephen	Private	1836	—	Farm labor	Discharged (disability) 11/10/62.
Ayers, Rufus	Private	1840	Wilson Co.	Farm labor	WIA 8/9/62. **Died of wounds, 9/1/62.**
Bland, Marion	Private	1825	Ponderella, Wilson Co.	Shoe maker	4th Sgt. 7/6/62. Captured 4/2/65.
Blythe, Nathaniel	Private	—	—	—	Discharged (disability) 4/5/62.
Blythe, William	Private	—	—	—	Deserted 8/7/62.
Bogle, Robert	Private	1820	Statesville, Wilson Co.	Farmer	Discharged (disability) 4/30/62.
Boyd, William R.	Private	—	—	—	Discharged (seniority) 8/28/62.
Chapman, Barry	Private	1836	Round Gap, Wilson Co.	Farm labor	Discharged (disability) 12/25/61.
Chapman, James L.	Private	1831	Wilson Co.	Farmer	Discharged (disability) 2/11/62.
Coley, Richard W.	Private	1835	Memphis, Shelby Co.	Tin smith	With reg't. until 12/63. No other records.
Craddock, Martin H.	Private	1842	Wilson Co.	Farm labor	Died of disease, 10/8/61.
Craddock, William C.	Private	1834	Statesville, Wilson Co.	Blacksmith	Discharged (disability) 6/20/62.
Davis, James H.	Private	1840	Wilson Co.	Farm labor	Discharged (disability) 11/8/61.
Davis, John W.	Private	1828	Laguardo, Wilson Co.	Carpenter	Discharged (furnished a substitute) 7/5/62.
Dunn, George W.	Private	1838	Statesville, Wilson Co.	Day laborer	Captured 4/2/65.
Dunn, John T.	Private	1834	Statesville, Wilson Co.	Farmer	Surrendered 4/9/65 (Appomattox).
Florida, James P.	Private	1813	Wilson Co.	Farmer	WIA 8/9/62. Discharged (wounds) 8/10/62.
Fuston, James W.	Private	1844	Wilson Co.	Day laborer	Discharged (disability) 6/25/62.
Gatton, Joseph W.	Private	1834	Round Gap, Wilson Co.	Farmer	Discharged (disability) 1/30/62.
Gray, George	Private	1830	Cainsville, Wilson Co.	Day laborer	Discharged (seniority) 8/20/62.
Hardwick, Thomas J.	Private	1840	Wilson Co.	Farm labor	**Killed, 5/31/62 (Seven Pines).**
Hollingsworth, Charles	Private	1830	Mt. Carmel, Wilson Co.	Boot maker	Accidently shot (foot) 7/20/62. In hospital. No other record.
Hutchison, Charles	Private	—	—	—	Discharged (disability) 4/5/62.

Name	Initial Rank	D.O.B.	Home	Prewar Occupation	Comments
Jennings, Francis "Frank"	Private	1841	Statesville, Wilson Co.	Farm labor	WIA 9/20/62. **Died of wounds, 11/1/62.**
Jennings, Gideon M.	Private	1843	Statesville, Wilson Co.	Farm labor	Captured 7/3/63. POW rest of war.
Jennings, James W.	Private	1841	Statesville, Wilson Co.	Farm labor	4th Sgt. 4/26/62. Discharged (furnished a substitute) 7/5/63.
Jennings, Thomas L.	Private	1839	Statesville, Wilson Co.	Farm labor	3rd Lt. 4/26/62. WIA 5/31/62. WIA 7/3/63. Captured 7/5/63. POW rest of war.
Jennings, William	Private	—	—	—	Discharged (disability) 4/5/62.
Jewell, James W.	Private	1838	—	Farm labor	1st Sgt. 4/26/62. WIA (right thigh) 8/9/62. In hospital until. Discharged (wounds) 3/30/63.
Johnson, Archibald	Private	1833	Wilson Co.	Farm labor	TDY (nurse) 2/15/62 to 4/63. Captured 7/3/63. POW rest of war.
Johnson, Freeling H.	Private	—	—	—	Discharged (disability) 4/5/62.
Johnson, William	Private	1835	Statesville, Wilson Co.	Farm labor	**Died of disease, 8/8/61.**
Jones, James D.	Private	1840	—	Farm labor	Discharged (disability) 11/27/61.
Jones, John M.	Private	1839	Wilson Co.	Farm labor	Discharged (disability) 6/25/62.
Jones, William N.	Private	1837	—	—	Captured 5/31/62. Exchanged. Captured 7/3/63. POW rest of war.
Keaton, John W.	Private	1834	Wilson Co.	Day laborer	1st Cpl. 6/25/62. Captured 7/3/63. POW until 11/10/63 — Took the Oath.
Keif, Roswell	Private	1827	—	Farmer	Discharged (disability) 2/11/62.
Lanier, John R.	Private	1841	Statesville, Wilson Co.	Farmer	5th Sgt. 7/16/62. WIA (right hand) 5/30/64. Surrendered 4/9/65 (Appomattox).
Lester, James W.	Private	1839	Wilson Co.	Farm labor	1st Cpl. 4/26/62. Discharged (disability) 6/25/62.
McMillen, Thomas	Private	1820	Wilson Co.	Farmer	Discharged (disability) 2/11/62.
Mullinax, Martin	Private	—	Round Gap, Wilson Co.	—	2nd Cpl. 4/26/62. Discharged (seniority) 8/20/62.
Parker, Hiram	Private	—	—	Farm labor	Discharged (disability) 2/11/62.
Patterson, John B.	Private	—	—	—	Deserted 1/8/63.
Patterson, William H.	Private	—	—	—	2nd Cpl. 8/20/62. Sick since 10/7/62 until. Discharged (disability) 12/31/63.
Patton, Commodore	Private	1822	Statesville, Wilson Co.	Carpenter	**Died of disease, 2/1/62.**
Phipps, James K.	Private	1845	Pelham, Grandy Co.	Farm labor	Discharged (minority) 8/20/62.
Quales, Littlebury J.	Private	1841	Wilson Co.	Farm labor	Discharged (disability) 11/17/61.
Ready, John A.	Private	1837	—	Teacher	5th Sgt. 10/31/61. Reduced (Pvt. 4/26/62. WIA 8/9/62. Discharged (wounds) 8/10/62.
Ricketts, James W.	Private	—	—	—	2nd Sgt. 6/16/63. Captured 5/31/64. Exchanged 10/11/64. Captured 4/9/65 (Appomattox).

Name	Initial Rank	D.O.B.	Home	Prewar Occupation	Comments
Ricketts, William D.	Private	1837	Wilson Co.	Farm labor	**Killed, 9/17/62 (Sharpsburg).**
Sanders, John R.	Private	1844	—	Farm labor	Discharged (minority) 8/20/62.
Sloan, John C. "Slick"	Private	1837	War Trace, Wilson Co.	—	2nd Lt. 4/26/62. Capt. 7/4/63. WIA (thigh) 6/2/64. Captured 4/2/65.
Smith, James M.	Private	—	—	—	Discharged (disability) 10/29/61.
Sneed, Thomas J.	Private	1844	Statesville, Wilson Co.	Day laborer	Discharged (disability) 6/20/62.
Stroud, James R.	Private	1818	Statesville, Wilson Co.	Farmer	Discharged (disability) 6/20/62.
Sullivan, Jefferson L.	Private	1833	—	Blacksmith	WIA (thigh) 8/9/62. Discharged (wounds) 10/6/62.
Sullivan, John D.	Private	—	—	—	Discharged (minority) 8/26/62.
Sullivan, Thomas P.	Private	1842	Rural Hill, Wilson Co.	Blacksmith	WIA 8/9/62. TDY (blacksmith) 8/63 to Deserted 3/1/64.
Thompson, Andrew J.	Private	1844	Wilson Co.	Farm labor	**Killed, 8/9/62 (Cedar Run).**
Thompson, James A.	Private	1841	Wilson Co.	Farm labor	5th Sgt. 4/26/62. WIA 6/26/62. **Died of wounds, 7/15/62.**
Turner, Jeremiah	Private	1837	—	Farm labor	WIA 8/9/62. Sick since 10/1/63 to 6/64. Captured 4/2/65.
Watson, Isaac L.	Private	1827	Pondville, Wilson Co.	Farmer	Discharged (disability) 2/11/62.
Webb, George C.	Private	1835	Round Gap, Wilson Co.	Farmer	WIA (left hand) 5/31/62. Discharged (wounds) 6/25/62.)
Whitlock, Robert F.	Private	1832	Statesville, Wilson Co.	Farmer	Surrendered 4/9/65 (Appomattox).
Williams, Thomas J.	Private	1825	—	Shoe maker	Discharged (seniority) 8/20/62.
Wilson, Isaac L.	Private	1837	—	Stone mason	Discharged (disability) 2/17/62.
Witt, Abner "Booker"	Private	1839	Statesville, Wilson	Farm labor	3rd Cpl. 4/26/62. 1st Cpl. 2/64. TDY (nurse) 3/64 to end of war.
Baird, Hugh	Conscript	—	Knox Co.	—	Drafted 8/3/63. WIA (foot) 8/19/64. WIA (foot) & captured 4/2/65.
Barker, Burrell	Conscript	—	Knox Co.	—	Drafted 8/3/63. Deserted 8/15/63.
Burgess, William	Entry	—	—	—	Listed only once as 2nd Lt. WIA & captured 7/3/63. No other record.
Celton, William	Conscript	—	Knox Co.	—	Drafted 7/21/62. WIA 5/5/64. In hospital rest of war.
Costeel, George	Conscript	—	Knox Co.	—	Drafted 7/24/63. Deserted 8/25/63.
Craft, James H.	Recruit	1845	Overton Co.	Farm labor	Enlisted 3/21/63. WIA (right leg amputated) 8/19/64.
Flanagan, Robert A.	Conscript	—	Knox Co.	—	Drafted 7/24/63. Deserted 9/14/63.
Fletcher, Franklin	Recruit	1841	Clairborne Co.	Farm labor	Enlisted 6/15/63. Captured 4/2/65.
Furgeson, Silas	Conscript	—	Knox Co.	—	Drafted 7/22/63. Deserted 9/14/63.
Henley, John A.	Conscript	—	McMinnville, Warren Co.	—	Drafted 3/12/63. Deserted 7/4/63.

Name	Initial Rank	D.O.B.	Home	Prewar Occupation	Comments
Hill, Asoph "Ate"	Transfer from Staff	1838	Cherry Valley, Wilson Co.	Farmer	Capt. 4/27/62. WIA 8/29/62. WIA 9/17/62. WIA (breast) & captured 7/3/63. **Died of wounds, 7/8/63.**
Hunter, John	Conscript	—	Richmond, VA	—	Drafted 7/10/63. Deserted 7/15/63.
Jester, Alberton	Conscript	—	Knox Co.	—	Drafted 7/21/63. Deserted 8/10/62.
Kirk, Henry	Conscript	—	Richmond, VA	—	Drafted 7/10/63. Deserted 7/15/63.
Lester, William H.	Recruit	—	Sevier Co.	—	Enlisted 9/7/61. Discharged (disability) 4/5/62.
Lewis, George W.	Recruit	—	Warm Spr., WV.	—	Enlisted 11/22/61. WIA 5/31/62. Medical furlough until. Deserted 3/10/64.
Martin, William	Conscript	—	Knox Co.	—	Drafted 8/3/63. Deserted 8/30/63.
Mathias, John W.	Conscript	—	Knox Co.	—	Drafted 7/23/63. Deserted 9/14/63.
Oliver, James T.	Transfer — Co. G	—	—	—	Transferred from Co. G, 10/1/63. Deserted 12/31/63.
Potter, Enoch	Recruit	—	Knox Co.	—	Enlisted 12/14/62. Transferred to Co. G, 10/1063.
Ragain, William	Recruit	—	McMinnville, Warren Co.	—	Enlisted 5/12/63. Captured 7/3/63. **POW — Died of disease, 3/20/64.**
Shoemaker, John W.	Conscript	—	Knox Co.	—	Drafted 4/20/63. Deserted 9/14/63.
Smith, William E.	Conscript	—	McMinnville, Warren Co.	—	Drafted 3/12/63. Deserted 7/4/63
Sutton, James H.	Recruit	—	McMinnville, Warren Co.	—	Enlisted 3/12/63. **Killed, 7/3/63 (Gettysburg).**
Thomas, William G.	Conscript	—	Richmond, VA.	—	Drafted 7/10/63. Deserted 7/15/63.
Viery, Daniel G.	Conscript	—	—	—	Drafted 7/63. Deserted 8/12/63.
White, Spencer P.	Conscript	—	—	—	Drafted 7/63. Deserted 8/30/63.

Company G. "Hurricane Rifles"

Name	Initial Rank	D.O.B.	Home	Prewar Occupation	Comments
Shepard, Samuel George	Captain	1830	Gladesville, Wilson Co.	Teacher	Maj. 9/19/62. Lt. Col. 4/8/63. Surrendered 4/9/65 (Appomattox).
Hobbs, James A. "Goat"	1st Lt.	1839	Tucker's Crossroads, Wilson Co.	Farm labor	Resigned (disability) 1/6/62.
Bond, Monroe M.	2nd Lt.	1843	Gladesville, Wilson Co.	Student	Resigned (disability) 6/5/62.
Graves, William Fox	3rd Lt.	1833	Lebanon, Wilson Co.	Clerk	1st Lt. 4/30/62. Capt. 10/7/62. WIA 7/3/63. WIA (leg) 5/7/64. Paroled 4/13/65.
Bond, James H.	1st Sgt.	1837	Ponderella, Wilson Co.	Physician	1st Lt. 1/2/62. Capt. 3/31/62. WIA 9/20/62. Resigned (wounds) 10/7/62.
Jennings, Newborn	2nd Sgt.	1837	Gladesville, Wilson Co.	Student (medical)	2nd Lt. 6/18/62. 1st Lt. 9/25/62. WIA (right shoulder) 12/13/62. In hospital until 9/63. WIA 5/5/64. In hospital until. Resigned (wounds) 8/19/64

Name	Initial Rank	D.O.B.	Home	Prewar Occupation	Comments
Ingram, John Calvin	3rd Sgt.	1838	Dixon Spr., Wilson Co.	Farmer	1st Sgt. 3/3/62. 3rd Lt. 4/26/62. 2nd Lt. 9/17/62. WIA 9/21/62. WIA & captured 7/3/63. POW rest of war.
Gwyn, Hugh Robert	4th Sgt.	1821	Wilson Co.	Farmer	Reduced (Pvt.) 3/26/62. Discharged (seniority) 8/20/62.
Sellars, Eli	1st Cpl.	1838	Cainsville, Wilson Co.	Farm labor	Reduced (Pvt.) 4/30/62. Discharged (disability) 7/22/62.
Ozment, John D.	2nd Cpl.	1832	Rural Hill, Wilson Co.	Farmer	4th Sgt. 4/30/62. WIA 5/3/63. **Died of wounds, 6/15/62.**
King, Medicus "Doc"	3rd Cpl.	1841	Rural Hill, Wilson Co.	Farm labor	Reduced (Pvt.) 4/30/62. Captured 4/3–8/65.
Richmond, Lovett Alex	4th Cpl.	1844	Rural Hill, Wilson	Farm labor	Reduced (Pvt.) 4/30/62. 3rd Cpl. 4/11/64. Captured 4/3–8/65.
Gwyn, John W.	Musician	—	—	—	Became Pvt. 4/26/62. Discharged (furnished a substitute) 10/24/62.
Rice, James T.	Musician	1837	Silver Spr., Wilson Co.	Salesman	Became Pvt. 12/31/62. **Killed, 5/31/62 (Seven Pines).**
Allen, William H.	Private	1842	Gladesville, Wilson Co.	Farm labor	Captured 7/3/63. POW — last record, 8/63.
Aubrey, Henry	Private	1825	Wilson Co.	Farmer	Discharged (seniority) 8/20.
Baird, William	Private	1837	Rural Hill, Wilson Co.	Farmer	1st Sgt. 5/1/63. **Killed, 7/3/63 (Gettysburg).**
Ballentine, Frederick "Cannon"	Private	—	Wilson Co.	—	TDY (teamster) 8/19/62 to 10/64. Captured 4/2/65.
Baskins, Robert A.	Private	1826	Gladesville, Wilson Co.	Farmer	Discharged (seniority) 8/20/62.
Blankenship, George	Private	1844	Wilson Co.	Farm labor	Discharged (minority) 8/20/62.
Bradshaw, Hartwell	Private	1835	Silver Spr., Wilson Co.	Clerk	WIA (right knee) & captured 7/3/63. **Died of wounds, 7/25/63.**
Bright, Joseph H.	Private	1837	Cainseville, Wilson Co.	Farm labor	WIA 5/3/63. **Died of wounds, 5/5/63.**
Cluck, Fountain W.	Private	1832	Ponderella, Wilson Co.	Teacher	Discharged (disability) 11/10/61.
Curry, Benjamin Frank	Private	1840	Gladesville, Wilson Co.	Farm labor	1st Cpl. 3/30/62. **Killed, 5/30/64 (Bethesda Church).**
Curry, John S.	Private	1846	Gladesville, Wilson Co.	Weaver's asst.	4th Cpl. 4/11/64. Captured 4/3–8/65.
Davis, William H.	Private	1839	Mt. Carmel, Wilson Co.	Farm labor	WIA 5/31/62. In hospital until. **Died of wounds, 5/15/63.**
Dement, John Luss	Private	1846	Ponderella, Wilson Co.	Farm labor	Discharged (minority) 8/20/62.
Doughterly, Nathan "Tip"	Private	—	—	—	Discharged (minority) 8/20/62.
Drennon, Thomas J.	Private	1832	Gladesville, Wilson Co.	Farm labor	WIA 12/13/62. In hospital until. Deserted 1/29/63.
Edwards, Eaton "Buck"	Private	1842	Ponderella, Wilson Co.	Farm labor	**Killed, 5/31/62 (Seven Pines).**

Name	Initial Rank	D.O.B.	Home	Prewar Occupation	Comments
Edwards, John B.	Private	1835	Ponderella, Wilson Co.	Farm labor	1st Sgt. 12/31/61. Reduced (Pvt.) 3/20/62. TDY (teamster) 8/2/62 to. Deserted 10/10/63.
Edwards, William H.	Private	1843	Ponderella, Wilson Co.	Farm labor	Discharged (disability) 2/10/62.
Foster, Andrew J.	Private	1840	Rural Hill, Wilson Co.	Farm labor	WIA 5/31/62. In hospital until 3/63. WIA (right arm amputated) & captured 7/3/63. No other records.
Grissom, James L. "Black Ram"	Private	1840	Lockport, Wilson Co.	Farm labor	**Killed, 7/3/63 (Gettysburg).**
Grissom, John D.	Private	1830	Ponderella, Wilson Co.	Farmer	Discharged (disability) 1/5/62.
Grissom, Thomas Albert	Private	1841	Lexington, Henderson Co.	Farm labor	WIA (left leg) 6/27/62. Sick since 5/25/63 to end of war.
Hackney, William Wallace	Private	1832	Ponderella, Wilson Co.	Day laborer	Discharged (seniority) 8/20/62.
Hagar, Reuben B.	Private	1832	Mt. Carmel	Blacksmith	WIA 12/13/62. On medical furlough to end of war.
Hamilton, Alexander	Private	1840	Wilson Co.	Farm labor	Discharged (disability) 9/28/62.
Harrison, James	Private	1824	Commerce, Wilson Co.	Farmer	Discharged (disability) 1/26/62.
Harrison, John	Private	1828	Gladesville, Wilson Co.	Farm labor	Discharged (disability) 3/20/62.
Harrison, John T.	Private	1841	Gladesville, Wilson Co.	Farm labor	Deserted 3/2/63.
Harrison, Thomas	Private	1832	Gladesville, Wilson Co.	Farm labor	2nd Sgt. 4/30/62. Deserted 3/2/63.
Harrison, William	Private	1840	Gladesville, Wilson Co.	Farm labor	Deserted 12/30/63.
Harrison, William Henry	Private	1837	Gladesville, Wilson Co.	Farm labor	**Killed, 7/1/63 (Gettysburg).**
Hawks, John Archer	Private	1831	Gladesville, Wilson Co.	Farmer	Deserted 12/30/63.
Hide, Edward	Private	1840	Lebanon, Wilson Co.	Day laborer	Deserted 7/16/63
Hide, Joseph	Private	1845	Lebanon, Wilson Co.	Farm labor	**Died of disease, 7/9/62.**
Hobbs, John H.	Private	1844	Lebanon, Wilson Co.	Farm labor	Discharged (disability) 2/10/62.
Huddleston, George W.	Private	1832	Ponderella, Wilson Co.	Farmer	3rd Sgt. 3/30/62. 1st Sgt. 12/31/63. WIA (left foot amputated) 6/6/64. **Died of wounds, 6/8/64.**
Hutchens, Aaron	Private	1841	Ponderella, Wilson Co.	Day laborer	Discharged (disability) 6/15/62.
Hutchens, Lafayette	Private	1835	Wilson Co.	Farm labor	WIA (chest) 12/13/62. **Died of wounds, 12/24/63.**
Jackson, John B.	Private	1828	Wilson Co.	Minister	Discharged (disability) 8/21/61.

Name	Initial Rank	D.O.B.	Home	Prewar Occupation	Comments
Jackson, Thomas R.	Private	1838	Laguardo, Wilson Co.	Farm labor	3rd Sgt. 4/26/62. WIA 8/30/62. 2nd Sgt. 10/62. Captured 11/15/64. Exchanged. Surrendered 9/5/65 (Appomattox).
Johns, William D.	Private	1840	Rural Hill, Wilson Co.	Farm labor	WIA 8/30/62. **Died of wounds, 9/1/62.**
Johnson, Littleton Halls	Private	1821	—	Farmer	WIA 8/9/62. **Died of wounds, 8/28/62.**
Johnson, William H.	Private	1806	Lebanon, Wilson Co.	Minister	TDY (hospital minister) 12/16/61 to 7/62. Discharged (disability) 7/29/62.
Jones, Robert F.	Private	—	—	—	Deserted 6/28/62.
Jones, William H. "Buck"	Private	1843	Rural Hill, Wilson Co.	Farm labor	WIA 6/27/62. Discharged (minority) 8/20/62.
Kennedy, John L.	Private	—	—	—	Captured 7/1/63. Exchanged. WIA 8/19/64. Discharged (wounds) 1/15/65.
Lannom, Andrew T.	Private	1839	Wilson Co.	Farm labor	Discharged (disability) 2/14/62.
Lannom, Joseph J.	Private	1827	Wilson Co.	Farmer	Discharged (seniority) 8/20/62.
Lannom, Nathan P. "Coon"	Private	—	—	—	4th Cpl. 4/26/62. 3rd Cpl. 7/62. WIA 8/9/62. Deserted 10/15/62.
Lannom, Peter Lafayette	Private	1837	Wilson Co.	Farm labor	Deserted 12/19/64.
Leonard, Frederick C.	Private	1805	Wilson Co.	Farmer	Discharged (disability) 11/25/61.
McCrary, James	Private	1826	Wilson Co.	Farmer	Discharged (disability) 6/15/62.
McCrary, John	Private	1830	Gladesville, Wilson Co.	Farm labor	Discharged (disability) 6/15/62.
Mount, John W.	Private	1836	Wilson Co.	Farm labor	**Died of disease, 12/2/61.**
Nelson, John W.	Private	1842	Ponderella, Wilson Co.	Farm labor	4th Cpl. 8/31/63. 2nd Cpl. 4/11/64. 2nd Sgt. 12/31/64. Surrendered 4/9/65 (Appomattox).
Nipper, John W.	Private	1837	Gladesville, Wilson Co.	Farm labor	Sick from 8/61. **Died of disease, 6/15/62.**
Oliver, James T.	Private	1836	Ponderella, Wilson Co.	Farm labor	WIA (hand) 5/3/63. Transferred to Co. F, 10/1/63.
Oliver, John M.	Private	1838	Ponderella, Wilson Co.	Farm labor	Discharged (disability) 7/20/61.
Oliver, William L.	Private	1825	Gallatin, Sumner Co.	Overseer	WIA (leg) 7/3/63. 4th Sgt. (color sgt.) 8/31/62. 3rd Sgt. 10/63. Ensign — 4/28/64. No other records.
Ozment, Robert B.	Private	1831	Oak Point, Wilson Co.	Blacksmith	WIA 8/27/62. WIA 9/14/62. On medical furlough until. Discharged (wounds) 4/18/63.
Patterson, Thomas	Private	1825	Ponderella, Wilson Co.	Day laborer	Discharged (seniority) 8/20/62.
Pickett, John B.	Private	1844	Lebanon, Wilson Co.	Farm labor	Discharged (minority) 8/20/62.
Poole, Wiley	Private	1844	Mt. Carmel, Wilson Co.	Farm labor	**Died of disease, 10/12/61.**

Name	Initial Rank	D.O.B.	Home	Prewar Occupation	Comments
Puckett, Paulding G.	Private	1836	Gladesville, Wilson Co.	Farm labor	Discharged (disability) 7/8/61.
Quesenbury, Hugh E.	Private	1830	Mt. Carmel	Farm labor	Discharged (disability) 5/15/62.
Quesenbury, Richard T.	Private	1842	Mt. Carmel	Farm labor	2nd Cpl. 8/31/62. Deserted 12/31/63.
Quesenbury, William J.	Private	1840	Mt. Carmel	Farm labor	WIA 9/17/62. Medical furlough until. Deserted 10/15/62.
Ray, James K.	Private	—	—	—	Deserted 6/13/63.
Richmond, James P.	Private	1821	Wilson Co.	Farmer	Discharged (seniority) 8/20/62.
Robbins, William H.	Private	1842	—	Farm labor	2nd Sgt. 4/30/62. 3rd Lt. 10/7/62. Captured 7/1/63. POW rest of war.
Roberts, John	Private	1826	Goodlettsville, Davidson Co.	Farmer	**Killed, 7/3/63 (Gettysburg).**
Robertson, George W.	Private	—	—	—	Discharged (disability) 12/16/61.
Robertson, Isaiah	Private	—	—	—	Discharged (disability) 2/1/62.
Robertson, Luke	Private	—	—	—	WIA 6/26/62. Medical furlough until 4/63. WIA (left arm) 5/3/63. 4th Sgt. 1/22/64. Deserted 10/11/64.
Rucker, Sterling Brown	Private	—	Wilson Co.	—	WIA (side) 5/3/63. Medical leave until. Captured 9/10/63 (Liberty, TN).
Rucker, Thomas W.	Private	—	Wilson Co	—	Discharged (disability) 12/16/61.
Simmons, Calvin J.	Private	1841	Wilson Co.	Farm labor	**Killed, 5/31/62 (Seven Pines).**
Sims, George G.	Private	1835	Lebanon, Wilson Co.	Farm labor	Deserted 1/25/64
Sullivan, Benjamin F.	Private	1837	Lebanon, Wilson Co.	Farm labor	Deserted 1/25/64.
Sullivan, Thomas J.	Private	1842	Rural Hill, Wilson Co.	Saddler	4th Cpl. 4/30/62. WIA 7/3/63. Medical furlough until. Deserted 12/31/63.
Sullivan, William H.	Private	1837	Rural Hill, Wilson Co.	Farm labor	WIA 5/31/62. Medical leave until. Deserted 9/15/72.
Summers, James H.	Private	1838	Lebanon, Wilson Co.	Farm labor	Sick since 7/26/62. TDY (nurse) 2/64, for rest of war.
Vann, John W.	Private	1836	Wilson Co.	Farm labor	Discharged (disability) 2/16/62.
Vaughn, Richard P.	Private	1840	—	Farm labor	5th Sgt. 8/31/61. WIA (right thigh) 7/3/63. Medical leave until. Deserted 7/31/64.
Vaughter, William G.	Private	1836	Gladesville, Wilson Co.	Farm labor	WIA 8/9/62. Medical furlough until. Deserted 10/15/62.
Woodrum, William F.	Private	1838	Gladesville, Wilson Co.	Farm labor	**Died of disease, 10/28/61.**
Young, Peter Bailey	Private	1828	Wilson Co.	Farmer	WIA (chest) 12/13/62. **Died of wounds, 12/29/62.**
Arnold, Granville	Conscript	—	Knox Co.	—	Drafted 7/19/63. Transferred to Co. F, 10/31/63.
Curry, James	Recruit	1844	Wilson Co.	Day laborer	Enlisted 10/24/62 (as a substitute for John Gwyn). **Died of disease, 4/17/63.**

Name	Initial Rank	D.O.B.	Home	Prewar Occupation	Comments
Potter, Enoch	Transfer	—	—	—	Transferred from Co. F, 10/1/63. Deserted 12/31/63.
Vickry, D. G.	Conscript	—	—	—	Drafted 7/63. Deserted 8/10/63.
Williams, Martin	Conscript	—	Knox Co.	—	Drafted 7/63. Deserted 11/63.

Company H. "The Grays"

Name	Initial Rank	D.O.B.	Home	Prewar Occupation	Comments
Williamson, William H.	Captain	1828	Lebanon, Wilson Co.	Lawyer	WIA 6/27/62. Maj. 4/7/63. WIA (right arm amputated) & captured 7/3/63. POW rest of war.
Blythe, David M.	1st Lt.	1828	Lebanon, Wilson Co.	Physician	**Died of disease, 1/12/62.**
Talbot, John B.	2nd Lt.	—	—	—	Relieved of duty, 4/26/62.
Martin, Andrew B.	3rd Lt.	1837	Lebanon, Wilson Co.	Lawyer	Relieved of duty, 4/26/62.
Crudup, Dempsey	1st Sgt.	1839	Rural Hill, Wilson Co.	Farm labor	1st Lt. 1/22/62. TDY (Richmond) 4/26/62. No other records.
Doak, Rufus P. "Ruff"	2nd Sgt.	—	—	—	1st Lt. 4/26/62. WIA 8/28/62. **Died of wounds, 9/16/62.**
Morris, Wilburn	3rd Sgt.	1835	Lebanon, Wilson Co.	Clerk	1st Sgt. 1/22/62. Reduced (Pvt.) 4/26/62. WIA (left hand) 5/31/62. Medical furlough until. Discharged (wounds) 8/27/62.
McCorkle, William M.	4th Sgt.	1836	Lebanon, Wilson Co.	Lawyer	2nd Lt. 4/26/62. Sick since 7/28/62. Resigned (sickness) 8/30/62.
McClain, James M.	5th Sgt.	1838	Lebanon, Wilson Co.	Lawyer	Reduced (Pvt.) 4/26/62. WIA (right leg amputated) 5/3/63. **Died of wounds, 7/22/63.**
Brackett, Anson	1st Cpl.	1836	—	Lawyer	Discharged (disability) 9/5/61.
Hank, Willis W.	2nd Cpl.	—	—	—	Transferred to Ashby's Cavalry, 2/18/62.
Williamson, John "Van"	3rd Cpl.	1831	Green Hill, Wilson Co.	Farm labor	Reduced (Pvt.) 4/26/62. 5th Sgt. 10/30/62. 4th Sgt. 1/29/63. WIA (right thigh) 7/3/63. WIA 8/19/64. TDY (engineers) 2/1/65 to end of war.
Allison, Andrew	4th Cpl.	1842	Lebanon, Wilson Co.	Student (law)	3rd Lt. 4/26/62. WIA 8/9/62. 1st Lt. 9/16/62. Sick since 1/5/63. Resigned (disability) 11/26/63.
Cloyd, Ezekial A.	Bugler	1820	Green Hill, Wilson Co.	Farmer	Discharged (disability) 3/25/62.
Cartmell, Robert D.	Drummer	1838	Lebanon, Wilson Co.	Harness maker	Discharged, 2/12/62. Re-enlisted (Pvt.) 3/24/63. Sick since, 3/1/64 to end of war.
Ahart, John	Private	1841	Green Hill, Wilson Co.	Farm labor	4th Cpl. 4/26/62. Discharged (disability) 7/15/62.
Alexander, Benjamin F. "Ben"	Private	1841	Cherry valley, Wilson Co.	Farm labor	2nd Cpl. 3/26/62. WIA 8/28/62. 1st Cpl. 1/63. Captured 7/3/63. POW until Exchange, 2/18/65. Captured 4/2/65.

Name	Initial Rank	D.O.B.	Home	Prewar Occupation	Comments
Alexander, Samuel	Private	1814	Cherry Valley, Wilson Co.	Farmer	TDY (teamster) 3/19/62 to 11/64. Captured 4/3–8/65.
Allison, Alexander	Private	1840	Lebanon, Wilson Co.	Student (law)	Appointed Lt. of artillery, 8/61.
Bashaw, Pierce	Private	1837	Green Hill, Wilson Co.	Farm labor	WIA 6/27/62. **Died of wounds (6/30/62.**
Beard, Joseph P.	Private	1842	Lebanon, Wilson Co.	Student (law)	**Killed, 5/31/62 (Seven Pines).**
Beard, Richard	Private	1842	Lebanon, Wilson Co.	Student (law)	WIA 5/31/62. Transferred to 5th Tenn. Inf. & promoted to 2nd Lt.
Blair, Henry H.	Private	—	—	—	WIA 5/31/62. In hospital until. Deserted 9/25/62.
Blair, James L.	Private	—	—	—	Discharged (furnished a substitute) 12/31/63.
Boydston, James G.	Private	1831	—	Minister	Discharged (sickness) 6/25/62.
Buford, Thomas E.	Private	1835	Lebanon, Wilson Co.	Stable keeper	**Killed, 5/31/62 (Seven Pines).**
Campbell, Frank M.	Private	1836	Wilson Co.	Farm labor	Discharged (injury—struck by a falling tree) 2/12/62.
Carroll, James	Private	1840	Lebanon, Wilson Co.	Farm labor	Discharged (disability) 11/8/61.
Criswell, John T.	Private	1834	Green Hill, Wilson Co.	Wheelwright	TDY (wheelwright) 10/62 to 6/65. Captured 4/2/65.
Dellis, Isham M.	Private	1840	Ponderella, Wilson Co.	Farm labor	**Died of disease, 12/16/61.**
Doak, John	Private	1836	Wilson Co.	Farm labor	Discharged (disability) 8/15/62.
Donnell, Benjamin F.	Private	1839	Mt. Carmel, Wilson Co.	Farm labor	Discharged (disability) 3/25/62.
Donnell, David K. "Davy"	Private	1805	Lebanon, Wilson Co.	Boarding house keeper	Discharged (disability) 11/25/61.
Donnell, Elihu Lahew	Private	1841	Mt. Carmel, Wilson Co.	Farm labor	WIA 8/9/62. **Died of wounds, 8/22/62.**
Etheridge, Tilmon	Private	1843	Cainsville, Wilson Co.	Farm labor	Captured 9/17/62. Exchanged. Deserted 2/15/65.
Grisham, George C.	Private	1841	Wilson Co.	Student	**Killed, 8/9/62 (Cedar Run).**
Guill, Benjamin	Private	1833	Rural Hill, Wilson Co.	Farm labor	WIA 5/3/63. TDY (hospital duty) 6/1/63 to 4/8/64. Medical furlough to end of war.
Hamilton, David D.	Private	1842	Nashville, Davidson Co.	Farm labor	WIA (left shoulder & skull) 5/31/62. WIA (hand) 12/13/62. WIA (foot) & captured 4/2/65.
Hamilton, John H.	Private	1836	Lebanon, Wilson Co.	Teacher	3rd Sgt. 12/31/61. 2nd Sgt. 11/62. WIA (shin) & captured 7/3/63. Paroled 9/4/63. Surrendered 4/9/65 (Appomattox).
Hamilton, Joseph P.	Private	1839	Nashville, Davidson Co.	Farm labor	TDY (commissary clerk) 10/22/62 to 7/63. Captured 2/5/65.
Harlin, John E.	Private	1839	Lebanon, Wilson Co.	Farm labor	WIA (arm) 7/1/63. Captured 4/2/65.

Name	Initial Rank	D.O.B.	Home	Prewar Occupation	Comments
Harlin, Samuel	Private	1841	Lebanon, Wilson Co.	Farm labor	WIA 9/17/62. **Died of wounds, 2/9/63.**
Harrington, Alpheus "Alf"	Private	1844	Wilson Co.	Student	Discharged (minority) 8/18/62.
Harris, Furgeson	Private	1840	Tucker's Crossroads, Wilson Co.	Farm labor	3rd Sgt. 4/26/62. WIA 8/28/62. 3rd Lt. 9/16/62. WIA 7/3/63. 1st Lt. 11/30/63. WIA (right leg) 4/2/65. Captured 4/3–8/65.
Harrison, Clark S.	Private	1836	Green Hill, Wilson Co.	Teacher	**Accidently killed, 11/23/61.**
Hawkins, Dick R.	Private	1831	—	—	TDY (commissary) 9/61 to 6/62/. Transferred to brigade commissary, 6/15/62. No other records.
Hearn, Orin	Private	1829	Shop Spr., Wilson Co.	Farmer	Discharged (furnished a substitute) 7/9/62.
Hewgley, Ashley	Private	1841	Wilson Co.	Farm labor	1st Cpl. 4/26/62. Sick since 7/28/62. Discharged (disability) 11/29/62.
Hewgley, John W.	Private	1835	Wilson Co.	Farm labor	Discharged (disability) 11/8/61.
Hewgley, William B.	Private	1842	Rural Hill, Wilson Co.	Farm labor	Captured 7/1/63. POW rest of war.
Hobbs, James A.	Private	1839	Tucker's Crossroads, Wilson Co.	Farm labor	TDY (pioneer corps) 6/62 to end of war.
Holloway, Thomas "Tom"	Private	1839	Lebanon, Wilson Co.	Teacher	WIA 12/13/62. **Killed, 7/3/63 (Gettysburg).**
Horn, William E.	Private	1829	Wilson Co.	Carpenter	Discharged (disability) 7/20/62.
Jackson, Robert N. "Bob"	Private	1838	Wilson Co.	Student	WIA 8/28/62. **Died of wounds, 10/8/62.**
King, Thomas B.	Private	1840	Murfreesboro, Rutherford Co.	Student	Captured 4/2/65.
Lindsey, John H.	Private	1838	Wilson Co.	Farm labor	Discharged (disability) 5/1/62.
Lindsey, Phillip	Private	—	—	—	Discharged (disability) 7/8/61.
Lindsey, Robert M.	Private	1841	Saltillo, Hardin Co.	Teacher	Captured 4/2/65.
Lowe, Marvelle	Private	1837	Wilson Co.	Farm labor	Discharged (furnished a substitute) 6/10/62.
Major, Samuel D.	Private	1832	Mt. Carmel, Wilson Co.	Teacher	2nd Sgt. 4/26/62. WIA 9/17/62. **Died of wounds, 10/23/62.**
Manson, Henry W. "Hal"	Private	1843	Lebanon, Wilson Co.	Day laborer	5th Sgt. 12/31/62. TDY (signal corps) 6/1/63 to 10/64. Captured 4/2/65.
Markham, Samuel P.	Private	1829	—	Stone mason	Discharged (disability) 2/12/62.
Massey, Archibald D.	Private	1831	Mt. Carmel	Farm labor	TDY (teamster) 6/10/62 to 1/63. Sick since 6/1/63 to 11/63. Deserted 5/4/64.
Matlock, Henry B.	Private	—	—	—	Discharged (disability) 10/18/61.
Matlock, William H.	Private	1838	Wilson Co.	Student	WIA (hip & knee) 6/27/62. Discharged (wounds) 6/28/62.

7th Tennessee Infantry Company H

Name	Initial Rank	D.O.B.	Home	Prewar Occupation	Comments
McDonald, John A.	Private	—	Lebanon, Wilson Co.	—	WIA (right thigh) & captured 9/17/62. Exchanged 11/12/62. Medical furlough 12/62 to 3/64. TDY (passport detective) 4/1/64 to end of war.
Miller, John T.	Private	1842	Lebanon, Wilson Co.	Shoe maker	4th Sgt. 4/26/62. 3rd Sgt. 11/62. Captured 7/1/63. POW rest of war.
Murray, Robert B.	Private	1824	—	Farmer	Discharged (seniority) 8/31/62.
Neal, Edward M.	Private	1841	Lebanon, Wilson Co.	Clerk	TDY (hospital steward) 9/61 to 5/62. TDY (Qtr. Mstr.) 5/62 to end of war.
Neal, James A.	Private	1843	Lebanon, Wilson Co.	Farm labor	TDY (ambulance driver) 3/62 to 12/62. TDY (Forage mstr.) 1/63 to end of war.
New, John D.	Private	1838	Lebanon, Wilson Co.	Farm labor	WIA (hand) 8/28/62. WIA 12/13/62. **Died of wounds, 1/12/63.**
New, Thomas J.	Private	1840	Lebanon, Wilson Co.	Farm labor	Discharged (disability) 8/4/62.
Organ, Rolly W.	Private	1838	Tucker's Crossroads, Wilson Co.	Clerk	**Died of disease, 9/15/61.**
Parker, William P.	Private	—	—	—	TDY (hospital physician) since 8/61. **Died of disease, 8/10/62.**
Patton, James T.	Private	1836	Lebanon, Wilson Co.	Farm labor	WIA 5/31/62. WIA 8/18/64. Sick since 11/15/64 to end of war.
Peyton, John C.	Private	1841	Sumner Co.	Student (law)	Discharged (disability) 6/15/62.
Ragland, John B.	Private	1838	Wilson Co.	Student	Discharged (disability) 2/20/62.
Ready, George W.	Private	1835	—	Teacher	5th Sgt. 4/26/62. Discharged (alienage) 9/3/62.
Reeves, John W.	Private	1842	Lebanon, Wilson Co.	Farm labor	**Killed, 8/9/62 (Cedar Run).**
Rutland, John B.	Private	1840	Rural Hill, Wilson Co.	Farm labor	WIA 5/31/62. Captured 7/3/63. POW rest of war.
Schofield, Cyrus J.	Private	1842	—	Student	Discharged (alienage) 8/30/62.
Settle, Leroy B.	Private	1838	—	Student	Transferred to Morgan's Artillery, 6/20/63, promoted to 2nd Lt.
Simmons, John S.	Private	1834	Cainsville, Wilson Co.	Farm labor	WIA (head) 7/3/63. **Died of wounds, 7/8/63.**
Stratton, Golliday	Private	1839	Lebanon, Wilson Co.	Clerk	Appointed (Staff) 2/20/62 to end of war.
Swain, Rolando	Private	1838	Lebanon, Wilson Co.	Clerk	TDY (brigade commissary) 7/22/62 to end of war.
Tate, John Bell	Private	1840	Green Hill, Wilson Co.	Farm labor	Discharged (disability) 8/1/62.
Tate, William Newton	Private	1839	Mt. Juliet, Wilson Co.	Farm labor	3rd Lt. 8/30/62. 2nd Lt. 9/16/62. WIA 7/3/63. Capt. 4/8/64. Captured 4/9/65 (Lynchburg).
Taylor, Robert R.	Private	1837	Big Springs, Wilson Co.	Stock dealer	WIA 5/31/62. Discharged (wounds) 10/1/62.

Name	Initial Rank	D.O.B.	Home	Prewar Occupation	Comments
Thompson, George A.	Private	1838	Wilson Co.	Farm labor	3rd Cpl. 4/26/62. WIA 8/28/62. 2nd Cpl. 1/63. Captured 7/3/63. Paroled. WIA 5/5/64. In hospital until. Discharged (wounds) 11/8/64.
Thompson, Zachariah "Zach"	Private	1844	Wilson Co.	Student	Transferred to Co. K, 9/1/61.
Tucker, John W.	Private	1831	Wilson Co.	Farmer	WIA 8/28/62. **Died of wounds, 8/31/62.**
Turner, Edward A.	Private	1838	Wilson Co.	Carpenter	Discharged (disability) 12/16/61.
Turner, Stephen L.	Private	1839	Wilson Co.	Farm labor	WIA(right hand & left arm) 5/31/62. Discharged (wounds) 8/11/62.
Westbrook, Lewis	Private	1836	Lebanon, Wilson Co.	Lawyer	1st Sgt. 4/26/62. Captured 7/1/63. POW rest of war.
Wharton, William H.	Private	1837	Lebanon, Wilson Co.	Clerk	TDY (brigade clerk) since 4/62 to 9/64. Captured 2/24/62.
White, James S.	Private	1841	Wilson Co.	Student	Discharged (disability) 1/12/62.
Wilkerson, Beverly J.	Private	1843	Wilson Co.	Post master	Discharged (disability) 2/12/62.
Williams, James A.	Private	—	—	—	Sick since 7/61. Discharged (disability) 10/31/62.
Williams, John N.	Private	1833	Wilson Co.	Farmer	Captured 7/3/63. POW rest of war.
Word, Roger Q. "Cu"	Private	1840	Lebanon, Wilson Co.	Farm labor	Captured 8/29/62. Exchanged. Captured 4/3–8/65.
Word, William "Bill"	Private	1824	Wilson Co.	Farmer	Discharged (seniority) 8/18/62.
Wormack, Joel E.	Private	1841	Wilson Co.	Farm labor	Discharged (disability) 2/12/62.
Wormack, Robert R.	Private	—	Wilson Co.	—	WIA 8/28/62. WIA (right arm amputated) & captured 7/3/63. POW rest of war.
Davis, John W.	Conscript	1838	—	—	Drafted 8/26/63. Captured 5/4/64. POW rest of war.
Eatherly, Martin A.	Transfer	—	—	—	Transferred from Co. I, 1/23/64. Captured 4/2/65.
Eatherly, Winfield S.	Recruit	1843	Silver Spr., Wilson Co.	Farm labor	Enlisted 4/26/63. Captured 4/3–8/65.
Jones, Timothy	Conscript	—	Richmond, VA	—	Drafted 6/10/62. Deserted 6/12/62.
Quinn, Patrick O.	Conscript	—	Harrisburg, VA	—	Drafted 3/1/64. TDY (teamster) since 4/1/64 to end of war.
Smith, Samuel	Conscript	—	—	—	Drafted 7/8/62. Deserted 7/9/62.
Stratton, James E.	Transfer	1839	—	—	Transferred from Co. D, 10/10/61. WIA 5/31/62. Discharged (wounds) 10/62.
Wade, William A.	Recruit	—	Nashville, Davidson Co.	—	Enlisted 2/12/62. WIA & captured 7/3/63. POW rest of war.
Wilkerson, Charles W.	Transfer	1836	Smithville, Dekalb Co.	—	Transferred from Co. K, 8/14/61. WIA (shoulder) 8/9/62. TDY (hospital) since 1/63 to 7/63. TDY (Qtr. Mstr.) since 7/63 to end of war.
Williams, Robert M.	Recruit	—	Valley Mt., WV	—	Enlisted 10/61. Deserted 12/63.

Name	Initial Rank	D.O.B.	Home	Prewar Occupation	Comments
Williamson, John A.	Recruit	1839	Valley Mt, WV	—	Enlisted 10/61. Discharged (alienage) 8/26/62.

Company I. "Silver Springs Guards"

Name	Initial Rank	D.O.B.	Home	Prewar Occupation	Comments
Anthony, Joseph "J.A"	Captain	1829	Silver Spr., Wilson, Co.	Manufacturer	Relieved of duty, 4/27/62.
Harris, William H.	1st Lt.	1822	Cainsville, Wilson Co.	Farm labor	Relieved of duty, 4/27/62.
Bass, James Oren	2nd Lt.	1838	Silver Spr., Wilson Co.	Farm labor	1st Lt. 4/30/62. Capt. 8/9/62. Captured 4/2/65.
Curd, William E. "Bill"	3rd Lt.	1836	Green Hill, Wilson Co.	Farm labor	Capt. 4/30/62. WIA 6/27/62. **Died of wounds, 7/16/62.**
Harkreader, Absalom "Gleaves"	1st Sgt.	1825	Silver, Spr., Wilson Co.	Farmer	Reduced (Pvt.) 4/30/62. Discharged (seniority) 8/20/62.
Vivrett, Thomas "Tom"	2nd Sgt.	1824	Mt. Carmel, Wilson Co.	Farmer	Reduced (Pvt.) 4/30/62. Discharged (seniority) 8/20/62.
Bayne, William T. "Bill"	3rd Sgt.	1825	Laguardo, Wilson Co.	Farmer	Reduced (Pvt.) 4/30/62. Discharged (seniority) 8/20/62.
Vivrette, John W.	1st Cpl.	—	Silver Spr., Wilson Co.	—	3rd Lt. 4/30/62. WIA (left leg) 5/31/62. Medical furlough until. Resigned (wounds) 1/10/63.
Kennedy, Horatio S. "H.S."	2nd Cpl.	1840	Silver Spr., Wilson Co.	Teacher	Reg't. Ord. Sgt. 4/30/62. Staff assignment until. Discharged (alienage) 12/7/62.
Anderson, Oren	3rd Cpl.	1836	Silver Spr., Wilson Co.	Trader	Reduced (Pvt.) 4/30/62. Captured 7/3/63. POW until 12/26/62. No other records.
Harkreader, William "Bill"	4th Cpl.	1839	Silver Spr., Wilson Co.	Farm labor	2nd Lt. 4/30/62. WIA (left arm amputated) 8/29/62. TDY (recruiter) until. Captured 5/18/64 (Rome, GA).
Bryant, Wesley "Wes"	Musician	1824	Green Hill, Wilson Co.	Farmer	Discharged (seniority) 8/20/62.
Jennings, Enos	Musician	1842	Green Hill, Wilson Co.	Farm labor	Captured 4/2/65.
Anderson, Mead "Clint"	Private	1841	Silver Spr., Wilson Co.	Farm labor	4th Cpl. 4/30/62. WIA (arm) & captured 7/3/63. Paroled. Captured 4/4/65.
Anderson, Thomas "Tom"	Private	1840	Silver Spr., Wilson Co.	Farm labor	2nd Sgt. 4/30/62. WIA 6/26/62. Medical furlough at home until. Captured 11/29/62. Paroled. WIA 5/3/63. **Died of wounds, 6/30/63.**
Baird, William C.	Private	1838	Rural Hill, Wilson Co.	Farmer	WIA 8/9/62. 3rd Lt. 10/15/62. **Killed, 12/13/62 (Fredericksburg).**
Bashaw, Joseph Peter "J.P."	Private	1842	Rural Hill, Wilson Co.	Clerk	1st Cpl. 12/31/61. WIA 6/26/62. WIA 7/3/63. Captured 7/5/63. Captured 8/19/64. Exchanged 11/1/64. Deserted 3/2/65.

Name	Initial Rank	D.O.B.	Home	Prewar Occupation	Comments
Bass, Francis "Fran"	Private	1835	Silver Spr., Wilson Co.	Farm labor	4th Sgt. 8/8/61. Reduced (Pvt.) 4/30/62. **Killed, 10/1/64 (Peeble's Farm).**
Brown, John E. "Pomp"	Private	—	—	—	Discharged (disability) 8/17/61.
Bryant, Ezekial "Zeke"	Private	1844	Green Hill, Wilson Co.	Farm labor	WIA 5/31/62. In hospital until. Deserted 1/1/63.
Buckner, John	Private	—	—	—	Transferred to 14th Tenn., 9/61.
Cawthorn, Charles	Private	1845	Green Hill, Wilson Co.	Farm labor	Sick since 4/10/62. Discharged (minority) 8/30/62.
Clemens, John W. "Jack"	Private	1839	Rural Hill, Wilson Co.	Farm labor	5th Sgt. 1/62. WIA (hand) 5/12/64. In hospital until. Discharged (wounds) 11/18/64.
Clemens, Thomas A. "T.A."	Private	1840	Rural Hill, Wilson Co.	Farm labor	3rd Lt. 12/20/62. 1st Lt. 3/21/64. WIA (abdomen) 4/2/65. Captured 4/3–8/65.
Criswell, James H. "Jim"	Private	1843	Green Hill, Wilson Co.	Farm labor	Captured 4/2/65.
Criswell, Robert F.	Private	1840	Rural Hill, Wilson Co.	Farm labor	TDY (nurse) 6/15/62 to 11/62. Captured 4/3–8/65.
Criswell, William "Turner"	Private	1834	Silver Spr., Wilson Co.	Farm labor	Sick since 6/5/62 for rest of war.
Curd, John T.	Private	1834	Green Hill, Wilson Co.	Farm labor	WIA 5/31/62. **Died of disease, 1/1/63.**
Davis, Richard T. "R.T."	Private	1843	Silver Spr., Wilson Co.	Farm labor	WIA (knee) 5/31/62. In hospital until 4/63. TDY (Qtr. Mster.) 4/8/63 to end of war.
Davis, Thomas	Private	—	Lebanon, Wilson Co.	—	Discharged (disability) 2/15/62.
Eatherly, Alexander F.	Private	1842	Silver Spr., Wilson Co.	Farm labor	Discharged (disability) 7/16/62.
Eatherly, James J. "Jim"	Private	—	Silver Spr., Wilson Co.	—	Discharged (disability) 2/10/62.
Eatherly, John W. "Wes"	Private	1845	Silver Spr., Wilson Co.	Farm labor	**Killed, 7/3/63 (Gettysburg).**
Eatherly, Martin A.	Private	1840	Silver Spr., Wilson Co.	Farm labor	Transferred to Co. H, 1/23/64.
Eatherly, Pleasant	Private	1835	—	Farm labor	**Killed, 5/31/62 (Seven Pines).**
Greer, George	Private	1839	Green Hill, Wilson Co.	Farm labor	WIA 9/7/61. Captured 4/2/65.
Grier, Elijah S. "Lige"	Private	1834	—	Farm labor	**Died of disease, 8/30/61.**
Griffin, Isaac G. "Ike"	Private	1843	Silver Spr., Wilson Co.	Farm labor	**Killed, 5/12/64 (Spotsylvania).**
Gwynn, William "Pos"	Private	1839	Laguardo, Wilson Co.	Farm labor	Deserted 9/15/63.
Haley, John B. "Jack"	Private	1834	Silver Spr., Wilson Co.	Carpenter	Discharged (disability) 9/24/61.
Hall, Andrew D. "Andy"	Private	1826	—	Mechanic	WIA 8/9/62. **Killed, 5/3/63 (Chancellorsville).**

Name	Initial Rank	D.O.B.	Home	Prewar Occupation	Comments
Hallum, George	Private	1840	Nashville, Davidson Co.	Farm labor	WIA 6/27/62. Deserted 2/5/65.
Hamblin, Joseph W. "Joe"	Private	1841	Silver Spr., Wilson Co.	Farm labor	WIA (shoulder) 5/12/64. Captured 4/3–8/65.
Hardaway, Purnel "Purn"	Private	1840	Silver Spr., Wilson Co.	Farm labor	Sick since 3/24/64 to end of war.
Harkreader, George G.	Private	1839	Silver Spr., Wilson Co.	Trader	Sick since 6/18/63. Deserted 12/20/63.
Harkreader, Henry	Private	1836	Rural Hill, Wilson Co.	Farm labor	WIA (forearm) 8/9/62. TDY (guard duty) 6/9/63 to end of war.
Harris, Jacob T. "Jake"	Private	—	Cainsville, Wilson Co.	—	TDY (teamster) 1/63 to 4/63. No other records.
Hill, Jesse E. "Jess"	Private	1842	Silver Spr., Wilson Co.	Farm labor	Discharged (disability) 6/15/62.
Jackson, John W.	Private	1841	Lockport, Wilson Co.	Farm labor	**Died of disease, 2/1/62.**
Jennings, Clem	Private	1839	Silver Spr., Wilson Co.	Farm labor	Dropped from rolls, 12/31/63.
Jennings, Jesse J. "Jess"	Private	1839	Green Hill, Wilson Co.	Farm labor	1st Sgt. 5/10/63. Sick since 2/15/65 to end of war.
Jennings, John Spencer	Private	1842	Statesville, Wilson Co.	Farm labor	3rd Sgt. 4/26/62. WIA 7/3/63. WIA 5/5/64. In hospital until. TDY (ambulance service) 9/64, to end of war.
Jetton, James F.	Private	—	—	—	WIA 5/31/62. Medical furlough until 6/63. TDY (wagon train guard) 6/10/63 to end of war.
Jetton, Persis D.	Private	1810	Rural Hill, Wilson Co.	Farmer	Discharged (disability) 8/7/61.
Jetton, William P. "Bill"	Private	1843	—	—	**Died of disease, 9/11/61.**
Johnson, Joseph A. "Joe"	Private	1833	Lebanon, Wilson Co.	Mechanic	Discharged (disability) 6/15/62.
Jones, Archey B. "Bat"	Private	1842	Rural Hill, Wilson Co.	Farm labor	WIA (both legs) 6/26/62. **Died of wounds, 6/28/62.**
Jones, John	Private	1844	Green Hill, Wilson Co.	Farm labor	Discharged (minority) 8/20/62.
Lane, Charles W. "Charlie"	Private	1845	Wilson Co.	Farm labor	WIA & captured 7/1/63. Exchanged. Captured 6/2/64. POW rest of war.
Lane, William T. "Turley"	Private	1841	Rural Hill, Wilson Co.	Farm labor	**Died of disease, 11/19/61.**
McClain, Alfred	Private	1839	—	Farm labor	**Killed, 5/31/62 (Seven Pines).**
McClain, Henry	Private	1839	Wilson Co.	Farm labor	3rd Sgt. 4/30/62. WIA (right thigh) 6/26/62. Discharged (wounds) 7/16/62.
Mims, Drury J.	Private	1834	—	Farm labor	Sick since 4/9/62 to 12/62. Sick since 6/5/63 to end of war.
Moore, James H. "Jack"	Private	1845	Green Hill, Wilson Co.	Farm labor	Discharged (minority) 8/20/62.

Name	Initial Rank	D.O.B.	Home	Prewar Occupation	Comments
Neal, John H.	Private	1837	Silver Spr., Wilson Co.	Farm labor	**Died of disease, 10/15/61.**
Neal, Ralph M.	Private	1824	—	Farmer	Discharged (seniority) 8/20/62.
Organ, William P.	Private	—	—	—	Deserted 12/31/63.
Parker, William T.	Private	1835	Davidson Co.	—	WIA (hip) 5/31/62. Sick since 6/10/63. Deserted 7/25/63.
Parton, John L.	Private	1825	Woodbury, Cannon Co.	Farmer	WIA 8/9/62. WIA 8/30/62. WIA 9/17/62 (thigh). Transferred to 45th Tenn., 12/62.
Peek, Sion "Sy"	Private	1836	Silver Spr., Wilson Co.	Farm labor	TDY (ambulance driver) 3/63 to 7/63. WIA (right breast) 6/3/64. **Died of wounds, 6/8/64.**
Rice, John	Private	1841	Silver Spr., Wilson Co.	Farm labor	**Died of disease, 5/20/62.**
Robison, Charles H. "Charlie"	Private	1842	Silver Spr., Wilson Co.	Farm labor	
Rutherford, Gideon M. "Gid"	Private	1829	Lebanon, Wilson Co.	Farmer	Discharged (disability) 11/28/61.
Scobey, Joseph B.	Private	1842	Green Hill, Wilson Co.	Farm labor	WIA 5/31/62. Medical furlough until 2/63. Transferred to Morgan's Cavalry, 3/63.
Searcy, Daniel D.	Private	1815	Green Hill, Wilson Co.	Farmer	5th Sgt. 10/31/61. Reduced (Pvt.) 4/30/62. Discharged (seniority) 8/20/62.
Searcy, Reuben "Sy"	Private	1837	Green Hill, Wilson Co.	Student (Literary)	Sick since 4/3/62. Deserted 4/5/62.
Smith, Andrew H. "Harv"	Private	1841	Wilson Co.	Farm labor	Discharged (disability) 2/1/62.
Smith, Eli	Private	1835	Green Hill, Wilson Co.	Farm labor	WIA 8/29/62. WIA & captured 7/3/63. POW rest of war.
Sullivan, Benjamin F. "Ben"	Private	1837	Lebanon, Wilson Co.	Farm labor	WIA 5/31/62. WIA 8/19/64. Captured 4/2/65.
Sullivan, Benjamin H. "Burl"	Private	1842	Rural Hill, Wilson Co.	Farm labor	Discharged (disability) 1/20/62.
Sullivan, Eclemuel	Private	—	—	—	WIA 6/26/62. Sick since 6/14/63. Deserted 6/15/63.
Sullivan, James A	Private	1844	Rural Hill, Wilson Co.	Farm labor	WIA 12/13/62. Sick since 7/22/63. Deserted 12/31/63.
Sullivan, James E.	Private	1844	Rural Hill, Wilson Co.	Farm labor	**Killed, 6/26/62 (Mechanicsville).**
Sullivan, John Elijah "Lige"	Private	1842	Rural Hill, Wilson Co.	Farm labor	2nd Cpl. 4/30/62. **Killed, 6/26/62 (Mechanicsville).**
Sullivan, John W.	Private	1825	Lebanon, Wilson Co.	Day laborer	WIA 7/3/63. WIA (left arm) 8/19/64. Captured 4/2/65.
Sullivan, William B.	Private	1840	Rural Hill, Wilson Co.	Farm labor	WIA (hip) 5/31/62. Sick since 6/18/62 to 12/62. Captured 4/2/65.
Tilford, James W.	Private	1835	Nashville, Davidson Co.	Carpenter	TDY (hospital) since 6/15/62 to 12/62. Deserted 3/31/65.
Vaughn, Dejohnson	Private	1838	Wilson Co.	—	WIA 5/31/62. Medical furlough until 1/63. TDY (wagon mstr.) 7/63 to end of war.

Name	Initial Rank	D.O.B.	Home	Prewar Occupation	Comments
Vivrett, John Bell "J.B."	Private	1839	Silver Spr., Wilson Co.	Farm labor	Captured 4/3–8/65.
Vivrett, John L. "Larry"	Private	1844	Green Hill, Wilson Co.	Farm labor	Discharged (disability) 2/10/62.
Vivrett, Rufus F. "Rufe"	Private	1842	Silver Spr., Wilson Co.	Farm labor	3rd Cpl. 4/30/62. WIA (hip) 5/12/64. Medical leave until. Deserted 7/26/64.
Vivrett, William Henry	Private	1841	Lebanon, Wilson Co.	Clerk	1st Sgt. 12/30/61. 3rd Lt. 4/30/62. WIA 9/17/62. **Died of wounds, 10/13/62.**
Walpole, James L. "Jim"	Private	1839	Green Hill, Wilson Co.	Teacher	WIA (foot) 8/9/62. WIA 8/29/62. Medical furlough until 1/63. WIA & captured 7/3/63. POW rest of war.
Webber, Simeon "Sim"	Private	1837	Rural Hill, Wilson Co.	Farm labor	Discharged (disability) 6/15/62.
Wilkerson, Albert V.	Private	1842	Rural Hill, Wilson Co.	Farm labor	WIA (left thigh) 7/3/63. Deserted 1/22/65.
Wilkerson, James W. "Jim"	Private	1837	Lebanon, Wilson Co.	Farm labor	**Killed, 12/13/62 (Fredericksburg).**
Wingo, Henry N.	Private	1840	Green Hill, Wilson Co.	Farm labor	1st Sgt. 7/18/62. **Killed, 5/3/63 (Chancellorsville).**
York, John F. "Frank"	Private	1842	Silver Spr., Wilson Co.	Farm labor	**Killed, 6/26/62 (Mechanicsville).**
Young, Andrew W. "Whit"	Private	1836	—	Farm labor	3rd Sgt. 6/62. WIA 5/3/63. **Died of wounds, 5/4/64.**
Young, James "Jim"	Private	1834	Cherry Valley, Wilson Co.	Farmer	4th Sgt. 5/62. **Killed, 5/31/62 (Seven Pines).**
Young, William H.	Private	1841	Rural Hill, Wilson Co.	Farm labor	4th Sgt. 7/30/62. 2nd Sgt. 1/64. WIA 5/12/64. Captured 4/2/65.
Anderson, Cader "Brad"	Transfer	1842	Silver Spr., Wilson Co.	Farm labor	Transferred from 45th Tenn., 12/14/62. Deserted 3/2/65.
McClain, John B.	Recruit	1842	Silver Spr., Wilson Co.	Farm labor	Transferred from 45th Tenn., 11/18/62. TDY (teamster) 1/1/63 to 9/64. Deserted 2/5/65.

Company K. "Wilson Blues"

Name	Initial Rank	D.O.B.	Home	Prewar Occupation	Comments
Bostick, Thomas H. "Tom"	Captain	1834	Lebanon, Wilson Co.	Lawyer	Resigned (sickness) 1/11/62.
Tolliver, Newman "Sol"	1st Lt.	1825	Lebanon, Wilson Co.	Coach maker	Transferred to brigade staff, 1/2/62. No other records.
Powell, Benjamin D.	2nd Lt.	1821	Lebanon, Wilson Co.	Master carpenter	Resigned 12/25/62.
Tarver, Benjamin J.	3rd Lt.	1825	Lebanon, Wilson Co.	Lawyer	Resigned (Sickness) 1/12/62.
Baird, Martin V.	1st Sgt.	1838	Lebanon, Wilson Co.	Farm labor	1st Lt. 4/26/62. WIA 8/29/62. Captured 7/3/63. **POW — Died of disease, 3/22/64.**

Name	Initial Rank	D.O.B.	Home	Prewar Occupation	Comments
Lane, John R.	2nd Sgt.	1837	Lebanon, Wilson Co.	Farm labor	Reduced (Pvt.) 4/30/62. WIA 8/9/62. WIA (left side) 8/19/64. WIA & captured 4/2/65.
Fakes, Daniel R.	3rd Sgt.	1828	Pondville, Wilson Co.	Merchant	2nd Lt. 4/26/62. Resigned 2/4/63.
Major, James H. "Jim"	4th Sgt.	1840	Mt. Carmel, Wilson Co.	Farm labor	Reduced (Pvt.) 4/26/62. TDY (ordnance) 4/26/62 to end of war.
Anderson, Mitchell	1st Cpl.	1839	Lebanon, Wilson Co.	Teacher	Reduced (Pvt.) 4/30/62. 3rd Lt. 5/6/63. WIA 7/3/63. **Died of wounds, 7/4/63.**
Brandon, Charles L.	2nd Cpl.	1833	Lebanon, Wilson Co.	Carriage maker	Reduced (Pvt.) 4/30/62. Captured 7/3/63. POW rest of war.
Benson, Ales D.	3rd Cpl.	—	Lebanon, Wilson Co.	—	Reduced (Pvt.) 4/30/62. Captured 11/28/63. Exchanged & paroled 2/10/65.
Chapman, William S.	4th Cpl.	1837	Lebanon, Wilson Co.	Farm labor	**Died of disease, 12/10/61.**
Blau, Julius	Musician	1838	Lebanon, Wilson Co.	Professor of Music	Discharged (disability) 5/12/62.
Rainy, Christopher	Musician	1843	Lebanon, Wilson Co.	Tailor	3rd Sgt. 4/30/62. Musician — 8/2/62. Transferred to staff band, 12/31/65. Sick in hospital to end of war.
Adams, Robert	Private	1840	—	—	Sick since 4/25/62 to 5/63. TDY (hospital steward) 5/15/63 to end of war.
Anderson, Robert	Private	—	—	—	4th Cpl. 2/28/63. Captured 7/3/63. POW rest of war.
Bass, Sion "Sy"	Private	1846	Silver Spr., Wilson Co.	Farm labor	TDY (butcher) 6/1/63 to 8/63. TDY (baggage guard) 12/5/63. No other records.
Bennett, John W.	Private	1844	Shop Spr., Wilson Co.	Farm labor	Discharged (minority) 8/18/62.
Bennett, William H.	Private	1844	Lebanon, Wilson Co.	Farm labor	Discharged (sickness) 11/5/61.
Bodine, Thomas	Private	1824	Hartsville, Sumner Co.	Carpenter	Discharged (Disability) 11/25/61.
Bostick, Abram	Private	1840	—	Teacher	Sgt. Maj. 5/28/62. **Killed, 6/27/62 (Gainsville).**
Bradshaw, Andrew S.	Private	—	—	—	Deserted 9/24/16.
Brothers, Andrew W.	Private	—	—	—	Transferred to 1st Tenn., 9/61.
Capehart, Thomas	Private	1844	—	Hostler	Discharged (minority) 8/18/62.
Cartwright, John A.	Private	1824	Cherry Valley, Wilson Co.	Merchant	Discharged (disability) 8/28/61.
Cartwright, John H. "Weaver"	Private	1844	Lebanon, Wilson Co.	Farm labor	2nd Cpl. 4/30/62. WIA (leg) 8/9/62. Discharged (wounds) 8/20/62.
Cato, William H. "Billy"	Private	1839	Dixon Spr., Smith Co.	Farm labor	4th Cpl. 4/30/62. 4th Sgt. 8/2/62. WIA 8/9/62. 3rd Sgt. 12/62. WIA 5/6/63. WIA 7/3/63. Captured 4/2/65.
Clemens, John G.	Private	1838	Wilson Co.	Farm labor	**Died of disease, 1/16/62.**

Name	Initial Rank	D.O.B.	Home	Prewar Occupation	Comments
Clemens, William E. "Billie"	Private	1836	Wilson Co.	—	Sick since 4/1/62 to 9/62. Sick since 2/24/64 to 10/62. Captured 4/2/65.
Connelly, George W.	Private	—	—	—	Sick since 6/5/62 to. Deserted 8/18/62.
Davenport, Joseph	Private	1830	Lebanon, Wilson Co.	Day laborer	Discharged (seniority) 8/18/62.
Derickson, Joseph S. "Seth"	Private	1842	Rainy, Smith Co.	Salesman	Transferred to Co. B, 5/1/62.
Derickson, Samuel W. "Sam"	Private	1839	Rainy, Smith Co.	Student (music)	Transferred to Co. B, 5/1/62.
Dill, Felix	Private	1818	—	Farmer	Discharged (disability) 8/2/62.
Dill, George	Private	1837	Lebanon, Wilson Co.	Farm labor	Discharged (disability) 8/9/62.
Donnell, Edison A. "Squire"	Private	1807	Wilson Co.	Farmer	Discharged (disability) 1/22/62.
Drake, Jackson	Private	1836	Lebanon, Wilson Co.	Saddler	Captured 7/14/63. POW rest of war.
Drake, Martin V.	Private	1834	Wilson Co.	Farm labor	WIA (right leg) 9/17/62. Discharged (wounds) 6/12/63.
Drake, William	Private	1845	Lebanon, Wilson Co.	Farm labor	Discharged (disability) 12/9/61.
Dukes, John T	Private	1836	Lebanon, Wilson Co.	Farm labor	Discharged (disability) 3/24/62.
Eddins, William A.	Private	1842	Lebanon, Wilson Co.	Farm labor	2nd Sgt. 4/26/62. **Killed, 6/27/62 (Gaines Mill).**
Forbis, Henry T.	Private	1840	Shop Spr., Wilson Co.	Farm labor	WIA & captured 7/3/63. **POW — Died of disease, 11/6/63.**
Forbis, Samuel F. "Sam"	Private	—	—	—	WIA 8/30/62. Sick on furlough rest of war.
Forrester, Isaac J.	Private	1834	—	Mechanic	**Died of disease, 1/19/62.**
Gann, George C.	Private	1845	Rainy, Smith Co.	Farm labor	Transferred to Co. B, 5/1/62.
Green, Walter	Private	1842	—	Brick maker	Discharged (alienage) 8/18/62.
Griffin, Charles T.	Private	1833	—	—	Transferred to Co. B, 5/1/62.
Griffin, James H. "Joab"	Private	—	—	—	Discharged (minority) 8/18/62.
Griffin, Joseph	Private	1826	—	Shoe maker	Discharged (seniority) 8/18/62.
Griffin, William W.	Private	1843	Lebanon, Wilson Co.	Saddler	4th Cpl. 8/2/62. 1st Cpl. 1/63. Deserted 1/23/65.
Hales, James B. "Jimmy"	Private	1833	Smith Co.	—	Transferred to Co. B, 5/1/62.
Hale, John C.	Private	1836	—	—	Transferred to Co. B, 5/1/62.
Hale, Thomas	Private	1837	Gladesville, Wilson Co.	Farm labor	**Died of disease, 3/2/62.**
Hale, Thomas R.	Private	1838	Smith Co.	Farm labor	**Died of disease, 10/15/61.**
Hill, James M.	Private	1844	Wilson Co.	Farm labor	Discharged (minority) 8/18/62.
Hill, Preston Y.	Private	—	Wilson Co.	—	WIA 8/29/62. 2nd Cpl. 12/31/62. Deserted 11/24/64.

Name	Initial Rank	D.O.B.	Home	Prewar Occupation	Comments
Hill, William G. "Tank"	Private	1836	Lebanon, Wilson Co.	Student (medicine)	TDY (medical asst.) 10/62 to end of war.
Hubbard, Thomas J.	Private	1839	—	—	Transferred to Co. B, 5/1/62.
Johnson, John R.	Private	1833	—	Farmer	WIA (right shoulder) 5/31/62. Discharged (wounds) 11/15/62.
Johnson, Thomas H. "Tom"	Private	1842	Lebanon, Wilson Co.	—	Captured 7/1/63. POW rest of war.
Johnson, William C.	Private	1839	Wilson Co.	Farm labor	WIA & captured 7/3/63. **Died of wounds, 7/16/63.**
Justiss, William H.	Private	1837	—	Farm labor	WIA 6/27/62. **Died of wounds, 7/28/62.**
Kirkpatrick, David F.	Private	1826	Wilson Co.	Saddler	Discharged (seniority) 8/18/62.
Kittrell, George M.	Private	1842	Lebanon, Wilson Co.	Farm labor	TDY (ordnance) 6/10/63 to 4/64. WIA (right leg) 5/12/64. Captured 4/2/65.
Lain, Abner G. "Abb"	Private	1838	Lebanon, Wilson Co.	Farm labor	**Died of disease, 6/26/62.**
Lane, John K. "Jack"	Private	1839	Rural Hill, Wilson Co.	Farm labor	WIA 8/9/62. WIA & captured 7/3/63. Paroled 9/25/63. WIA 11/27/63. In hospital until. Deserted 12/26/63.
Lane, William B. "Billy"	Private	1841	Rural Hill, Wilson Co.	Farm labor	3rd Cpl. 2/5/63. WIA 7/3/63. 12/64 — Last on rolls.
Lester, James L.	Private	1844	Lebanon, Wilson Co.	Student	Discharged (minority) 8/18/62.
Lester, William H.	Private	1834	Lebanon, Wilson Co.	Saddler	1st Cpl. 4/30/62. **Killed, 8/29/62 (2nd Manassas).**
Liggon, Charles W.	Private	1839	—	—	Discharged (disability) 8/2/62.
Lindsey, William	Private	1838	Grundy, Jefferson Co.	Day laborer	TDY (teamster) 8/30/62 to 8/63. WIA (right thigh) & captured 6/2/64. Exchanged 10/29/64. In hospital to end of war.
Martin, James "Jim"	Private	1839	Lebanon, Wilson Co.	—	Last on rolls, 12/31/63.
McIntyre, Henry M.	Private	1840	Wilson Co.	Farm labor	**Killed, 5/3/63 (Chancellorsville).**
McIntyre, James C.	Private	1815	Lebanon, Wilson Co.	Day laborer	4th Cpl. 4/30/62. Discharged (seniority) 8/18/62.
McKenzie, Ephraim L.	Private	1835	Lincoln Co.	Student	WIA 8/29/62. In hospital until. **Died of wounds, 1/15/63.**
Moses, William J.	Private	—	—	—	Transferred to Artillery, 6/1/61.
Moxley, James H.	Private	1839	Mt. Carmel, Wilson Co.	Farm labor	Sick since 4/15/62 to 9/62. WIA 7/3/63. **Died of wounds, 7/16/63.**
Moxley, Joseph P.	Private	1815	Mt. Carmel, Wilson Co.	Farmer	Discharged (disability) 8/14/61.
Moxley, Richard N. "Reese"	Private	—	—	—	1st Sgt. 4/30/62. WIA (shoulder) 5/3/63. WIA (face) & captured 4/2/65.
Nettles, John A.	Private	—	Wilson Co.	—	WIA 5/10/64. Captured 4/2/65.
Norris, Archibald "Archie," "A.D."	Private	1838	Rome, Wilson Co.	Teacher	Capt. 4/26/62. Captured 4/2/65.

Name	Initial Rank	D.O.B.	Home	Prewar Occupation	Comments
Organ, Cornelius	Private	—	—	—	TDY (teamster) 12/16/61 to 1/65. **Died of disease, 1/31/65.**
Organ, Moses L.	Private	1841	—	Farm labor	**Killed, 5/31/62 (Seven Pines).**
Paul, Andrew F.	Private	1840	Lebanon, Wilson Co.	Student	3rd Sgt. 8/2/62. 2nd Lt. 8/30/62. **Killed, 5/3/63 (Chancellorsville).**
Perkins, Leroy W. "Lee"	Private	1842	Lebanon, Wilson Co.	Farm labor	**Died of disease, 8/13/61.**
Peyton, John S.	Private	1842	Lebanon, Wilson Co.	Teacher	1st Cpl. 4/30/62. **Killed, 5/31/62 (Seven Pines).**
Phillips, David L.	Private	1839	Cainsville, Wilson Co.	Teacher	Captured 5/31/62. Exchanged 8/6/62. 3rd Lt. 2/27/63. 2nd Lt. 5/8/63. Captured 7/3/63. POW rest of war.
Polston, Joseph	Private	1843	Dixon Spr., Smith Co.	Farm labor	Captured 4/3–8/65.
Powell, John M.	Private	1841	Lebanon, Wilson Co.	Farm labor	Sick since 4/9/62 to 8/62. 5th Sgt. 8/2/62. TDY (baggage guard) 9/62 to 5/63. 4th Sgt. 5/63. WIA (left hand) 8/18/64. Captured 4/2/65.
Reed, John D.	Private	1840	Lebanon, Wilson Co.	Farm labor	TDY (pioneer corps) 6/62 to end of war. Surrendered 4/9/65 (Appomattox).
Rice, William P.	Private	1841	Lebanon, Wilson Co.	Farm labor	**Killed, 5/31/62 (Seven Pines).**
Riggans, Daniel N.	Private	—	Wilson Co.	—	WIA 8/29/62. Deserted 1/23/65.
Rucks, Howell T.	Private	1839	Rainy, Smith Co.	Farm labor	Transferred to Co. B, 5/1/62.
Rutland, Isaac A.	Private	1838	Wilson Co.	Blacksmith	Discharged (disability) 8/21/61.
Scheib, Charles	Private	1816	Lebanon, Wilson Co.	Upholster	Discharged (disability) 12/9/61.
Scoby, Burchett	Private	1838	Lebanon, Wilson Co.	Farm labor	WIA 5/3/63. Captured 4/3–8/65.
Seat, James L.	Private	1840	Nashville, Davidson Co.	Farm labor	WIA (face) 7/3/63. Captured 7/5/63. POW rest of war.
Shannon, John W.	Private	1839	Mt. Carmel	Farm labor	WIA 9/17/62. **Died of wounds, 9/20/62.**
Sherrill, James P.	Private	1834	Tucker's Crossroads, Wilson Co.	Farmer	5th Sgt. 4/30/62. Reduced (Pvt.) 6/6/62. TDY (ambulance driver) 1/63 to 4/64. Captured 4/3–8/65.
Shipper, Frank	Private	—	—	—	Discharged (seniority) 8/24/62.
Smart, James P.	Private	1843	Gladesville, Wilson Co.	Farm labor	Captured 6/2/64. POW rest of war.
Steed, William N.	Private	—	Wilson Co.	—	WIA (right hand) 6/1/64. Captured 4/2/65.
Stewart, Alexander	Private	1816	Allen Co., KY	Painter	Discharged (seniority) 8/18/62.
Tapley, James W.	Private	1841	Cainsville, Wilson Co.	Farm labor	WIA 12/13/62. Captured 5/5/64. POW rest of war.
Tate, James	Private	1843	Lebanon, Wilson Co.	Farm labor	**Killed, 12/13/62 (Fredericksburg).**

Name	Initial Rank	D.O.B.	Home	Prewar Occupation	Comments
Tinsbloom, Thomas	Private	—	Wilson Co.	—	Sick since, 4/28/62 to 11/62. TDY (nurse) 11/62 to 7/63. Captured 5/5/64. POW rest of war.
Walls, William	Private	1834	Wilson Co.	Blacksmith	Discharged (disability) 11/25/61.
Watkins, William A.	Private	1838	Lockport, Wilson Co.	Farm labor	**Killed, 8/30/62 (2nd Manassas).**
Weaver, James	Private	1841	—	—	WIA (left thigh) 9/17/62. Medical furlough until 7/63. TDY (ambulance driver) 7/63 to. Deserted 12/31/63.
Wilkerson, Charles W.	Private	1836	Smithville, Dekalb Co.	—	Transferred to Co. H, 8/14/61.
Williams, Henry T.	Private	1835	Sandersville, Sumner Co.	Store laborer	4th Sgt. 4/30/62. 2nd Sgt. 8/2/62. Captured 7/1/63. POW rest of war.
Woollard, James A. "Jim"	Private	1834	Lebanon, Wilson Co.	Farm labor	5th Sgt. 2/28/63. Captured 7/1/63. POW rest of war.
Wray, Richard E.	Private	1826	Lebanon, Wilson Co.	Carpenter	5th Sgt. 10/10/61. 3rd Lt. 4/26/62. Resigned (sickness) 8/30/62.
Baumbach, Anthony J.	Recruit	—	Harrisburg, VA	—	Enlisted 1/64. Captured 4/12/65.
Thompson, Zachariah "Zack"	Transfer	1844	Wilson Co.	Student	Transferred from Co. H, 9/1/61. Discharged (minority) 8/24/62.

Part I Notes

Chapter 1

1. Tennessee Civil War Centennial Commission, *Tennesseans in the Civil War: A Military History of Confederate and Union Units with available Rosters of Personnel* (Nashville: Civil War Centennial Commission, 1964), vol. 1, 188. Ezra J. Warner, *Generals in Gray: Lives of the Confederate Commanders* (Baton Rouge: Louisiana State University Press, 1959), 128.
2. D. C. Kelley, *Confederate Veteran*, 552. The *Confederate Veteran* is hereafter referred to as *CV*.
3. D. C. Kelley, *CV*, 552.
4. H. T. Childs, *CV*, 111.
5. Robert Hatton, speech presented to the House of Representatives, 10 January 1861, *CV*, 554.
6. Robert Hatton, letter to Sophie Hatton, in James Vaulx Drake, *Life of General Robert Hatton: Including His Most Important Speeches* (Nashville: Marshall and Bruce, 1867). Hereafter referred to as Drake, Robert Hatton letters.
7. Jack Cato, personal communication, 30 April 1999.
8. Drake, Robert Hatton letters, 23 May 1861.
9. William Robbins (Co. G) letter, which states, "Miss Fannie Shepard Presented to this Company a beautiful Confederate flag." James Miller, personal communication, 31 April 1999.
10. G. W. Williams, "Those Battle Flags: A Correspondent Who Claims to Know About Them," *The Weekly American*, 13 July 1887.
11. James Miller, personal communication, 31 April 1999.
12. "Military Movement in Wilson County," *Lebanon Herald*, 2 May 1861.
13. Drake, Robert Hatton letters, 2 June 1861.
14. Drake, Robert Hatton letters, 31 May 1861.
15. Archibald Norris, 10 January 1861, "Book of Small Things," self-published manuscript, n.d. Hereafter referred to as Archibald Norris Journal.
16. Archibald Norris Journal, 5 February 1861.
17. Archibald Norris Journal, 11 May 1861.
18. Archibald Norris Journal, 11 February 1861
19. David Phillips, in Harry Phillips, *Phillips Family History* (Lebanon, TN: Lebanon Democrat, 1935), 84. Hereafter referred to as David Phillips Journal.
20. Archibald Norris Journal, 12 March 1861.
21. Cody Naramore, personal communication, 22 June 2011.
22. Drake, Robert Hatton letters, 18 June 1861.
23. John A. Fite, "Short and Uninteresting History of a Small and Unimportant Man," (Lebanon, TN: unpublished manuscript, 1910), 25. Hereafter referred to as John A. Fite, Reminiscences.
24. John A. Fite, Reminiscences, 38–9.
25. U.S. National Archives, *Compiled Service Records of Confederate Soldiers Who Served in Organizations From the State of Tennessee* (Washington, DC: National Archives, 1959). Hereafter referred to as the CSRCS.
26. CSRCS. James A. Hobbs and Monroe M. Bond both resigned their lieutenant's positions in 1862.
27. Reta Moser, and Alice Hughes Shepard Carver, *Colonel S. G. Shepard, CSA: Commander of the Seventh Tennessee Infantry Regiment—A Missing Page in Civil War History* (Bloomington, IN: iUniverse, 2010), 35.
28. Reta Moser, and Alice Hughes Shepard Carver, *Colonel S. G. Shepard, CSA*, 35.
29. Drake, Robert Hatton letters, 12 June 1861.
30. Archibald Norris Journal, 16 July 1861.
31. John K. Howard, "Lebanon Grays Journal," 4 June 1861. Sandy Springs Baptist Church Records (Iredell Co.), Wake Forest University Special Collections and Archives, Z. Smith-Reynolds Library.
32. Lamont Wade, personal communication, 6 June 2011.
33. Archibald Norris Journal, 11 July 1861.
34. John A. Fite, Reminiscences, 38.
35. Gerald F. Linderman, *Embattled Courage: The Experience of Combat in the American Civil War* (New York: The Free Press, 1987).
36. Joe B. McBrien, *The Tennessee Brigade* (Chattanooga, TN: Hudson, 1977), 3.
37. John Goodner, letter to Lizzie Floyd, 28 June 1861, in William T. Hale, *History of DeKalb County,*

Tennessee (Nashville: Hunter, 1915). Hereafter referred to as John Goodner letters.
 38. Reta Moser, and Alice Hughes Shepard Carver, *Colonel S. G. Shepard, CSA*, 8.
 39. Drake, Robert Hatton letters, 18 June 1861.
 40. Drake, Robert Hatton letters, 14 July 1861.
 41. Jack Cato, personal communication, 30 April 1999.
 42. Archibald Norris Journal, 15 July 1861.
 43. Joe B. McBrien, *The Tennessee Brigade*, 2.
 44. Joe B. McBrien, *The Tennessee Brigade*, 2.
 45. Archibald Norris Journal, 24 July 1861.
 46. John A. Fite, Reminiscences, 40.
 47. John A. Fite, Reminiscences, 40.
 48. Drake, Robert Hatton letters, 24 July 1861.
 49. John A. Fite, Reminiscences, 40.
 50. Ezra J. Warner, *Generals in Gray*, 10.
 51. John A. Fite, Reminiscences, 41.
 52. John A. Fite, Reminiscences, 41–2.
 53. Drake, Robert Hatton letters, 1 August 1861.
 54. Drake, Robert Hatton letters, 1 August 1861.
 55. Archibald Norris Journal, 1 August 1861.
 56. John A. Fite, Reminiscences, 42.
 57. Drake, Robert Hatton letters, 1 August 1861.
 58. C. Wallace Cross, *Ordeal By Fire: A History of the Fourteenth Tennessee Volunteer Infantry Regiment, CSA* (Clarksville, TN: Clarksville Montgomery County Museum, 1990), 14–15.
 59. Archibald Norris Journal, 3 August 1861.
 60. John B. Lindsley, *The Military Annals of Tennessee* (Nashville: Lindsley, 1886), 228. Hereafter referred to as *MAT*.
 61. John Ingram, in the Tennessee Civil War Questionnaire, compiled by Gus Dyer and John T. Moore (Nashville: Tennessee Historical Commission, 1914–1920). Hereafter referred to as TCWQ.
 62. Ferguson Harris, "Last of a Series of Interesting Articles to the Old 7th Tennessee. *Lebanon Democrat*, 17 August 1899. Hereafter referred to as *Lebanon Democrat*.

Chapter 2

 1. John Goodner, 10 August 1861, in William T. Hale, *History of DeKalb County, Tennessee* (Nashville: Hunter, 1915). Hereafter referred to as John Goodner letters.
 2. Drake, Robert Hatton letters, 12 August 1861.
 3. Drake, Robert Hatton letters, 14 August 1861.
 4. Drake, Robert Hatton letters, 23 August 1861.
 5. John A. Fite, Reminiscences, 44.
 6. Drake, Robert Hatton letters, 18 August 1861.
 7. Drake, Robert Hatton letters, 18 August 1861.
 8. Drake, Robert Hatton letters, 18 August 1861.
 9. John A. Fite, Reminiscences, 46.
 10. John Goodner letters, 29 August 1861.
 11. John A. Fite, Reminiscences, 49.
 12. Ferguson Harris, *Lebanon Democrat*, 17 August 1899.
 13. Drake, Robert Hatton letters, 18 August 1861.
 14. John A. Fite, Reminiscences, 47.
 15. David Phillips, *Phillips Family History*, 3 September 1861.
 16. Archibald Norris Journal, 6 September 1861.
 17. David Phillips, *Phillips Family History*, 9 September 1861.
 18. David Phillips, *Phillips Family History*, 9 September 1861.
 19. David Phillips, *Phillips Family History*, 10 September 1861.
 20. David Phillips, *Phillips Family History*, 11 September 1861.
 21. David Phillips, *Phillips Family History*, 9 September 1861.
 22. David Phillips, *Phillips Family History*, 13 September 1861.
 23. David Phillips, *Phillips Family History*, 13 September 1861.
 24. Joseph Bashaw, TCWQ.
 25. CSRCS.
 26. John A. Fite, Reminiscences, 49.
 27. Joe B. McBrien, *The Tennessee Brigade*, 8–9.
 28. Drake, Robert Hatton letters, 18 August 1861.
 29. David Phillips, *Phillips Family History*, 4 November 1861.
 30. Harry Phillips, *Phillips Family History*, 29 October 1861.
 31. John Goodner letters, 28 October 1861.
 32. David Phillips, *Phillips Family History*, 17 November 1861.
 33. Drake, Robert Hatton letters, 2 November 1861.
 34. Drake, Robert Hatton letters, 28 October 1861.
 35. Drake, Robert Hatton letters, 2 November 1861.
 36. David Phillips, *Phillips Family History*, 20 November 1861.
 37. John A. Fite, Reminiscences, 50–1.
 38. David Phillips, *Phillips Family History*, 29 November 1861.
 39. David Phillips, *Phillips Family History*, 30 November 1861.
 40. David Phillips, *Phillips Family History*, 17 December 1861.
 41. Drake, Robert Hatton letters, 16 December 1861.
 42. William Andrews, *Footprints of a Regiment: A Recollection of the 1st Georgia Regulars* (Atlanta: Longstreet Press, 1992), 27.
 43. David Phillips, *Phillips Family History*, 19–20 December 1861.
 44. David Phillips, *Phillips Family History*, 21 December 1861.
 45. David Phillips, *Phillips Family History*, 23 December 1861.
 46. William Andrews, 24.
 47. John A. Fite, Reminiscences, 49–50.
 48. John A. Fite, Reminiscences, 51.
 49. David Phillips, *Phillips Family History*, 31 December 1861.
 50. David Phillips, *Phillips Family History*, 3 January 1862.
 51. David Phillips, *Phillips Family History*, 3 January 1862.
 52. David Phillips, *Phillips Family History*, 4 January 1862.
 53. David Phillips, *Phillips Family History*, 4 January 1862.
 54. Thomas Yoseloff, *Confederate Military History*

55. David Phillips, *Phillips Family History*, 4 January 1862.
56. David Phillips, *Phillips Family History*, 5 January 1862.
57. John A. Fite, Reminiscences, 52.
58. David Phillips, *Phillips Family History*, 27–28 January 1862.
59. Drake, Robert Hatton letters, 7 February 1862.
60. Drake, Robert Hatton letters, 1 February 1862.
61. Drake, Robert Hatton letters, 11 February 1862.
62. David Phillips, *Phillips Family History*, 12 February 1862.
63. David Phillips, *Phillips Family History*, 18 February 1862.
64. David Phillips, *Phillips Family History*, 18–19 February 1862.
65. Drake, Robert Hatton letters, 21 February 1862.
66. Drake, Robert Hatton letters, 26 February 1862.
67. David Phillips, *Phillips Family History*, 2 March 1862.
68. David Phillips, *Phillips Family History*, 2 March 1862.
69. Thomas Hastings letter, Houston Davis family history, 8 June 1862.
70. Drake, Robert Hatton letters, 5 March 1862.
71. Drake, Robert Hatton letters, 5 March 1862.
72. Drake, Robert Hatton letters, 5 March 1862.
73. David Phillips, *Phillips Family History*, 14 March 1862.
74. David Phillips, *Phillips Family History*, 14 March 1862.
75. David Phillips, *Phillips Family History*, 6 April 1862.
76. David Phillips, *Phillips Family History*, 8 April 1862.
77. Douglas S. Freeman, *Lee's Lieutenants: A Study in Command* (New York: Charles Scribner's Sons, 1942), 1: 171.
78. David Phillips, *Phillips Family History*, 24 April 1862.
79. Drake, Robert Hatton letters, 30 April 1862.
80. David Phillips, *Phillips Family History*, 26 April 1862.
81. Jeremy Spires, personal communication, 23 December 2010. Records are from the Wilson County, Tennessee, Circuit Court Records, 1858–1867, 19 September 1866.
82. CSRCS.
83. CSRCS.
84. Lamont Wade, personal communication, 1 May 2012.

Chapter 3

1. Ferguson Harris, *Lebanon Democrat*, 2 August 1900.
2. David Phillips, *Phillips Family History*, 28 April 1862.
3. Thomas Yoseloff, *CMH*, vol. 8:181.
4. William Andrews, *Footprints of a Regiment: A Recollection of the 1st Georgia Regulars* (Atlanta: Longstreet Press, 1992), 33.
5. David Phillips, *Phillips Family History*, 10 May 1862.
6. Drake, Robert Hatton letters, 21 May 1862.
7. Drake, Robert Hatton letters, 21 May 1862.
8. David Phillips, *Phillips Family History*, 10 May 1862.
9. Frank Burns, ed., *History of Wilson County, Tennessee: Its Land and Its Life* (Lebanon, TN: Wilson County Library Board, 1987), 328.
10. Absolom Harrison, *The Civil War Gazette*, 10 May 1862.
11. Frank Burns, 328.
12. Drake, Robert Hatton letters, 30 April 1862.
13. David Phillips, *Phillips Family History*, 11 May 1862.
14. William T. Hale, *History of DeKalb County, Tennessee (*Nashville: Hunter, 1915), 156.
15. David Phillips, *Phillips Family History*, 24 May 1862.
16. Drake, Robert Hatton letters, 28 May 1862.
17. Drake, Robert Hatton letters, 28 May 1862.
18. Andrew Martin letter, in *Life of General Robert Hatton*, 31 May 1862.
19. John A. Fite, Reminiscences, 62.
20. H. T. Childs, *CV*, 19.
21. John Lindsley, *MAT*, 231.
22. H. T. Childs, *CV*: 19–20.
23. David Phillips, *Phillips Family History*, 31 May 1862.
24. James Drake, *Life of General Robert Hatton, Including His Most Important Public Speeches* (Nashville: Marshall and Bruce, 1867), 456.
25. John A. Fite, Reminiscences, 62.
26. John H. Moore, in John Lindsley, *MAT*, 231.
27. J. H. Richardson, in *War of the Rebellion: The Official Records of the Union and Confederate Armies*, Ser. 1, Vol. 12, Pt. 1: 811. Hereafter referred to as *OR*.
28. Ferguson Harris, *Lebanon Democrat*, 24 June 1904.
29. Ferguson Harris, *Lebanon Democrat*, 24 June 1904.
30. Paul Clements, *A Past Remembered: A Collection of Antebellum Homes in Davidson County* (Nashville: Clearville Press, 1987).
31. William Sewell letter, 1915, in Teresa W. Rogers, personal communication, 20 May 2012.
32. Gerald Linderman, *Embattled Courage: The Experience of Combat in the American Civil War* (New York: The Free Press, 1987), 9.
33. Ferguson Harris, *Lebanon Democrat*, 24 June 1904.
34. J. H. Richardson, *OR*: 811.
35. H. T. Childs, *CV*, 19–20.
36. Ferguson Harris, *Lebanon Democrat*, 24 June 1904.
37. John H. Moore, *MAT*, 231
38. David Phillips, *Phillips Family History*, 31 May 1862.
39. John A. Fite, Reminiscences, 62.
40. CSRCS.
41. Shepherd Pryor letter, 26 May 1862.

42. Richard Beard, TCWQ.
43. "The Daily Dispatch," *Richmond Dispatch*, 9 June 1862.
44. CSRCS.
45. C. Wallace Cross, *Ordeal By Fire: A History of the Fourteenth Tennessee Volunteer Infantry Regiment, CSA* (Clarksville, TN: Clarksville Montgomery County Museum, 1990), 28.
46. David Phillips, *Phillips Family History*, 31 May 1862.
47. David Phillips, *Phillips Family History*, 6 August 1862.
48. John A. Fite, Reminiscences, 62.
49. John A. Fite, Reminiscences, 62.
50. Joe B. McBrien, *The Tennessee Brigade*, 24.
51. Ferguson Harris, *CV*, 18.
52. Abram Bostick letter, 20 June 1862.
53. James Archer, *OR*, 347.
54. John Williams letter. Williams family history.
55. CSRCS. Sgt. James Thompson (Co. F) died of his wounds on 26 June 1862. Pvt. Archey Jones (Co. I) died of his wounds on 28 June 1862.
56. Ferguson Harris, *Lebanon Democrat*, 26 July 1900.
57. John A. Fite, Reminiscences, 67–68.
58. Ferguson Harris, *Lebanon Democrat*, 26 July 1900.
59. C. Wallace Cross, *Ordeal By Fire*, 31–32.
60. Douglas S. Freeman, *Lee's Lieutenants: A Study in Command* (New York: Charles Scribner's Sons, 1942), 1: 520.
61. James Archer, *CV*, 66.
62. Ferguson Harris, *Lebanon Democrat*, 26 July 1900.
63. Shepard Gleason, *OR*, 126.
64. CSRCS. Captain William Curd died of his wounds on 16 July 1862.
65. CSRCS.
66. Ferguson Harris, *Lebanon Democrat*, 26 July 1900.
67. CSRCS.
68. Ferguson Harris, *Lebanon Democrat*, 26 July 1900.
69. Ambrose P. Hill, *OR*, 326.
70. Ferguson Harris, *Lebanon Democrat*, 26 July 1900.
71. John Martindale, *OR*, 119.
72. Ferguson Harris, *Lebanon Democrat*, 26 July 1900.
73. John Hurst, *CV*, 507.
74. Francis Schoeffel, *OR*, 125.
75. Joe B. McBrien, *The Tennessee Brigade*, 30.
76. James Archer, *OR*, 347.
77. John H. Moore, *MAT*, 233.
78. John Williams letter, 29 June 1862.
79. James Fite, letter, 30 March 1863, CSRCS.
80. John Goodner, letter, 30 March 1863, CSRCS.
81. Douglas S. Freeman, *Lee's Lieutenants*, 1: 567.
82. John A. Fite, Reminiscences, 68.
83. John A. Fite, Reminiscences, 70.
84. Ambrose Hill, *OR*, 50.
85. James Archer, *OR*, 52. James Archer reported that his brigade was "about 1,200 strong." That would have been with all five units on the line. With the 14th Tennessee not directly attached to the brigade's battle line, Archer had about 1,000 men.
86. John A. Fite, Reminiscences, 70.
87. John A. Fite, Reminiscences, 70.
88. G. F. Henderson, *Stonewall Jackson and the American Civil War* (New York: Konecky & Konecky, 1898), 2: 91.
89. John A. Fite, Reminiscences, 70.
90. George Andrews, *OR*, 9.
91. CSRCS.
92. CSRCS.
93. John A. Fite, Reminiscences, 70.
94. CSRCS.
95. George Andrews, *OR*, 9.
96. CSRCS.
97. James Crofutt, personal communication, 13 October 2011.
98. Silas Cosgrove, *OR*, 10.
99. CSRCS.
100. George Andrews, *OR*, 9.
101. Silas Cosgrove, *OR*, 10.
102. John H. Moore, *MAT*, 234.
103. CSRCS.
104. James Archer, *OR*, 52.
105. James Archer, *OR*, 52.
106. Jedediah Hotchkiss, *Make Me a Map of the Valley: The Civil War Journal of Stonewall Jackson's Topographer* (Dallas: Southern Methodist University Press, 1973), 66.
107. John A. Fite, Reminiscences, 71.
108. Henry Harkreader, *CV*, 307.
109. Ferguson Harris, *CV*, 18.

Chapter 4

1. Douglas S. Freeman, *Lee's Lieutenants*, 2: 66.
2. James Archer, *CMH*, 189.
3. John Ingram, TCWQ.
4. Douglas S. Freeman, *Lee's Lieutenants*, 2: 85.
5. G. F. Henderson, *Stonewall Jackson*, 2: 98–9.
6. G. F. Henderson, *Stonewall Jackson*, 2: 98–9.
7. G. F. Henderson, *Stonewall Jackson*, 2: 98–9.
8. A.P. Hill, *OR*, 176.
9. C. Wallace Cross, *Ordeal By Fire*, 39.
10. Douglas S. Freeman, *Lee's Lieutenants*, 2: 96.
11. James Archer, *OR*, 188.
12. John Lindsley, *MAT*, 235.
13. William A. Clendening, *Civil War Times Illustrated* Collection, U.S. Army Military Historical Institute, Carlisle Barracks, PA. Hereafter referred to as Clendening letters.
14. Henry Slocum, *OR*, 117.
15. Clendening letters.
16. Henry Brown, *OR*, 121.
17. John Lindsley, *MAT*, 235.
18. Ferguson Harris, *Lebanon Democrat*, 22 June 1899.
19. John H. Moore, *MAT*, 235.
20. James Archer, *OR*, 188.
21. Robert Johnson and Clarence Buel, eds., *Battles and Leaders of the Civil War* (New York: Century, 1887), 2: 498.

22. CSRCS.
23. CSRCS.
24. CSRCS.
25. John Lindsley, *MAT*, 235.
26. Joseph Peter Bashaw, TCWQ.
27. Robert Johnson and Clarence Buel, eds., *Battles and Leaders of the Civil War*, 2: 498.
28. James I. Robertson, *General A. P. Hill* (New York: Vintage Books, 1987), 122.
29. James Archer, *OR*, 188.
30. Ferguson Harris, *Lebanon Democrat*, 22 June 1899.
31. Joseph Peter Bashaw, TCWQ.
32. CSRCS.
33. Ferguson Harris, *Lebanon Democrat*, 22 June 1899.
34. William H. Andrews, *Footprints of a Regiment: A Recollection of the 1st Georgia Regulars* (Atlanta: Longstreet Press, 1992), 68.
35. James Archer, *OR*, 188.
36. Douglas S. Freeman, *Lee's Lieutenants*, 2: 121.
37. CSRCS.
38. John Williams letters.
39. William H. Andrews, *Footprints of a Regiment*, 69.
40. James Archer, *OR, 1*88.
41. William H. Andrews, *Footprints of a Regiment*, 71.
42. Jedediah Hotchkiss, *Make Me a Map of the Valley*, 79.
43. James I. Robertson, *General A. P. Hill*, 131–132.
44. Joseph Peter Bashaw, TCWQ.
45. Douglas S. Freeman, *Lee's Lieutenants*, 2: 130.
46. C. Wallace Cross, *Ordeal By Fire*, 45.
47. Douglas S. Freeman, *Lee's Lieutenants*, 2: 151, 165.
48. Douglas S. Freeman, *Lee's Lieutenants*, 2: 151, 165.
49. David Phillips, *Phillips Family History*, 30 September 1862.
50. James Archer, *OR*, 282.
51. Jedediah Hotchkiss, *Make Me a Map of the Valley*, 79.
52. George Willard, *OR*, 199.
53. Compiled Service Records of Confederate Soldiers.
54. James Neal, *OR*, 284.
55. Preston Hill, TCWQ.
56. CSRCS.
57. Joe B. McBrien, *The Tennessee Brigade*, 46.
58. C. Wallace Cross, *Ordeal By Fire*, 46.
59. James I. Robertson, *General A. P. Hill*, 140.
60. Reta Moser, and Alice Hughes Shepard Carver, *Colonel S. G. Shepard, CSA*, 50.
61. Jedediah Hotchkiss, *Make Me a Map of the Valley*, 82.
62. Amy Boyce, "Directions For A. P. Hill March," (Harper's Ferry, WV: pamphlet, 1979).
63. William H. Andrews, *Footprints of a Regiment*, 78.
64. James Archer, *OR*, 282.
65. Amy Boyce, 1979.
66. James Archer, *OR*, 282.
67. Ferguson Harris, *CV*, 38.
68. James Archer, *OR*, 282.
69. John H. Moore, *MAT*, 237
70. John Priest, *Antietam: The Soldiers' Battle* (Shippensburg, PA: White Mane, 1989), 272.
71. James Archer, *OR*, 282.
72. James Comly, *OR*, 159.
73. James Comly, *OR*, 159.
74. CSRCS.
75. Edwin L. Ferguson, *Sumner County, Tennessee in the Civil War* (Gallatin, TN: printed privately, 1972).
76. CSRCS.
77. David Woodward, "Captain Robert G. Miller: Military Service During Civil War: 1861–1865" (David Woodward family history: unpublished manuscript, n.d.).
78. Edward Harland, *OR*, 151.
79. CSRCS.
80. James Archer, *OR*, 282.
81. CSRCS.
82. John Priest, *Antietam: The Soldiers' Battle*, 340–341.
83. Ambrose Hill, *OR*, 273.
84. James Barnes, *OR*, 88.
85. James Gwyn, *OR*, 89.
86. CSRCS.
87. CSRCS.
88. James Gwyn, *OR*, 89.
89. James Archer, *OR*, 282.
90. James Bond, letter in CSRCS, 30 September 1862.
91. Reta Moser, and Alice Hughes Shepard Carver, *Colonel S. G. Shepard, CSA*, 48.
92. Jedediah Hotchkiss, *Make Me a Map of the Valley*, 84.
93. John A. Fite, Reminiscences, 77.
94. William H. Andrews, *Footprints of a Regiment*, 89.
95. William H. Andrews, *Footprints of a Regiment*, 89.
96. Mary Ella Hale, Hale family history, November 1862.
97. Reta Moser, and Alice Hughes Shepard Carver, *Colonel S. G. Shepard, CSA*, 52.
98. Joseph P. Hamilton letter, 31 October 1862. Lewis Leigh Jr. collection. Reprinted in *Lincoln Herald*, Vol. 81, No. 3 (1979), 207.
99. William H. Andrews, *Footprints of a Regiment*, 94.
100. David Phillips, *Phillips Family History*, 30 September 1862.
101. William H. Andrews, *Footprints of a Regiment*, 91.
102. William H. Andrews, *Footprints of a Regiment*, 91.
103. Jedediah Hotchkiss, *Make Me a Map of the Valley*, 97.
104. James Archer, *OR*, 314.
105. C. G. Chamberlayne, *Ham Chamberlayne—Virginian: Letters and Papers of an Artillery Officer in the War for Southern Independence 1861–1865* (Richmond, VA: Dietz, 1932), 141.

106. William T. Venner, *Hoosiers' Honor: The Iron Brigade's 19th Indiana Regiment* (Shippensburg, PA: Burd Street Press, 1998), 387.
107. Ferguson Harris, *Lebanon Democrat*, 27 July 1899.
108. Ambrose P. Hill, *OR*, 308.
109. John A. Fite, Reminiscences, 79–80.
110. J. Hawkins, *OR*, 317.
111. John Goodner, *OR*, 318.
112. James Lockert, *OR*, 319.
113. James Lockert, *OR*, 319.
114. John H. Moore, "Fredericksburg," *The Southern Bivouac*, Vol. 2 (1883): 179–184.
115. Andrew Hutchens, *OR*, 316.
116. James Lockert, *OR*, 319.
117. Francis Goodall, in John H. Moore, "Fredericksburg," 179–184.
118. CSRCS.
119. William McCall, *CV*, 19.
120. Ferguson Harris, *Lebanon Democrat*, 27 July 1899.
121. CSRCS.
122. A. P. Hill, *OR*, 308.
123. Albert Magilton, *OR*, 250.
124. Edward J. Stackpole, *Drama on the Rappahannock: The Fredericksburg Campaign* (Harrisburg, PA: Stackpole, 1957), 82.
125. William H. Andrews, 13 December 1862.
126. William H. Andrews, *Footprints of a Regiment*, 95.

Chapter 5

1. Jedediah Hotchkiss, *Make Me a Map of the Valley*, 100.
2. John Johnson, TCWQ.
3. Douglas S. Freeman, *Lee's Lieutenants*, 2: 380.
4. Edgar Q. Rooker, manuscript, n.d.
5. Joe B. McBrien, *The Tennessee Brigade*, 56.
6. James Robertson, *General A. P. Hill*, 165.
7. John N. Williams, Williams Diary, n.d.
8. Joe B. McBrien, *The Tennessee Brigade*, 56.
9. John Johnson, TCWQ.
10. James B. Hale letter, 26 February 1863.
11. John N. Williams, Williams Diary, 23 February 1863.
12. William H. Andrews, *Footprints of a Regiment*, 109.
13. James Archer letter, 3 February 1863.
14. James Fite letter, 30 March 1863.
15. John Goodner letter, 30 March 1863.
16. John A. Fite Reminiscences, 81.
17. Newton George, *OR*, 362.
18. John Hurst, *CV*, 261.
19. James Archer, *OR*, 359.
20. Newton George, *OR*, 362.
21. John A. Fite, *OR*, 363.
22. John A. Fite, *OR*, 363.
23. John H. Moore, *MAT*, 3 May 63.
24. John A. Fite, *OR*, 363.
25. CSRCS.
26. CSRCS.
27. Newton George, *OR*, 362.
28. A. N. Porter, *OR*, 361.
29. Newton George, *OR*, 362.
30. William Pegram, *OR*, 367.
31. Ferguson Harris, *CV*, 261.
32. James Archer, *OR*, 359.
33. Ferguson Harris, *CV*, 261.
34. Birkett Fry, *OR*, 360.
35. CSRCS.
36. CSRCS.
37. John A. Fite, Reminiscences, 81–82.
38. Ferguson Harris, *CV*, 261.
39. Ferguson Harris, *CV*, 261.
40. Newton George, *OR*, 362.
41. CSRCS.
42. John A. Fite, *OR*, 363.
43. August Wright, *OR*, 328.
44. Henry Heth, *OR*, 339.
45. James Archer, *OR*, 339.
46. CSRCS.
47. Joseph Peter Bashaw, TCWQ.
48. Newton George, *OR*, 362.
49. James Archer, in *Official Records*, Ser. 1, Vol. 25, Pt. 1, No. 335.
50. John A. Fite, Reminiscences, 82.
51. John A. Fite, Reminiscences, 82.
52. Elizabeth Roberson, ed., *In Care of Yellow River: The Complete Civil War Letters of Pvt. Eli Pinson Landers to His Mother* (Gretna, LA: Pelican, 1997).
53. Ezra J. Warner, *Generals in Gray*, 135.
54. Ezra J. Warner, *Generals in Gray*, 113.
55. Joe B. McBrien, *The Tennessee Brigade*, 82.
56. Tally Simpson letter to Mary Simpson, 13 June 1863, *in Far, Far From Home: The War Time Letters of Dick and Tally Simpson, 3rd South Carolina Volunteers*, edited by Guy Everson and Edward Simpson (New York: Oxford University Press, 1994).
57. John A. Fite, Reminiscences, 82.
58. Isaac A. Caldwell letter, the Caldwell family collection, East Tennessee Historical Society, Knoxville, TN.
59. E. Brunson, *OR*, 364.
60. Ham Chamberlayne letter, 25 June 1863.
61. E. Brunson, *OR*, 364.
62. John Ingram, TCWQ.
63. Rod Gragg, *Covered with Glory: The 26th North Carolina at the Battle of Gettysburg* (New York: Harper Collins, 2000), 65–6.
64. Tally Simpson letter, 28 June 1863.
65. Rod Gragg, *Covered With Glory*, 66.
66. Rod Gragg, *Covered With Glory*, 64.
67. Thomas Cockrell and Michael Ballard, eds., *A Mississippi Rebel in the Army of Northern Virginia* (Baton Rouge: Louisiana State University Press, 1995), 192.
68. W. H. Bird, *Stories of the Civil War, Company C, 13th Regiment of Alabama Volunteers* (Columbiana, AL: Advocate Print, n.d.), 6.
69. Tally Simpson letter, 28 June 1863.
70. CSRCS.
71. CSRCS. An analysis of the 7th Tennessee personnel records reveals that at the time of the Gettys-

Chapter 6

1. John A. Fite, Reminiscences, 86.
2. Harry W. Pfanz, *Gettysburg: The First Day* (Chapel Hill: University of North Carolina, 2001), 25.
3. James L. Morrison, ed., *The Memoirs of Henry Heth* (Westport, CT: Greenwood Press, 1974), 173.
4. John A. Fite, Reminiscences, 83–4.
5. John A. Fite, Reminiscences, 84.
6. John A. Fite, Reminiscences, 84.
7. David Phillips Journal.
8. Harry W. Pfanz, *Gettysburg: The First Day*, 53
9. Archibald Norris Journal.
10. John A. Fite, Reminiscences, 86.
11. John A. Fite, Reminiscences, 85.
12. Joseph Peter Bashaw, TCWQ.
13. J. C. Bingham, *CV.*
14. George R. Wood, *CV*. 35.
15. Noah A. Trudeau, *Gettysburg: A Testing of Courage* (New York: Harper Collins Books, 2002), 164.
16. J. B. Turney, *CV*, 535.
17. Noah A. Trudeau, *Gettysburg: A Testing of Courage*, 166.
18. Rod Gragg, *Covered With Glory*, 7.
19. J. B. Turney, *CV,* 535.
20. James Miller, personal communication, 31 April 1999. The flag carried in the Battle of Gettysburg was the third flag presented to the 7th Tennessee. This flag, which James Miller refers to as the "white border flag — with honors," was issued in late May or early June 1863. The crossed bars of dark blue contained 13 stars laid over a field of red. A 1-inch strip of white bordered the flag. Battle honors were placed in each red-field portion of the flag. The top contained Seven Pines, Mechanicsville, and Cold Harbor. The right section had Ox Hill, Harper's Ferry, and Sharpsburg. The left section had Frazier's Farm, Cedar Run, and Manassas. The bottom section had Shepherdstown, Fredericksburg, and Chancellorsville. In the center of the flag was the number "7."
21. Marc Storch and Beth Storch, "What a Deadly Trap We Were In: Archer's Brigade on July 1, 1863," *Gettysburg Magazine: Historical Articles of Lasting Interest* 6 (January 1992), 20.
22. Marc Storch and Beth Storch, *Gettysburg Magazine*, 20.
23. George W. Lamberson, TCWQ.
24. Noah A. Trudeau, *Gettysburg: A Testing of Courage*, 179.
25. Ferguson Harris, *Lebanon Democrat*, 9 August 1900.
26. Archibald Norris Journal.
27. CSRCS.
28. Harry Pfanz, *Gettysburg: The First Day*, 66.
29. Robert Johnson and Clarence Buel, eds., *Battles and Leaders of the Civil War*, Vol. 3: 437.
30. Ferguson Harris, *Lebanon Democrat,* 10 August 1899.
31. Ferguson Harris, *Lebanon Democrat,* 10 August 1899.
32. CSRCS.
33. W. H. Moon, *CV*, 449.
34. John T. McCall, *Louisville Journal*, 1902, 2.
35. Samuel G. Shepard, *OR*: 646.
36. Ferguson Harris, *Lebanon Democrat,* 10 August 1899.
37. Harry Pfanz, *Gettysburg: The First Day*, 66.
38. Ferguson Harris, *Lebanon Democrat,* 10 August 1899.
39. J. B. Turney, *CV*, 535.
40. Ferguson Harris, *Lebanon Democrat,* 10 August 1899.
41. John T. McCall, *Louisville Journal*, 1902, 2.
42. CSRCS.
43. Noah A. Trudeau, *Gettysburg: A Testing of Courage*, 182.
44. Marc Storch and Beth Storch, *Gettysburg Magazine*, 22.
45. Marc Storch and Beth Storch, *Gettysburg Magazine*, 21.
46. John T. McCall, *Louisville Journal*, 1902, 2.
47. Alan T. Nolan, *The Iron Brigade* (Ann Arbor, MI: Hardscrabble Books, 1983), 233.
48. Alan T. Nolan, *The Iron Brigade*, 236.
49. CSRCS.
50. William Dudley, *The Iron Brigade at Gettysburg: Official Report of the Part Born by the 1st Brigade, 1st Division, 1st Army Corps of the Army of the Potomac, in Action at the Battle of Gettysburg* (Cincinnati: privately printed, 1879), 214
51. William H. Bird, *Stories of the Civil War, Company C, 13th Regiment of Alabama Volunteers* (Columbiana, AL: Advocate Print, n. d.), 7.
52. E. T. Boland, *CV*, 308.
53. E. T. Boland, *CV*, 308.
54. George Otis, and Alan Gaff, eds., *The Second Wisconsin Infantry* (Dayton, OH: Morningside Bookshop, 1984), 274.
55. CSRCS.
56. Samuel Shepard, *OR*: 646.
57. CSRCS.
58. Noah A. Trudeau, *Gettysburg: A Testing of Courage*, 186.
59. Joseph Peter Bashaw, TCWQ.
60. John A. Fite, Reminiscences, 86.
61. E. T. Boland, *CV,* 308.
62. CSRCS.
63. William T. Venner, *Hoosiers' Honor*, 63.
64. Rod Gragg, *Covered With Glory*, 98.
65. CSRCS.
66. Ezra J. Warner, *Generals in Gray*, 95.
67. Harry Pfanz, *Gettysburg: The First Day*, 118.
68. Marc Storch and Beth Storch, *Gettysburg Magazine*, 26.
69. Rod Gragg, *Covered With Glory*, 31–34.
70. James J. Pettigrew, *Notes on Spain and the Spaniards, in the Summer of 1859, with a Glance at Sardinia* (Charleston, SC: Pettigrew, 1861).

71. Samuel G. Shepard, *OR*: 552.
72. O. B. Curtis, *History of the Twenty-Fourth Michigan of the Iron Brigade* (Detroit: Winn & Hammond, 1891), 160.
73. Rod Gragg, *Covered With Glory*, 115.
74. O. B. Curtis, *History of the Twenty-Fourth Michigan of the Iron Brigade*, 159.
75. Holand Richardson, in *Cambridge City Tribune*, 13 August 1871, 1.
76. William T. Venner, *Hoosiers' Honor*, 67.
77. Harry Pfanz, *Gettysburg: The First Day*, 269.
78. William Robinson, *OR*: 280.
79. Samuel G. Shepard, *OR*: 552.
80. Rod Gragg, *Covered With Glory*, 118.
81. Rod Gragg, *Covered With Glory*, 118.
82. Harry Pfanz, *Gettysburg: The First Day*, 288.
83. Samuel G. Shepard, *OR*: 552.
84. Ambrose P. Hill, *OR*: 44
85. Noah A. Trudeau, *Gettysburg: A Testing of Courage*, 257.
86. O. B. Curtis, *History of the Twenty-Fourth Michigan of the Iron Brigade*, 162.
87. Rod Gragg, *Covered With Glory*, 101.
88. Noah A. Trudeau, *Gettysburg: A Testing of Courage*, 258.
89. Noah A. Trudeau, *Gettysburg: A Testing of Courage*, 258.
90. William T. Venner, *Hoosiers' Honor*, 5.
91. Alan T. Nolan, *The Iron Brigade*, 365.
92. Rod Gragg, *Covered With Glory*, 101.
93. Rod Gragg, *Covered With Glory*, 144.
94. Noah A. Trudeau, *Gettysburg: A Testing of Courage*, 258.
95. William T. Venner, *Hoosiers' Honor*, 5.
96. J. Howard Wert, in Michael A. Dreese, *The Hospital at Seminary Ridge at the Battle of Gettysburg* (Jefferson, NC: McFarland, 2002), 120.
97. Noah A. Trudeau, *Gettysburg: A Testing of Courage*, 266.
98. Noah A. Trudeau, *Gettysburg: A Testing of Courage*, 266.
99. James J. Archer, journal, 8 July 1863, C. A. Porter Hopkins, ed., "The James J. Archer Letters: A Marylander in the Civil War," *Maryland Historical Magazine* 56 (June 1961), 355. Hereafter referred to as "James J. Archer, letter."
100. James J. Archer, letter, 28 July 1863.
101. James J. Archer, letter, 28 August 1863.
102. James J. Archer, letter, 6 February 1864.
103. James J. Archer, letter, 20 May 1864.
104. James J. Archer, letter, 20 July 1864.
105. John Goodner letters, 9 March 1863.
106. Noah A. Trudeau, *Gettysburg: A Testing of Courage*, 291.
107. Samuel G. Shepard, *OR*: 552.
108. Noah A. Trudeau, *Gettysburg: A Testing of Courage*, 422.
109. Samuel G. Shepard, *OR*: 552.

Chapter 7

1. John B. Lindsley, *MAT*, 246.
2. John Priest, *Into the Fight: Pickett's Charge at Gettysburg* (Shippensburg, PA: White Mane Books, 1998), 199.
3. Jonas Cook, in J. B. Polley, *CV*, 524.
4. Jonas Cook, in J. B. Polley, *CV*, 524.
5. Samuel G. Shepard, *OR*: 552.
6. Skip Smith, personal communication, 31 December 2010.
7. John H. Moore, *MAT*, 249.
8. James Miller, personal communication, 12 August 1999.
9. Edmund Berkeley, *CV*, 175.
10. Noah A. Trudeau, *Gettysburg: A Testing of Courage*, 458.
11. Noah A. Trudeau, *Gettysburg: A Testing of Courage*, 451.
12. Harry Stevens, *Souvenir of the Excursions of the 14th Connecticut* (Washington, DC: Gibson Brothers, 1893), 15–24.
13. John H. Moore, *CV*, 15–16.
14. Harry Stevens, *Souvenir of the Excursions of the 14th Connecticut*, 15–24.
15. James L. Morrison, *The Memoirs of Henry Heth*, 175.
16. Jennings C. Wise, *The Long Arm of Lee: The History of the Artillery of Northern Virginia* (New York: Oxford University Press, 1959).
17. George R. Stewart, *Pickett's Charge: A Microhistory of the Final Attack at Gettysburg, July 3, 1863* (Boston: Houghton Mifflin, 1959), 97.
18. John H. Moore, *MAT*, 248.
19. John H. Moore, *The Southern Bivouac*, 389.
20. Noah A. Trudeau, *Gettysburg: A Testing of Courage*, 440.
21. John H. Moore, *The Southern Bivouac*, 389.
22. D. Scott Hartwig, "It Struck Horror to Us All," *Gettysburg Magazine* 4 (January 1991), 94.
23. Noah A. Trudeau, *Gettysburg: A Testing of Courage*, 451.
24. John Priest, 31.
25. George R. Stewart, *Pickett's Charge*, 93.
26. D. Scott Hartwig, *Gettysburg Magazine*, 94.
27. David Johnston, *The Story of a Confederate Boy in the Civil War* (Radford, VA: Johnston, 1914), 203–208.
28. Randolph Shotwell, "Three Years in Battle and Three in Federal Prisons," in J. G. de Roulhac Hamilton, ed., *The Papers of Randolph Shotwell* (Raleigh: North Carolina Historical Commission, 1929–1931), 1–31.
29. George R. Stewart, *Pickett's Charge*, 138.
30. John H. Moore, *MAT*, 249.
31. George R. Stewart, *Pickett's Charge*, 135.
32. John Gibbon, *Personal Recollections of the Civil War* (Dayton, OH: Morningside Press, 1978), 146.
33. John Gibbon, *Personal Recollections of the Civil War*, 147.
34. John Gibbon, *Personal Recollections of the Civil War*, 147.
35. Thomas Osborn, "Experiences at the Battle of Gettysburg," in Herbert Crumb, ed., *The Papers of Thomas Osborn; The Eleventh Corps Artillery at Gettysburg* (Hamilton, NY: Edmonston, 1992).
36. John Gibbon, *Personal Recollections of the Civil War*, 148.

37. Francis M. Wafer, "Diary of Francis Moses Wafer," (Kingston, ON: Queen's University Library, manuscript, n.d.).
38. Waitt, Ernest Linden, comp., *History of the Nineteenth Massachusetts Volunteer Infantry 1861–1865* (Salem: MA: Salem Press, 1906), 234–235.
39. Samuel McIntyre letter, 27 June 1890, in David Ladd and Audrey J. Ladd, *The Bachelder Papers* (Dayton, OH: Morningside Bookshop, 1995).
40. Alonzo Silsby letter, 5 August 1863, *Portage County Newspaper*.
41. John B. Turney, *CV*, 536.
42. David Johnston, *The Story of a Confederate Boy in the Civil War*, 206.
43. D. Scott Hartwig, *Gettysburg Magazine*, 95.
44. John McCall, *Louisville Journal*, 1902.
45. John A. Fite, Reminiscences, 86.
46. Erasmus Williams letter, n. d., in John Daniels Papers, University of Virginia, Charlottesville, VA.
47. David Johnston, *The Story of a Confederate Boy in the Civil War*, 206.
48. D. Scott Hartwig, *Gettysburg Magazine*, 95.
49. George R. Stewart, *Pickett's Charge*, 138.
50. Birkett Fry, "Pettigrew's Charge At Gettysburg," *Southern Historical Society Papers* 8 (1879), 92–93. Hereafter referred to as *SHSP*.
51. John Holt, in Maud M. Brown, *The University Greys: Company A, Eleventh Mississippi Regiment, Army of Northern Virginia, 1861–1865* (Richmond, VA: Garrett and Massie, 1940), 37–40.
52. John H. Lewis, *Recollections from 1860 to 1865* (Portsmouth, VA: privately printed, 1893), 84–85.
53. John T. McCall, *Louisville Journal*, 1902.
54. John H. Lewis, *Recollections from 1860 to 1865*, 84–85.
55. Ferguson S. Harris, *Lebanon Democrat*, 10 August 1899.
56. Birkett Fry, *SHSP*, 92–93.
57. John H. Lewis, *Recollections from 1860 to 1865*, 84–85.
58. Birkett Fry, *SHSP*, 92–93.
59. Rod Gragg, *Covered With Glory*, 176.
60. John H. Moore, *MAT*, 248.
61. John Dooley, *Confederate Soldier: His War Journal* (Washington, DC: Georgetown University Press, 1945), 101–107.
62. Rawley Martin, "Rawley Martin's Account," *SHSP*, 184–194.
63. George R. Stewart, *Pickett's Charge*, 95.
64. John Johnson, *CTWQ*.
65. Rawley Martin, *SHSP*, 184–194.
66. June Kimble, *CV*: 460–461.
67. Rawley Martin, *SHSP*, 184–194.
68. John Priest, *Into the Fight*, 84–85.
69. John Dooley, *Confederate Soldier: His War Journal*, 101–107.
70. Robert A. Bright, *CV*, 263–266.
71. John H. Moore, *The Southern Bivouac*, 390.
72. James Crocker, *Gettysburg: Pickett's Charge and Other War Addresses* (Portsmouth, VA: Fisk, 1915), 37.
73. William H. Swallow, *The Southern Bivouac* 4 (1886), 564–565.
74. Wiley Woods, *CV*, Battles, 1861–1932, n.d., Box 1, Special Collections Department, William R. Perkins Library, Duke University, Durham, NC.
75. James Crocker, *Gettysburg: Pickett's Charge and Other War Addresses*, 38.
76. James Crocker, *Gettysburg: Pickett's Charge and Other War Addresses*, 38.
77. William T. Venner, "Walking Pickett's Charge: The 7th Tennessee's Route."
78. George R. Stewart, *Pickett's Charge*, 185.
79. James Crocker, *Gettysburg: Pickett's Charge and Other War Addresses*, 42.
80. Rawley Martin, *SHSP*, 184–194.
81. Charles T. Loehr, *SHSP*, 32, 33–40.
82. William T. Venner, "Walking Pickett's Charge." Deborah Fit, "Gettysburg Replants Five Orchards," *Civil War News*, January 2005.
83. David Woodward, "Captain Robert G. Miller: Military Service During Civil War: 1861–1865," 1–23.
84. James Crocker, *Gettysburg: Pickett's Charge and Other War Addresses*, 42.
85. Rod Gragg, *Covered With Glory*, 187.
86. William T. Venner, "Walking Pickett's Charge."
87. William M. McCall letter, 6 September 1907.
88. CSRCS.
89. CSRCS.
90. Ferguson S. Harris, *Lebanon Democrat*, 10 August 1899.
91. Mike Ferrell, personal communication, 2 January 2011.
92. James Crocker, *Gettysburg: Pickett's Charge and Other War Addresses*, 43.
93. John T. McCall, *Louisville Journal*, 1902.
94. William N. Tate, *CV*, 275.
95. CSRCS.
96. CSRCS.
97. William T. Venner, "Walking Pickett's Charge."
98. Charles D. Page, *History of the Fourteenth Regiment, Connecticut Volunteer Infantry* (Meridian, CT: Horton, 1906), 142–156.
99. Charles D. Page, *History of the Fourteenth Regiment, Connecticut Volunteer Infantry*, 142–156.
100. John H. Moore, *MAT*, 249.
101. Charles P. Hamblen, *Connecticut Yankees at Gettysburg* (Kent, OH: Kent State University Press, 1993), 116.
102. Ezra D. Simmons, *A Regimental History: The 125th New York State Volunteers* (New York: Ezra D. Simmons, 1888), 136–138.
103. Charles P. Hamblen, *Connecticut Yankees at Gettysburg*, 104.
104. Samuel G. Shepard, *OR*: 552.
105. John T. McCall, *Louisville Journal*, 1902.
106. CSRCS.
107. CSRCS.
108. CSRCS.
109. CSRCS.
110. CSRCS.
111. John H. Moore, *The Southern Bivouac*, 390.
112. John B. Turney, *CV*, 536.

113. Joseph Peter Bashaw, "Some of the Experiences of Joseph Peter Bashaw Confederate Soldier 1861 to 1865," (manuscript, 1932), 8.
114. Joseph P. Bashaw, "Experiences," 8.
115. John H. Moore, *MAT*, 250.
116. Charles D. Page, *History of the Fourteenth Regiment, Connecticut Volunteer Infantry*, 142–156.
117. John H. Moore, *MAT*, 250.
118. CSRCS.
119. John H. Moore, *The Southern Bivouac*, 390.
120. CSRCS.
121. Mead Anderson, in Maurie Yearly, ed., *Reminiscences of the Boys in Gray, 1861–1865* (Dallas: Wilkerson, 1912), 21.
122. Rod Gragg, *Covered With Glory*, 192.
123. John A. Fite, Reminiscences, 87.
124. John H. Moore, *The Southern Bivouac*, 390.
125. William Wood, *Reminiscences of Big I* (Wilmington, NC: Broadfoot, 1987), 43–48.
126. Joseph C. Mayo, *Southern Historical Society Papers* 34 (1906), 328–335.
127. John B. Lindsley, *MAT*, 250.
128. Randolph Shotwell, *Our Living and Our Dead*, Vol. 4, 1876, 90–95.
129. Noah A. Trudeau, *Gettysburg: A Testing of Courage*, 506.
130. Noah A. Trudeau, *Gettysburg: A Testing of Courage*, 506.
131. Rod Gragg, *Covered With Glory*, 197.
132. John H. Moore, *MAT*, 250.
133. John A. Fite, Reminiscences, 87. CSRCS.
134. John B. Turney, *CV*, 536.
135. John A. Fite, Reminiscences, 86.
136. Thomas Smyth, *OR*: 43.
137. Rod Gragg, *Covered With Glory*, 194.
138. Samuel G. Shepard, *OR*: 552.
139. George R. Stewart, *Pickett's Charge*, 209.
140. George R. Stewart, *Pickett's Charge*, 198.
141. James Johnson letter, n.d., William Walker collection.
142. John Dooley, *Confederate Soldier: His War Journal*, 101–107.
143. CSRCS.
144. William Oliver, *The Weekly American*, 6 July 1887.
145. George R. Stewart, *Pickett's Charge*, 202.
146. Thomas Smyth, *OR*: 43.
147. CSRCS.
148. CSRCS.
149. Ferguson S. Harris, *Lebanon Democrat*, 10 August 1899.
150. Joseph P. Bashaw, "Experiences," 9.
151. Samuel G. Shepard, *OR*: 552.
152. D. Scott Hartwig, *Gettysburg Magazine*, 97.
153. John Dooley, *Confederate Soldier: His War Journal*, 101–107.
154. CSRCS.
155. Samuel G. Shepard, *OR*: 552.
156. Joseph P. Bashaw, "Experiences," 9.
157. John B. Turney, *CV*, 536.
158. CSRCS
159. George W. Lewis, TCWQ.
160. John B. Turney, *CV*, 536.
161. Charles D. Page, *History of the Fourteenth Regiment, Connecticut Volunteer Infantry*, 142–156.
162. Thomas Smyth, *OR*: 43.
163. June Kimble, *CV*, 460–1.
164. John McCall, *Louisville Journal*, 1902.
165. Noah A. Trudeau, *Gettysburg: A Testing of Courage*, 511.
166. John A. Fite, Reminiscences, 87.
167. Birkett Fry, *SHSP*, 92–93.
168. Ferguson S. Harris, *Lebanon Democrat*, 10 August 1899.
169. Ferguson S. Harris, *Lebanon Democrat*, 10 August 1899.
170. John B. Turney, *CV*, 536.
171. George R. Stewart, *Pickett's Charge*, 204.
172. Ralph S. Thompson, *Gettysburg Papers*, Vol. 2, 964.
173. John H. Moore, *The Southern Bivouac*, 390.
174. John Johnson, *CTWQ*
175. Samuel G. Shepard, *OR*: 552.
176. John H. Moore, "The Battle of Gettysburg," *Weekly Philadelphia Times*, 4 November 1882.
177. John H. Moore, 914.
178. Joseph P. Bashaw, "Experiences," 9.
179. Ferguson S. Harris, *Lebanon Democrat*, 10 August 1899.
180. Ferguson S. Harris, *Lebanon Democrat*, 10 August 1899.
181. John A. Fite, Reminiscences, 87.
182. Samuel G. Shepard letter, 8 February 1882.
183. Samuel G. Shepard, *OR*: 552.

Chapter 8

1. Joseph P. Bashaw, "Experiences," 10.
2. Charles T. Loehr, *SHSP*, 33–4.
3. John A. Fite, Reminiscences, 90.
4. Jennings C. Wise, 914.
5. John Priest, 163.
6. Gregory A. Coco, *Gettysburg: Historical Articles of Lasting Interest*, July 1990, No. 3, 95–108.
7. D. Scott Hartwig, *Gettysburg Magazine*, 89–100.
8. Joe B. McBrien, *The Tennessee Brigade*, 84.
9. D. Scott Hartwig, *Gettysburg Magazine*, 89–100.
10. Heather K. Peake, "General John D. Imboden and the Confederate Retreat from Gettysburg," *Civil War Interactive*. http://www.civilwarinteractive.com/ArticleGeneralJohnDImboden.htm.
11. Joseph P. Bashaw, "Experiences," 10.
12. Heather K. Peake, *Civil War Interactive*.
13. Ferguson Harris, *Lebanon Democrat*, 17 August 1899.
14. John Imboden, *Battles and Leaders*, 3: 420.
15. John Imboden, *Battles and Leaders*, 3: 420.
16. Heather K. Peake, *Civil War Interactive*.
17. CSRCS.
18. Joseph P. Bashaw, "Experiences," 10.
19. Joseph P. Bashaw, "Experiences," 10.
20. Joseph P. Bashaw, TCWQ.
21. Kent M. Brown, *Retreat from Gettysburg*

(Chapel Hill: University of North Carolina Press, 2005).
22. Edwin B. Coddington, *The Gettysburg Campaign: A Study in Command* (New York: Simon and Schuster, 1968), 565–566.
23. Ferguson S. Harris, *Lebanon Democrat*, 17 August 1899.
24. Noah A. Trudeau, *Gettysburg: A Testing of Courage*, 550.
25. C. Wallace Cross, *Ordeal By Fire*, 77–78.
26. Henry Heth, *OR*: 44.
27. James L. Morrison, *The Memoirs of Henry Heth*, 178.
28. *CMH*, 8, 203.
29. James L. Morrison, *The Memoirs of Henry Heth*, 178.
30. Henry Heth, *OR*: 44.
31. Samuel G. Shepard, *OR*: 552.
32. Samuel G. Shepard, *OR*: 552.
33. John H. Moore, *MAT*, 255.
34. CSRCS.
35. Joseph P. Bashaw, TCWQ.
36. Ezra J. Warner, *Generals in Gray*, 318.
37. Emory Upton, *The Military Policy of the United States* (Washington, DC: Government Printing Office, 1916), 470
38. CSRCS.
39. CSRCS.
40. Douglas S. Freeman, *Lee's Lieutenants*, 3: 241.
41. James L. Morrison, *The Memoirs of Henry Heth*, 180.
42. Douglas S. Freeman, *Lee's Lieutenants*, 3, 245.
43. Henry H. Walker, "Report of Brigadier-General H. H. Walker, October 21, 1863," *The Rebellion Record*, Vol. 10 (New York: Van Nostrum, 1867), 615.
44. Henry H. Walker, *The Rebellion Record*, 615.
45. CSCRS.
46. James L. Morrison, *The Memoirs of Henry Heth*, 180.
47. Douglas S. Freeman, *Lee's Lieutenants*, 3: 247.
48. Reta Moser, and Alice Hughes Shepard Carver, *Colonel S. G. Shepard, CSA*, 123.
49. Douglas S. Freeman, *Lee's Lieutenants*, 3: 269.
50. Douglas S. Freeman, *Lee's Lieutenants*, 3: 272.
51. Joe B. McBrien, *The Tennessee Brigade*, 87.
52. CSRCS.
53. "Richmond Dispatch Account," *The Rebellion Record*, 29 November 1863.
54. "Richmond Dispatch Account," 29 November 1863.
55. James L. Morrison, *The Memoirs of Henry Heth*, 180.
56. *New York Tribune* account in Walker, *The Rebellion Record*, 12 December 1863.
57. *New York Tribune* account in Walker, *The Rebellion Record*, 12 December 1863.
58. C. Wallace Cross, *Ordeal By Fire*, epilogue.
59. Joe B. McBrien, *The Tennessee Brigade*, 88.
60. Thomas Capehart letter, 27 November 1863. Sue Goodwin collection.
61. Thomas Capehart letter, 27 November 1863. Sue Goodwin collection.
62. Alice Williamson, Journal, 19 February 1864. Special Collections Library, Duke University, Chapel Hill, NC.
63. Alice Williamson, Journal, 12 March 1864.
64. Archibald Norris letter, 15 April 1864.

Chapter 9

1. Robert Carter, *Four Brothers in Blue: From Bull Run to Appomattox* (Washington, DC: Gibson Brothers, 1913), 388.
2. Homer D. Musselman, *The 47th Virginia Infantry* (Madison: University of Wisconsin, 1991): 1.
3. Joe B. McBrien, *The Tennessee Brigade*, 90.
4. John H. Moore, *Weekly Philadelphia Times*, 26 November 1882.
5. Douglas S. Freeman, *Lee's Lieutenants*, 3: 349.
6. Joe B. McBrien, *The Tennessee Brigade*, 91.
7. Homer D. Musselman, *The 47th Virginia Infantry*, 1.
8. CSRCS.
9. Douglas S. Freeman, *Lee's Lieutenants*, 3: 351.
10. CSRCS.
11. CSRCS.
12. James L. Morrison, *The Memoirs of Henry Heth*, 182–3.
13. James L. Morrison, *The Memoirs of Henry Heth*, 183.
14. Douglas S. Freeman, *Lee's Lieutenants*, 3: 352.
15. James L. Morrison, *The Memoirs of Henry Heth*, 183.
16. CSRCS.
17. CSRCS.
18. CSRCS.
19. Douglas S. Freeman, *Lee's Lieutenants*, 3: 352.
20. Douglas S. Freeman, *Lee's Lieutenants*, 3: 354.
21. James L. Morrison, *The Memoirs of Henry Heth*, 184.
22. Joseph P. Bashaw, "Experiences," 11.
23. Douglas S. Freeman, *Lee's Lieutenants*, 3: 354.
24. Joe B. McBrien, *The Tennessee Brigade*, 92.
25. James L. Morrison, *The Memoirs of Henry Heth*, 185.
26. Joseph P. Bashaw, "Experiences," 11.
27. Douglas S. Freeman, *Lee's Lieutenants*, 3: 358.
28. Joseph P. Bashaw, "Experiences," 11.
29. Douglas S. Freeman, *Lee's Lieutenants*, 3: 358.
30. J. K. Miller, *CV*, 239.
31. Joe B. McBrien, *The Tennessee Brigade*, 93.
32. Douglas S. Freeman, *Lee's Lieutenants*, 3: 365.
33. Douglas S. Freeman, *Lee's Lieutenants*, 3: 372.
34. Douglas S. Freeman, *Lee's Lieutenants*, 3: 372.
35. Joe B. McBrien, *The Tennessee Brigade*, 92.
36. James L. Morrison, *The Memoirs of Henry Heth*, 185.
37. Joseph P. Bashaw, "Experiences," 13.
38. Homer D. Musselman, *The 47th Virginia Infantry*, 2.
39. CSRCS.
40. John H. Moore, *Weekly Philadelphia Times*, 26 November 1882.
41. John H. Moore, *Weekly Philadelphia Times*, 26 November 1882.

42. John H. Moore, *Weekly Philadelphia Times*, 26 November 1882.
43. Homer D. Musselman, *The 47th Virginia Infantry*, 2.
44. John H. Moore, *Weekly Philadelphia Times*, 26 November 1882.
45. John H. Moore, *Weekly Philadelphia Times*, 26 November 1882.
46. James L. Morrison, *The Memoirs of Henry Heth*, 186.
47. John H. Moore, *Weekly Philadelphia Times*, 26 November 1882.
48. John H. Moore, *Weekly Philadelphia Times*, 26 November 1882.
49. CSRCS.
50. James L. Morrison, *The Memoirs of Henry Heth*, 186.
51. James L. Morrison, *The Memoirs of Henry Heth*, 186.
52. William J. Jones letter, 25 August 1880.
53. CSRCS.
54. CSRCS.
55. Joe B. McBrien, *The Tennessee Brigade*, 96.
56. Clendening letters.
57. Joseph P. Bashaw, "Experiences," 12.
58. Karlton Smith, "James Longstreet and Pickett's Charge," Gettysburg Seminary Paper, Gettysburg, PA, 1998.
59. Joe B. McBrien, *The Tennessee Brigade*, 98.
60. CSRCS.
61. Homer D. Musselman, *The 47th Virginia Infantry*, 3.
62. CSRCS.
63. CSRCS.
64. CSRCS.
65. Homer D. Musselman, *The 47th Virginia Infantry*, 3.
66. Mark Grimsley, *And Keep Moving On: The Virginia Campaign, May–June 1864* (Lincoln: University of Nebraska Press, 2002), 209–210.
67. Mark Grimsley, 209–210.
68. CSRCS.
69. CSRCS.
70. John H. Moore, *Weekly Philadelphia Times*, 26 November 1882.
71. CSRCS.
72. Homer D. Musselman, *The 47th Virginia Infantry*, 3.
73. Douglas S. Freeman, *Lee's Lieutenants*, 3: 515.
74. David Macrae, *The Americans at Home* (New York: Dutton, 1952), 1: 170.
75. Homer D. Musselman, *The 47th Virginia Infantry*, 3.
76. Joseph P. Bashaw, "Experiences," 13.
77. Joseph P. Bashaw, "Experiences," 13.
78. Homer D. Musselman, *The 47th Virginia Infantry*, 3.
79. Joseph P. Bashaw, "Experiences," 13–14.
80. Joseph P. Bashaw, "Experiences," 14.
81. Joseph P. Bashaw, "Experiences," 15.
82. Joseph P. Bashaw, "Experiences," 15.
83. CSRCS.
84. Joseph P. Bashaw, "Experiences," 15.
85. Joseph P. Bashaw, "Experiences," 15.
86. William Goldsborough, *The Maryland Line in the Confederate Army, 1861–1865* (Baltimore: Guggenheim, Weil, 1902), 133–134.
87. William Goldsborough, *The Maryland Line in the Confederate Army*, 135.
88. Joseph P. Bashaw, "Experiences," 14.
89. Douglas S. Freeman, *Lee's Lieutenants*, 3: 543–4.
90. Joseph P. Bashaw, TCWQ.
91. William Goldsborough, *The Maryland Line in the Confederate Army*, 134.
92. Douglas S. Freeman, *Lee's Lieutenants*, 3: 614–5.
93. Ezra J. Warner, *Generals in Gray*, 96.
94. Orlando B. Wilcox, *Battles and Leaders of the Civil War*, 4: 568.
95. William Goldsborough, *The Maryland Line in the Confederate Army*, 135.
96. CSRCS.
97. William Goldsborough, *The Maryland Line in the Confederate Army*, 135.
98. CSRCS.
99. William Goldsborough, *The Maryland Line in the Confederate Army*, 135.
100. Homer D. Musselman, *The 47th Virginia Infantry*, 4.
101. William Goldsborough, *The Maryland Line in the Confederate Army*, 135.
102. William Goldsborough, *The Maryland Line in the Confederate Army*, 135.
103. William Goldsborough, *The Maryland Line in the Confederate Army*, 136.
104. CSRCS.
105. Orlando B. Wilcox, *Battles and Leaders of the Civil War*, 4: 569.
106. William Goldsborough, *The Maryland Line in the Confederate Army*, 136.
107. CSRCS.
108. Somervell Sollers letter, 12 September 1864.
109. William Goldsborough, *The Maryland Line in the Confederate Army*, 136.
110. CSRCS.
111. Joseph P. Bashaw, "Experiences," 15.
112. Orlando B. Wilcox, *Battles and Leaders of the Civil War*, 4: 569.
113. CSRCS.
114. Orlando B. Wilcox, *Battles and Leaders of the Civil War*, 4: 570.
115. CSRCS.
116. CSRCS.
117. Orlando B. Wilcox, *Battles and Leaders of the Civil War* 4: 570.
118. James L. Morrison, *The Memoirs of Henry Heth*, 191.
119. William Goldsborough, *The Maryland Line in the Confederate Army*, 139.

Chapter 10

1. William T. Venner, "The 7th Tennessee Reached the End of the Line on the Muddy Banks of Hatcher's Run," *America's Civil War*, January 1999.

Notes — Chapter 10

2. Allethia Mayes, "Five Daughters of Capt. John C. Allen," *Confederate Veteran* 9 (1901), 495.
3. Joe B. McBrien, *The Tennessee Brigade*, 104.
4. Richard Hephner, "Where Youth and Laughter Go: The Experience of Trench Warfare from Petersburg to the Western Front," Virginia Polytechnic Institute and State University, 1997.
5. James J. Archer letters, *Maryland Historical Magazine*, 16 October 1864.
6. R. T. Mockbee, *CV*, 31.
7. Ferguson Harris, *Lebanon Democrat*, 18 July 1900.
8. Austin C. Dobbs, ed., *Franklin L. Riley—Grandfather's Journal: Company B, 16th Mississippi Infantry Volunteers* (Shippensburg, PA: Morningside Books, 1988), 200–210.
9. Robert Graves, *Good-bye to All That* (New York: Penguin, 1929), 104.
10. Ferguson S. Harris, *Lebanon Democrat*, n. d.
11. Porter Alexander, in *Fighting for the Confederacy*, Gary Gallagher, ed. (Chapel Hill: University of North Carolina Press, 1989), 435.
12. Ferguson S. Harris, *CV*, 73–4.
13. Somervell Sollers letters, 12 September 1864.
14. Frederick S. Rees letters, 23 July 1864.
15. Ferguson S. Harris, *Lebanon Democrat*, n. d.
16. N. D. Bachman, *CV*, 70–1.
17. C. P. Mooney, *CV*, 117.
18. Richard Wheeler, *Witness to Appomattox* (New York: Harper and Row, 1989), 17.
19. John Coxe, *CV*, 359.
20. John Coxe, *CV*, 359.
21. Richard Wheeler, *Witness to Appomattox*, 17.
22. Callie Sneed letters, 21 October 21 1864.
23. John Hale letters, 3 October 1864.
24. Sidney A. Williams letters, 19 December 1864
25. Mary Frayhouse letters, 7 November 1864.
26. William W. Ward letters, November 1864.
27. William W. Ward letters, September 28, 1864.
28. John Hale letters, 3 October 1864.
29. Lizzie Fackler letters, 18 November 1864.
30. Addie Garber letters, 19 January 1862.
31. Callie Sneed letter to Tom Sneed, October 21, 1864.
32. Mary Frayhouse letters, 7 November 1864.
33. William W. Ward letters, November 1864.
34. Myrta Lockett Avary, *A Virginia Girl in the Civil War: 1861–1865* (New York: Appleton, 1903), 288.
35. Dolly Sumner Lunt, journal entry, 25 December 1864, in *A Woman's Wartime Journal* (New York: Century, 1918), 24–5.
36. Elizabeth Russell Stiner letters, 17 December 1864.
37. CSRCS.
38. Jack L. Dickinson, *The Confederate Peace Resolutions and Negotiations of 1864–1865* (Huntington, WV: Marshall University, 2010), 3.
39. "Southern Conscription of Slaves," *Harper's Weekly*, November 19, 1864.
40. Richard Wheeler, *Witness to Appomattox*, 19.
41. William Goldsborough, *The Maryland Line in the Confederate Army*, 144.
42. CSRCS.
43. Joseph P. Bashaw, TCWQ.
44. Richard Wheeler, *Witness to Appomattox*, 17.
45. Joseph P. Bashaw, TCWQ.
46. Joseph P. Bashaw, "Experiences," 17.
47. Joseph P. Bashaw, TCWQ.
48. Douglas S. Freeman, *Lee's Lieutenants*, 3: 623–5.
49. Ferguson S. Harris, *CV*, 73–4.
50. Benjamin D. Rogers letters, in "Minutes: United Confederate Veterans Camp #941," 20 September 1926.
51. Somervell Sollers letters, 12 September 1864.
52. Ferguson Harris, *Lebanon Democrat*, 16 August 1900.
53. Roger Harrell, *The Second North Carolina Cavalry* (Jefferson, NC: McFarland, 2004), 360.
54. Roger Harrell, *The Second North Carolina Cavalry*, 366.
55. John B. Lindsley, *MAT*, 241.
56. Thomas Hyde, in A. Wilson Green, *The Final Battles in the Petersburg Campaign* (Nashville: University of Tennessee, 2008), 203.
57. Richard Wheeler, *Witness to Appomattox*, 85.
58. Richard Wheeler, *Witness to Appomattox*, 84.
59. Edward Wiley, ed., *The United States: Its Beginnings, Progress and Modern Development* (New York: American Education Alliance, 1913), 120.
60. William T. Venner, *America's Civil War*, January 1999.
61. William McComb, *CV*, 37.
62. John B. Lindsley, *MAT*, 242.
63. CSRCS.
64. John B. Lindsley, *MAT*, 242.
65. Edward Wiley, *The United States: Its Beginnings, Progress and Modern Development*, 120.
66. Andrew A. Humphreys, "The Virginia Campaign of '64 and '65," in *Campaigns of The Civil War*, Vol. 12, John S. Pierson, ed. (New York: Charles Scribner's Sons, 1883), 366.
67. William J. Barton, *CV*, 565.
68. CSRCS.
69. George W. Getty, *OR*: 955.
70. Andrew A. Humphreys, "The Virginia Campaign of '64 and '65," 367.
71. William J. Barton, *CV*, 565.
72. William J. Barton, *CV*, 565.
73. R. T. Mockbee, *CV*, 31.
74. James Hale letters, 27 May 1865.
75. Henry Heth, *CV*, 320.
76. John B. Lindsley, *MAT*, 242.
77. R. T. Mockbee, *CV*, 31.
78. CSRCS.
79. "Noble Veteran is Laid to Rest," *Lebanon Democrat*, 20 April 1926.
80. R. T. Mockbee, *CV*, 31.
81. Merritt Barber, *OR*, 970.
82. Edward Wiley, *The United States: Its Beginnings, Progress and Modern Development*, 120.
83. Merritt Barber, *OR*: 969.
84. Andrew Miller, TCWQ.
85. CSRCS.

86. R. T. Mockbee, *CV*, 31.
87. Joe B. McBrien, *The Tennessee Brigade*, 109–10.
88. J. F. Caldwell, *The History of a Brigade of South Carolinians Known First as Gregg's and Subsequently as McGowan's Brigade* (Philadelphia: King and Baird, 1866), 220.
89. J. F. Caldwell, *The History of a Brigade of South Carolinians*, 223.
90. Andrew A. Humphreys, "The Virginia Campaign of '64 and '65," 368.
91. J. F. Caldwell, *The History of a Brigade of South Carolinians*, 225.
92. Joe B. McBrien, *The Tennessee Brigade*, 110.
93. William Goldsborough, *The Maryland Line in the Confederate Army*, 149.
94. J. F. Caldwell, *The History of a Brigade of South Carolinians*, 226.
95. J. F. Caldwell, *The History of a Brigade of South Carolinians*, 226.
96. CSRCS.
97. J. F. Caldwell, *The History of a Brigade of South Carolinians*, 228.
98. J. F. Caldwell, *The History of a Brigade of South Carolinians*, 229.
99. J. F. Caldwell, *The History of a Brigade of South Carolinians*, 230.
100. J. F. Caldwell, *The History of a Brigade of South Carolinians*, 233.
101. J. F. Caldwell, *The History of a Brigade of South Carolinians*, 234.
102. J. F. Caldwell, *The History of a Brigade of South Carolinians*, 234.
103. CSRCS.
104. J. F. Caldwell, *The History of a Brigade of South Carolinians*, 236.
105. J. F. Caldwell, *The History of a Brigade of South Carolinians*, 237.
106. J. F. Caldwell, *The History of a Brigade of South Carolinians*, 243.
107. William C. Boze, *CV*, 28.
108. James Hale letters, 27 May 1865.

Bibliography

Books

Andrews, William H. *Footprints of a Regiment: A Recollection of the 1st Georgia Regulars*. Atlanta: Longstreet Press, 1992.

Avary, Myrta Lockett. *A Virginia Girl in the Civil War: 1861–1865*. New York: Appleton, 1903.

Brown, Kent M. *Retreat from Gettysburg: Lee, Logistics and the Pennsylvania Campaign*. Chapel Hill: University of North Carolina Press, 2005.

Brown, Maud M. *The University Greys: Company A, Eleventh Mississippi Regiment, Army of Northern Virginia, 1861–1865*. Richmond, VA: Garrett and Massie, 1940.

Burns, Frank. ed. *History of Wilson County, Tennessee: Its Land and Its Life*. Lebanon, TN: Wilson County Library Board, 1987.

Caldwell, J. F. *The History of a Brigade of South Carolinians Known First as Gregg's and Subsequently as McGowan's Brigade*. Philadelphia: King and Baird, Printers, 1866.

Carter, Robert. *Four Brothers in Blue: From Bull Run to Appomattox*. Washington, DC: Washington Press of Gibson Brothers, 1913.

Chamberlayne, C. G. *Ham Chamberlayne — Virginian: Letters and Papers of an Artillery Officer in the War for Southern Independence 1861–1865*. Richmond, VA: Dietz, 1932.

Clements, Paul. *A Past Remembered: A Collection of Antebellum Homes in Davidson County*. Nashville: Clearville Press, 1987.

Coddington, Edwin B. *The Gettysburg Campaign: A Study in Command*. New York: Simon and Schuster, 1968.

Crocker, James. *Gettysburg: Pickett's Charge and Other War Addresses*. Portsmouth, VA: Fisk, 1915.

Cockrell, Thomas, and Michael Ballard, eds. *A Mississippi Rebel in the Army of Northern Virginia*. Baton Rouge: Louisiana State University Press, 1995.

Cross, C. Wallace. *Ordeal By Fire: A History of the Fourteenth Tennessee Volunteer Infantry Regiment, CSA*. Clarksville, TN: Clarksville Montgomery County Museum, 1990.

Crumb, Herbert. ed. *The Papers of Thomas Osborn; The Eleventh Corps Artillery at Gettysburg*. Hamilton, NY: Edmonston, 1992.

Curtis, Orson B. *History of the Twenty-Fourth Michigan of the Iron Brigade*. Detroit: Winn & Hammond, 1891.

Dickinson, Jack L. *The Confederate Peace Resolutions and Negotiations of 1864–1865*. Huntington, WV: Marshall University, 2010.

Dooley, John. *Confederate Soldier: His War Journal*. Washington, DC: Georgetown University Press, 1945.

Drake, James Vaulx. *Life of General Robert Hatton: Including His Most Important Speeches*. Nashville: Marshall and Bruce, 1867.

Dreese, Michael A. *The Hospital at Seminary Ridge at the Battle of Gettysburg*. Jefferson, NC: McFarland, 2002.

Everson, Guy, and Edward Simpson, eds. *Far, Far from Home: The War Time Letters of Dick and Tally Simpson, 3rd South Carolina Volunteers*. New York: Oxford University Press, 1994.

Freeman, Douglas. *Lee's Lieutenants: A Study in Command*. New York: Charles Scribner's Sons, 1942.

Gallagher, Gary, ed. *Fighting for the Confederacy*. Chapel Hill: University of North Carolina Press, 1989.

Gibbon, John. *Personal Recollections of the Civil War*. Dayton, OH: Morningside Press, 1978.

Goldsborough, William. *The Maryland Line in the Confederate Army, 1861–1865*. Baltimore: Guggenheim, Weil, 1902.

Gragg, Rod. *Covered With Glory: The 26th North Carolina at the Battle of Gettysburg*. New York: Harper Collins, 2000.

Graves, Robert. *Good-bye to All That*. New York: Penguin, 1929.

Green, A. Wilson. *The Final Battles in the Petersburg Campaign*. Nashville: University of Tennessee, 2008.

Grimsley, Mark. *And Keep Moving On: The Virginia Campaign, May–June 1864*. Lincoln: University of Nebraska Press, 2002.

Hale, William T. *History of Dekalb County, Tennessee*. Nashville: Paul Hunter, 1915.

Hamblen, Charles P. *Connecticut Yankees at Gettysburg*. Kent, OH: Kent State University Press, 1993.

Hamilton, J. G. de Roulhac, ed. *The Papers of Randolph Shotwell*. Raleigh: North Carolina Historical Commission, 1929–1931.

Harrell, Roger. *The Second North Carolina Cavalry*. Jefferson, NC: McFarland, 2004.

Henderson, G. F. *Stonewall Jackson and the American Civil War*. New York: Konecky & Konecky, 1898.

Horn, Stanley. *Tennesseans in the Civil War: A Military History of Confederate and Union Units*. Nashville: Civil War Centennial Commission, 1964.

Hotchkiss, Jedediah. *Make Me a Map of the Valley: The Civil War Journal of Stonewall Jackson's Topographer*. Dallas: Southern Methodist University Press, 1973.

Johnson, Robert, and Clarence Buel, eds. *Battles and Leaders of the Civil War*. New York: Century, 1887.

Johnston, David. *The Story of a Confederate Boy in the Civil War*. Radford, VA: Johnston, 1914.

Ladd, David, and Audrey J. Ladd. *The Bachelder Papers*. Dayton, OH: Morningside Bookshop, 1995.

Linderman, Gerald F. *Embattled Courage: The Experience of Combat in the American Civil War*. New York: The Free Press, 1987.

Lindsley, John B. *The Military Annals of Tennessee*. Nashville: Lindsley, 1886.

Lunt, Dolly Sumner. *A Woman's Wartime Journal*. New York: Century, 1918.

Macrae, David. *The Americans at Home*. New York: Dutton, 1952.

McBrien, Joe B. *The Tennessee Brigade*. Chattanooga, TN: Hudson, 1977.

Magee, Benjamin F. *History of the 72nd Indiana of the Mounted Lightning Brigade*. Lafayette, IN: Vater, 1882.

Morrison, James L., ed. *The Memoirs of Henry Heth*. Westport, CT: Greenwood Press, 1974.

Moser, Reta, and Alice Hughes Shepard Carver. *Colonel S. G. Shepard, CSA: Commander of the Seventh Tennessee Infantry Regiment—A Missing Page in Civil War History*. Bloomington, IN: iUniverse, 2010.

Musselman, Homer D. *The 47th Virginia Infantry*. Madison: University of Wisconsin, 1991.

Nolan, Alan T. *The Iron Brigade*. Ann Arbor, MI: Hardscrabble Books, 1983.

Otis, George, and Alan Gaff, eds. *The Second Wisconsin Infantry*. Dayton, OH: Morningside Bookshop, 1984.

Page, Charles D. *History of the Fourteenth Regiment, Connecticut Volunteer Infantry*. Meridian, CT: Horton, 1906.

Pfanz, Harry W. *Gettysburg: The First Day*. Chapel Hill: University of North Carolina, Chapel Hill, 2001.

Pierson, John S., ed. *Campaigns of the Civil War*. New York: Charles Scribner's Sons, 1883.

Priest, John. *Antietam: The Soldiers' Battle*. Shippensburg, PA: White Mane, 1989.

_____. *Into the Fight: Pickett's Charge at Gettysburg*. Shippensburg, PA: White Mane Books, 1998.

Ridley, Bromfield. *Battles and Sketches of the Army of Tennessee*. Mexico, MO: Missouri, 1906.

Roberson, Elizabeth, ed. *In Care of Yellow River: The Complete Civil War Letters of Pvt. Eli Pinson Landers to His Mother*. Gretna, LA: Pelican, 1997.

Robertson, James I. *General A. P. Hill: The Story of a Confederate Warrior*. New York: Vintage Books, 1987.

Simmons, Ezra D. *A Regimental History: The 125th New York State Volunteers*. New York: Simmons, 1888.

Stackpole, Edward J. *Drama on the Rappahannock: The Fredericksburg Campaign*. Harrisburg, PA: Stackpole, 1957.

Stevens, Harry. *Souvenir of the Excursions of the 14th Connecticut*. Washington, DC: Gibson Brothers, 1893.

Stewart, George R. *Pickett's Charge: A Microhistory of the Final Attack at Gettysburg, July 3, 1863*. Boston: Houghton Mifflin, 1959.

Tennessee Civil War Centennial Commission. *Tennesseans in the Civil War: A Military History of Confederate and Union Units with available Rosters of Personnel*. Nashville: Civil War Centennial Commission, 1964.

Trudeau, Noah A. *Gettysburg; A Testing of Courage*. New York: Harper Collins Books, 2002.

Upton, Emory. *The Military Policy of the United States*. Washington, DC: Government Printing Office, 1916.

Venner, William T. *Hoosiers' Honor: The Iron Brigade's 19th Indiana Regiment*. Shippensburg, PA: Burd Street Press, 1998.

Waitt, Ernest Linden, comp. *History of the Nineteenth Massachusetts Volunteer Infantry 1861–1865*. Salem: MA: Salem Press, 1906.

Warner, Ezra J. *Generals in Gray*. Baton Rouge: Louisiana State University Press, 1959.

Wheeler, Richard. *Witness to Appomattox*. New York: Harper and Row, 1989.

Wiley, Edward, ed. *The United States: Its Beginnings, Progress and Modern Development*. New York: American Education Alliance, 1913.

Wise, Jennings C. *The Long Arm of Lee: The History of the Artillery of Northern Virginia*. New York: Oxford University Press, 1959.

Wood, William. *Reminiscences of Big I*. Wilmington, NC: Broadfoot, 1987.

Yearly, Maurie, ed. *Reminiscences of the Boys in Gray, 1861–1865*. Dallas: Wilkerson, 1912.

Yoseloff, Thomas. *Confederate Military History*. New York: Yoseloff, 1962.

Newspapers and Periodicals

America's Civil War. January 1999.
Cambridge City Tribune. 13 August 1871
Civil War Gazette. 10 May 1862.
Civil War Interactive.
Civil War Times Illustrated.
Civil War News. January 2005.
Confederate Veteran.
    Archer, James. Vol. 8 (1900): 66.
    Bachman, N. D. Vol. 26 (1918): 70–1.
    Barton, William. Vol. 5 (1897): 565.
    Berkeley, Edmund. Vol. 38 (1930): 175.
    Bingham, J. C. Vol. 5 (1897): 565.
    Boland, E. T. Vol. 14 (1906): 308.
    Boze, William C. Vol. 5 (1897): 28.
    Bright, Robert A. Vol. 38 (1930): 263–266.
    Childs, H. T. Vol. 8 (1900): 111.
    Childs, H. T. Vol. 25 (1917): 19.
    Coxe, John. Vol. 22 (1914): 359.
    Harkreader, Henry. Vol. 34 (1926): 307.
    Harris, Ferguson. Vol. 3 (1895): 261.
    Harris, Ferguson. Vol. 6 (1898): 73–4.
    Harris, Ferguson. Vol. 8 (1900): 38.
    Harris, Ferguson. Vol. 13 (1905): 18.
    Hatton, Robert. Vol. 7 (1899): 554.
    Heth, Henry. Vol. 10 (1902): 320.
    Hurst, John. Vol. 15 (1907): 507.
    Hurst, John. Vol. 28 (1920): 261.
    Kelley, D. C. Vol. 7 (1899): 552.
    McCall, William. Vol. 3 (1895): 19.
    McComb, William. Vol. 7 (1899): 37.
    Mayes, Allethia. Vol. 9 (1901): 495.
    Miller, J. K. Vol. 3 (1895): 239.
    Mockbee, R. T. Vol. 6 (1898): 31.
    Moon, W. H. Vol. 33 (1925): 449.
    Mooney, C. P. Vol. 22 (1914): 117.
    Moore, John H. Vol. 9 (1901): 15–16.
    Polley, J. B. Vol. 18 (1910): 524.
    Tate, William N. Vol. 6 (1897): 275.
    Trimble, June. Vol. 18 (1910): 460–1.
    Turney, J. B. Vol. 8 (1900): 535.
    Wood, George R. Vol. 22 (1914): 35.

Gettysburg Magazine: Historical Articles of Lasting Interest.
    Vol. 3 (July 1990): 95–108.
    Vol. 4 (January 1991): 89–100.
    Vol. 6 (January 1992): 20.

Gettysburg Papers. Vol. 2. 1986.
Harpers Weekly. 19 November 1864.
Lebanon Democrat.
    22 June 1899.
    27 July 1899.
    10 August 1899.
    17 August 1899.
    18 July 1900.
    26 July 1900.
    2 August 1900.
    9 August 1900.
    24 June 1904.

Lebanon Herald. 2 May 1861.
Lincoln Herald. 31 October 1862.
Louisville Journal. 1902.
Maryland Historical Magazine. June 1961.
Our Living and Our Dead. Vol. 4, 1876.
Portage County Newspaper. 5 August 1863
Rebellion Record.
    Vol. 10 (21 October 1863): 615.
    Vol. 8 (29 November 1863): 243.
    Vol. 8 (12 December 1863): 241.

Richmond Dispatch. 9 June 1862.
Southern Bivouac.
    Vol. 2, 1883.
    Vol. 4, 1886.

Southern Historical Society Papers
    Vol. 7, 1879.
    Vol. 32, 1904.
    Vol. 34, 1906.
    Vol. 39, 1914.

Dyer, Gus, and John T. Moore, comp. Tennessee Civil War Questionnaire. Nashville: Tennessee Historical Commission, 1914–1920.
    Bashaw, Joseph P. Co. I.
    Beard, Richard. Co. H.
    Hill, Preston. Co. K.
    Ingram, John. Co. G.
    Johnson, John. Co. A.
    Lamberson, George W. Co. A.
    Miller, Andrew. Co. D.

United Confederate Veterans #941. 20 September 1926.

War of the Rebellion: The Official Records of the Union and Confederate Armies. U.S. War Department. Washington, DC: Government Printing Office, 1880–1901.
    Anderson, Robert. Vol. 21: 251.
    Andrews, George. Vol. 16: 9.
    Archer, James. Vol. 13: 347.

Archer, James. Vol. 16: 52.
Archer, James. Vol. 16: 188.
Archer, James. Vol.19: 282.
Archer, James. Vol. 21: 314.
Archer, James. Vol. 25: 359.
Barber, Merritt. Vol. 46: 970.
Barnes, James. Vol. 19: 88.
Brown, Henry. Vol. 16: 121.
Brunson, E. Vol. 27: 364.
Comly, James. Vol. 19: 159.
Cosgrove, Silas. Vol. 16: 10.
Fite, John. Vol. 25: 363.
Fry, Birkett. Vol. 25: 360.
George, Newton. Vol. 25: 362.
Getty, George. Vol. 46: 955.
Gleason, Shepard. Vol. 13: 126.
Goodner, John. Vol. 21: 318.
Gwyn, James. Vol. 19: 89.
Harland, Edward. Vol. 19: 151.
Hawkins, J. Vol. 21: 317.
Heth, Henry. Vol. 25: 339.
Heth, Henry. Vol. 27: 44.
Hill, Ambrose. Vol. 16: 50.
Hill, Ambrose. Vol. 16: 176.
Hill, Ambrose. Vol. 19: 273.
Hill, Ambrose. Vol. 21: 308.
Hill, Ambrose. Vol. 27: 44.
Hutchens, Andrew. Vol. 21: 316.
Lockert, James. Vol. 21: 319.
Magilton, Albert. Vol. 21: 250.
Martindale, John. Vol. 13: 119.
Neal, James. Vol. 19: 284.
Pegram, William. Vol. 25: 367.
Porter, A. N. Vol. 25: 361.
Richardson, J. H. Vol. 12: 1.
Robinson, William. Vol. 27: 280.
Schoeffel, Francis. Vol. 13: 125.
Shepard, Samuel G. Vol. 27: 552.
Shepard, Samuel G. Vol. 27: 646.
Slocum, Henry. Vol. 16: 117.
Smyth, Thomas Vol. 27: 43.
Willard, George, Vol. 19: 199.
Wright, August. Vol. 25: 328.

Weekly American. 13 July 1887.
Weekly Philadelphia Times. 5 November 1882.

Manuscripts

Bashaw, Joseph Peter. "Some of the Experiences of Joseph Peter Bashaw Confederate Soldier 1861 to 1865." Manuscript, 1932.

Bird, William H. *Stories of the Civil War, Company C, 13th Regiment of Alabama Volunteers.* Columbiana, AL: Advocate Print, n. d.

Boyce, Amy. "Directions for A. P. Hill March." Harper's Ferry, WV, 1979.

Dudley, William Dudley. *The Iron Brigade at Gettysburg: Official Report of the Part Born by the 1st Brigade, 1st Division, 1st Army Corps of the Army of the Potomac, in Action at the Battle of Gettysburg.* Cincinnati: n.p., 1879.

Ferguson, Edwin L. *Sumner County, Tennessee, in the Civil War.* Gallatin, TN: n.p., 1972.

Fite, John A. "Short and Uninteresting History of a Small and Unimportant Man." Lebanon, TN: unpublished manuscript, 1910.

Hephner, Richard. "Where Youth and Laughter Go: The Experience of Trench Warfare from Petersburg to the Western Front," Blacksburg: Virginia Polytechnic Institute and State University, 1997.

Lewis, John H. *Recollections from 1860 to 1865.* Portsmouth, VA: n.p., 1893.

Norris, Archibald. *Book of Small Things.* N.p.: Norris, n. d.

Pettigrew, James J. *Notes on Spain and the Spaniards, in the Summer of 1859, with a Glance at Sardinia.* Charleston, SC: Pettigrew, 1861.

Edgar Q. Rooker. "Asoph Hill, 'Statesville Tiger': A Chronological Outline of the Military Career of Asoph Hill With Particular Emphasis on the Seventh Tennessee Infantry Regiment and The Tennessee. Archer's Brigade." N.d.

Smith, Karlton. "James Longstreet and Pickett's Charge." Gettysburg, PA: Gettysburg Seminary Paper, 1998.

U.S. National Archives. *Compiled Service Records of Confederate Soldiers Who Served in Organizations From the State of Tennessee.* Washington, DC: National Archives, 1959.

Venner, William T. "Walking Pickett's Charge: The 7th Tennessee's Route." www.thomasvenner.com, 2011.

Wafer, Francis M. "Diary of Francis Moses Wafer." Kingston, ON: Queen's University Library, manuscript, n.d.

Woodward, David. "Captain Robert G. Miller: Military Service During Civil War: 1861–1865." David Woodward family history: unpublished manuscript, n.d.

Diaries and Journals

Howard, John. "Lebanon Grays Journal." Sandy Springs Baptist Church Records. Iredell County. Wake Forest University Special Collections and Archives, Z. Smith-Reynolds Library.

Phillips, David. Journal, in Harry Phillips, *Phillips Family History.* Lebanon, TN: Lebanon Democrat, 1935.

Williams, John N. Diary, in Williams family history, Nashville.

Williamson, Alice. Journal. Special Collections Library, Duke University, Chapel Hill.

Family History Collections

Bostick family papers. Nashville.
Caldwell family collection. Knoxville, TN.
Daniels family collection. Charlottesville, VA.
Davis family history. Jefferson City, MO.
Goodwin family history. Atlas, OK.
Hale family history. Mt. Juliet, TN.
Leigh family history. Lincoln, NE.
Pryor family history. Atlanta, GA.
Walker family history. Chattanooga, TN.
Williams family history. Nashville.
Woodward family history. Huntington, WV.

Personal Communications

Cato, Jack. Personal communication, 30 April 1999. Lebanon, TN.
Crofutt, James. Personal communication, 13 October 2011. Jefferson City, MO.
Ferrell, Mike. Personal communication, 2 January 2011. Smyrna, TN
Miller, James. Personal communication, 31 April 1999 and 12 August 1999. Lebanon, TN.
Naramore, Cody. Personal communication, 22 June 2011, Quenemo, KS.
Smith, Skip. Personal communication, 31 December 2010. Lenoir, NC.
Spires, Jeremy. Personal communication, 23 December 2010, Mt. Juliet, TN.
Wade, Lamont. Personal communication, 6 June 2011. Richmond, VA.

Website

Peake, Heather K. "General John D. Imboden and the Confederate Retreat from Gettysburg," *Civil War Interactive*. http://www.civilwarinteractive.com/ArticleGeneralJohnDImboden.htm.

Index

Numbers in ***bold italics*** indicate pages with photographs.

Abbott, Henry (Co. C) 170
Abner, James (Co. B) 164
Adams, James (Co. F) 184
Adams, Robert (Co. K) 202
Ahart, John (Co. H) 192
Alabama Infantry (5th Btn) 39, 43, 45, 67, 70, 83, 90, 95
Alabama Infantry (13th) 70, 83, 85, 88, 89, 90, 95, 116
Alexander, Benjamin (Co. H) 192
Alexander, Charles (Co. E) 178
Alexander, George (Co. D) 173
Alexander, Samuel (Co. H) 193
Alexandria, Tennessee 32, 123
Allegheny College, Pennsylvania 3, 8
Allen, Armstrong (Co. B) 164
Allen, Elden (Co. E) 182
Allen, Frank (Co. D) 173
Allen, John 159
Allen, John (Co. B) 9, 10, 13, 83, 84, 87, 95, 104, 105, 106, 143, 151, 163
Allen, William (Co. G) 188
Allison, Alexander (Co. H) 193
Allison, Andrew (Co. H) 192
Allison, Robert (Co. A) 27, 160
Alsup, Henry (Co. F) 184
Amelia Court House, Virginia 156
Anderson, Cader (Co. I) 201
Anderson, Dewitt (Co. D) 173
Anderson, James M. (Co. D) 173
Anderson, Joseph 31
Anderson, Joseph (Co. C) 52, 170
Anderson, Mary 31
Anderson, Mead (Co. I) 105, 106, 197
Anderson, Mitchell (Co. K) 103, 202
Anderson, Monroe (Co. D) 83
Anderson, Oren (Co. I) 106, 197
Anderson, Overton (Co. B) 164

Anderson, Robert (Co. K) 105, 202
Anderson, Samuel A 13, 29, 32
Anderson, Sarah 31
Anderson, Stephen (Co. F) 184
Anderson, Thomas (Co. I) 73, 197
Anderson, William (Co. A) 160
Anderson, William (Co. I) 106
Anderson's Brigade 25, 26, 30
Anthony, Joseph (Co. I) 83, 197
Apple, Anthony (Co. B) 164
Apple, Henderson (Co. B) 164
Appomattox Court House, Virginia 157
Appomattox River 135, 155
Appomattox surrender 4
Aquia Creek, Virginia 25
Archer, James J. 38, 39, 40, 41, 43, 45, 46, 48, 49, 50, 51, 52, 53, 54, 57, 58, 59, 62, 64, 67, 70, 71, 73, 74, 75, 76, 80, 81, 83, 84, 86, 88, 89, 90, 93, 137, 138, 139, 141, 144
Archer's Brigade 2, 42, 44, 45, 51, 60, 62, 64, 65, 66, 70, 71, 73, 74, 84, 92, 95, 107, 125, 139, 143
Armstrong, William 159
Arnold, Granville (Co. G) 191
Ashby, Samuel (Co. A) 163
Atchley, David (Co. C) 172
Athens, Tennessee 32
Atlanta, Georgia 18
Atwell, William (Co. A) 160
Aubrey, Henry (Co. G) 188
Ayers, Rufus (Co. F) 47, 48, 184

Baber, James (Co. C) 18, 21, 83, 169
Baber, John (Co. C) 170
Baber, Joseph (Co. C) 170

Baber, William (Co. C) 87, 135, 170
Bailey, Thomas (Co. D) 47, 48, 173
Bailiff, Joab (Co. A) 87, 160
Bailiff, William (Co. A) 160
Baird, Hugh (Co. F) 141, 186
Baird, Martin (Co. K) 53, 105, 201
Baird, Sarah 8
Baird, William (Co. G) 108, 188
Baird, William (Co. I) 67, 197
Baker, Samuel (Co. D) 173
Baldwin, Nicholas (Co. D) 177
Ballentine, Frederick (Co. G) 188
Barber, James (Co. A)
Barker, Burrell (Co. F) 186
Barkley, Joseph (Co. D) 174
Barnard, Robert (Co. D) 177
Barner, William (Co. D) 138, 177
Bartholomew, Thomas (Co. E) 178
Bartlett, William (Co. A) 160
Bashaw, Joseph Peter (Co. I) 18, 53, 55, 76, ***82***, 83, 89, 103, 104, 108, 110, 112, 113, 114, 117, 126, 127, 128, 133, 135, 136, 137, 140, 148, 149, 197
Bashaw, Pierce (Co. H) 193
Baskins, Robert (Co. G) 188
Bass, Francis (Co. I) 145, 149, 198
Bass, James (Co. I) 111, 113, 118, 143, 197
Bass, Oren (Co. I) 41
Bass, Sion (Co. K) 202
Batts, A.W. (Co. A) 163
Baumbach, Anthony (Co. K) 206
Bayne, William (Co. I) 197
Beals, Amos (Co. D) 177
Beard, Joseph (Co. H) 193
Beard, Richard (Co. H) 37, 193
Beard, Thomas (Co. I) 35
Beasley, Henry (Co. B) 164

Beasley, John (Co. B) 164
Beaver Dam Creek, Virginia 39
Beck, Armstrong (Co. B) 164
Bennett, John (Co. K) 202
Bennett, William (Co. K) 202
Benning, Col. Henry 59
Benson, Ales (Co. K) 202
Berry, Harris (Co. D) 174
Berryville, Virginia 63
Birney, David 52, 124
Black, David (Co. B) 164
Blackburn, Elisha (Co. E) 118, 179
Blackburn, William (Co. E) 182
Blair, Andrew (Co. B) 168
Blair, Henry (Co. H) 193
Blair, Henry (Co. I) 35
Blair, James (Co. H) 193
Bland, Marion (Co. F) 184
Blankenship, George (Co. G) 188
Blau, Julius (Co. K) 202
Bledsoe, Alexander (Co. E) 60, 179
Bliss, Adeline 96
Bliss, William 96
Blythe, David (Co. H) 192
Blythe, Nathaniel (Co. F) 184
Blythe, William (Co. F) 184
Boatswain's Swamp, Virginia 40
Boddy, Elijah (Co. C) 169
Bodine, Thomas (Co. K) 202
Bogle, Robert (Co. F) 184
Bolen, Milem (Co. D) 177
Bond, James (Co. G) 10, 62, 187
Bond, Monroe (Co. G) 10, 187
Bone, Robert (Co. A) 160
Bonner, John (Co. B) 168
Bostick, Abram 36, 39, 202
Bostick, Thomas (Co. K) 23, 27, 83, 86, 201
Bottom Bridge, Virginia 29, 30
Boulton, Edward (Co. B) 168
Boulton, James (Co. B) 164
Boulton, John (Co. B) 164
Boulton, William (Co. B) 168
Bowers, Joseph (Co. D) 174
Boyd, William (Co. F) 184
Boyd, William (19th GA) 39
Boydston, James (Co. H) 193
Boydton Plank Road, Virginia 135, 141
Boze, William (Co. B) 164
Brackett, Anson (Co. H) 192
Bradley, Andrew (Co. B) 106, 164
Bradley, Jack (Co. B) 41, 164
Bradley, James 99, 144, 159
Bradley, James (Co. B) 165
Bradley, Leonard (Co. B) 165
Bradley, William (Co. B) 104, 154, 165
Bradshaw, Andrew (Co. K) 202
Bradshaw, Hartwell (Co. G) 105, 188
Bradshaw, William (Co. D) 42, 174
Brady, Alven (Co. D) 177
Brady's Gate, West Virginia 19
Branch, Lawrence 45, 55
Brandon, Charles (Co. K) 202

Brandon, Thomas (Co. E) 179
Branham, Daniel (Co. C) 170
Brashnahan, Thomas (Co. C) 102, 170
Braxton's battery 32
Breckinridge, Maj. Gen. John 134
Brier Creek, Tennessee 124
Bright, Joseph (Co. G) 188
Brockenbrough, Col. John 117
Brothers, Andrew (Co. K) 202
Brown, Alfred (Co. C) 103, 170
Brown, Enoch (Co. B) 27, 165
Brown, John E. (Co. I) 198
Brown, John J. (Co. C) 170
Brown, Milton (Co. E) 103, 179
Brown, Thomas (Co. D) 67, 174
Browning, Robert (Co. D) 177
Bruce, Harriet 16
Bruce, James (Co. E) 179
Bruce, William (Co. D) 16, 174
Bryant, Ezekial (Co. I) 198
Bryant, Wesley (Co. I) 197
Buchanan, Felix 90
Buck, Calvin (Co. C) 170
Buck, James (Co. C) 35, 170
Buck, Madison (Co. C) 36, 170
Buckner, John (Co. I) 198
Buford, John 115
Buford, Thomas (Co. H) **36**, 193
Bullard, Thomas (Co. D) 174
Burgess, William (Co. F) 186
Burgess Mill Pond, Virginia 153
Burke, James (Co. C) 170
Burnett, David (Co. B) 165
Busby, John (Co. C) 170

Cage, Jesse (Co. E) 126, 150, 179
Cage, John (Co. E) 179
Calef, John 86
Calhoun, Samuel (Co. D) 174
Callis, John (Co. E) 179
Camp Gregg, Virginia 69, 90
Camp Trousdale, Tennessee 6, 7, 9, 10, 11
Campbell, Frank (Co. H) 24, 193
Campbell, George (Co. C) 170
Campbell, John (Co. B) 165
Canary, John (Co. K) 114, 177
Cantrell, Stephen (Co. C) 170
Capehart, Thomas (Co. K) 120, 202
Carlisle, George (Co. B) 57, 165
Carlisle, William (Co. B) 72, 165
Carroll, James (Co. H) 193
Carson, Benjamin (Co. D) 174
Carter, Henry (Co. D) 174
Carter, John 53
Carter, John (Co. D) 174
Carthage, Tennessee 9, 83, 136
Cartmell, Robert (Co. H) 192
Cartwright, John (Co. K) 47, 202
Cartwright, John H. (Co. K) 202
Cashtown, Pennsylvania 80
Castleman, Gad (Co. C) 169
Cato, Jack 3
Cato, Ruth 3
Cato, William (Co. K) 3, 81, 82, 86, 104, 105, 108, 109, 123, 124, 151, 202
Catron, Lizzie 14
Cawthorn, Charles (Co. I) 198
Cedar Run, battle of 44–49
Celton, William (Co. F) 186
Chamberlain, Foster (Co. D) 53, 174
Chamberlain, James (Co. D) 53, 174
Chambers, Peter (Co. B) 165
Chambers, William (Co. D) 173
Chambersburg Pike, Pennsylvania 80, 85
Chancellorsville, battle of 71–77
Chapman, Barry (Co. F) 184
Chapman, Chesley (Co. A) 40, 160
Chapman, James (Co. F) 184
Chapman, William (Co. K) 202
Charlottesville, Virginia 12
Chastin, John (Co. D) 174
Chattanooga, Tennessee 12
Cheat Mountain, West Virginia 17, 19
Cheek, Andrew (Co. A) 163
Cheek, James (Co. E) 72, 179
Cheek, John (Co. A) 103, 125, 160
Cheek, Joseph (Co. C) 172
Cherry Valley, Tennessee 14
Chestnut Mount, Tennessee 16
Chickahominy River 29, 30, 32
Chimborazo hospital 37
Clark, Edward (Co. E) 53, 170
Clark, Reuben (Co. C) 170
Clarke, Edward (Co. C) 170
Clary, James (Co. D) 174
Clemens, John (Co. I) 132, 198
Clemens, John G. (Co. K) 202
Clemens, Thomas (Co. I) 154, 198
Clemens, William (Co. K) 203
Clendening, James (Co. C) 170
Clendening, John S. (Co. E) 178
Clendening, William (Co. E) 51, 53, 132, 179
Cleney, Henry (Co. C) 170
Close, John (Co. A) 59, 132, 160
Cloyd, Ezekial (Co. H) 192
Cluck, Fountain (Co. G) 188
Cochran, Joshua (Co. C) 170
Coe, Andrew (Co. A) 9
Coe, Andrew (Co. D) 41, 174
Coe, Martin Van Buren (Co. A) 9, 19, 160
Coe, William (Co. E) 179
Coley, Richard (Co. F) 184
Collier, James (Co. C) 170
Compton, Jasper (Co. A) 160
Conditt, William (Co. B) 114, 165
Conke, Higgins (Co. E) 182
Conley, Patrick (Co. D) 177
Connecticut Infantry (8th) 61
Connecticut Infantry (14th) 102, 107, 111
Connelly, George (Co. K) 203
Conscription Act 26, 27
Cook, Salura 82

Cooley, Joseph (Co. E) 179
Copeland, Thomas (Co. E) 62, 179
Corder, James (Co. B) 9, 144, 164
Corley, Daniel (Co. B) 165
Cosby, John (Co. A) 161
Costeel, George (Co. F) 186
Cowen, George (Co. A) 88, 95, 108, 161
Craddock, Martin (Co. F) 184
Craddock, Mary 101
Craddock, William (Co. F) 184
Craft, James (Co. F) 141, 186
Craig, N.S. (Co. E) 179
Crane, James 136
Crawford, John (Co. C) 172
Criswell, James (Co. I) 198
Criswell, John (Co. H) 193
Criswell, Robert (Co. I) 198
Criswell, William (Co. I) 198
Crudup, Dempsey (Co. H) 192
Crump, John (Co. C) 41, 170
Crump, William (Co. C) 170
Cuffman, Benjamin (Co. E) 179
Cumberland River 31
Cumberland University, Tennessee 5, 7, 9, 25, 30, 31, 36, 38, 56, 72, 74, 120
Curd, John T. (Co. I) 198
Curd, William (Co. I) 41, 197
Curry, Benjamin (Co. G) 134, 188
Curry, James (Co. G) 191
Curry, John (Co. G) 188
Curtis, Hiram (Co. A) 161
Custer, George 149, 157

Dailey, John (Co. D) 173
Dana, N 34
Davenport, Joseph (Co. K) 203
Davis, James (Co. F) 184
Davis, Jefferson 25, 34, 148
Davis, John (Co. C) 171
Davis, John (Co. F) 184
Davis, John W. (Co. H) 196
Davis, Joseph 85, 89, 90, 137, 150
Davis, Richard (Co. I) 35, 198
Davis, S.L. (Co. A) 163
Davis, Squire (Co. F) 35
Davis, Thomas (Co. A) 36, 140, 161
Davis, Thomas (Co. I) 198
Davis, William (Co. G) 188
Dawson, Henry (Co. B) 165
Dawson, Isaac (Co. B) 13, 87, 165
Dawson, James (Co. B) 165
Dawson, John (Co. B) 165
Dekalb County, Tennessee 3, 6, 49, 55, 85, 120, 135
Delaware Infantry (1st) 102, 107
Dellis, Isham (Co. H) 193
Dement, John (Co. G) 188
Derickson, Joseph (Co. B) 54, 168
Derickson, Joseph (Co. K) 203
Derickson, Samuel (Co. B) 168
Derickson, Samuel (Co. K) 203
Devin, Thomas 149
Dias, Jesse (Co. D) 174
Dill, Felix (Co. K) 203

Dill, George (Co. K) 203
Dillard, Paleaman (Co. B) 108, 165
Dillard, Pleasant (Co. D) 174
Dillon, George (Co. E) 179
Dixon Springs, Tennessee 99
Doak, Rufus (Co. H) 52, 192, 193
Dockey, Oliver (Co. E) 182
Donelson, James (Co. E) 178
Donnell, Benjamin (Co. H) 193
Donnell, David (Co. H) 193
Donnell, Edison (Co. K) 203
Donnell, Elihu (Co. H) 48, 193
Donnell, James (Co. A) 105, 160
Donnell, John (Co. D) 174
Donnell, Stephen (Co. D) 174
Dorris, Isaiah (Co. E) 182
Dorris, Samuel (Co. E) 62, 179
Dorris, Thomsberry (Co. E) 179
Doughterly, Nathan (Co. G) 188
Douglas, Dewitt (Co. E) 12, 83, 178
Douglas, George (Co. E) 179
Douglas, James (Co. C) 171
Dowell, Jonathan (Co. A) 35, 83, 87, 88, 90, 160
Dowell's Tavern, Virginia 71
Drake, Jackson (Co. K) 203
Drake, Martin (Co. K) 61, 203
Drake, William (Co. K) 203
Drennon, Thomas (Co. G) 188
Driver, George (Co. A) 161
Dugger, Andrew (Co. E) 178
Duke, Felix (Co. B) 165
Duke, Samuel (Co. B) 165
Duke, Wesley (Co. B) 165
Dukes, John T. (Co. K) 203
Dumont, Brig. Gen. Ebenezer 31
Dunavin, James (Co. E) 179
Dunn, Blackwell (Co. E) 110, 179
Dunn, George (Co. F) 184
Dunn, John (Co. F) 184

Early, Jubal 68
Eatherly, Alexander (Co. I) 198
Eatherly, James J. (Co. I) 198
Eatherly, John (Co. I) 105, 108, 198
Eatherly, Martin (Co. H) 196
Eatherly, Martin A. (Co. I) 198
Eatherly, Pleasant (Co. I) 35, 198
Eatherly, William (Co. H) 140
Eatherly, Winfield (Co. H) 196
Eddins, William (Co. K) 41, 203
Elam, Daniel (Co. E) 179
Elliott, William (Co. C) 141
Ellis, Theodore 102, 111
Elston, John (Co. E) 179
Emmitsburg Road, Pennsylvania 103, 104, 106, 109, 110
Enfield Rifles 40, 145
Edward, John (Co. G) 189
Edwards, Eaton "Buck" (Co. G) 36, 188
Edwards, Julius (Co. C) 171
Edwards, William (Co. G) 189
Elkin, Colby (Co. C) 171
Elliott, James (Co. C) 171
Elliott, William (Co. C) 171

Emerique, Alphonso (Co. A) 40, 126, 161
Etheridge, Tilmond (Co. H) 193
Etson, John (Co. E) 108
Eubanks, Gilmore (Co. C) 67, 171
Evitts, Samuel (Co. D) 174
Evitts, William (Co. D) 174
Ewell, Richard 156

Faidley, Edward (Co. C) 171
Fairchild, Jesse (Co. D) 177
Fakes, Daniel (Co. K) 202
Falling Waters, battle of 115–117
Ferguson, Benjamin (Co. B) 20, 165
Ferrell, James (Co. B) 165
Ferrill, Andrew (Co. B) 164
Ferrill, Benjamin (Co. D) 144, 174
Ferrill, James (Co. B) 47, 165
Fields, James (Co. B) 165
Fish, Jonas (Co. E) 182
Fish, John (Co. D) 177
Fite, James 27, 35, 37, 40, 43, 44, 48, 70, 98, 102, 112, 113, 119, 138, 143, 146, 159
Fite, John (Co. B) 9, 10, 12, 13, 14, 16, 19, 20, 22, 23, 27, 34, 35, 37, 39, 40, 44, 45, 46, 47, 48, 63, 64, 65, 72, 74, 75, 76, 80, 81, 83, 84, 85, 87, 88, 89, 90, 95, 98, 99, 100, 104, 105, 106, 109, 111, 112, 163
Five Forks, battle of 149
Flanagan, Robert (Co. F) 186
Fletcher, Franklin (Co. F) 186
Florida, James (Co. F) 184
Floyd, Robert (Co. A) 161
Floyd, William (Co. A) 161
Foley, Edward (Co. C) 171
Forbes, William (14th TN) 34
Forbis, Henry (Co. K) 104, 203
Forbis, Samuel (Co. K) 203
Forbiss, John (Co. C) 171
Forrester, Isaac (Co. K) 203
Forrester, Thomas (Co. C) 47, 48, 171
Fort Archer, Virginia 150
Fort Delaware prison 93
Fort Donelson, Tennessee 24
Foster, Andrew (Co. A) 104, 189
Foster, Oliver (Co. C) 67, 74, 169
Foster, William (Co. A) 161
Foutch, Dixon (Co. A) 161
Foutch, Elijah (Co. A) 161
Foutch, Francis (Co. A) 161
Foutch, Levi (Co. A) 161
Franklin, James (Co. E) 46, 100, 179
Franklin, John (Co. C) 169
Franklin, Tennessee 24
Frazer, Francis (Co. E) 104, 180
Frazer, George (Co. E) 180
Fredericksburg, battle of 65–68
Freeman, George (Co. E) 144, 180
Freeman, James (Co. D) 174
Freeman, Robert (Co. D) 20, 174

Fry, Birkett 76, 77, 90, 91, 92, 93, 95, 96, 98, 99, 100, 108, 109, 112, 133, 134, 136, 137
Fry, John (Co. C) 27, 75, 169
Furgeson, Silas (Co. F) 186
Fuston, James (Co. F) 184

Gallatin, Tennessee 5, 21, 27, 120
Gann, George (Co. B) 168
Gann, George (Co. K) 203
Garrett, Allen (Co. E) 180
Garrett, James (Co. E) 101, 180
Garrett, William (Co. E) 108, 180
Garrison, John (Co. A) 161
Gatton, Joseph (Co. F) 184
George, Newton 112
Georgia Infantry (19th) 39, 43, 45, 52, 59, 66, 67, 70
Getty, George 124
Gettysburg, battle of 81–111
Gibbs, Frederick (Co. B) 75, 165
Gibbs, Richard (Co. B) 47, 141, 151, 165
Gibson, Jesse (Co. D) 177
Gibson, Uriah (Co. D) 177
Gillespie, Foster (Co. C) 171
Gillespie, James (Co. B) 166
Gillespie, Jesse (Co. E) 180
Gladesville, Tennessee 10, 88
Goin, Leroy (Co. E) 182
Goodall, Francis (Co. B) 67, 132, 166
Goodner, John 4, 7, 11, 12, 15, 16, 19, 21, 27, 32, 34, 36, 37, 38, 40, 41, 44, 65, 70, 94, 159
Goodner, Thomas (Co. A) 161
Goostree, Malkijah (Co. C) 171
Gordon, George 45
Gordonsville, Virginia 44
Grant, Ulysses 121, 122, 134, 135, 137, 149
Granville, Tennessee 20
Graves, Henry (Co. E) 180
Graves, James (Co. D) 36, 174
Graves, John (Co. D) 174
Graves, Samuel (Co. D) 174
Graves, William (Co. G) 10, 63, 67, 103, 125, 143, 187
Graves, William D. (Co. E) 180
Gray, George (Co. F) 184
Gray, James (Co. E) 60, 104, 105, 180
Gray, William (Co. E) 180
Green, Thomas (Co. D) 177
Green, Walter (Co. K) 203
Green Hill, Tennessee 21, 41
Greenbrier Bridge, West Virginia 19
Greencastle, Pennsylvania 114
Greer, George (Co. I) 198
Greer, Joseph (Co. B) 9, 10, 164
Gregg, Maxcy 40, 52
Gregston, George (Co. A) 72, 161
Grier, Elijah (Co. I) 16, 198
Griffin, Charles (Co. B) 168
Griffin, Charles (Co. D) 175
Griffin, Charles (Co. K) 203

Griffin, Isaac (Co. I) 130, 198
Griffin, James (Co. K) 203
Griffin, Joseph (Co. K) 203
Griffin, William (Co. A) 161
Griffin, William W. (Co. K) 203
Grisham, George (Co. H) 47, 193
Grissom, James (Co. G) 111, 189
Grissom, John (Co. G) 189
Grissom, Thomas (Co. G) 41, 189
Guill, Benjamin (Co. H) 193
Guinea Station, Virginia 69
Gutheridge, Dr. Robinson 27
Guthrie, Nathan (Co. C) 171
Guthrie, William (Co. E) 72, 180
Gwyn, Hugh (Co. G) 188
Gwyn, John W. (Co. G) 188
Gwynn, William (Co. I) 198

Hackney, William (Co. G) 189
Hagar, Reuben (Co. G) 67, 189
Hagerstown, Maryland 80, 114
Hagerstown Road 91, 92
Hale, Armstead (Co. C) 173
Hale, George (Co. C) 173
Hale, James (Co. B) 70, 104, 109, 158, 169
Hale, John (Co. B) 72, 125, 169
Hale, John C. (Co. K) 203
Hale, Thomas (Co. K) 203
Hale, Thomas R. (Co. K) 203
Hales, James (Co. K) 203
Haley, John (Co. I) 198
Hall, Andrew (Co. I) 72, 198
Hall, John (Co. B) 108, 166
Hallum, George (Co. I) 199
Hamblin, Joseph (Co. I) 199
Hamilton, Alexander (Co. G) 189
Hamilton, David (Co. H) 35, 140, 151, 193
Hamilton, George (Co. E) 108, 180
Hamilton, Joe (Co. F) 14
Hamilton, John (Co. H) 104, 157, 193
Hamilton, Joseph (Co. H) 64, 193
Hancock, Winfield 127
Haney, Martin (Co. B) 166
Hank, Willis (Co. H) 192
Hardaway, Purnel (Co. I) 199
Hardwick, Thomas (Co. E) 35, 184
Harkreader, Absalom (Co. I) 197
Harkreader, George (Co. I) 199
Harkreader, Henry (Co. I) 47, 48, 49, 199
Harkreader, William (Co. I) 52, 53, 54, 197
Harlin, John (Co. H) 75, 88, 193
Harlin, Samuel (Co. H) 194
Harpers Ferry, battle of 56–58
Harrington, Alpheus (Co. H) 194
Harris, Ferguson (Co. H) 14, 36, 39, 40, 41, 51, 58, 65, 67, 74, 75, 86, 87, 96, 99, 102, 111, 113, 115, 122, 130, 131, 132, 144, 145, 146, 149, 153, 194
Harris, Hart (Co. D) 67, 103, 173
Harris, Isham 5, *6*, 12, 13

Harris, Jacob (Co. I) 199
Harris, James 144
Harris, James (Co. A) 161
Harris, William (Co. I) 197
Harrison, Clark (Co. H) 21, 22, 194
Harrison, James (Co. G) 189
Harrison, John (Co. G) 189
Harrison, John T. (Co. G) 189
Harrison, Thomas (Co. G) 189
Harrison, William (Co. G) 189
Harrison, William H. (Co. G) 88, 93, 189
Hastings, Thomas (23rd KY) 25
Hatcher, Thomas (Co. D) 114, 175
Hatcher's Run, battle of 150–154
Hatton, Robert 5, 6, *7*, 9, 11, 12, 13, 14, 15, 16, 17, 18, 20, 22, 23, 24, 25, 27, 29, 30, 32, 33, 34, 35, 37, 159
Hawkins, Dick (Co. H) **120**, 194
Hawkins, John (Co. D) 175
Hawkins, William (Co. D) 103, 175
Hawks, John (Co. G) 189
Haynie, James (Co. B) 166
Hays, Henry (Co. B) 166
Hazel Grove, Virginia 73, 74, 76
Hearn, Albert R. (Co. D) 52, 175
Hearn, Albert W. (Co. D) 175
Hearn, George (Co. D) 173
Hearn, Hardy (Co. D) 175
Hearn, James D. (Co. D) 108, 175
Hearn, James E. (Co. D) 175
Hearn, James L. (Co. D) 175
Hearn, Mathew (Co. D) 175
Hearn, Orin (Co. H) 194
Hearn, Richard (Co. D) 175
Hearn, Thomas (Co. D) 125, 175
Helleman, George (Co. D) 175
Hellman, George (Co. D) 35, 175
Helton, Tennessee 87
Hendricks, Mac (Co. C) 171
Hendrickson, Abram (Co. A) 161
Henley, John (Co. F) 186
Henry, Jacob (Co. C) 171
Henry, M. 11
Herne, James (Co. C) 171
Herne, James W. (Co. D) 177
Hester, Rufus (Co. C) 171
Heth, Henry 76, 77, 88, 90, 91, 96, 116, 117, 118, 119, 122, 123, 124, 126, 127, 128, 129, 130, 133, 135, 136, 140, 144, 153, 155
Hewgley, Ashley (Co. H) 194
Hewgley, John (Co. H) 194
Hewgley, William (Co. H) 194
Hide, Edward (Co. G) 189
Hide, Joseph (Co. G) 189
High, Branch (Co. B) 166
Hill, Ambrose P. 39, 44, 55, 56, 61, 65, 77, 80, 92, 118, 155
Hill, Asoph (Co. F) 56, 61, 83, 108, 159, 187
Hill, Henry (Co. F) 184
Hill, James M. (Co. K) 203

Hill, Jesse (Co. I) 199
Hill, John (Co. C) 171
Hill, Preston (Co. K) 53, 57, 203
Hill, William (Co. K) 204
Hinsley, William (Co. A) 161
Hobbs, James (Co. G) 10, 24, 187
Hobbs, James A. (Co. H) 194
Hobbs, John (Co. G) 189
Hobson, Francis (Co. A) 160
Hogan, Alexander (Co. E) 180
Hollingsworth, Charles (Co. F) 184
Holloman, Coon (Co. D) 175
Holloway, Thomas (Co. H) 35, 67, 82, 83, 102, 103, 104, 105, 109, 110, 194
Honeycutt, Thomas (Co. E) 180
Hood, Benjamin (Co. A) 163
Hood, Henry (Co. A) 163
Hooker, Josephy 70
Hope, Samuel (Co. C) 18, 171
Hopkins, Joseph (Co. B) 166
Horn, James (Co. B) 16, 166
Horn, William (Co. H) 194
Hot Springs, West Virginia 20
Howard, George 111, 159
Howard, John 26, 27, 32, 40, 41, 44, 56, 58, 59, 74, 159
Hubbard, James (Co. C) 36, 171
Hubbard, Thomas (Co. B) 168
Hubbard, Thomas (Co. K) 204
Huddleston, George (Co. G) 135, 189
Hughes, Faustulus (Co. E) 180
Hughes, George (Co. B) 166
Hughes, Joseph (Co. E) 180
Hughes, Robert (Co. D) 89, 175
Hullett, William (Co. A) 161
Hunter, Burchett (Co. D) 72, 175
Hunter, John (Co. F) 187
Huntersville, West Virginia 14, 19
Hurricane Rifles 10
Hurst, Marcus (Co. E) 178
Hutchens, Aaron (Co. G) 189
Hutchens, Lafayette (Co. G) 67, 189
Hutchinson, James (Co. E) 178
Hutchison, Charles (Co. F) 184

Idson, John (Co. E) 180
Idson, Joseph (Co. E) 180
Idson, Josiah (Co. E) 180
Illinois Cavalry (8th) 82, 86, 92
Imboden, John 114, 115
Indiana Infantry (19th) 2, 89, 90
Indiana Infantry (27th) 45, 47
Ingram, Cassius (Co. C) 35, 169
Ingram, John (Co. G) 50, 62, 78, 10, 188
Irby, Robert (Co. D) 53, 119, 175
Iron Brigade 2, 84, 88, 91, 92
Iverson, Brig. Gen. Alfred 71

Jackson, Bailey (Co. C) 171
Jackson, John (Co. G) 189
Jackson, John W. (Co. I) 199
Jackson, Robert (Co. H) 51, 194

Jackson, Thomas (Co. G) 146, 190
Jackson, Thomas "Stonewall" 23, 51, 53, 55, 58, 64, 76, 77
Jaco, Andrew (Co. D) 175
Jacobs, Sarah 25
James, Alvy (Co. F) 183
James, William (Co. B) 13, 166
Jarred, William (Co. B) 166
Jennett, David (Co. C) 119, 171
Jennings, Clem (Co. I) 199
Jennings, Enos (Co. I) 197
Jennings, Francis (Co. F) 62, 185
Jennings, Gideon (Co. F) 185
Jennings, James W. (Co. F) 185
Jennings, Jesse (Co. I) 199
Jennings, John (Co. F) 59, 183
Jennings, John (Co. I) 103, 125, 198
Jennings, Newborn (Co. G) 25, 67, 126, 187
Jennings, Samuel (Co. D) 36, 111, 175
Jennings, Thomas (Co. D) 175
Jennings, Thomas L. (Co. F) 185
Jennings, William (Co. F) 185
Jester, Alberton (Co. F) 187
Jetton, James (Co. I) 199
Jetton, Persis (Co. I) 199
Jetton, William (Co. I) 199
Jewell, James (Co. F) 47, 185
Johns, William (Co. G) 52, 190
Johnson, Archibald (Co. F) 185
Johnson, Bushrod 149
Johnson, Freeling (Co. F) 185
Johnson, James (Co. B) 41, 166
Johnson, John (Co. A) 69, 99, 110, 161
Johnson, John (Co. B) 169
Johnson, John (Co. K) 37, 204
Johnson, Joseph (Co. I) 199
Johnson, Littleton (Co. G) 47, 48, 190
Johnson, Richard (Co. B) 166
Johnson, Thomas (Co. D) 175
Johnson, Thomas H. (Co. D) 175
Johnson, Thomas H. (Co. K) 204
Johnson, William (Co. D) 177
Johnson, William (Co. F) 15, 185
Johnson, William (Co. K) 104, 204
Johnson's William H. (Co. G) 190
Johnson's Island prison, 54, 93
Johnston, Joseph E. 34
Jones, Archey (Co. I) 199
Jones, Buck (Co. G) 42
Jones, David 37, 43, 159
Jones, Elyah (Co. A) 163
Jones, Henry (Co. B) 166
Jones, James (Co. E) 180
Jones, James D. (Co. F) 185
Jones, John (Co. I) 199
Jones, John M. (Co. F) 185
Jones, Lorenzo (Co. D) 175
Jones, Marcellus 82
Jones, Robert (Co. G) 190
Jones, Timothy (Co. H) 196
Jones, William 131
Jones, William (Co. E) 180

Jones, William (Co. F) 185
Jones, William "Buck" (Co. G) 190
Jordan Springs, Virginia 61
Justiss, William (Co. K) 204

Kavanaugh, John (Co. D) 176
Kearney, Phillip 52, 53
Keaton, John (Co. F) 185
Keif, Roswell (Co. F) 185
Kelly, John (Co. C) 171
Kennedy, Elijah (Co. F) 183
Kennedy, Horatio (Co. I) 197
Kennedy, John (Co. G) 140, 190
Kentucky Infantry (23rd) 25
Key, George (Co. B) 166
King, Medicus (Co. G) 188
King, Samuel (Co. B) 107, 166
King, Thomas (Co. H) 194
Kirk, Henry (Co. F) 187
Kirkland, William 136
Kirkpatrick, David (Co. K) 204
Kirkpatrick, Hugh, Jr. (Co. E) 180
Kirkpatrick, Hugh, Sr. (Co. E) 181
Kirkpatrick, Peterfield (Co. E) 181
Kirkpatrick, William (Co. C) 171
Kirkpatrick, William (Co. E) 178, 181
Kittrell, George (Co. K) 132, 204
Knight, Elijah (Co. B) 166
Knight, James (Co. B) 42, 166
Knight, John (Co. D) 177
Know Nothing Party 6
Knox, William (Co. F) 183
Knoxville, Tennessee 12, 117
Koeph, William (Co. E) 181

Laguardo, Tennessee 49
Lain, Abner (Co. K) 204
Lambertson, George (Co. A) 86, 162
Lambertson, William (Co. A) 162
Lamkins, William (Co. D) 176
Lane, Charles (Co. I) 89, 199
Lane, Jack (Co. K) 87, 145, 204
Lane, John (Co. K) 103, 141, 202
Lane, William (Co. K) 103, 204
Lane, William T. (Co. I) 199
Lang, John (Co. B) 169
Lanier, John (Co. F) 101, 103, 111, 134, 185
Lannom, Andrew (Co. G) 190
Lannom, Joseph (Co. G) 27, 190
Lannom, Nathan (Co. G) 190
Lannom, Peter (Co. G) 190
Lapsey, John (Co. B) 134, 164
Lapsey, Norvell (Co. B) 166
Lebanon Herald 3
Lebanon, Tennessee 5, 7, 8, 25, 30, 31, 36, 37, 38, 44, 53, 56, 61, 74, 82, 86, 120
Leddy, Andrew (Co. C) 171
Lee, Robert E. 17, 34, 44, 56, 58, 63, 64, 70, 74, 77, 95, 97, 104,

Index

105, 108, 111, 113, 115, 117, 118, 128, 129, 130, 137, 149
Leonard, Frederick (Co. G) 190
Lester, Henry (Co. D) 173
Lester, James (Co. D) 176
Lester, James L. (Co. K) 204
Lester, James W. (Co. F) 185
Lester, Joshua (Co. D) 176
Lester, William (Co. K) 53
Lester, William H. (Co. F) 187
Lester, William H. (Co. K) 204
Lewis, George (Co. F) 187
Lewis, John (Co. C) 171
Lewis, William (Co. E) 181
Liberty, Tennessee 86
Liggon, Charles (Co. K) 204
Light, Thomas (Co. A) 163
Lincoln, Lewis (Co. A) 162
Lindsey, Charles (Co. E) 182
Lindsey, John (Co. H) 194
Lindsey, Phillip (Co. H) 194
Lindsey, Robert (Co. H) 194
Lindsey, William (Co. K) 134, 204
Little, Romanzoff (Co. D) 176
Longstreet, Gen. James 44, 127
Love, James (Co. C) 67, 171
Love, Joseph (Co. E) 104, 181
Loveall, James (Co. C) 173
Loveall, Joseph (Co. C) 171
Lowe, Marvelle (Co. H) 194
Lownsborough, Thomas (Co. B) 13, 86, 171
Lowry, Jefferson (Co. C) 172
Lucas, John (Co. C) 170
Luck, John (Co. A) 107, 162
Lum, Nathan (Co. C) 172
Lynch, David (Co. B) 166
Lynch, John (Co. B) 169

MacRae, William 150
Mahone, William 140
Major, James H. (Co. K) 202
Major, Samuel (Co. H) 61, 194
Malone, David (Co. C) 172
Malone, Edward
Malone, Robert (Co. A) 162
Manassas, battle of (First) 12
Manassas, battle of (Second) 51–54
Manassas Junction, Virginia 50, 51, 52
Maney, George (1st TN) 16, 23, 24
Mann, Stephen (Co. B) 164
Manson, Henry "Hal" (Co. H) 75, 154, 194
Markham, Samuel (Co. H) 194
Marsh Creek, Pennsylvania 85
Martin, Andrew (Co. H) *30*, 192
Martin, James (Co. D) 53, 101, 144, 154, 173
Martin, James (Co. K) 204
Martin, John (Co. A) 162
Martin, Joseph (Co. A) 162
Martin, William (Co. D) 16, 173
Martin, William (Co. F) 187
Maryland Infantry (2nd) 136
Mason, Phillip (Co. A) 162

Massachusetts Infantry (2nd) 45, 47
Massachusetts Infantry (20th) 34
Massey, Archibald (Co. H) 194
Matherly, Daniel (Co. E) 181
Matherly, William (Co. E) 181
Mathias, John (Co. F) 187
Matlock, Henry (Co. H) 194
Matlock, William (Co. H) 42, 194
Mayo, Robert 129, 132, 133
McCall, John (Co. B) 87, 88, 98, 103, 109, 166
McCall, William (Co. E) 67, 181
McClain, Alfred (Co. I) 35, 199
McClain, Charles (Co. B) 75, 105, 166
McClain, Henry (Co. I) 41, 199
McClain, James (Co. H) *72*, 192
McClain, John B. (Co. I) 201
McClain, Rufus 32, 79, 159
McClendenon, William (Co. D) 176
McComb, William (14th TN) 39, 144, 148, 149, 150, 151, 152, 153, 155, 157
McCorkle, William (Co. H) 36, 192
McCrary, James (Co. G) 190
McCrary, John (Co. G) 190
McDonald, Henry (Co. B) 167
McDonald, John (Co. H) 59, 195
McDonald, William (Co. B) 164
McGee, William (Co. B) 104, 167
McGlothin, Sarah 11
McGuffey, Levi (Co. A) 162
McGuire, Hugh (Co. E) 57, 181
McGuire, William (Co. E) 178
McIntyre, Henry (Co. K) 75, 204
McIntyre, James C. (Co. K) 204
McKeehan, John (Co. E) 182
McKeehan, Robert (Co. E) 182
McKeehan, Samuel (Co. E) 182
McKenzie, Ephraim (Co. K) 204
McKenzie, Parson (Co. K) 51
McKinley, William (Co. C) 172
McKinney, George (Co. B) 146, 154, 167
McMillen, Thomas (Co. F) 185
McMurtry, Thomas (Co. E) 181
McPherson's Ridge, Pennsylvania 90, 92
Mechanicsville, battle of 40–44
Mercersburg, Pennsylvania 14
Meredith, Solomon 84
Mexican War 7, 13, 24, 32, 38, 77, 90
Michigan Cavalry (4th) 116
Michigan Infantry (7th) 34, 35
Michigan Infantry (24th) 89, 90
Miles, Nelson 155
Millboro, Virginia 13, 21
Miller, Andrew (Co. D) 75, 144, 154, 176
Miller, James (Co. D) 176
Miller, John T. (Co. H) 195

Miller, Robert (Co. E) 61, 100, 101, 111, 143, 157, 181
Miller, Samuel (Co. D) 177
Mims, Drury (Co. I) 199
Mingo Flats, West Virginia 17, 18, 19
Miser, Thomas (Co. D) 177
Mississippi Rifles 7
Mitchell, Henry (Co. B) 167
Monocacy River 55
Montgomery, James (Co. E) 181
Moore, James (Co. I) 199
Moore, John "Jack" (Co. B) 9, 35, 36, 44, 47, 51, 59, 65, 71, 87, 95, 96, 97, 99, 100, 102, 103, 104, 105, 108, 109, 110, 111, 116, 129, 130, 135, 143, 157, 164
Moore, Theodore (Co. A) 162
Morgan, John Hunt 30, 31, 32
Morris, Wilburn (Co. H) 192
Moses, William (Co. K) 204
Mott, Gershom 124
Mount, John (Co. G) 190
Mount, Richard 27
Mount Carmel, Tennessee 78
Moxley, James (Co. K) 103, 204
Moxley, Joseph (Co. K) 204
Moxley, Richard (Co. K) 75, 150, 204
Mullinax, Martin (Co. F) 185
Mundy, Marcellus (23rd KY) 25
Munsley, William (Co. E) 135, 182
Murfee, Ervin (Co. A) 162
Murray, George (Co. A) 154, 162
Murray, Robert (Co. H) 195
Myers, James (Co. E) 183

Nashville, Tennessee 12, 24, 88
Neal, Edward (Co. H) 195
Neal, James (Co. H) 195
Neal, John H. (Co. I) 200
Neal, Ralph (Co. I) 200
Nelson, John (Co. G) 190
Nettles, John (Co. K) 129, 204
Nettles, Joseph (Co. D) 176
New, John (Co. H) 53, 195
New, Thomas (Co. H) 195
New Jersey Infantry (2nd) 51
New Jersey Infantry (3rd) 51
New Jersey Infantry (4th) 51
New Jersey Infantry (12th) 96
New Market, Virginia 21
New York Infantry (13th) 41
New York Infantry (25th) 41
Newby, Thomas (Co. A) 162
Newsom, Horace (Co. A) 162
Newsom, James (Co. A) 160
Newsom, Richard (Co. A) 162
Nipper, John (Co. G) 190
Nix, John (Co. A) 57, 162
Norris, Archibald (Co. K) 3, *8*, 9, 11, 12, 14, 27, 29, 56, 70, 83, 86, 95, 103, 105, 110, 111, 113, 117, 118, 119, 121, 122, 123, 126, 128, 129, 132, 133, 138, 140, 141, 143, 145, 148, 149, 150, 151, 153, 154, 204

Index

Oak Point, Tennessee 57
Oakley, Nathan (Co. F) 83, 183
Ohio Infantry (23rd) 61
Ohio Infantry (30th) 61
Oliver, Andrew (Co. B) 167
Oliver, James (Co. G) 75, 190
Oliver, James T. (Co. F) 187
Oliver, John (Co. G) 190
Oliver, William (Co. G) 105, 121, 190
Orange Court House, Virginia 44, 117
Orange Plank Road, Virginia 122, 123
Orange Turnpike, Virginia 77
Organ, Cornelius (Co. K) 205
Organ, Moses (Co. K) 205
Organ, Rolly (Co. H) 195
Organ, William (Co. I) 200
Ozment, John (Co. G) 75, 188
Ozment, Robert (Co. G) 51, 57, 190

Palmer, Richard (Co. D) 144, 176
Pardon, Benjamin (Co. D) 178
Parker, Hiram (Co. F) 185
Parker, William (Co. I) 35, 200
Parker, William P. (Co. H) 195
Parkinson, Littleton (Co. A) 75, 162
Parrow, William (Co. D) 176
Parton, John (Co. I) 61, 200
Parvine, Lafayette (Co. B) 138, 167
Patterson, John (Co. B) 167
Patterson, John B. (Co. F) 185
Patterson, Thomas (Co. G) 190
Patterson, William (Co. F) 185
Patton, Commodore (Co. F) 185
Patton, James (Co. H) 36, 138, 195
Paty, Burr (Co. A) 162
Paty, James H. (Co. B) 53, 106, 167
Paty, James M. (Co. B) 167
Paty, John (Co. B) 167
Paty, Oren (Co. B) 167
Paul, Andrew (Co. K) 73, **74**, 204
Payne, Greenwood (Co. E) 181
Pearce, Richard (Co. E) 183
Peek, Sion (Co. I) 134, 200
Pegram, William 74
Pender, William 48, 51, 54, 62, 76
Pendleton, John (Co. A) 162
Pennsylvania Cavalry (1st) 45, 46
Pennsylvania Infantry (72nd) 108
Perkins, Leroy (Co. K) 16, 205
Perry, Benjamin (Co. B) 167
Petersburg, Virginia 135, 136, 141
Pettigrew, James 90, 96, 111, 116
Peyton, John (Co. K) 35
Peyton, John C. (Co. H) 195
Peyton, John S. (Co. K) 205
Phelps, Silas (Co. B) 164
Phillips, Bruce 90
Phillips, David (Co. K) 8, 17, 19, 21, 22, 23, 25, 26, 27, 30, 32, 33, 36, 38, 56, 64, 105, 205

Phillips, James (Co. F) 9
Phillips, John (Co. D) 178
Phillips, Nelson (Co. D) 178
Phillips, William (Co. B) 167
Phillips, William (Co. C) 169
Phipps, James (Co. F) 185
Pickett, James 100, 101
Pickett, John (Co. G) 190
Pierce, G.L. (Co. E) 181
Piper, Alexander (Co. B) 42, 167
Piper, James (Co. B) 167
Plainville, Indiana 2
Plank Road, Virginia 70
Poague, William 112
Polston, Joseph (Co. K) 205
Ponderella, Tennessee 62
Poole, Wiley (Co. G) 190
Porter, Alexander (Co. B) 167
Porterfield, John (Co. F) 183
Potomac River 23, 55, 61, 62, 78, 114, 116
Potter, Enoch (Co. F) 187
Potter, Enoch (Co. G) 192
Potter, Robert 134
Powell, Benjamin (Co. K) 201
Powell, John (Co. K) 138, 205
Pratt, Andrew (Co. A) 163
Prewett, Silas (Co. C) 172
Price, Helen "Hattie" 81
Puckett, John (Co. E) 105, 181
Puckett, Paulding (Co. G) 191
Purcell, Francis (Co. E) 181
Purcell, Henry (Co. E) 36, 181

Quales, Littlebury (Co. F) 185
Quesenbury, Hugh (Co. G) 191
Quesenbury, Richard (Co. G) 191
Quesenbury, William (Co. G) 191
Quinn, Patrick (Co. H) 196

Rabeck, William (Co. D) 129, 178
Ragain, William (Co. F) 187
Ragland, Agnes 14
Ragland, John B. (Co. H) 195
Ragland, Samuel (Co. D) 36, 176
Rainy, Christopher (Co. K) 202
Rainy, Tennessee 16
Ralston, Luther (Co. D) 104, 173
Ralston, William (Co. D) 173
Ramsey, Thomas (Co. D) 176
Randolf, Sec. of War George 32
Rappahannock River 69, 118
Ray, James (Co. G) 191
Read, John (Co. A) 162
Ready, George (Co. H) 195
Ready, Horace 150
Ready, John A. (Co. F) 185
Ready, Martha Morgan 56
Reasonover, George (Co. A) 162
Reaves, Algernon 90
Reed, John (Co. K) 205
Reed, Thomas (Co. C) 172
Reeves, Francis (Co. B) 164
Reeves, John (Co. H) 47, 195
Reilly (Hatton), Sophie 6, 7, 34
Renfro, Francis (Co. E) 75, 181
Rhea, Sterling (Co. D) 124, 178

Rice, James (Co. G) 188
Rice, John (Co. I) 200
Rice, William (Co. K) 36, 205
Richards, Bailey (Co. B) 46, 167
Richardson, John (7th MI) 36
Richmond, James (Co. G) 191
Richmond, Lovett (Co. G) 188
Richmond, Virginia 29, 32, 33, 39, 40, 44, 118, 144
Ricketts, James (Co. F) 185
Ricketts, William (Co. F) 60, 186
Riggans, Daniel (Co. K) 53, 205
Risden, James (Co. A) 163
Rison, Henry (Co. B) 87, 167
Roark, Jesse (Co. E) 183
Robbins William (Co. G) 90, 191
Roberts, John (Co. G) 108, 191
Robertson, George (Co. G) 191
Robertson, Isaiah (Co. G) 191
Robertson, John (Co. D) 178
Robertson, Luke (Co. G) 40, 72, 191
Robinson, Andrew (Co. A) 160
Robinson, John 52
Robinson, Gutheridge 159
Robison, Charles (Co. I) 140, 200
Robison, James (Co. B) 167
Rogers, John (Co. D) 176
Rogers, William (Co. D) 140, 178
Roland, James (Co. C) 172
Rome, Tennessee 8, 14
Romney, Virginia 22
Roney, Elmore (Co. C) 172
Rose, Thomas (Co. C) 27, 172
Royster, Ira (Co. B) 135, 167
Rucker, Sterling (Co. G) 75, 191
Rucker, Thomas (Co. G) 191
Rucks, Howell (Co. B) 169
Rucks, Howell (Co. K) 205
Rural Hill, Tennessee 82, 83
Rutherford, Benjamin (Co. C) 173
Rutherford, Benjamin (Co. E) 182
Rutherford, Gideon (Co. I) 200
Rutland, Isaac (Co. K) 205
Rutland, John (Co. H) 195
Rutledge, Richard (Co. C) 172

Sanders, James (Co. E) 182
Sanders, John (Co. F) 186
Sandlin, Isaac (Co. A) 162
Saunders, William (Co. E) 183
Saylor's Creek, battle of 156
Scheib, Charles (Co. K) 205
Schofield, Cyrus (Co. H) 195
Scobey, Joseph (Co. I) 200
Scoby, Burchett (Co. K) 205
Scott, Thomas (Co. E) 182
Searcy, Daniel (Co. I) 200
Searcy, Reuben (Co. C) 170
Searcy, Reuben (Co. I) 200
Seat, Hiram (Co. D) 176
Seat, James (Co. K) 103, 205
Seat, John (Co. D) 176
Sellars, Eli (Co. G) 27, 188
Settle, Leroy (Co. H) 195

Index

Seven Pines, battle of 33–39
Sewell, Daniel Watts (Co. A) 35, 162
Sewell, William (Co. A) 35, 162
Sewell Mountain, West Virginia 19
Sexton, James (Co. B) 167
Sexton, Robert (Co. B) 169
Shanks, John (Co. A) 162
Shannon, John (Co. K) 59, 205
Sharp, William (Co. E) 183
Sharpsburg, battle of 58–61
Shaub, Charles (Co. C) 172
Shaver, Charles (Co. A) 162
Shaw, James (Co. D) 176
Shelton, Lewis (Co. E) 183
Shelton, Solomon (Co. E) 183
Shenandoah River 25
Shepard Samuel George (Co. G) 10, 17, 23, 27, 43, 44, 47, 53, 56, 58, 63, 64, 70, 81, 83, 87, 89, 91, 94, 102, 105, 106, 108, 110, 111, 112, 113, 115, 116, 117, 118, 121, 122, 123, 126, 127, 128, 129, 130, 132, 133, 134, 135, 137, 138, 140, 141, 143, 144, 145, 148, 149, 150, 151, 152, 154, 155, 157, 187
Sherrill, James (Co. K) 205
Shiloh, battle of 26
Shipper, Frank (Co. K) 205
Shoemaker, Germain (Co. B) 136, 167
Shoemaker, James (Co. B) 75, 169
Shoemaker, John (Co. B) 168
Shoemaker, John W. (Co. F) 187
Shoemaker, William (Co. D) 41, 176
Shop Springs, Tennessee 119
Short, James (Co. C) 172
Shutt, George (Co. D) 176
Silver Springs, Tennessee 32, 41, 54, 79, 149
Simmons, Calvin (Co. G) 191
Simmons, John (Co. H) 103, 195
Simpson, Charles (Co. F) 22, 183
Sims, George (Co. G) 191
Sims, William (Co. A) 162
Sloan, John (Co. F) 134, 143, 186
Smart, James (Co. K) 134, 205
Smith, Andrew (Co. I) 200
Smith, Elezear (Co. B) 168
Smith, Eli (Co. I) 53, 105, 200
Smith, James M. (Co. F) 186
Smith, John (Co. C) 173
Smith, Nelson (Co. B) 57, 168
Smith, Samuel (Co. H) 196
Smith, William (Co. D) 176
Smith, William E. (Co. F) 187
Smith County, Tennessee 3, 6, 49, 55, 85, 87, 120, 135, 147
Sneed, Thomas (Co. A) 88, 163
Sneed, Thomas J. (Co. F) 186
Snickers Gap, Virginia 64
Snickersville, Virginia 25
Snider, George (Co. D) 178
Snyder, Daniel (Co. A) 163

Spencer, Noah (Co. C) 173
Spotsylvania, battle of 128–133
Springfield Rifles 40
Spurgeon, Thomas (Co. D) 178
Stallings, Catherine 147
Stallings, Harrison 147
Stallings, Lydia 147
Stanfield, Joseph (Co. B) 168
Statesville, Tennessee 15, 81, 101
Staunton, Virginia 12, 13, 18, 21, 120
Steed, William (Co. K) 134, 205
Stevens, Bartholomew (Co. D) 176
Stewart, Alexander (Co. K) 205
Stiles, Allen (Co. D) 176
Stiner, Peter (Co. E) 148, 183
Stott, William (Co. B) 6, 168
Strasburg, Virginia 21
Stratton, Golliday (Co. H) 195
Stratton, James (Co. D) 173
Stratton, John (Co. H) 196
Stroud, Andrew (Co. F) 183
Stroud, James (Co. F) 186
Stroud, Lester (Co. F) 46, 183
Stroud, Oliver (Co. F) 132, 184
Sudley Springs, Virginia 52
Sullins, Walter (Co. A) 163
Sullivan, Benjamin F. (Co. G) 191
Sullivan, Benjamin F. (Co. I) 141, 200
Sullivan, Benjamin H. (Co. I) 200
Sullivan, Eclemuel (Co. I) 200
Sullivan, James A. (Co. I) 200
Sullivan, James E. (Co. I) 40, 200
Sullivan, Jefferson (Co. F) 186
Sullivan, John D. (Co. F) 186
Sullivan, John E. (Co. I) 40, 200
Sullivan, John W. (Co. I) 103, 140, 200
Sullivan, Thomas J. (Co. G) 103, 191
Sullivan, Thomas P. (Co. F) 186
Sullivan, William B (Co. I) 200
Sullivan, William H. (Co. G) 191
Summers, James (Co. G) 191
Sumner County, Tennessee 3, 6, 7, 49, 55, 85, 120, 135
Sutton, James (Co. F) 106, 187
Swain, Rolando (Co. H) 195
Sweet, David (Co. E) 140, 183
Sweetwater, Tennessee 18

Talbot, John (Co. H) 192
Tallant, William (Co. C) 173
Tapley, James (Co. K) 205
Tarver, Benjamin (Co. K) 24, 201
Tate, James (Co. K) 67, 205
Tate, John (Co. H) 195
Tate, William (Co. H) 102, 125, 143, 195
Tatum, Frank (Co. D) 176
Taylor, Alexander (Co. E) 62, 182
Taylor, Robert (Co. E) 178
Taylor, Robert (Co. I) 35
Taylor, Robert R. (Co. H) 195

Taylor, William (Co. C) 172
Tennessee Infantry (1st; Maney) 18, 24
Tennessee Infantry (1st; Turney) 26, 32, 37, 39, 43, 45, 54, 59, 67, 85, 90, 95, 108
Tennessee Infantry (14th) 24, 32, 37, 39, 43, 59, 85, 88, 90, 95, 112, 116
Tennessee Infantry (17th) 150
Tennessee Infantry (23rd) 150
Terry, William (Co. A) 163
Thackston, Benjamin (Co. B) 103, 154, 168
Thackston, Blake (Co. B) 67, 168
Thomas, William (Co. F) 187
Thompson, Andrew (Co. F) 47, 186
Thompson, George (Co. H) 51, 196
Thompson, James (Co. F) 40, 186
Thompson, Leonidas (Co. B) 168
Thompson, Robert (Co. B) 164
Thompson, Zachariah (Co. H) 196, 206
Tilford, James (Co. I) 200
Timberlake, Fountain (Co. B) 168
Timberlake, Francis (Co. B) 67, 105, 108, 164
Tinsbloom, Thomas (Co. K) 206
Tolliver, Newman (Co. K) 201
Tracy, Andrew (Co. A) 163
Tribble, Haney (Co. D) 176
Trimble, Nathaniel (Co. B) 168
Trousdale, William (Co. A) 163
Tubb, William (Co. B) 168
Tucker, John (Co. H) 51, 196
Tucker's Crossroads, Tennessee 9, 96
Tuckett, J.H. 159
Tumlin, George (Co. B) 168
Turnage, James (Co. C) 36, 119, 150, 151, 172
Turner, Edward (Co. H) 196
Turner, Jeremiah (Co. F) 11, 154, 186
Turner, Stephen (Co. I) 35
Turner, Stephen L. (Co. H) 196
Turney, Peter (1st TN) 26, 34, 58
Turpin, Thomas (Co. E) 182
Tyree, George (Co. C) 172

Vanatta, James (Co. A) 36, 160
Van de Graff, Abram (5th AL Btn) 39, 90
Vann, John (Co. G) 191
Van Tooth, James (19th IN) 2
Vaughn, Dejohnson (Co. I) 200
Vaughn, Richard (Co. G) 103, 191
Vaughter, William (Co. G) 191
Vermont Infantry (18th) 131
Vick, Alexander **38**, 159
Vickry, D.G. (Co. G) 192
Vicksburg, Mississippi 18, 49
Viery, Daniel (Co. F) 187
Vivrette, John B. (Co. I) 201
Vivrette, John L. (Co. I) 201

Vivrette, John W. (Co. I) 197
Vivrette, Rufus (Co. I) 201
Vivrette, Thomas (Co. I) 197
Vivrette, William (Co. I) 60, 61, 201

Wade, William (Co. H) 108, 196
Wagoner, Daniel (Co. E) 183
Walker, Daniel (Co. E) 183
Walker, Henry 117, 118, 122, 123, 126, 127, 129
Walker, John (Co. E) 183
Walker, William (Co. C) 172
Wallace, Jehu (Co. C) 169
Walls, William (Co. K) 206
Walpole, James (Co. I) 47, 105, 107, 108, 201
Walsh, Lafayette (Co. D) 14, 17, 42, 78, 79, 112, 113, 117, 126, 128, 143, 154, 173
Walsh, Shelby (Co. D) 176
Walton, Robert (Co. D) 176
Ward, William (Co. B) 168
Warford, Bartlett (Co. A) 62, 160
Warm Springs, Virginia 13, 14, 16, 19, 20
Warmack, Albert (Co. B) 168
Warren, Gouverneur 119, 149
Warren, Joshua (Co. C) 172
Warrenton Springs Ford, Virginia 50
Washam, William (Co. B) 168
Watkins, Charles (Co. C) 172
Watkins, James (Co. D) 47, 134, 176
Watkins, William (Co. K) 54, 206
Watkins, Zarah (Co. C) 176
Watson, Isaac (Co. F) 186
Weaver, James (Co. K) 37, 61, 206
Webb, George (Co. F) 36, 186
Webb, Thomas 143
Webb, Thomas (Co. A) 163
Webb, William (Co. F) 183
Webber, Simeon (Co. I) 201
Webster, John (Co. D) 106, 177
Weldon Road, battle of 137–141
Wells, Joseph (Co. C) 172
Westbrook, Lewis (Co. H) 90, 102, 196
Wharton, Jesse (Co. D) 173
Wharton, Joseph (Co. D) 173
Wharton, William (Co. H) 196

Wheeler, Gen. Joseph 30
White, Henry (Co. C) 172
White, James (Co. H) 196
White, Joseph (Co. E) 182
White, Spencer (Co. F) 187
Whitehead, Andrew (Co. D) 108, 177
Whitlock, Pleasant 31
Whitlock, Robert (Co. F) 186
Widow Tapp farm, Virginia 126
Wilderness, the battle 122–128
Wilkerson, Albert (Co. I) 103, 201
Wilkerson, Beverly (Co. H) 196
Wilkerson, Charles (Co. H) 47, 196
Wilkerson, Charles (Co. K) 206
Wilkerson, James (Co. I) 201
Williams, Andrew (Co. E) 182
Williams, David (Co. D) 177
Williams, Francis (Co. E) 182
Williams, George (Co. E) 182
Williams, Henry (Co. E) 62, 182
Williams, Henry (Co. K) 105, 206
Williams, James (Co. E) 141, 182
Williams, James A. (Co. H) 196
Williams, John (Co. A) 102, 163
Williams, John (Co. D) 40, 44, 54, 177
Williams, John (Co. H) 69, 70, 197
Williams, John A. (Co. H) 197
Williams, John N. (Co. H) 196
Williams, Joseph (Co. E) 182
Williams, Martin (Co. G) 192
Williams, Owen (Co. A) 163
Williams, Robert (Co. H) 196
Williams, Solomon (Co. D) 177
Williams, Thomas (Co. E) 183
Williams, Thomas J. (Co. F) 186
Williams, William H. (Co. E) 182
Williamsburg, Virginia 26
Williamson, John (Co. H) 103, 140, 192
Williamson, William (Co. H) 27, 51, **56**, 58, 70, 83, 108, 192
Williamsport, Maryland 114, 115
Willoughby, William (Co. A) 163
Willoughby Run, Pennsylvania 86, 91
Wilmouth, Burgess (Co. A) 122, 123, 124, 126, 127, 128, 130, 132, 160

Wilson, Charles (Co. E) 182
Wilson, Isaac (Co. F) 186
Wilson, R.M. (Co. A) 163
Wilson Blues 6, 86
Wilson County, Tennessee 3, 6, 21, 25, 27, 30, 49, 55, 85, 120, 135
Winchester, Virginia 22
Windham, Charles (Co. C) 119, 172
Windham, James (Co. C) 172
Winfrey, James (Co. A) 104, 163
Wingo, Henry (Co. I) 75, 201
Winkler, Abraham (Co. D) 178
Wisconsin Infantry (2nd) 88, 89, 90
Wisconsin Infantry (6th) 90
Wisconsin Infantry (7th) 90
Wise, John (Co. E) 47, 178
Witt, Abner (Co. F) 186
Woodall, Thomas (Co. C) 172
Woodrum, William (Co. G) 191
Woodstock, Virginia 21
Woollard, James (Co. K) 206
Wooten, John (Co. E) 183
Word, Roger (Co. H) 43, 53, 196
Word, William (Co. H) 196
Wormack, Henry (Co. D) 36
Wormack, Joel (Co. H) 196
Wormack, John (Co. D) 177
Wormack, Robert (Co. H) 51, 108, 196
Wray, Richard (Co. K) 206
Wright, Augustus 76
Wright, Horatio 150
Wright, Robert (Co. A) 83, 160
Wynne, William (Co. C) 75, 172

Yeaman, Robert (Co. B) 168
Yeargin, Thomas (Co. A) 163
Yeargin, Wesley (Co. A) 163
Yoakum, Robert (Co. E) 183
York, John (Co. I) 40, 201
Yorktown, Virginia 26
Young, Andrew (Co. I) 201
Young, James (Co. C) 172
Young, James (Co. I) 35, 201
Young, Peter (Co. G) 67, 191
Young, William (Co. I) 132, 201

www.ingramcontent.com/pod-product-compliance
Lightning Source LLC
Chambersburg PA
CBHW081551300426
44116CB00015B/2844